THE NEW MIDDLE AGES

BONNIE WHEELER, *Series Editor*

The New Middle Ages presents transdisciplinary studies of medieval cultures. It includes both scholarly monographs and essay collections.

PUBLISHED BY PALGRAVE:

Women in the Medieval Islamic World: Power, Patronage, and Piety
edited by Gavin R. G. Hambly

The Ethics of Nature in the Middle Ages: On Boccaccio's Poetaphysics
by Gregory B. Stone

Presence and Presentation: Women in the Chinese Literati Tradition
by Sherry J. Mou

The Lost Love Letters of Heloise and Abelard: Perceptions of Dialogue in Twelfth-Century France
by Constant J. Mews

Understanding Scholastic Thought with Foucault
by Philipp W. Rosemann

For Her Good Estate: The Life of Elizabeth de Burgh
by Frances A. Underhill

Constructions of Widowhood and Virginity in the Middle Ages
edited by Cindy L. Carlson and Angela Jane Weisl

Motherhood and Mothering in Anglo-Saxon England
by Mary Dockray-Miller

Listening to Heloise: The Voice of a Twelfth-Century Woman
edited by Bonnie Wheeler

The Postcolonial Middle Ages
edited by Jeffrey Jerome Cohen

Chaucer's Pardoner and Gender Theory
by Robert S. Sturges

Crossing the Bridge: Comparative Essays on Medieval European and Heian Japanese Women Writers
edited by Barbara Stevenson and Cynthia Ho

Engaging Words: The Culture of Reading in the Later Middle Ages
by Laurel Amtower

Robes and Honor: The Medieval World of Investiture
edited by Stewart Gordon

Representing Rape in Medieval and Early Modern Literature
edited by Elizabeth Robertson and Christine M. Rose

Same Sex Love and Desire Among Women in the Middle Ages
edited by Francesca Canadé Sautman and Pamela Sheingorn

Sight and Embodiment in the Middle Ages: Ocular Desires
by Suzannah Biernoff

Listen Daughter: The Speculum virginum and the Formation of Religious Women in the Middle Ages
edited by Constant J. Mews

Science, the Singular, and the Question of Theology
by Richard A. Lee, Jr.

Gender in Debate from the Early Middle Ages to the Renaissance
edited by Thelma S. Fenster and Clare A. Lees

Malory's Morte Darthur: *Remaking Arthurian Tradition*
by Catherine Batt

The Vernacular Spirit: Essays on Medieval Religious Literature
edited by Renate Blumenfeld-Kosinski, Duncan Robertson, and Nancy Warren

Popular Piety and Art in the Late Middle Ages: Image Worship and Idolatry in England 1350–1500
by Kathleen Kamerick

Absent Narratives, Manuscript Textuality, and Literary Structure in Late Medieval England
by Elizabeth Scala

Creating Community with Food and Drink in Merovingian Gaul
by Bonnie Effros

Representations of Early Byzantine Empresses: Image and Empire
by Anne McClanan

Encountering Medieval Textiles and Dress
edited by Désirée G. Koslin and Janet Snyder

Eleanor of Aquitaine: Lord and Lady
edited by Bonnie Wheeler and John Carmi Parsons

Isabel La Católica, Queen of Castile
edited by David A. Boruchoff

Homoeroticism and Chivalry: Discourses of Male Same-Sex Desire in the Fourteenth Century
by Richard Zeikowitz

Portraits of Medieval Women: Family, Marriage, and Politics in England 1225–1350
by Linda E. Mitchell

Eloquent Virgins: From Thecla to Joan of Arc
by Maud Burnett McInerney

The Persistence of Medievalism: Narrative Adventures in Contemporary Culture
by Angela Jane Weisl

Capetian Women
edited by Kathleen Nolan

Joan of Arc and Spirituality
edited by Ann Astell and Bonnie Wheeler

The Texture of Society: Medieval Women in the Southern Low Countries
edited by Ellen E. Kittell and Mary A. Suydam

JOAN OF ARC AND SPIRITUALITY

Edited by

Ann W. Astell and Bonnie Wheeler

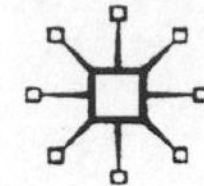

JOAN OF ARC AND SPIRITUALITY
© Ann W. Astell and Bonnie Wheeler, 2003

All rights reserved. No part of this book may be used or reproduced in any manner whatsoever without written permission except in the case of brief quotations embodied in critical articles or reviews.

First published 2003 by
PALGRAVE MACMILLAN™
175 Fifth Avenue, New York, N.Y. 10010 and
Houndmills, Basingstoke, Hampshire, England RG21 6XS
Companies and representatives throughout the world

PALGRAVE MACMILLAN is the global academic imprint of the Palgrave Macmillan division of St. Martin's Press, LLC and of Palgrave Macmillan Ltd. Macmillan® is a registered trademark in the United States, United Kingdom and other countries. Palgrave is a registered trademark in the European Union and other countries.

ISBN 1–4039–6222–7 hardback

Library of Congress Cataloging-in-Publication Data
Joan of Arc and spirituality/edited by Ann W. Astell and Bonnie Wheeler.
p. cm.
Includes bibliographical references and index.
ISBN 1–4039–6222–7
1. Joan, of Arc, Saint, 1412–1431. 2. Spirituality—France—History—To 1500. 3. Christian women saints—France—Biography. I. Astell, Ann W. II. Wheeler, Bonnie, 1944–

DC103.J629 2003
282'.092—dc21 2003050576

A catalogue record for this book is available from the British Library.

Design by Newgen Imaging Systems (P) Ltd., Chennai, India.

First edition: December, 2003
10 9 8 7 6 5 4 3 2 1

Printed in the United States of America.

CONTENTS

TABLE OF ILLUSTRATIONS

JOAN OF ARC AND SPIRITUALITY

Ann W. Astell and Bonnie Wheeler

Politics, piety, and militancy are often intermingled. We observe this in our own time (often to our pain), just as we note it in figures from the past. This intermingling is one of the more unusual and widely noted characteristics of Joan of Arc (1412?–31). Joan of Arc is an unusual saint. Canonized in 1920 as a virgin, she died in 1431 as a condemned heretic. Uneducated and youthful, she obeyed "voices" that counseled her to pursue an unprecedented militant vocation. This collection explores multiple facets of Joan's prayerful life. Two-thirds of our chapters consider Joan in her own time. Her various trial documents provide a rich and tantalizing range of evidence about ways in which Joan understood her spiritual life as well as ways in which it was understood by others. Joan also figures in lively late medieval debates about spiritual discernment and about the expression and control of popular religion, and the middle chapters consider these matters. The later chapters merely hint at the broad spectrum of postmedieval receptions of *La Pucelle* by women writers, artists, and saints, while the final chapter presents responses by contemporary women who find Joan a force in their own lives. Taken together, these essays offer new perspectives on the heroism of Joan's original way of sanctity.

How can we see the spiritual in the militant Joan of Arc? What forms of piety have been provoked by reflecting on the Maid of Orléans, who died as a condemned heretic? Though her condemnation in 1431 was retracted in the nullification trial of 1455–56, Joan was not elevated to the status of saint in the Roman Catholic tradition until 1920. Over the long centuries between, Joan's own virtue and piety were treated variously—sometimes dismissed with contempt, sometimes accepted with reverence. Her canonization in the aftermath of World War I was institutionally masked as a reward for her virginity rather than her valor, her martyrdom, or even her status as a "confessor" or "doctor", as many believe her to be.[1] Joan herself did not consider her vaunted and oft-tested virginity a virtue or a vocation—it was a temporary necessity rather than a necessarily permanent condition. Most who prize Joan regret this backhanded slap of sanctity, and some hope that other categories of sanctity might be added to her current status.

This book continues in the tradition which recognizes that Joan transcends a merely nationalist agenda and has become a global figure of heroic sanctity. Joan shaped her life, mission, and goals at the direction of her "heavenly voices"—the archangel Michael, Saint Margaret, and Saint Catherine. She saw her life as animated by her spirituality: a just war, for her as for all crusaders, was a form of prayer. Yet, as George Tavard reminds us, "it is not easy to place Jeanne la Pucelle in one of the classical schools of spirituality."[2] As the essays in this volume show, there are multiple facets of Joan's prayerful life. We are aware above all of her inward looking in her attention to her spiritual voices; over and over she voices her desire to mold her actions on the basis of her divinely inspired mission. She thus embodies and symbolizes the active consequences of living out (and out of) profound religious faith.

*

Inspired by Anne Barstow's survey questions (found in chapter 15 of this volume), we decided that it would be fitting for us as coeditors of this volume to enter into that dialogue by making a brief, personal statement about the importance of Joan of Arc within our own lives. At this point, therefore, our separate voices must be heard.

Bonnie writes:
I had no interest in Joan of Arc when I was a girl. I thought she was either crazed or fictional or both, and she was certainly on the wrong side of all my secular, democratic, antiwar sentiments. I first became curious about Joan when I began to study seriously the roles of Jean Gerson and Christine de Pizan in the *querelle des dames*. Though it remains an imaginative speculation, I was intrigued by the question of whether there might be any causal relation between Gerson's death on July 12, 1429 and Christine's composition of the *Ditié de Jehanne d'Arc*, which she dated July 31, 1429. I wondered whether the proximity of her partisan Gerson's death to Joan's success in Orléans and in leading Charles to his coronation on July 17 of that year inspired Christine to compose her final tribute to female heroism. These two powerful intellectuals helped shape contemporary responses to Joan; they propelled one strain of instant mythologizing that validated her

status as warrior heroine in biblical and classical traditions. In any case, the intersection of the dates in July is portentous.

Only then did I read Joan's trial records. As we all know, those documents are staggering—in all senses. I was entirely swept away by them. In these documents we hear the piercingly clear voice of a young woman whose spirit and psyche are being probed by men who are largely convinced that she is a menace to spiritual and worldly authority. I was startled by Joan's confessional habits of self-examination and her respect for clerical authority, revealed in her initial willingness when on trial to probe her own conscience, to expose her anxieties as well as proclaim her piety. I now read voraciously about Joan and frequently teach a course on Joan to undergraduates, all of whom are older than was Joan when she was burned at the stake (for Ann's and my and other syllabi, see the pedagogy pages on the International Joan of Arc Society's website at http://www.smu.edu/ijas).

For me, Joan's spirituality is like the unmentionable elephant-in-the-room: it is impossible to avoid, utterly undeniable, yet inexplicable. Her faith been represented, admitted, and denied in several contradictory fashions. Some of us as scholars are embarrassed by the simple beliefs of the subjects we study; others of us yearn for faith that seems unattainable. Others condescend to or are embarrassed by persons of faith. I am troubled by an academic tendency to dismiss Joan's spirituality as adolescent fantasy since this strikes me as both sexist and ageist. Who is to say that a teenaged girl doesn't have a fully mature spiritual self-understanding? Mystics and maniacs may be closely allied but they are not necessarily identical.

Wonderful colleagues, including those whose work is found in this volume (and especially my brilliant coeditor Ann Astell), have generously taught me about Joan, and she fascinates me as Augustine always has: I live inside the questions she provokes if not the answers she provides. As I read and think about Joan, I encounter the limits of my spiritual horizons. Her own intense devotional life sustained her as it sustains others. If I can't quite find her anyplace else, I can't get her out of my head.

Ann writes:

Like many of Barstow's respondents, I was first drawn to Saint Joan as a teenaged girl. I read *The Lark*, shortly after viewing a made-for-television movie about Joan of Arc, starring Genevieve Bujold. My identification with Joan was so strong and immediate that I wrote a declamation, based on Joan's speeches to her judges at Rouen, and delivered it onstage before the student body at Jefferson Junior High, playing Joan's part, my hair cut short. A pious and serious girl raised on a farm in Wisconsin, I identified easily with Joan's rural, peasant origins and love of nature. Like her, I could hear the church bells ringing the Angelus from across the fields. The sound of their ringing mingled with my adolescent yearning to discover my own calling in life. Joan's short life, intensely lived, confirmed my urgent sense, already as a youth, that each one is granted only a few years on earth, that each day is precious, and that we are not allowed to waste the little time we have; rather, we are obliged to spend it doing good, in keeping with our vocation.

Unlike many of the women in Barstow's survey, I have always seen Joan as a saint and a martyr; it is precisely the heroic, religious quality of her spirituality that attracted me as a youth and that still draws me to her. A saint of ardent love and intense prayer, she heard God's call, and she obeyed, come what may, even after the voices fell silent. She let God use her in the world; she withheld nothing from him, neither action nor suffering. For Joan, a radical instrumentality—the lonely fulfillment of her mission—became a unique way of holiness that assimilated her to Mary and Jesus. What amazes me more today than ever is the spiritual discernment, the charity, and the moral courage that enabled Joan to accept a vocation that was without precedent for a woman—one that exposed her to severe trials, that tested her faith, and that required of her great purity of soul and body. Accepting her vocation, she accepted also her martyrdom, for she knew what her "yes" would cost her.

When I became a Schoenstatt Sister of Mary twenty-five years ago, I was happy to discover in the pages of the founding document of the Schoenstatt Movement a reference to Saint Joan of Arc. Speaking at a minor seminary on October 18, 1914, to a group of boys who were soon to be drafted as soldiers in World War I, Fr. Joseph Kentenich (+1968) compared the little Schoenstatt Shrine, which was originally dedicated to Saint Michael the Archangel, to the Shrine of Saint Catherine of Fierbois, where the sword of Saint Joan was discovered. Addressing the boys as Saint Michael had once called to Joan of Arc, Fr. Kentenich urged them to take up the spiritual armor of prayer and practice virtue and to place their lives bravely at the service of the Mother of God.

As I write these lines, the newspapers are again filled with reports of war. When Bonnie and I began to envision this collection, we could not have foreseen these developments, which suggest a new relevance of Joan's story for contemporary spirituality. Some will follow Joan as soldiers, some as protesters against war, but no one can rightly claim Saint Joan as a guide who does not act in obedience to the inner voice of conscience, which commands us all. One thing, I think, is sure: the lonely courage of Joan of Arc means that no one who simply follows the crowd can be said to follow her. Joan's discipleship is different.

Notes

1. See the work of Henry Ansgar Kelly, especially "The Right to Remain Silent: Before and After Joan of Arc," *Speculum* 68 (1993): 992–1026, and "Joan of Arc's Last Trial: The Attack of the Devil's Advocates," *Fresh Verdicts on Joan of Arc*, ed. Bonnie Wheeler and Charles T. Wood (New York, Garland, 1996), pp. 205–36.
2. George H. Tavard, "The Spirituality of Saint Joan," in *Joan of Arc at the University*, ed. Mary Elizabeth Tallon (Milwaukee: Marquette University Press, 1997), p. 56 [43–58].

PART ONE

JOAN'S OWN SPIRITUALITY

CHAPTER 1

THE MORTAL BODY AS DIVINE PROOF: A SPIRITUAL–PHYSICAL BLAZON OF JOAN OF ARC

Nadia Margolis

In this chapter, Joan's mortal body is presented as a key facet of her spiritual persona in her cultural reception history, first in terms of a sacramental anatomy linking her to Christ as savior, then in relation to the fleur-de-lis as co-icon sacred to France, and finally as prophetic agent.

Prologue: "Corps pour corps"

In around March 22, 1429, Joan dictated a challenge, as part of her famous "Letter to the English," urging them to surrender peacefully or suffer dire consequences: "Roy d'Angleterre, se ainsi ne le faictes, je sui chef de guerre, et en quelque lieu que j'actandray voz gens en France, [. . .] si ne vuellent obeir, *je les feray tous occire; je sui cy envoiee par Dieu, le Roy du Ciel, corps pour corps*, pour vous bouter hors de toute France"[1] [King of England, if you do not do so, I am commander of the armies, and wherever I meet your men in France, [. . .] should they wish not to obey, *I shall have them all killed, every last one, for I am sent here by God, King of Heaven*, to kick you all out of France] (emphasis mine). These words, so astounding from a young girl addressing the conqueror of her homeland, reflect the essence of how Joan perceived her mission: sent by God, she, normally a gentle, pious country girl, would kill as often as necessary and without hesitation to achieve her goal. The locution "corps pour corps"—literally "body for body" or "body by body"—connotes more than the mortality exchange, part of the fatal economy, mandated by a Just War (the secular equivalent of Holy War).[2] Joan's body, unlike the other soldiers' of both sides, even the commanding officers', represented not only a unit of military might but also an incarnation of divine will, as she endured various assaults and afflictions. Plus she was, as she states, "chef de guerre"—literally *head* of the army. These ordeals and responsibilities too, like the commands of her voices, she accepted unquestioningly as the fate of a mortal body playing a divinely ordained role. Furthermore, I shall argue that, like other martyrs, but in a more aggressive way, especially for a woman, Joan's lone mortal body, in war and in death, both whole and in part, offered the ultimate proof of her divine inspiration sufficient to dispel all suspicion of any manifestation of satanic influence.

Why did Joan accept her voices' mandate unquestioningly, and what does this indicate about her spirituality? Etienne Delaruelle, in his classic essay on Joan's spirituality, affirms that some of the more outwardly obscure, or vague and incoherent, aspects of Joan's piety actually serve to underscore the divinity of her inspiration:

> Ignorante de l'Ecriture, elle ne savait pas clairement comment le Seigneur avait parlé aux prophètes; étrangère à toute école de spiritualité, on ne lui avait parlé non plus jamais des motions de l'Esprit Saint dans une âme. Elle ne sait que ce qu'elle éprouve au jour le jour, définissant mal—on le lui a reproché—cette expérience ineffable, employant le mot approximatif de <<voix>> pour désigner cette action de Dieu en elle, qui désormais y fait loi. Elle vit alors en état d'attente.[3]
>
> [Ignorant of the Scriptures, she did not know clearly how the Lord had spoken to the prophets; an outsider to any school of spiritual belief, she had also been told nothing of the movements of the Holy Ghost within a soul. She knows only what she experiences from day to day, never properly articulating—for which she was reproached—this ineffable experience, using the approximating term <<voices>> to designate God's agency within her, which henceforth became the rule. She thus lived in a state of expectation.]

In other words, it is an oversimplification to say that she "bypassed the Church Militant" (Church on Earth), as her accusers, threatened by her voices, would have us believe. More precisely, Joan received her brand of Christian doctrine—the truths by which she lived and thought as a virtuous person—in their purest form: via her angelic voices and visions. Initiated into the faith by listening to her mother's teachings and reciting the Paternoster (the prayer "Our Father"), Joan possessed only rudimentary knowledge of Christian teaching, but yet lived it more perfectly than those learned and exalted theologians governing the Church Militant. While aware of this superiority over her persecutors, as symbolized by her voices, she also urgently needed to partake of the key sacraments these priests alone could administer. Likewise, Bishop Cauchon and the others needed to disprove, or have her recant, the truth of her voices—this "direct line" to God—in order to conquer her, body and soul. This mutual recognition between captors and captive of the power of Joan's inspiration, as shown by her physical presence and actions, adds to the literal cruxes constituting her passion: the quandary of her obedience to the Church Militant versus the Church Triumphant (Church in Heaven) thus joins the other interrelated conflicts she incarnated: political-military force versus divine right; male versus female hegemony; official, public versus personal spirituality; body versus soul.

In her the Word was made flesh, as revealed in practice. As this chapter will attempt to show, her mortal body also belongs to this concrete, yet elusive or self-contradictory category of her spiritual manifestations: one not only proving "God's agency within her" (and not Satan's, as her detractors maintained) but also one elevating her status from that of one *waiting* (Delaruelle's "expectation") to that of one *awaited*, to accomplish a distinctly finite, temporal goal. This goal was to help rescue her country during a perilous phase of France's self-determination, the final phase of the Hundred Years War.

In executing her mission, her persona constantly self-regenerated among three different, yet interrelated, primary signs: her body, her country's icon (the fleur-de-lis), and the divine word (prophecies applicable to and by her, as well as God's Word via her voices). This study purports to chart how her mortal body functioned as an intensifying vehicle for the other two expressions of her personhood, to make her own type of trinity, uniting divine theology and earthly politics to fulfill her mission for France. I shall underscore that it was no coincidence that she would be compared to Christ by her compatriots after her death and was even revered as a cult figure in life,[4] a connection informed by French kingship theory and political-theological polemic, as much as by her own personal piety and patriotism.[5] Unlike her fictional precursors, the mysterious serpent-woman protector Mélusine and the more fact-based Roland—two originally French folkloric legends later elaborated by clerkly propagandists into nationalistic founding figures and literary heroes—Joan was a real-life person. All were endowed with natural, supernatural, and martyrological attributes profusely represented by bodily gestures and metaphors, but Joan, rivaling another true-life hero, Saint Louis, merits separate examination as a more full-fledged analogue of Christ.[6]

Throughout our entire analysis, we must remain mindful of a pervasive tension between Joan's increasingly deliberate self-fashioning and those qualities ascribed to her by chroniclers and other authors who fashioned her image, just as the Gospels and later Church Fathers portrayed Jesus, eternalizing Him. It is significant, for example, that Joan was celebrated by authors other than hagiographers, and often those casting a colder, more secular, eye. Equally meaningful, among hagiographers, is the possibility that Joan is not the first *woman* to be directly likened to Christ, but she may be the first woman to be so linked for her more stereotypically masculine role, that of soldier, in which physical violence is endured as part of the saintly exploit preceding the martyrdom itself; the latter qualifying phase often inflicting equal physical torment upon female and male saints.[7] Therefore, any study of Joan's spiritual–bodily mapping must involve the historiographical, even mythographical, traditions generated by her literal body and its metaphoricity, whether in structure, gesture, or speech. Although this essay's scope does not necessitate a full review of posterity's allusions to her body's religious symbolism, we do expect to reveal its basic importance in understanding her cultural reception as a vital spiritual figure even today.

Of Arms and the Woman: The Anatomy of a Female Warrior–Saint

Any investigation of this sort automatically engages the medieval theological doctrines concerning mortal and divine bodies, and the more secular, specific characteristics of Joan's corporeality as recorded by her contemporaries and later authors. While space does not allow for anything approaching a proper discussion of the first category here, the following overview should help acquaint the reader with the prevailing doctrines and dogmas applicable to Joan's sacramental role as well as to Christ's—a parallelism noted by the heroine's later apologists.

Commentators on Joan's life and death could draw upon the abundant, painstakingly evolved Christian doctrines on the mortal body, perhaps most eloquently articulated in Saint Paul's epistles, especially the body as temple of the Holy Spirit/Holy Ghost. First and foremost, Christ's body in all its manifestations inspired the sacraments: outward rituals imparting grace and through which the pious observer participates in His inner "mystery": that which makes him uniquely, ineffably, Jesus Christ. His most important mystery is the Incarnation: how, through the flesh of his human mother, Mary,[8] he assumed the form of a man in order to fulfill and thus to communicate his Father's will on earth. Joan's duality is evident here: on the one hand, analogous to Mary, she became imbued with a sense of His will through her eyes and ears, hearing His emissaries' voices rather than receiving His seed through her womb; on the other hand, pursuing the Joan-as-Christ track, we could compare Joan's mother, Isabel Romée, to Mary and Jacques d'Arc to Joseph.[9] The most profound sacrament, the Eucharist—the body and blood of Christ ritually consumed via the communion wafer and wine through the phenomenon called transubstantiation—was fervently practiced by Joan. The power of relics (remains of Christ's and other saints' bodies as healing objects) is also evident in Joan's story after her death, as we shall see, as are the doctrines of the glorification and Resurrection of Christ's body after the Crucifixion, at least analogously.[10]

In 1894, during Joan's case for Beatification, the Congregation's prefect, Cardinal Aloisi-Masella, frequently emphasized her body, both wholly and in part, as indicators of her saintly servitude, in his decree of January 27. He deployed such phrases as "fearing God in the simplicity and innocence of her heart," "her fingers worked the spindle," "put her hand to the great work" to laud the "good and simple maiden, sustained only by the spirit of obedience and animated by a wonderful charity."[11]

Obviously, allusions of this sort belong to the realm of metaphor, or at least to metonymy, especially synecdoche, depending on the magnitude of the divine presence we perceive in Joan's members and gestures. To qualify Joan's body as metaphoric would make her a sort of reflection of God; whereas to interpret her as metonymic would render her more an extension of God, his "right hand" as it were, just as when she deliberately stands at Charles's right at the Reims coronation. In all, Joan's function may arguably vary from episode to episode, between metaphoric and metonymic. That her actions belong as much to these abstract realms as to literal truth is typical enough of hagiographic portraiture.

Joan used her body more literally as a soldier of God than most other saints have done before the supreme consummation of a horrific death.[12] This fact blurs the distinction between metaphor and reality all the more, making her a euhemeristic heroine, especially in the so-called Rehabilitation trial testimony gathered from 1452 to 1456. Since virtually no eyewitness visual-arts portraits of her survive, we must depend completely on verbal descriptions.[13] These are too often colored by each witness's—and in some cases, the recorders'—political agenda. The Rehabilitation contained more details of Joan's physiognomy than the Rouen trial. It was also more positive in tone, as part of its overall intent to save Charles's good name at least as much as Joan's. Other sources, from outside the trials, like Perceval de Boulainvilliers's letter to the duke of Milan, contain many details but lack accuracy, sometimes contradicting others' reports. Not surprisingly, a degree of reciprocity arose between Joan's reality and each narrator's intention, with the positive ones coloring her description from the heroic, hagiographical, or even Christlike palette while the detractors highlighted diabolical or witchlike traits. But whatever the motives behind each portrait, we concur with Colette Beaune that Joan, like other saintly women, manifested a "progressive spiritualization of the body."[14]

What we can determine to some extent is that Joan had almost black hair and eyes, a rather dark complexion, and sturdy build.[15] As with the putatively olive-skinned Christ often depicted with a fair complexion and light-brown hair for Western audiences,[16] such facts did not prevent later artists from lightening her hair and complexion to enhance her saintly aura. And it is not surprising that the Joan imaged by the Vichy government—Pro-Nazi collaborators in World War II—was often "Aryanized" to blonde, as in the notorious woodcut by M. Albe.[17]

Epic heroes drawn from history but aggrandized in literature, from weak-heeled Achilles to beardless Njal, have often borne some sort of physical mark, usually an absurdly incongruous deficiency in relation to their overall superhuman attributes. Joan was no exception. Her various physical deformities to be surveyed here—eliciting either awe, fear, or curiosity—form an integral part of her mystique. Joan's various corporeal strata follow a hierarchy of spiritual significance, though not a strictly vertical one; rather, one radiating from her religious-symbolic "center": her virginity.

Virginity is by far her most important attribute, confirmed simultaneously with the Poitiers examination prior to Orléans and also during her imprisonment at Rouen.[18] Her self-naming as "La Pucelle" in her "Lettre aux Anglais" (March 22, 1429) and her motto, "Jesus Mary," demonstrate her awareness of her virginity's religious-symbolic force and her exceptional need to stave off accusations of sexual promiscuity by preemptively asserting that she was not a lowly camp follower. The success of her self-fashioning as virgin warrior is reflected in the profusion of contemporary treatises devoted to her that focus primarily on this trait and its political-theological implications.[19] Following the example of her favorite saints, Margaret of Antioch and Catherine of Alexandria, Joan supposedly made a vow of chastity when she first heard her voices. She was also later sued for breach of marriage promise—unsuccessfully—by a young man at Toul.[20] Joan thus underwent, as a real-life person, what martyrs to chastity, like her saints Catherine and Margaret, avoided by being legends.[21] In a characteristic leap of heuristic faith as an historian, Colette Beaune suggests that because Joan's famous ring was connected with Saint Catherine's ring, and because Catherine was a mystical bride of Christ, Joan too was a bride of Christ.[22]

Perhaps more directly, we could perceive Joan's wearing of armor as outwardly reflecting her anatomical virginity, itself evidence of her spiritual flawlessness. By undertaking a male military mission and assuming clothing of the most masculine kind, she merges with and then transcends both the already redoubtable performative "militant" virginity of her favorite saints and other martyrs and also the "bridal" virginity of the quieter majority of female religious, in order to live her virginity as a true third gender.[23] Joan's chastity apparently enshrouded her within a veritable force-field of chivalric honor. It was respected by her men-at-arms to deferential extremes, as with Jean d'Aulon, who testified that although he had seen her naked and found her body attractive, he never felt carnal desire for her;[24] the duke of Alençon claims similar self-restraint upon catching a glimpse of her breasts.[25] Her virginity also promoted her, a humble provincial, to a kind of elite status before the various noblewomen entrusted first with examining, then supervising her during her imprisonment, causing even the duchess of Bedford to be fiercely protective of Joan's person.

Joan's burning was the climax of her performance of ultra-militant virginity as much to her contemporaries as to us moderns, since witnesses reported seeing a dove fly up to Heaven from her expiring body. Then, as a jarring contrast, in an act of seeming earthly, morbid prurience as much as standard post-execution procedure, the executioner pushed back the flames and revealed her naked, ashen corpse to the public, so that all might concur, once and for all, that she was indeed female, dead, and thus had not escaped, as a witch might have.[26]

Allied to her virginity/chastity and the purity of her closed, intact body (and therefore, soul) immured against sin,[27] is Joan's supposed amenorrhea, again per testimony of Jean d'Aulon in the Rehabilitation trial: "oncques n'avoit eu la secrecte maladie des femmes" [never did she have the woman's secret malady].[28] The most meaningful side of this bit of hearsay gathered by Jean d'Aulon from Joan's female attendants is that Jean d'Aulon meant this as a compliment, as part of Joan's supra-feminine purity before the prevailing misogynistic clerical attitude.[29] She will spill blood in the name of God and her king, but not in this flawed—if one listens to misogynist clerics linking it to Eve's sin—banally female way. Likewise witnesses like Simon Charles, president of the royal treasury, testified to never having seen her perspire nor urinate.[30] Joan does often shed tears,[31] however—in confession, for her people, and for her own cruel fate prior to her execution in a manner comparable to Christ.[32]

Second in importance to her virginity, but perhaps foremost in revealing the role of Joan's mortal body as divine proof, would be her heart. If her virginity stood as her religious-symbolic center, her heart functioned as her material-bodily center. Yet this organ certainly does not lack for sacrosanct connotations. Like Joan herself, her heart offered the most dramatic, immediate proof of her superlative devotion to God and His approval of her mission and vengeance against her enemies, during her lifetime and even more after her death. After her burning, witnesses like Jean Massieu, citing the executioner, tell us that despite efforts to reduce it to ashes, Joan's heart "remained intact and full of blood" [remansit cor illesum et sanguine plenum] and then was thrown into the Seine with her ashes.[33] Such reports verge on hagiography; in this case as if to explain why no relics of Joan remain.[34] In fact this was the same executioner who confided to Martin Ladvenu and other priests his fears of damnation for having burned a saint,[35] as did the notary Jean Tressart.[36] Indeed, notary Boisguillaume (Guillaume Colles) acknowledges the dreadful end suffered by all those responsible for Joan's death.[37] Apart from its folkloric resonances,[38] Joan's heart, then, lay at the vortex of earthly versus divine justice—and of her contemporaries' unprecedented awareness of this retribution, both tropologically and in reality.

The meaning of blood itself, apart from menstrual blood and the blood-filled heart mentioned earlier, deserves special mention as an overt manifestation of Joan's devotion. Many a female religious martyr (including Catherine) endured emitting some sort of epiphanic gore during her ordeal, but only Joan spilled hers as part of the positive, or pre-martyrdom, phase of her exploit. Not surprisingly, blood shed in warfare bore a dual significance for Joan: while it was right that English blood should flow, the sight of French blood spilling always made her hair stand on end.[39] Medically speaking, Joan's war-induced blood came under scrutiny when she was wounded and especially during her imprisonment, where she was bled with leeches in accordance with accepted medical procedure to cure her food poisoning.[40] Since it was the duke of Bedford who had ordered these doctors' visits, we can discern another interested party in the value of Joan's mortal body as proof: Bedford did not wish to let her die of incidental illness, but rather to endure punishment as a victim of his authority. Finally, her dynastic blood, having become ennobled by Charles through letters patent to her family, would be revered in the nineteenth century, as her "glorious blood" became traceable through numerous French notables—including none less than the seventeenth-century moralist Fénelon and the colonizing Marshal Lyautey (1854–1934)—over succeeding centuries.[41] (The next section of this chapter will discuss her role in purifying the Blood Royal associated with the fleur-de-lis, another icon linking her to her country's destiny.)

Third would come her eyes and ears, primary receptors of her voices and visions and aids in discerning their false counterparts. That she was touched by these Voices is signaled by a birthmark behind her right ear—"tabes rubea retro aurem dextram," as Jean Bréhal records in his Rehabilitation review.[42] Her ears enabled her to hear Mass, which she did whenever possible,[43] and also her beloved church bells in her native Domremy. She hated hearing vulgar language, whose usage she forbade among her men. The judges repeatedly asked about her visions, what she precisely saw and heard, their tone rife with sarcasm. Her adamantly evasive and sometimes flippant answers rendered ridiculous such questions as whether her angels came naked or clothed, making the judges, who sought to discredit her as a diabolical lunatic, look like infidels. As Delaruelle comments, what she really saw and heard matters less than what her unquestioning belief in them inspired within her and her people, as evidenced by her exploits.[44] Her angels' earthly forms, pseudo-bodies—the sole concern of the judges—mattered little to Joan because they were just that: simply guises for assimilation by mortal eyes. It was Joan's mortal body that counted because it was the operative vehicle for what she believed to be her voices', or God's, commands.

Her mouth too played a role. From it emanated her own, reputedly sweet, yet commanding, sometimes insolent, voice,[45] suppressed as direct discourse in trial records, arguably to diminish her charismatic persona for posterity.[46] It was also the instrument of her confession, several times per week or even per day during combat situations, as a way of "preserving the virginity of her soul."[47] Perhaps her most memorable vocalism was at the stake, when she cried "Jesus" three times before expiring—an outcry that moved onlookers to weeping, as reported by several Rehabilitation witnesses.[48] In another routine oral capacity, Joan did not usually consume much food and drink.[49] Like Jesus and Mary, Joan was mainly a vegetarian who also ate fish, in keeping with her predilection for scriptural symbolism, but no meat, except for taking the Communion host, the Eucharist, symbolic of Christ's flesh, which she did more frequently than the Church then prescribed.[50] Much has been made by her interrogators and modern historians of her fasting and possible tendency toward anorexia, often linked by her detractors to her "hallucinatory" voices and visions, and by her apologists to her supposed amenorrhea.[51]

Turning now to the major part of Joan's body—her trunk and limbs, plus a rather short neck[52]—we think of Christine de Pizan, among others, who marveled at how "une fillette de XVI ans" [such a lithe sixteen-year-old girl] could wear and wield such heavy armaments, as if to assert that the more diminutive her physique, the greater her faith and assistance from God, which Christine equates with "nourriture" [nourishment].[53] The poet's view also coincides with the heroine's wish, as expressed at her Rouen trial, to have her miraculous exploits seen as solely the work of God.[54] As uplifting as this may seem, Christine's propaganda harmonizes with her military doppelganger's but not with the impressions of such contemporaries as Perceval de Boulainvilliers,[55] who affirms Joan's unusual physical strength and skilled horsemanship.

From another significant angle concerning her physique and armor, Delaruelle, always seeking to interpret the impact of Joan's physical presence through fifteenth-century eyes, emphasizes that the clerics took offense at *any* form of male dress, the armor being so secondary that it is not mentioned specifically during the trial, in contrast to her ring, sword, and banner, which, as Delaruelle deduces about how her wearing of armor, was more tacitly construed to be a series of religious emblems from the Christian Soldier motif, rather than mere weapons.[56] If we accept this, then we can go on to suggest that Joan's body, as well as her armor, rendered material what had heretofore been metaphorical in sermon, hymn, and prayer. She could be perceived as a real-life incarnation of Saint Michael, the soldier saint of France, and his female homologue, Catherine—as it happens, two saints from Joan's visions, with whose cults her own seemed later to intertwine.[57]

The topic of saintly cults recalls a related one, earlier touched upon briefly—namely, that of relics. Though her remains were deliberately dumped into the Seine to avert veneration and thus inevitably helped to promote her case for sainthood in 1894,[58] it could be said that Joan's spirituality and overwhelming charisma during her lifetime made her not only a living cult but also a movable reliquary: healing the demoralized French populace through her touch and, more abstractly, healing France's rifts through her wounds. Unlike certain other female mystics, Joan's mortal body did not undergo ecstatic-pain symptoms of its union with Christ's on the Cross: no stigmata appear on her hands and feet as we find in accounts of the lives of such saints as Catherine of Siena and Catherine of Genoa. Those wounds she does experience, in her breast, foot (both at Orléans), and thigh (outside Paris), result from actual contact with weapons, or in one additional instance, from long hours in the saddle[59]—not from extreme privation and self-mortification during contemplation. Joan's wounds result from active, not metaphorical, service, nor did they occur out of static devotion and veneration.[60] Her tolerance for pain befits both saint and soldier.[61] Joan's wounds represent Christ's and participate in His Passion as manifestations of her obedience to the divine voices, commanding her to use her body as a male soldier's, in both dress and gesture.

Even more than with Christ and other martyrs, Joan's self-contradicting gender and sexuality attracted the most attention of all her physical qualities, both in her day and in ours, because she made it so visible, supposedly at the behest of her voices. She cultivated her personal charisma by assuming male dress, either as a cross-dresser or transvestite, a subtopic whose fascination for scholars has only increased over the ages.[62]

Examination of medieval theological writings and the art inspired by them yields two principal, often deliberate, sources of visceral–allegorical parallelisms between Joan's and Christ's abnegation of sexuality, and also, paradoxically, fostered each figure's maternal image: first, the infant or young Jesus as the Ever-virgin, yet genitally exposed,[63] and second, the concept of Jesus-as-Mother, according to which Jesus suckles the faithful from his breasts and shelters them within his womb-like wounds.[64] Joan too is a "pucelle" plus warrior—ergo an Amazon, as Gerson, Montigny, and Bréhal noted[65]—yet one whom Christine de Pizan, for example, also evokes as offering her breast to nourish France on peace.[66] Because Christine is speaking to a lay public more than to theologians, she proclaims the un- or rather, super-naturalness of this condition: "Véez bien chose oultre nature!" [See how extraordinary (lit. = beyond nature) this is!] (v. 192). In these respects, Joan, like Jesus, incarnates the spiritual reconciliation of fecundity with purity and unconditional, nurturing love.

Each figure possesses key virtues normally identifying the opposite sex while avoiding that gender's impurities. Given the misogynistic attitude of the Church's doctrines, Joan's iconography entailed more "unnatural" disparities to reconcile than Christ's. For example, Amazons, whose name in Greek means "without breasts," cut off (usually, only) their right breast so as not to impede the bowstring when shooting an arrow, thus making them equal to men at archery. This deliberate, gender-blurring, combat-effective aspect of the Amazon precedent derived from pagan myth, which Joan's example commingles with Christian allegory.[67] The bizarre, indeed shocking, physiological impossibility of such recombinations within a single sex, as exemplified in both figures, arrests our attention. Moreover, both Joan and Jesus deploy their uniquely bisexual powers toward greater self-sacrifice and suffering, instead of greater material gain and pleasure. This sets an example that can move us to extremes of devotion, or, in more secular terms, obsession. Furthermore, the relentless calculation behind these Joan-as-Christ similarities drawn or hinted at by Joan's apologists is justified. For even though Joan did not found a church as did Christ's followers—such was not part of her mission—she did significantly help to move a nation toward self-actualization both spiritually and militarily.

Her polemicists' persistence was also necessary to stave off pro-English maneuvers to distort her bodily purity. Anglo-Burgundian historians like Hall, Holinshed, and later followers like Fabyan often labeled her everything from a witch or harlot to a monster, a pythoness; depicting her as an evil being who feigned pregnancy to escape execution.[68] Fortunately, her rapid entrenchment within the Christological register allowed her image to withstand such calumny over the centuries. For all their flights of spuriousness, by the late nineteenth century, the historiography and hagiography of Joan and Christ taught us at least one valuable lesson: that the most valid reading is not necessarily a gendered one. In other words, the interrelation of her body with that of Christ's makes her not so much a bride of Christ but instead patterns itself on the difference between sacrament and sacramental. For if we consider Christ's body to be the foundation of the sacraments as mentioned here, then Joan's body may be viewed as a "sacramental": it does not attain Christ's sanctity, but nonetheless outwardly signifies God's inward action, mediating His presence in time and space; and making His will known through her against the English in France.

In the Beauty of the Lilies. . .: Joan's Body as Icon

Toward the end of his recently rediscovered 1917 film, *Joan the Woman*, Cecil B. De Mille ends his prologue scene on a surrealistic note of prophecy via text and image. As the intertitle reads: "She gave her all for France, and her reward was martyrdom," Joan (Geraldine Farrar) strikes the pose of Christ-like crucifixion against a human-sized, illuminated fleur-de-lis shadow on the wall. Her arms and head are upraised first in glory, then hang in suffering, as her head slumps sideways, then bobs, finally forward. Despite the fortyish Farrar's corporeal heft, the diva's talent for gesture and De Mille's then-burgeoning gift for visual symbolism make this scene plausible, and more trenchant than either artist may have fully realized at the time. For it is not only a redeeming moment in a kitsch-ridden, though worthy, contribution to Joan's filmic history, but also, like certain other scenes, extremely clever in its manipulation of prevailing political and religious sentiment during World War I, as part of its general goal to jolt the United States out of its isolationism. In its choice of superimposed icons—Joan, Christ crucified, and the fleur-de-lis—this scene inscribes itself, whether consciously or unconsciously, within a centuries-old, primarily verbal, tradition of Johannic political–martyrological iconography, rendering it with unprecedented visual effectiveness and originality. For De Mille's Joan is not only crucified like Christ on the cross, but also specifically on the French national symbol, the fleur-de-lis—an ornate torture rack—signifying her fidelity to her king and her apotheosis as national savior.[69]

De Mille's cinematic symbolism sprang from more than Hollywood's random brainstorming, since Joan's own banner, as dictated by her voices, was a white field sprinkled with gold fleurs-de-lis, thereby uniting her with this earthly patriotic symbol from the beginning of her campaign. Her banner's more distinctive elements—the King of Heaven atop the world, an orb flanked by the angels Michael and Gabriel, and the motto, "Jhesu Maria" [Jesus Mary] boldly inscribed—left no doubt as to her divine claims and also to those of Valois kingship, both of which were deemed by her pro-English Rouen trial interrogators as heretical. Modern historian Colette Beaune notes that only a few locales and persons have been identified with the fleur-de-lis besides Joan. Foremost among these was the hallowed thirteenth-century lawgiver and crusader, Saint Louis (Louis IX), whose family, the Capetians, preceded the Valois.[70] To this list, Marina Warner adds some more romantic, though dubiously spiritual, honorees like Gilles de Rais and Lord Darnley.[71] King Charles VII also strengthened Joan's connection with the lily symbol by conferring nobility upon her family, granting a coat of arms to her brothers and the noble family name of "Du Lys" [Of the Lily].[72]

The fleur-de-lis, the lily flower, was one of the dominant symbols of France well before Joan's era, ever since its prototype appeared on the insignia of Hugh Capet's son, Robert the Pious (996–1031). In adopting it as an integral part of their great seal, which originally displayed King Henry I holding the lily in his right hand,[73] the French kings distinguished their right to rule as deriving not from brute force and fear—as proclaimed in most other countries' royal seals adorned with eagles, dragons, and lions—but from "Wisdom, Faith and Chivalry."[74] These serene facets of mental, spiritual, and moral purity united the ruler, his dynasty, and his domain first through Saint Denis, who supposedly introduced these virtues into France, and then through the Virgin and resurrected Christ; followed by militant defense of these ideals whenever necessary. The fleur-de-lis's aspects were glossed and even extolled by thirteenth- and fourteenth-century chroniclers, commentators, and poets like Guillaume de Nangis, Yves of Saint-Denis, Philippe de Vitry, and Geoffroy of Paris, who related the three petals to the Holy Trinity and the flower's whiteness to chastity (Hinkle, 15–21). In botanical-medical lore, Bernard de Gordon maintained that all parts of the white lily plant possessed therapeutic powers (Hinkle, 2). This last property we may link in particular to part of Joan's mandate, heralded in the so-called Merlin prophecy of her as a "maiden who shall give care to healing."[75] In many representations the pronounced central petal of the conventionally feminine flower assumed a sword-like, even phallic symbolism for military and dynastic-male potency—all the more essential to a country forging its rules of royal succession under Salic Law, thereby barring female rulers. Retroactively, historical "spin doctors" would conjoin the fleur-de-lis with the heaven-sent victories over the German tribes of France's first holy king, Clovis, baptized with equally divine chrism at Reims ca. 496 (Hinkle, 23–26, 72).

The lily's innate reconciliations and unifications—of the sacred versus the profane, of medical versus magical powers, of male versus female succession, and of France's pagan foundation versus Christian continuity—all point to Joan of Arc as divinely chosen savior of France, emphasizing her mortal body. The lily's literal and figurative whiteness and polysemy, just as physical whiteness combines all colors of the spectrum, parallel her various interrelated aspects: virginity, divine appointment, curative abilities, martyrdom, capacity for militant action to protect royal succession under Salic Law. Whenever we credit women with dynastic preservation and reinforcement, we usually think of flamboyant, serial polygamist matriarchal queens, like Eleanor of Aquitaine, who generated entire ruling classes from a single womb, and concomitantly brilliant cultural legacies from a single court. Joan is probably the only female protector of the Blood Royal to do so by nonreproductive means, indeed, by exploiting the antithesis, her virginity—just as the lily's symbolic potency resides within its canonical three petals, its unblemished whiteness; indeed every part but its reproductive corm. At the same time, both Joan and the lily, as shall gradually be seen here, operate via what we might call a gendered virginity, affording one of many abstract links between her and Christ.

In his most thorough history of the fleur-de-lis, William Hinkle demonstrates how, by Joan's time, the Anglo-Burgundian propagandists commanded by the duke of Bedford sought to subvert this quintessentially French lily, just as they attempted to defame Joan's bodily purity. They reworked the fleur-de-lis pedigree pattern not only to resolve the problems of royal succession within England after the Wars of the Roses, but also to hallow symbolically, through more politicized flora, what they had recently wrested by military might outside the kingdom. The Anglicized fleur-de-lis, a revised ideological spoil of war, thus furnished a proleptic prophecy, in word and image, for Henry V's miraculous victory over the French at Agincourt in 1415 and the resultant 1422 Treaty of Troyes that made Henry VI king of both England and France. First inspired by verses commissioned by the duke of Bedford in 1423, the ingenious fleur-de-lis-shaped genealogical chart shows the usurping heir, Henry VI, at the flower's base, suggestively parting the petals in the center.[76] Saint Louis appears at the top of the central, dominant petal, with the French Valois suggestively on the less favored left [*sinister*] petal, while Henry V's lineage occupies the right (Hinkle, 66–75, pl. 21). That the entire English claim in this scheme is guaranteed by female succession—through Charles VI's daughter Catherine, mother of Henry VI—in contrast to the French Salic Law barring such hereditary rights, perfectly delineates the disparity between French and English theories of kingship.[77] In addition, by eradicating Charles VII from all petals of the pedigree, it accentuates by absence the essence of Joan's mission to restore the Dauphin's legitimacy. Again we think of the Merlin prophecy: Joan would heal France's ills as the virgin warrior, restoring the lily of the Valois lineage compromised by Queen Isabel's infidelity and now mis-grafted by France's enemies.

More ironic symmetries present themselves, though on a strictly factual, rather than image–text–credo, level. The author of the verses and probably of the fleur-de-lis schema was one Laurent Calot, a royal secretary and Warwick's intimate, who also figures nefariously in Joan's trial: it was he who handed her the infamous cedula of Abjuration, and helped her sign it by guiding her hand.[78]

A further ironic coincidence occurred in 1445, the year of Henry VI's marriage to Margaret of Anjou. Though copies of both Calot's poem and pictorial fleur-de-lis pedigree were thought to have been posted in several major churches of northern France, particularly Notre Dame at Paris (Hinkle, 198), one of the finest examples of Calot's occupies all of folio 3r of

British Library MS Royal 15.E.VI, a splendidly produced anthology of French narrative texts and treatises compiled as a wedding gift from no less than John Talbot, first earl of Shrewsbury—Joan's legendary English counterpart and prisoner at the battle of Patay back in 1429—to Margaret. One principal work in this highly significant collection is Christine de Pizan's famous military treatise, the *Livre des Fais d'armes et de chevalerie* [Feats of Arms and Chivalry] of 1410, which was soon to attain great popularity in England.[79] Michel-André Bossy has insightfully explicated Calot's illustration in relation to Christine's *Fais d'armes* and the entire anthology's literary context.[80] Less emphasized by Bossy and beyond Hinkle's scope is that here we have a military manual by Christine, from her large oeuvre aimed at enlightening her adoptive country of France, now used fifteen years later, in Queen Margaret's anthology, to undermine the legitimacy of the French Valois, the dynasty of Christine's esteemed patrons, in favor of the English claim to the throne.

That the ardently patriotic Christine should find herself posthumously serving the enemy cause is bitter enough. Still closer investigation of Christine's relation to Joan's mission yields further ironies and convergences, involving not only the fleur-de-lis but also another hotly contested flower, more dissonantly embodying Christological elements and their quasi-obscene antithesis: the rose. Christine had begun her polemical career demolishing Lorris's and Jean de Meun's *Roman de la rose*, itself an allegory of female deflowering, as a defamation of women created, then applauded, by a sacrosanct segment of male society—high-ranking Parisian notaries and other officials—that should have known better. Twenty-five years later she crowned her prolific, richly varied literary career with the only non-anonymous vernacular work from Joan's lifetime. Christine not only defended but also celebrated Joan's virtuous androgyny as divinely inspired and "natural," and as divine proof of the "unerring fleur-de-lis," that is, Charles VII's claim to the throne (*Ditié de Jehanne d'Arc*, stanza 12).[81] As many a scholar has written, Christine finds in Joan the military incarnation of her own literary-polemical persona.[82] To this we might add that Joan also embodies Christine's poetic-autobiographical androgyny, commanded not so much by God as by a more pagan divinity, Fortuna, as graphically expressed in her *Livre de la Mutacion de Fortune* [Book of Fortune's Mutability] (vv. 1236–1405).[83] In both Christine and Joan, transgendering occurs beyond each woman's mortal will, as part of each woman's sibylline endowment, by force of earthly circumstance (widowhood, military service) and supernatural election—all of which the aged poet recognized more omnisciently than did the young heroine.

To return to the immediate historical context of Calot's lily, Henry VI's and Marguerite's union represented an attempt to redress the public-relations failure of Henry's ill-starred Paris coronation in December 1431.[84] This preposterous event was organized by another gray English eminence, along with Bedford and Warwick, Henry Beaufort, also known as Cardinal Winchester. Beaufort sought to offset, as the royal secretary Calot did the fleur-de-lis pedigree, the authentic 1429 Reims coronation of Charles VII, at which Joan was a keynote presence.

Within Joan's family, her later descendants (via her brothers' lines) came to realize that because of the Maid's increasing posthumous renown, especially in the nineteenth century, the name "d'Arc" carried more cachet than the royally conferred "du Lys," and thus shifted to the former, as in the case of Pierre Lanéry d'Arc, her most accomplished nineteenth-century descendant and scholar. And this is but one of the instances in which Joan's body would ally itself with the verbal, as well as the forementioned visual dimension to fulfill her mission.

The Flesh Made Word: Joan's Speaking Body

This final phase attempts to show how Joan, through her mortal body, verbally announced "Good News" for the French. She fulfilled the prophecies of "Merlin, Sibyl and Bede," as cited in Christine de Pizan's lapidary *Ditié* verses encompassing the Celtic, the antique pagan, and early Christian elements of France's cultural heritage, while simultaneously validating Joan as its rescuer.[85] These prophecies furnish much of the discursive parallel to the visual icon of her relation to the fleurs-de-lis, in her time and thereafter. In terms of her physical role, she also made her own predictions concerning the length of her mission and when she would be wounded. Throughout her career, from that of one foretold to one sanctified, Joan's immortality is indebted to the spoken and written word and to her seeming awareness of this phenomenon. A parallel progression also occurs onomastically, as seen at the end of this essay's previous section, when Joan's ennobled descendants, the Du Lys family, reverted to calling themselves "d'Arc" in the nineteenth century because of Joan's renascent glory, the champion of the symbol eclipsing the symbol itself.

During her lifetime, before her death, she knew herself to be in a state of grace—she felt God's presence within her—as we learn from her trial testimony [May 27] after she retracted her abjuration of her voices: again, powerful utterances.[86] Delaruelle signals this conviction as quite uncommon in her era, at a time when saintliness defined itself instead by penance and prayer within cloistered spaces (Delaruelle, 376).

Her closed, virginal body bespoke, and aroused others to speak not only of her soul's purity but also of its purging of the kingdom's body politic. Joan's virginity compensated for failings in Isabel's "open" promiscuous body and in the fissures wrought by the mental illness of the Dauphin's father, Charles VI, the troubled head of France's government. More than one commentator has opined that the English entered France through Louis of Orléans's and John the Fearless's bashed skulls: icons of the fratricidal civil war that weakened the country much more than did her external enemies. Such a bodily metaphor is apparent not only to modern scholars but also to her contemporaries, as manifested most comprehensively in several writings by Christine de Pizan in addition to her *Ditié de Jehanne d'Arc*: her pre-Joan works including the *Lamentacion, Corps de Policie, Mutacion de Fortune* and others.[87] Religiously oriented witnesses, like Martin Ladvenu and Isambart de la Pierre, also enveloped Joan's already captivating presence in their own innate idea of divine grace. Isambart adds the detail of a dove—another Christological symbol—flying upward from Joan's expiring corpse, as she cries the name of Jesus, thus further unifying her martyrdom with His.[88] This final corporeal *re*union between Joan and Christ may also be seen as the perfect completion of the process initiated by her having received *comm*union (the Eucharist) prior to her execution.[89]

Warner has trenchantly equated the discovery of Joan's unburned heart as immaculate vessel amidst the ashes with the Eucharist: "The pattern of the Word made flesh must repeat among all strata of the Christian bedrock [. . .] the image of Joan's unconsumed heart became a new touchstone, of her integrity, her incorruptibility, her charity, her love for God and God's love for her."[90]

But all these manifestations, as marvelous as they are, still belong to the realm of performance.[91] Joan's body also did actually speak and create, as well as hear and enact. She was more than a vessel or vehicle. By way of heuristic clarification, since "speaking bodies" have received much critical attention among medievalists, my use of such terms relates less to the secular–literary approach articulated by Jane Burns, for thematic reasons, and more to the theologically based analyses of Dyan Elliott and others.[92] By drawing upon Elliott's "physiology," we could consider Joan's entire mission, from her first visions and hearing of voices through her burning, as one sustained state of mystical rapture in which her soul followed her body. But as Elliott also observes, specifically stating Joan as an example, because of the heightened insecurity among late medieval male clerics concerning the overweening power of female mystical devotion, Joan's exceptional exploits did little to distinguish her as divinely inspired rather than diabolical.[93]

Despite the uncanny forcefulness of Joan's actions, her words in her testimony and letters spoke just as loudly. By deploying the body rhetoric (the corpus known as the arts of rhetoric) as well as by physical acts (*her* body *as* rhetoric), she helped to identify and restore France's rightful body politic, particularly its "head" (Charles VII as rightful king) and "reproductive system" (re-sanctifying the Blood Royal for guaranteeing future kings), and in so doing, she helped to redeem the French State as an organism, as united with the Mystical Body of Christ.[94] Her phrase "body for body" thus attains a higher meaning through her special mission.

To step back a bit in order to clarify this point: the truly divine—and to mortals, fearsome—proof offered by Joan's mortal, that is, literal, body lay in that she accomplished what was normally reserved only for allegorical or mythical figures, not out of grand ambition, but because, as Delaruelle indicates (e.g., 376–78), the literal level of devotion was all she knew. Or rather, to modify Delaruelle's assessment, such was all Joan *wanted us to think* she knew, as reflected in her *verbal* avowal of her simplistic obedience to divine will. Her outwardly anti-exegetical mindset, that is, her professed refusal to read the commands of her voices on any level but literally, formed the basis of her defiantly pure spirituality, while also disconcerting her trial interrogators. We can envision this speech, untainted by interpolation (interpretive commentary, as in law or scripture) to parallel her virginity. Her voices had commanded her to answer "boldly" [audacter].[95] And like preserving her virginity, maintaining simple yet firm speech was her best defense, as well as part of her promise to her angels. For to practice exegesis—to gloss her actions along the canonical four levels of scriptural interpretation—would have ensnared her further into playing her Church-Militant adversaries' bad-faith game.[96] Bypassing their questions was part of her larger spiritual program leading directly to the Church Triumphant.

Yet to avoid succumbing to Joan's own ruse, we remind ourselves that it took more than a simple, pious automaton to convince the dauphin—whether by words or sign, or both—of her credibility during their secret conversation at Chinon.[97] Furthermore, letters like the one cited at the outset of this chapter were dictated by no mere uppity bumpkin. Nor were many other of her utterances during the trial. This suggestion of feint or deceit may at first jar us as antithetical to Joan's image, until we grasp that such manipulation participates in her self-fashioning as a more effective agent of divine will. At least as much as Saint Francis, she understood how virginity, clothing, gesture, and certain trademark locutions—like her stubborn usage of "Transeatis ultra / Passez outre" [Move on]—when parrying a question or words she used when urging her men into battle (Jesus Mary!) or her last words at the stake ("Jesus!" uttered three times), could join her banner, rings, and swords as part of her unique personal iconography, her body rhetoric.

We might conclude, then, by affirming Joan's spirituality as a trivalent phenomenon involving her as body, symbol, and word. She accepted going to war without question, just as she would hear Mass every week. Yet she was also shrewdly conscious of the various symbolic patterns and personal associations linked with war as essential to her mission: *athleta Christi*,

Judith, Saint Michael, and so forth. By her intransigent adherence to her military mission, or what she thought it to be, her material body converted abstract spirituality into action, both verbal and physical, which bore the weight of symbolic-allegorical interpretation on every level. If, in so doing, her body met with immolation, this also guaranteed her immortality by its symbolic value, ironically thanks to the exegetes of her career and its multivalent implications, including the same learned, subtle minds that also engineered her burning. There again, she did more than *perform* as a virgin, martyr, or war hero; by her unique combination of aspects and actions she also *created* new dimensions of mortal spirituality, through her own mystical body, as a link with the divine and as a force for France's eventual unification on earth. Consequently, her spiritual effectiveness as protective saint of France eventually equaled and even surpassed that of Saint Michael in modern times, during her country's moments of gravest self-doubt and despair: what Joan would have called its "grant pitié" [gravely pitiful state], most notably during the German Occupation in World War II, as evidenced, for example, in the writings of leftist philosopher Simone Weil.[98] By this time, her image as a symbol of hope had spread beyond France and throughout the world.

Notes

1. Cited in (Modern French trans. only) Régine Pernoud and Marie-Véronique Clin, *Jeanne d'Arc* (Paris: Fayard, 1986), p. 379; for the original Middle French with an English trans., see Pernoud and Clin, *Joan of Arc: Her Story*, ed. and trans. Jeremy duQ. Adams (New York: St. Martin's, 1998), pp. 33–34. Future references to this work in its French original will henceforth read "Pernoud & Clin," followed by the equivalent English citation, "Adams trans.," where possible.
2. This also was one of the phrases reiterated early in the trial record itself when Joan denied having said them, Latinized to "corpus pro corpore" along with another corporeal one, "caput guerrae" [head of the army] (February 22, 1431, session 2). Some scholars believe them to have been added later by detractors seeking to portray her as bloodthirsty. See Jules Quicherat, ed., *Procès de Condamnation et de Réhabilitation de Jeanne d'Arc*, Société de l'Histoire de France, 5 vols. (Paris: Jules Renouard, 1841–49; New York: Johnson reprint, 1965), 1:55. For the medieval ideal of Just War, signaling Joan as one of the few whose pure motives made the Hundred Years War a just war, see Philippe Contamine, "La Théologie de la guerre à la fin du Moyen Age: la Guerre de Cent Ans fut-elle une guerre juste?" In *Jeanne d'Arc: Une époque, un rayonnement. Colloque d'histoire médiévale, Orléans, octobre 1979* (Paris: CNRS, 1982), pp. 9–22.
3. Etienne Delaruelle, "La Spiritualité de Jeanne d'Arc," *Bulletin de Littérature Ecclésiastique* 65 (1964): 17–33; 81–98; the quotation is from the reprint in

Delaruelle, *La Piété populaire au Moyen âge*, ed. Raoul Manselli and André Vauchez (Turin: Bottega d'Erasmo, 1975), p. 378, as are all further references to Delaruelle in this chapter.

4. Onlookers would ask to touch her or have her touch their bibles; she supposedly brought a dead infant back to life long enough for it to receive last rites at Lagny, whose church commemorates the occasion via a plaque visible today. See Pierre Lanéry d'Arc, *Le Culte de Jeanne d'Arc au XVe siècle* (Orléans: Herluison, 1887). For her cult after her death into the present, see Michel Winock, "Jeanne d'Arc," in vol. 3 of *Les France*, which is vol. 3 of Pierre Nora, ed., *Les Lieux de mémoire* (Paris: Gallimard, 1992), pp. 674–733.
5. See, e. g., her letters "To the English," "To the City of Troyes," and "To Philip the Good, Duke of Burgundy" in Pernoud and Clin and trans. Adams, for such phrases alluding to France as "saincte royaume à l'ayde du roy Jésus" [a holy kingdom aided by King Jesus].
6. For Joan of Arc and Mélusine as deformed women yet saviors of the French royal dynasty, see N. Margolis, "Myths in Progress: A Literary-Typological Comparison of Mélusine and Joan of Arc," in Donald Maddox and Sara Sturm-Maddox, *Melusine of Lusignan: Founding Fiction in Late Medieval France* (Athens: University of Georgia Press, 1996), pp. 241–66. Saint. Louis was France's Crusader-king, alongside whom Joan was also invoked. See Colette Beaune, *Naissance de la nation France* (Paris: Gallimard/NRF, 1985), p. 251, and further discussion later in this chapter.
7. See, e.g., Philippe de Mézières's (ca. 1390) treatise for the comfort of married ladies, *Le Livre de la vertu du sacrement de mariage*, ed. Joan B. Williamson (Washington, D. C.: Catholic University of America Press, 1993), p. 274, in which he recounts the story of Saint Cecilia, emphasizing her quiet suffering and humility in her marriage: traits more "feminine" in contrast to Joan's more violent, "masculine" warrior exploits involving greater physical suffering. Philippe transgenders these virtues so that "suivant le Cruxefis" [following the Crucifix, i.e. her marriage as martyrdom], Cecilia eventually converted her husband and brother-in-law to Christianity, and thus rendered her marital conduct, recalling the "Passion of the sweet, slain Lamb," a "mirror" for wives.
8. For Joan and the Cult of the Virgin, see Ann Astell, chapter 2, in this volume.
9. Adding to Joan's heroic, otherworldly mystique are her father's prescience and *agon:* Joan, in her testimony in prison (March 12, 1431) reports her father's dream that his daughter would one day run away with soldiers, a nightmare that provoked him to contemplate drowning her in order to prevent her flight (see, e.g., Quicherat 1:131–32, 219). This pathos was later augmented by French theologian Valerand de Varanne's 1501 Latin poem, which invents Jacques's death by grief after her death (in Quicherat 5:83). Joseph of Nazareth was far more compliant and sporting, dying happily as he had lived obediently, thus earning him his own saintly cult. See Francis L. Filas, *The Man Nearest to Christ: The Complete Life, Theology, and Devotional History of St. Joseph* (Boston: St. Paul Editions, 1962).

10. For definitions, history, and bibliography on each of these, see *The Oxford Dictionary of the Christian Church*, ed. F.L. Cross, 3rd ed. E. A. Livingstone (Oxford: Oxford University Press, 1997).
11. Excerpts cited in English translation of decree reproduced in Louis Petit de Julleville, *Joan of Arc*, trans. Hester Davenport, Coll. The Saints (London: Duckworth; New York: Benziger, 1901), pp. 186–87.
12. For an analysis of Joan's body in modern philosophical and literary theorizations of subjectivity, see Françoise Meltzer, *For Fear of the Fire: Joan of Arc and the Limits of Subjectivity* (Chicago and London: University of Chicago Press, 2001); see also Katherine Crawford's astute review for *H-France* (http://www3.uakron.edu/hfrance/reviews/crawford.html).
13. For a discussion of Joan's physical person as given in the trials, etc., see the inspired analysis by Colette Beaune, "Jeanne la Pucelle," *Perspectives médiévales* 27 (2001): 21–36, esp. 24–27; Beaune's shoddy documentation can be remedied by consulting Pierre Duparc's essay in vol. 5: 142–43 of his edition of the Rehabilitation. All references to Rehabilitation trial testimony are from the definitive critical edition of the Latin text (vols. 1–2) with modern French translation of testimony but not of all documents (vols. 3–4): *Procès en nullité de la réhabilitation de Jeanne d'Arc*, ed. Pierre Duparc, Société de l'Histoire de France, 5 vols. (Paris: Klincksieck, 1977–88), henceforth "Duparc," with "=" separating Latin text cit. from French translation cit. where available.
14. Beaune, "Jeanne la Pucelle," p. 25.
15. Duparc 5: 142–43. For other proof of her black hair, see below, under discussion of her relics, esp. note 34.
16. If his one facial relic-imprint, as enhanced in studies of the Holy Shroud of Turin can be believed. Inconclusive tests (e.g., carbon dating) have, however, called the Shroud's authenticity into question. See, e.g., Odile Celier, *Le Signe du linceul: le saint suaire de Turin. De la relique à l'image* (Paris: Le Cerf, 1992).
17. Analyzed and reproduced in N. Margolis, "The 'Joan Phenomenon' and the French Right," in *Fresh Verdicts on Joan of Arc*, ed. Bonnie Wheeler and Charles T. Wood (New York: Garland, 1996), p. 273.
18. On medical examinations of Joan, see Marie-Véronique Clin, "Joan of Arc and Her Doctors," in *Fresh Verdicts on Joan of Arc*, esp. pp. 299–300. Clin cites the testimony of Guillaume de la Chambre as given in Duparc 1:350 = 4:35.
19. See Deborah Fraioli, *Joan of Arc: The Early Debate* (Woodbridge, Suffolk: Boydell Press, 2000), passim for early fifteenth-century writings on Joan and her own letters, all much preoccupied with her virginity.
20. See Condemnation trial testimony for March 12 and 26, 1431; for commentary on what is known of the lawsuit and Joan's chastity vow, see Pernoud and Clin, pp. 188–89; Adams's translation, 119.
21. According to the most widely read source in Joan's time, the *Légende Dorée* (Golden Legend, or Legenda Aurea), by Jacobus de Voragine (see trans. William G. Ryan, *The Golden Legend: Readings on the Saints* [Princeton, N. J.: Princeton University Press, 1993], 1: 232–33), Margaret of Antioch eluded her (parents') marriage promise to Olybrius by stealing away during

her wedding night and donning male attire, living as a monk for the rest of her life. Also like Joan (or like a prevailing, spurious image of Joan, perhaps to effect another line to Christ, the Good Shepherd [Jn. 10:7–18, etc.]), Margaret tended sheep; and both Joan and Margaret did spinning. Catherine of Alexandria not only zealously refused the advances of Maxentius, but also out-debated, and even converted, the pagan philosophers at her trial before suffering death by decapitation, whereupon milk—not blood—flowed from her severed neck (2: 334–41). In ca. 1450, Charles VII's celebrated portraitist, Jean Fouquet, illustrated the lives of these saints and also of Saint Michael, Joan's foremost saint, for his *Hours of Etienne Chevalier* (New York: George Braziller, 1971), plates 28, 42, 43.

22. Beaune, "Jeanne la Pucelle," p. 24. The "Bride of Christ" (German = "Brautmystik" [bridal mysticism]) theme is actually a contemplative practice derived in various forms from the biblical marriage symbolism of the Old and New Testaments, especially the Song of Songs, to represent the union of the soul with God. The Church Fathers and particularly Saint Bernard of Clairvaux developed this metaphor to illustrate the place of the Church in Heaven and on Earth: just as the Old Testament saw Israel as the "Bride" and Jehovah as the "Bridegroom," so the Catholic Church became the collective Bride, with Christ as the most perfect Bridegroom. Sometimes Mary was considered the bride in cases where an individual figure was required. After further elaboration by twelfth-century German mystics like Hildegard of Bingen and the more secular Beguines in thirteenth-century France and the Low Countries (esp. Mechtild and Hadewijch), such nuns, having renounced marriage or their mortal husbands in favor of this loftier love, believed their souls to ascend nearer to heaven through intense, even erotic, contemplation of this mystical marriage to Christ. See Barbara Newman, *From Virile Woman to WomanChrist: Studies in Medieval Religion and Literature* (Philadelphia: University of Pennsylvania Press, 1995), pp. 139, 143–51. Though not without merit, Beaune's interpretation requires additional refinement surpassing the scope of this study. For instance, the element of waiting, as we find in our Delaruelle quotation and as part of the Bride of Christ typology (Newman, p. 144), would be another point of comparison, along with others less concerned with the body.
23. For the concepts of "bridal" versus "militant" virginity and "third gender," see, most recently, Sarah Salih, *Versions of Virginity in Late Medieval England* (Cambridge: D. S. Brewer, 2001), and Barbara Newman's online review in TMR of September 8, 2002.
24. Duparc 1:486.
25. Duparc 1:387.
26. Duparc 1:461 = 4:141. Meltzer, *Fear of the Fire*, p. 200, taking a more modern critical viewpoint, deems this display procedure one of the most "heinous" of many "violations" of Joan.
27. Several witnesses during the Rehabilitation hearings attested to Joan's chastity, e.g., seneschal Jean d'Aulon; see Duparc 1:325 = 4:10.
28. Duparc 1:486.

29. See Frances Gies, *Joan of Arc: The Legend and the Reality* (New York: Harper & Row, 1981), p. 26.
30. Duparc 1:402.
31. On her profuse weeping see, e.g., Perceval de Boulainvilliers's 1429 Latin letter on her to Duke Filippo Maria Visconti of Milan, in Quicherat 5:120. All future references henceforth will read "Boulainvilliers." For an English summary of this letter, see Gies, p. 48 and passim.
32. For example, Duparc 1:352 = 4:37; 1:456 = 4:136; see Beaune, "Jeanne la Pucelle," 25.
33. Duparc 1:435 = 4:116.
34. Not that this absence prevented nineteenth-century investigators from claiming to have seen such items as a strand of her black hair once embedded in the sealing wax of her "Letter to the Inhabitants of Riom," as reported by Quicherat in 1849 (ed. *Procès* 5:147)—doubtless more credible than the Chinon pharmacist, one Tourlet, who claimed to possess a jar labeled as containing her remains in 1895 (see Jacques Dalarun, "Le Troisième Procès de Jeanne d'Arc," in *Images de Jeanne d'Arc: Actes du Colloque de Rouen, 25–27 mai 1999*, ed. Jean Maurice and Daniel Couty [Paris: Presses Universitaires de France, 2000], p. 58). Both "relics" have since disappeared.
35. Duparc 1:225 = 3:212–13.
36. Duparc 1:454 = 4:133.
37. Duparc 1:440 = 4:120.
38. For tales relating to Joan's unburned heart, and for a similar anecdote concerning the poet Shelley's cremation, see Warner, *Image*, p. 282, n. 72.
39. Duparc 1:479.
40. Clin, "Joan and Her Doctors," p. 299.
41. See Georges de Morant, *Le Sang Glorieux de Jeanne d'Arc*, vol. 4 of *Le Nobiliaire du XXe siècle* (Paris: Le Nobiliaire du XXe siècle, 1912).
42. Duparc 2:474; 5:143.
43. Beaune, "Jeanne la Pucelle," p. 26.
44. Delaruelle, p. 366.
45. Boulainvilliers, p. 120.
46. Pernoud and Clin, trans. Adams, p. 112.
47. Beaune, "Jeanne la Pucelle," p. 26.
48. Duparc 1:352 = 4:137; 1:461 = 4:141.
49. Boulainvilliers, p. 120.
50. Beaune, "Jeanne la Pucelle," p. 26. For the evolving interpretations of ingesting the Eucharist as Christ's flesh as a source of strength in facing martyrdom, guarantee of incorruption and resurrection, as a relic, etc., see Caroline W. Bynum, *The Resurrection of the Body in Western Christianity, 200–1300*, Lectures on the History of Religions, n. s. 15 (New York: Columbia University Press, 1995), esp. pp. 39, 41, 47, 55–56, 140, 149, 221, 316.
51. Warner, 21. See Joan's February 24 interrogation.
52. Duparc 2:474 = 5:143.
53. *Ditié*, stanza 35, vv. 274–77.

54. February 27, March 15, 28, 31.
55. Boulainvilliers, p. 120.
56. Delaruelle, pp. 368–69.
57. Beaune, *Naissance*, pp. 166–69, 195–96.
58. Warner, pp. 29–30. See also notes 33 and 34 above.
59. Duparc 1:359 = 4:45.
60. For this distinction between Joan and other visionaries—though not specifically in conjunction with wounds—see Delaruelle, p. 380; for the more traditionally perceived similarities between Christ and Joan, see Delaruelle, p. 349. We might therefore characterize Joan's wounds as "masculine," given their direct-active origin, as opposed to the passive, "feminine" afflictions of more typical female mystics, but to pursue such terminology is to risk falling into an essentialist quagmire. This is not only essentialist but also anachronistic, since like many dualisms (body and soul, or masculine versus feminine—especially attempting to deduce medieval gender theory from grammatical-lexical gender) moderns tend to ascribe to the medieval thinking about the body are either distorted or simply fallacious. See, e.g., Caroline W. Bynum, "Why all the Fuss About the Body? A Medievalist's Perspective," in *Beyond the Cultural Turn*, ed. Victoria E. Bonnell and Lynn Hunt, Studies in the History of Society and Culture 34 (Berkeley and Los Angeles: University of California Press, 1999), pp. 241–80.
61. See Esther Cohen, "The Animated Pain of the Body," *American Historical Review* 105 (2000): 36–68.
62. For this see, most recently, Susan Crane, *The Performance of Self: Ritual, Clothing and Identity During the Hundred Years War* (Philadelphia: University of Pennsylvania Press, 2002), esp. pp. 73–106 and notes.
63. See Leo Steinberg, *The Sexuality of Christ in Renaissance Art and in Modern Oblivion* (New York: Pantheon/October, 1983).
64. A theme perhaps first systematically explored, albeit uncomfortably, by André Cabassut in 1949. For this and other bibliography, see Carolyn W. Bynum, "Jesus as Mother and Abbot as Mother: Some Themes in Twelfth-Century Cistercian Writing," in Bynum, *Jesus as Mother: Studies in the Spirituality of the High Middle Ages* (Berkeley: University of California Press, 1982), pp. 110–69. For more in-depth studies of medieval gender doctrines of the body, see the essays in *Medieval Theology and the Natural Body*, ed. Peter Biller and A. J. Minnis, York Studies in Medieval Theology, 1 (York/Woodbridge, Suffolk/Rochester, N. Y.: York Medieval Press/Boydell & Brewer, 1997). Most recently, see also Crane, *Performance*, passim.
65. Duparc 2:39, 284, 469, respectively.
66. *Ditié*, vv. 189–90.
67. Joan was likened to the Amazons but was named instead the tenth Worthy Lady in that important pagan-Christian-chivalric pantheon, just as another hero of the Hundred Years War, Du Guesclin, was named the tenth Worthy. See Deborah Fraioli, "Why Joan of Arc Never Became an Amazon," in *Fresh Verdicts on Joan of Arc*, pp. 189–204.

68. These excerpts can be found in vols. 4–5 of Quicherat's edition, with the guidance of the index (under "Jeanne") in vol. 5:529–31.
69. For a recent, accessible reproduction of this shot, and an analysis from an American feminist film historian's point of view, see Robin Blaetz, *Visions of the Maid: Joan of Arc in American Film and Culture* (Charlottesville: University Press of Virginia, 2002), p. 64. Farrar herself remarked in a publicity interview for the movie page of the *New York Times* in December 1916, "Joan of Arc is the Woman Christ of all ages" [cited in Leslie Midkiff DeBauche, *Reel Patriotism: The Movies and World War I* (Madison: University of Wisconsin Press, 1997), p. 17]. De Mille's image most closely resembles Octave Guillonnet's cover illustration for Franz Funck-Brentano's history, *Jeanne d'Arc* (Paris: Boivin, 1912), although De Mille uses one large fleur-de-lis *as* the cross whereas Guillonnet has a cross covered with small fleurs-de-lis. For Guillonnet and other right-wing icons of Joan, see "Joan and the French Right," esp. pp. 274–76.
70. Beaune, *Naissance*, p. 251.
71. Marina Warner, *Joan of Arc: The Image of Female Heroism* (New York: Knopf, 1982), p. 167.
72. *Procès de Jeanne d'Arc*, ed. and trans. Pierre Tisset and Yvonne Lanhers, Société de l'Histoire de France, 3 vols. (Paris: Klincksieck, 1960–71), 2:51–2. For an annotated English translation (based on P. Champion's 1920 ed.) see W. P. Barrett, trans., *The Trial of Joan of Arc* (New York: Gotham House, 1932).
73. Henry I, Robert's son, was the direct lineal ancestor of Philip IV [d. 1314].
74. See William M. Hinkle, *The Fleurs de Lis of the Kings of France: 1285–1488* (Carbondale: Southern Illinois University Press, 1991), esp. pp. 1–18. Warner, *Image*, also mentions the fleurs-de-lis legend and Joan, pp. 167–68.
75. The complete line of prophecy ascribed to the legendary Merlin by Geoffrey of Monmouth (early twelfth century) in his widely read history of the kings of Britain, the *Historia Regum Britanniae*, reads: *Ex nemore canuto puella eliminabitur ut medelae ad curam adhibeat* [From out of an oak forest a maiden shall come to give care to healing]. Much has been made of Joan's oak forest ("bois chenu") origins in connecting her mission specifically to this prophecy, both just before and certainly after her Orléans victory (see Charles T. Wood, *Joan of Arc and Richard III: Sex, Saints, and Government in the Middle Ages* [New York: Oxford University Press, 1988], ch. 7, passim). This Celtic-based lore, like the various scriptural precedents cited by Joan's examiners at Poitiers in 1428, served to underscore Joan's credibility as heaven-sent redeemer of France among her apologists.
76. Henry was in reality too young to engage in such matters—as usual, Bedford's ambition was the true petal-pusher in this verbal–visual stratagem.
77. See Wood, *Joan of Arc & Richard III*, ch. 1.
78. For pertinent excerpts of Calot's poem commissioned by Bedford see Benedicta J.H. Rowe, "King Henry's Claims to France in Picture and Poetry," *The Library*, 4th Ser., 12 (1932–33): 77–88. For Calot's role in Joan's trial, see Pernoud and Clin, pp. 208, 225; Adams's translation, pp. 131, 142.

79. Despite her pro-French patriotism as displayed in the later *Ditié de Jehanne d'Arc* and other works, Christine did have strong ties to the English nobility, established well before the crucial Battle of Agincourt (1415) and Treaty of Troyes (1420), particularly for her adolescent son's benefit, since Jean de Castel served the earl of Salisbury from 1397 to 1400. Even during the anti-French apogee of Bedford's reign, however, Christine's work was coveted by English collectors both in manuscript and, by the 1480s, in translations printed by Caxton. See Charity C. Willard, *Christine de Pizan: Her Life and Works* (New York: Persea, 1984), esp. pp. 42–43; 213–16.
80. Michel-André Bossy, "Arms and the Bride: Christine de Pizan's Military Treatise as a Wedding Gift for Margaret of Anjou," in *Christine de Pizan and the Categories of Difference*, ed. Marilynn Desmond, Medieval Cultures 14 (Minneapolis and London: University of Minnesota Press, 1998), pp. 236–56. Like Hinkle, though independently, Bossy also reproduces the revised lily from London, BL Roy. MS 15E.VI, fol. 3.
81. Vv. 95–97 read: ". . .En l'estat royal, dont je lix / Qu'onques [. . .] En foy n'errerent fleurs de lix." Ed. and trans. Angus J. Kennedy and Kenneth Varty, Medium Aevum Monographs, n.s. 9 (Oxford: Society for the Study of Mediaeval Languages and Literature, 1977), p. 30, Eng. translation, p. 42.
82. The most recent example being Jean-François Kosta-Théfaine, "Une prière politique pour la France: Le *Ditié de Jehanne d'Arc* de Christine de Pizan," *Lendemains* 94 (1999): 109–22, with very complete notes to previous scholarship.
83. *Livre de la Mutacion de Fortune*, ed. Suzanne Solente (Paris: Picard, 1959), vol. 1. For English translations of this excerpt, see those by N. Margolis (in verse) in *The Writings of Christine de Pizan*, ed. Charity C. Willard (New York: Persea, 1994), pp. 124–27, and, in prose, by R. Blumenfeld-Kosinski and K. Brownlee in *The Selected Writings of Christine de Pizan*, ed. R. Blumenfeld-Kosinski, Norton Critical Editions (New York: W.W. Norton, 1997), pp. 105–107.
84. Hinkle, pp. 73 ff.
85. See notes to Christine's *Ditié*, ed. Kennedy and Varty, pp. 68–69, for more information on these three sets of prophecies during Joan's time. For further political and literary insights, see Kevin Brownlee, "Structures of Authority in Christine de Pizan' *Ditié de Jehanne d'Arc*," in *Discourses of Authority in Medieval and Renaissance Literature*, ed. K. Brownlee and Walter Stephens (Dartmouth, N. H.: University Press of New England, 1989), pp. 134–50, 274–76; rpt. in Blumenfeld-Kosinski and Brownlee, *The Selected Writings*, pp. 371–90.
86. So powerful that they would provoke the trial recorder to note in that page's margin: "deadly reply" [responsio mortifera]. See Pernoud and Clin, trans. Adams, p. 133.
87. See Renate Blumenfeld-Kosinski, " 'Enemies Within/Enemies Without': Threats to the Body Politic in Christine de Pizan," *Medievalia et Humanistica*, n.s. 26 (1999): 1–15.
88. Duparc 1:225 = 3: 212–13.

89. Perhaps the most dramatic emphasis upon Joan's taking communion is found in Carl Dreyer's 1928 film, *La Passion de Jeanne d'Arc.*
90. Warner, p. 29.
91. I mean by this no denigration of the concept of performance as recently examined among late medieval women mystics by such fine scholars as those contained in, e.g., Mary Suydam and Joanna Ziegler, eds., *Performance and Transformation: New Approaches to Late Medieval Spirituality* (New York: St. Martins, 1999).
92. E. Jane Burns, *Bodytalk: When Women Speak in Old French Literature* (Philadelphia: University of Pennsylvania Press, 1993) discusses primarily secular texts in obscene (for the fabliaux) and erotic contexts. Although devotional expressivity can share imagery and themes with secular love poetry, Joan's piety and her contemporaries' attitude toward it have more in common with the cases examined in Dyan Elliott, *Fallen Bodies: Pollution, Sexuality, and Demonology in the Middle Ages* (Philadelphia: University of Pennsylvania Press, 1999) and "The Physiology of Rapture and Female Spirituality," along with Rosalynn Voaden, "Beholding Men's Members: The Sexualizing of Transgression in *The Book of Margery Kempe*," both in Biller and Minnis, *Medieval Theology and the Natural Body*, pp. 141–73, 175–90, resp. Nevertheless, Burns's insights into how women in Old French courtly literature "talk back" with their bodies against their male idealizers can be profitably read as a counterpoint to women's saintly and demonic body language as defined in Voaden, Elliott, Bynum and others.
93. Elliott, "Physiology," p. 167: "As the famous example of Joan of Arc would suggest [. . .] women as vessels of devotion and vessels of depravity were fast becoming virtually indistinguishable."
94. I am aware of the limitations of this play on the Latin "corpus," used to denote both a physical "body" and, more abstractly, a body of written material, often rules. The term "Body Politic," so dear to medieval political theorists, exploited both meanings, especially the first, to emphasize the harmonious, hierarchical interworkings of ideal government. The classic source on this concept is F.W. Maitland's annotated translation of Otto Gierke's *Political Theories of the Middle Age* (Cambridge: Cambridge University Press, 1900; repr. 1987): for "society as organism" and the State's and Church's union toward the Mystical Body of Christ, see esp. pp. 22–23. By contrast, one rarely sees the term "body rhetoric," perhaps because medieval theorists feared excessive tautology, since the speaker's body is *de facto* so profoundly engaged in rhetoric. Also, medieval theorists found it more effective to seek to isolate and fenestrate the rhetorical and dictaminal arts (epistolary writing) and their related faculties (esp. memory). Whenever the corpus of these arts was represented as an integrated whole, it was more often through such images as trees.
95. February 27, 1431, session 4, see, e.g., Quicherat 1:71.
96. These four levels (literal, allegorical, tropological, anagogical) formed the basis of medieval exegesis scripture as taught in theological schools, the learned and morally correct way of reading—finally any book or event—so

as to come closer to understanding and preaching God's mysteries. See Harry Caplan, *Of Eloquence*, ed. Anne King and Helen North (Ithaca, NY.: Cornell University Press, 1970), esp. pp. 93–104.

97. For a recent in-depth discussion of this "secret" or "prayer" between Joan and the Dauphin, and indeed the entire trial transcript as a collaborative literary text between Joan and her judges, to be perpetuated over succeeding centuries, see Karen Sullivan, *The Interrogation of Joan of Arc*, Medieval Cultures 20 (Minneapolis: University of Minnesota Press, 1999), esp. pp. 64–81 (King's prayer).

98. A graduate of the elite Ecole Normale Supérieure where she was branded the "Red Virgin" because of her political activism, Jewish-born convert to mystical Catholicism via Buddhism and self-imposed privation, Simone Weil (1909–43) penned in her *Notebooks* of 1941–42 that the fundamental difference between the spirit of the *Bhagavad Gita* and Joan of Arc lies in that the former "makes war although inspired by God" and Joan "makes war because inspired by God." See Dorothy T. McFarland, *Simone Weil* (New York: Frederick Ungar, 1983), p. 117.

CHAPTER 2

THE VIRGIN MARY AND THE "VOICES" OF JOAN OF ARC

Ann W. Astell

The fervent Marian devotion of the historical Joan of Arc has largely been ignored. This chapter surveys the evidence for that devotion, arguing that the Maid identified closely with the Virgin and was perceived by her followers and enemies alike as an "altera Maria."

When I told a colleague of mine that I was studying Joan of Arc and the Virgin Mary, he replied, "I'll be curious to learn what you discover. It's hard to imagine that virago [Joan] and the humble Handmaid [Mary] together." Many scholars who have taken a more considerate view of Joan's spirituality seem to share my colleague's spontaneous reaction. Although, as Renée Grisel wrote long ago, "Joan participated from her infancy in the cult of the Virgin," for some unknown reason scholarly studies of Joan and modern renditions of her legend often pass in silence over this aspect of her devotional life.[1] Indeed, judging by the account given by some Jehannine historians, the example of Joan of Arc confirms the assertion of Caroline Walker Bynum: "Mary is not really as important as one might expect in [medieval] women's spirituality," which focuses instead on the humanity of Christ.[2]

Much in the historical record, however, suggests the opposite—namely, that Mary was important to Joan, and that Joan's love for Jesus, on the one hand, and her devotion to Mary, on the other, formed an organic whole. In this essay I wish, first of all, to survey briefly the historical evidence for

Joan of Arc's Marian devotion. Second, to comment on reasons for the scholarly and artistic neglect of this evidence. Third, to offer new ways of interpreting the historical evidence from a double perspective. I argue that the voice of Mary sounds among Joan's voices and that Joan identified herself with Mary in startling ways that challenge currently dominant academic accounts of the medieval *imitatio Mariae*.

The Signs of Mary

First of all, the historical evidence. The trial records include Joan's statement that she learned the "Pater Noster, Ave Maria, [and] Credo" from her mother.[3] The testimonies given by eleven different eyewitnesses during the Rehabilitation of 1456 confirm her devotion to our Lady of Bermont (figure 2.1). Michel Lebuin reports, "When I was young, I went with her on pilgrimage to Notre Dame de Bermont, the hermitage. She went almost every Saturday to that hermitage, with her sister, and put candles there."[4] Perrin Drappier, the church warden of Domremy, and Colin, son of Jean Colin of Greux similarly bear witness: "Almost every Saturday afternoon Joan, with her sister and other women, went to the hermitage of Notre Dame de Bermont, bearing candles."[5] Jean Moreau, Joan's godfather, adds that Joan went "often and of her own will. . .to the hermitage of Notre Dame de Bermont near to the town of Domremy, when her parents thought she was ploughing or working elsewhere in the fields."[6]

Also in reference to her childhood devotion to Mary, Joan describes herself gathering "garlands [of flowers] for the image of Our Lady of Domremy" [*pro imagine Beatae Mariae de Dompremi*].[7] She did so near the so-called Ladies' Tree or Fairies' tree, where the villagers gathered every year on Laetare Sunday for a traditional springtime festival.[8] From that same tree, according to Joan, Maypoles [*gallice le beau may*] were cut.[9]

At Vaucouleurs, according to the testimony of Jean le Fumeux, Joan went every morning to the chapel of Robert de Baudricourt's castle, which was called our Lady of the Vaults. After hearing morning mass, she would stay there a long time to pray, "on her knees before the holy Virgin, sometimes with bowed head, sometimes with her head raised" [. . . *genibus flexis ante beatam Mariam, aliquotiens vultu projecto, et aliquotiens vultu erecta*].[10] Similarly, Henri Arnolini describes Joan praying "sometimes prone before the crucifix, and sometimes with her hands joined and fixed, but her face and eyes raised toward the crucifix or toward Holy Mary."[11] During her trial she begged repeatedly to be allowed to hear Mass "in honor of God and Blessed Mary"[*in honorem Dei et Beatae Mariae*].[12]

While still in Domremy Joan received from her father and mother through the hands of her brother the treasured ring that was later taken

NOTRE-DAME DE BERMONT.

2.1 Our Lady of Bermont. Courtesy of Jean Frisk, Marian Library, University of Dayton.

from her by her Burgundian captors.[13] In the trial record, Joan describes it as a metallic ring "not of pure gold," inscribed with "three crosses and no other sign. . .excepting Jhesus Maria."[14] The holy names of Jesus and Mary appear regularly in Joan's letters, linked as a kind of motto or dedication at the top, preceding the salutation.[15] Joan describes the standard that she carried onto the battlefield as "sewn with fleur-de-lys": "And there, it seems to me, were written the names of Jesus and of Mary, and they were embroidered with silk."[16]

During the Rehabilitation, Jean Pasquerel refers to a second banner, on which was painted "the image of our Lord crucified." Joan ordered it to be made, according to Pasquerel, as a device "to rally the priests" who followed the royal army as chaplains.[17] Both Pasquerel and Count Dunois, the Bastard of Orléans, report that Joan commanded the daily gathering of the mendicant friars for prayer and their singing, in particular, of "anthems and hymns to Saint Mary," a devotion "to the Blessed Virgin, the Mother of God," in which Joan herself participated, along with the clerics.[18] The *Journal of the Siege*, which describes in detail Joan's first entry into Orléans on April 29, 1429, reports: "she ordered her standard to be borne before her. . .and on the pennon was painted an annunciation (this is the image of our Lady having before her an angel giving her a lily)."[19]

The use of an annunciation scene on Joan's banner at Orléans is striking when interpreted in the context of *The Poitiers Conclusions*. As Deborah Fraioli has documented, Joan's claim to have been sent by God to the dauphin led to a serious, ecclesiastical trial at Chinon and Poitiers in March 1429, during which leading clergymen tested Joan's prophetic status and attempted through a process of discernment of spirits [*discretio spirituum*] to answer the question whether or not she should be believed and obeyed. The judges determined first of all that Joan's faith and personal character merited trust: "In her is found no evil, only goodness, humility, virginity, piety, honesty, and simplicity."[20] As a second step in the discernment process, they asked her for a sign: "Thus God commanded Ahaz to ask for a sign, when God promised him victory, telling him: *pete signum a Domino*; and the same with Gideon, who requested a sign."[21] According to the *Conclusions*, Joan replied that she would show the required sign only later at Orléans, in the form of a miraculous victory.

The name of Mary does not appear in the summary document known as *The Poitiers Conclusions*. The list of Joan's virtues is reminiscent of Mary's, however. More important, perhaps, from the perspective of Joan's Marian devotion and identification are the scriptural examples of Ahaz and Gideon, which provided the proof texts used by Joan's judges at Poitiers. The sign given to the warrior Gideon in Judges 6:36–40, that of the dew-covered fleece, was regularly interpreted by exegetes as a typological foreshadowing of the Virgin Birth. Similarly, the Lord answered the request of King Ahaz for a sign with a Marian promise: "Behold, a young woman shall conceive and bear a son and shall call his name Immanuel" (Isaiah 7:14). The use of these two prophetic texts indicates that Joan's judges at Poitiers associated her with the Virgin Mary.

On Tuesday, March 22, 1429 at the end of the hearings at Poitiers, Joan dictated her famous "Letter to the English," a spirited summons to the king of England, the duke of Bedford, and his lieutenants, demanding that they "surrender to the Maid who is sent here by God, the King of Heaven, the keys of all the good towns which [they] have taken and violated in France."[22] The letter bears the superscription "Jhesus Maria." In it Joan links God and Mary his Mother, at one level; and the rightful king of France and Joan the Maid at another, lower level; even as she establishes vital links between the king of France and the King of Heaven, on one side, and between Mary and the Maid, on the other. To the English she declares: "You will not hold the kingdom of France from God the King of Heaven, son of Saint Mary; for the king Charles, the true heir [*vray héritier*], will hold it, as revealed to him by the Maid."[23] Joan's employ of an annunciation scene at her first entrance into Orléans suggests not only that she had played the part of an angel to Charles at Chinon, revealing to him his rightful claim to the throne against his own mother's intimation that he was illegitimate,[24] but also that she identified herself with Mary, the handmaid of the Lord, to whom the angel Gabriel had come.

A neglected early source confirms this early understanding of Joan as an *altera Maria*. Jules Quicherat's five-volume edition of fifteenth-century texts related to Joan of Arc includes a fragmentary, undated, unsigned letter. It may have been written, as Quicherat suggests, by a participant in the siege at Orléans to his commander, whom he addresses as "our most reverend father and revered preceptor" [*Reverendissime pater et praeceptor noster metuendissime*].[25] Knights of the Order of Saint John of Jerusalem fought under the banner of the Maid at Orléans, among them Nicole de Giresme, the grand master of the order in France.[26] Quicherat speculates that the letter was written by one of his knights. Judging only by the contents of the letter, I would date it during the time period between Joan's first meeting with the dauphin on Sunday, March 6, 1429, and her departure for Orléans at the end of April.

In that fragmentary letter, the writer marvels at the favor of God that has been shown to the poor, oppressed people of France through a maiden of eighteen years, whom God has sent "for the complete cure and reformation of a most Christian kingdom" to the French king, the true heir and rightful successor [*validus successor*] to the throne. The writer goes on to echo the Magnificat of Mary in Luke 1:46–55 and to compare the Virgin Mary to Joan the Maid:

> Let your most reverend Power hear, I beg you, and your mind exult [*exultet animus*] in the gift of so heavenly a girl [*puellari tam coelesti*], which the Almighty has deigned to present in our times. A heavenly maiden [*Puella*] has come, and [she has done so] because the Almighty Father himself has honored the Virgin Mary above all others, with the intended result that he has drawn away from every earthly desire those seeing her to be so beautiful, no matter who they might be and from what kind of immoral life. Will not God, moreover, be said to have ordained the same about the virgin sent to us [*de virgine nobis missa*], Joan by name? Joan, I say, the Maid [*Puella*], clothed in the dress of a shepherdess, and yet somehow manlike [*quasi virile*], has come by the command of almighty God to the king through diverse and

> dangerous routes, without violence, unwounded, unharmed, accompanied by other persons; she has come to the king, and. . .it was ordained by the decision of the royal council that she should speak not to the king, but to many men and excellent clerics, doctors of theology, and be examined diligently by others. But as it happened, that decision notwithstanding, the Maid went without delay to the queen and asked [to see] the king whom she was calling the dauphin. The king did not hold back, but immediately came to her. . . .[27]

This remarkable letter, which likens Joan of Arc to the Virgin Mary, calling them both "puella" and "virgo," gives us a fresh and somewhat startling insight into what may be called a fifteenth-century "liberation theology."[28] Drawing a parallel between the spiritual freedom from worldly desires and the political freedom from foreign oppression, the writer suggests that Joan the Maid has been sent to accomplish a two-fold liberation for the French people. Saint Bridget of Sweden had prophesied in 1360 in the Fourth Book of her *Revelations* that the sufferings of France were permitted as a punishment for sin. Calling the prophecy of Saint Bridget "the most elusive but potentially the most significant" of the prophecies applied to Joan of Arc, Deborah Fraioli points out, "the prophecy begins with the Virgin Mary asking Christ to 'have pity on the unhappy realm of France' [*miserere isti regno*] since he has commanded generally that sins be forgiven."[29] The Bridgittine prophecy strongly favors the English cause, but concludes: "When the French acquire true humility, the kingdom will devolve to the true heir [*legittimum heredem*] and experience a good peace."[30] Quoting this last line and interpreting it somewhat out of context as a reference to Charles VII, rather than Henry VI, Walter Bower applies the prophecy to Joan in his *Scotichronicon* (ca. 1437).[31] Valeran Varanius also makes Joan of Arc the instrument of Mary's merciful intercession with her Son. His late fifteenth-century Latin epic *De gestis Joannae virginis Franciae egregiae bellatricis* begins with Charles's prayer to the Virgin Mary, begging for peace; Mary's prayer to her Son for the French; Christ's response; Mary's speech to Charles; and the sending of an angel to Joan.[32] The German chronicler, Eberhard von Windecken (1380–1442), Joan's contemporary and notary to Emperor Sigismund, suggestively links Joan "die Jungfrau" to the "Jungfrau Maria" through the repeated use of the same noun and states that Joan accomplished the great victories of 1429 with the help of God and Mary.[33]

The utter helplessness of the French and their long suffering gave them in the eyes of many a certain claim to God's mercy and the right to hope for a miraculous, divine intervention, since all human efforts to expel the English invaders had failed. If the French had sinned, they had also offered atonement and begged for mercy. Writing shortly after the victory at

Orléans, the promised sign of God's favor, the theologian Jacques Gélu dares to ask: "if God sent his son for the salvation of the world, why should he not send Joan [*unam de suis creaturis*] to free a king and save his people from the jaws of their enemies?"[34] Similarly, as we have seen, the anonymous letter that Quicherat ascribes to a knight of the order of Saint John compares the appearance of Mary at the dawn of salvation to the arrival of Joan of Arc.

A strong pattern of biblical concordance unites the anonymous letter with three other early documents—*De quadam puella, The Poitiers Conclusions*, and the *Dissertatio* of Jacques Gélu, all of which date from 1429. The "animus exultet" of the letter, as we have seen, alludes to the Magnificat of Mary: "Magnificat anima mea Dominum / Et exultavit spiritus meus" (Luke 1.46–47). Like the Magnificat, which celebrates the mighty arm of God, which deposes the proud and exalts the humble, 1 Corinthians 1.27 declares: "And the weak things of the world hath God chosen, that he may confound the strong." The latter text appears, as Deborah Fraioli notes, in both *De quadam puella* and in the *Dissertatio* of Jacques Gélu as a scriptural proof for Joan's divine instrumentality.[35] Like *The Poitiers Conclusions*, which cites the examples of Gideon and Ahaz, the letter combines the sign of the virgin—both Mary and Joan—with the promise of moral and military victory.

When Joan first arrived at Chinon, her appearance was seen as the fulfillment of yet another prophecy with Marian resonance. After the Treaty of Troyes in 1420, it was a commonplace prophecy that even as France had been lost by a woman, Isabeau de Bavière, it would be saved by a woman. The *Sibylla Francica* (1429) shows that this prophecy was current even in Germany. Joan applied it to herself when she asked her uncle, Durant Lassois, for his help, reminding him, "Was it not said that France would be ruined by a woman, and afterwards restored by a virgin?" [*Nonne alias dictum fuit 'quod Francia per mulierem desolaretur, et postea per virginem restaurari debebat'?*].[36] As Fraioli and others have noted, this prophecy stands as a version of the EVA/AVE prophecy, whereby the disobedience of the first woman, Eve, was redeemed at the hour of the annunciation by the Virgin Mary's obedience to the call of the angel: "Ave." The Italian chronicle of Joan's contemporary, Antonio Morisini, declares, "Just as through a woman, through Notre-Dame Saint Mary, [God] saved the human race, so through this young girl, pure and unsullied, he saved the most beautiful part of Christianity."[37] Writing somewhat later, in 1456 at the request of the future king Louis XI, then dauphin, Mathieu Thomassin makes the same connection. Referring to Mary as "la pucelle Vierge Marie" and to Joan as "laditte Pucelle Jehanne," Thomassin draws a parallel between Mary, who was responsible for the "reparation and restoration of the human lineage," and Joan, who brought about the "reparation and restoration of the kingdom of France."[38]

In support of his claim, Thomassin quotes the *Ditié de Jehanne d'Arc* of Christine de Pisan, a poem she completed on July 31, 1429, shortly after the coronation of Charles VII at Reims. In stanza 28 Christine likens Joan explicitly to the Old Testament heroines Esther, Judith, and Deborah—all of them biblical and liturgical types of Mary—and she praises Joan in stanza 22 in language usually applied to Mary herself as a being specially created by God, a "Maiden sent from God, into whom the Holy Spirit poured His great grace, in whom there was and is an abundance of noble gifts," such that "never did Providence refuse any [of Joan's] request[s]."[39]

Among the miracles worked at Joan's petition, one of the most striking is that performed at Lagny. There, according to Joan's own testimony during the trial, Joan knelt, "praying on [her] knees" before "the image of Our Lady of Lagny," begging "God and our Lady" for the life of a three-day-old infant, who did miraculously revive long enough to be baptized.[40] The scene is vividly described and paints the memorable picture of Joan, holding in her arms the seemingly lifeless baby boy, whose skin is "black," the color of Joan's own coat of mail. In the company of the young women of the town [*cum aliis puellis*] Joan kneels before the Virgin Mary as her mirror image, another *Mater Dolorosa*, a *pietà*, clasping to her breast a newborn son who has, to all appearances, been dead for three days: "Et fuerant tres dies." Suddenly in a mysterious repetition of Christ's own resurrection, the child comes to life, gasps for air three times, is baptized, and buried in consecrated ground. The striking paschal symbolism of the account—three days of death, three gasps of life-giving air, resurrection, birth to the new life of grace, and entombment—must have struck Joan's judges, ever suspicious of witchcraft, for they asked Joan specifically about the child's age.

Even as Joan entrusted the infant of Lagny to the intercession of the Virgin Mary, so too she entrusted herself after her capture by the Burgundians. Before she leapt from the tower of Beaurevoir, where she had been imprisoned, Joan mentions that she had "commended [herself] to God and to the Virgin Mary."[41] Finally, in answer to her interrogators at Rouen, Joan asserted "she came to the king of France from God and the Virgin Mary, and all the saints in paradise and the Church Victorious above and by their commandment."[42] She died at the stake on May 30, 1431, at the end of the month dedicated to Mary.

Mary, the Visions, and the "Voices"

Despite this substantial body of historical evidence, Joan of Arc has seldom been regarded as a Marian saint. As notable exceptions to this rule, the imaginative medievalist writings of Paul Claudel and Friedrich Schiller accord a prominent place to the Virgin Mary in the story of Joan of Arc and attempt (albeit in radically different ways) to integrate the historical evidence for Joan's Marian devotion into the larger narrative of her mission. In his *Die Jungfrau von Orleans* (1801) Schiller, on the one hand, displaces the Christian saints traditionally identified as Joan's voices—namely, Saint Michael the Archangel, Saint Catherine of Alexandria, and Saint Margaret of Antioch—replacing them with a single, numinous figure, the holy Virgin, who resembles a classical goddess more than the Virgin Mary.[43] Claudel, on the other hand, removes Saint Michael in order to allow the Virgin Mary herself to complement Saints Margaret and Catherine in their appeals to, and comfort of, Joan the Maid.[44] In Claudel's poetic text for Arthur Honegger's 1938 oratorio, *Jeanne d'Arc au bûcher*, the votive candles that Joan lights at Mary's altar merge symbolically with Joan's final self-oblation in the fire that consumes her at the stake.

Schiller and Claudel stand virtually alone, however. According to Karen Sullivan, the fifteenth-century "*Miroir des femmes vertueuses* portrays Joan receiving her mission from the Virgin Mary, St. Catherine, and St. Agnes, though no other document links the Virgin or Agnes with Joan."[45] When Sullivan claims that no document beside the *Miroir* "links the Virgin. . .with Joan," she means, I presume, that "no other document" from the medieval period specifically names the Virgin Mary as the one who called and commissioned Joan.

But is this true? One might quibble with Sullivan and cite the hostile Burgundian chronicle of Jean Lefèvre de Saint-Remi, a contemporary of Joan's and an eyewitness to some of her exploits, who reports that the Virgin Mary is said to have appeared to Joan, accompanied by angels and saints, including the prophet David, and that God is said to have revealed to Joan through the mouth of Mary [*par la bouche de la Vierge Marie*] that she should take up arms and lead Charles to Reims for his coronation.[46] Quicherat, however, dismisses this account in a footnote, calling it an "erreur du chroniqueur," because no French author refers to a Marian apparition, and because Joan's judges at Rouen do not question her about any vision of the Virgin Mary.[47]

No apparition then. But an audition? In the legend of Joan of Arc, her "voices" are much more important than the accounts of visions. As we have just noted, Joan herself claims in the trial record to have been sent to the king of France by God, the Virgin Mary, and all the saints. Karen Sullivan's own remarkable work on the interrogations of Joan of Arc helps us in fact to understand Joan's voices as inclusive of the voice of Mary. Whereas Sullivan argues, however, that Joan's references to the voices of individual saints is belated and enforced—the psychological result of prolonged and torturous interrogations—and represents a breakdown at odds with her original testimony, I maintain that Joan's organic sense of the heavenly unison between God and the saints remained constant throughout and allowed her to name individual intercessors and models in answer to those who questioned her without contradicting her earlier, more general witness to her voices. Indeed, the later references to particular saints illumine the meaning of Joan's earlier mentions of voices. The Virgin Mary and the saints were always already there for Joan, speaking in harmony with God, willing his will, inseparable from him.

Sullivan observes that prior to Joan's trial at Rouen and also in its early stages, Joan consistently describes her source of inspiration as a heavenly "voice" or "voices," alternating between the singular and the plural forms of that word. She speaks again and again of having been sent by God. Only as the trial progresses does Joan's story change in response to the persistent questions of the theologians who ask her to name and describe the individuals who counsel her. Under unrelenting pressure, Joan singles out, from out of the vast company of angels and saints, three figures to whom she was genuinely devoted, whose *legenda* are parallel to hers in various ways, and who could therefore fittingly serve as role models and heavenly patrons for her: namely, Saints Michael, Margaret, and Catherine.[48] Occasionally she adds to the list of her counselors none other than Saint Gabriel, the archangel who was sent by God to the Virgin Mary.[49]

When I first ran across the references to Saint Gabriel in the trial records, I was astonished, because scholarly and popular accounts of Joan's history seldom mention him. There are five such references. When asked whether Saint Gabriel was with Saint Michael when the latter first appeared to her, she says that she cannot recall: "respondit quod de hoc non recordatur."[50] When asked whether she believes that Saints Michael and Gabriel have "natural heads," she replies, "I have seen them with my own eyes" [*Ego vidi ipsos oculis meis*].[51] Later she confesses that, beginning at age thirteen, Saints Michael and Gabriel appeared to her often in corporeal form, and sometimes they were accompanied by hosts of angels and by Saints Catherine and Margaret.[52] Pressed for details about the sign that she had given to king Charles at Chinon in order to win his trust, she speaks about a vision of angels, who appeared to her and to the king, paying him homage and giving him a crown. Calling such a claim presumptuous, audacious, and a blatant fiction [*praesumptuosum, temerarium, confictum*], her judges at Rouen reminded her that nowhere is it recorded that such reverence was ever paid by angels and archangels to any human being, even the purest—not even to the Blessed Virgin, the Mother of God: "imo etiam nec Beatae Virgini, genetrici Dei."[53] And yet, according to the trial records, Joan insisted that Saint Gabriel had come to her often, with Saint Michael, and sometimes with thousands of angels.[54] The last mention of Saint Gabriel is especially poignant. Threatened with torture, on May 3rd, the feast of the Invention of the Cross, Joan reports to her judges that she has been comforted by Saint Gabriel: "And she believes that it was St. Gabriel; and she knew by her voices [*per suas voces*] that it was St. Gabriel."[55]

Joan names particular saints, but she persists nevertheless in referring to her "voices" and in her insistence that her judges are tearing apart a heavenly reality that is, for her, an organic whole. Asked whether she invoked spirits to her aid, as one might conjure up demons, she replies, "I call to God and our Lady, [asking] that they send me counsel and comfort; and thereafter they send [the voices] to me."[56] Asked to submit herself to the judgment of the Church, she declares, "I commit myself to Our Lord, Who sent me, to our Lady, and to all the blessed saints," asserting, "our Lord and the Church [are] all one" and cannot be separated from one another.[57] Similarly, when she is asked "whether when she puts the candles before the image of Saint Catherine she does it in honor of her who appears to her, she answer[s]: 'I do it in honour of God, of our Lady, of St. Catherine, who is in heaven, and of her who appears to me. . . .and I make no difference between St. Catherine who is in heaven and her who appears to me.'"[58]

Keeping Company with Mary

If, then, Joan experienced Saint Catherine in vital union with God and our Lady, and if she heard Mary's voice among her other voices, why does she not single the Virgin Mary out to the same degree as she does the three saints Michael, Margaret, and Catherine? The long dominant, feminist answer to this question is that Christian women, even the saints among them, necessarily have a conflicted relationship to the Virgin Mary who, "alone of all her sex," possessed an unobtainable excellence and surpassing gifts that by their very nature preclude imitation, enhance their sense of inferiority, and enforce their submission to patriarchy.[59] Judging purely on the basis of the number of explicit references to Mary, Donald Weinstein and Rudolph Bell have concluded that only one-third of the medieval saints characterized by devotion to Mary were women.[60]

As Caroline Walker Bynum has argued, however (albeit in another context), an analysis that is purely quantitative, rather than qualitative, can be extremely misleading.[61] I would add to Bynum's general caveat about quantitative analysis the observation that quantitative analysis assumes that the one to whom a person is deeply devoted must be named as an "other," whereas in fact the opposite may be true. If a saint's psychological structure of devotion to Mary is so deep as to constitute identification with her, then there are likely to be fewer, rather than more, mentions of her as a separate person.

Building upon Julia Kristeva's powerful psychological insight that the image of the Virgin Mother Mary countered a variety of forms of female paranoia and was "able to attract women's wishes for identification" with her,[62] Pamela Sheingorn and Barbara Newman have argued that many medieval women saw "in Mary's life a reassuring image of their own situation," imitated her in their own fantasy romances, and "revelled in the same familial endearments—daughter, sister, mother, bride—that belonged *par excellence* to Mary."[63] Late medieval Eucharistic theology encouraged all

2.2 Albrechtsalter, Stiftsmuseum, Klosterneuberg, Austria. Courtesy of the Curator, Stiftsmuseum.

Christians to understand themselves as welcoming the whole Christ—body, blood, soul, and divinity—into their body and souls in the reception of Communion—a teaching that reinforced women's psychological identification with Mary. Many saw her (in Newman's words) "not as standing 'alone of all her sex', but as supremely imitable."[64] Indeed, a growing number of qualitative studies suggests that not only recognized mystics like Hadejwich, Angela of Foligno, Julian of Norwich, and Bridget of Sweden, but also ordinary laywomen identified so closely with Mary in their multiform relationships to God that they were virtually incorporated into her and came, without displacing her, to occupy Mary's affective and ethical position in relation to the Father, the Incarnate Son, and the Holy Spirit.[65]

Such, I posit, holds true in the case of Joan of Arc. Devoted as a child to our Lady of Bermont, Joan's soul-life was assimilated to hers. When Joan received a special call from God through the voice of an archangel, she vowed her virginity to God, as Mary had done.[66] Joan's coming to save France had been prophesied, even as Mary's special role in the plan of salvation had been foretold by the prophet Isaiah. Joan communed with God through audition, through the hearing of voices, even as Mary was represented as conceiving Christ through the ear of obedience at the hour of the Annunciation.[67] Joan often heard her voices, moreover, including that of Saint Gabriel, at the ringing of the angelus bells, at the very hour when the Ave Maria was being prayed in remembrance and renewal of the Annunciation.[68]

Joan heard God and the saints calling her the "daughter of God," a title especially associated with Mary, the highly favored daughter of the Father.[69] She called herself and was called by others "Joan the Maid" [*la Pucelle*], even as Mary was the Virgin [*la Vierge*]. As Marina Warner notes, "*Pucelle* means 'virgin'. . .It is the equivalent of the Hebrew '-*almah*, used of. . .the Virgin Mary. . .in the Bible."[70] A well-known medieval French Christmas carol refers to Mary as the "pucelle" of prophecy, using the same word Joan used to name herself: "Chantons a ce Noël joly, / —Ne vivons plus piteusement, / Une pucelle, / De Dieu ancelle, / A enfanté, comme était dict, / Un beau mignon a plein minuit" [Let us sing on this lovely Christmas, / We no longer live in misery, / A virgin, / God's handmaiden, / has, as prophesied, / borne a beautiful little darling, / in the middle of the night].[71]

Enduring repeated and humiliating examinations to test her virginity, as well as accusations of whoredom, Joan may have drawn comfort, remembering the scriptural doubts of Saint Joseph about Mary's own purity (Matthew 1:18–25). Echoing Mary's Magnificat (Luke 1:46–55), Joan herself declared before her judges that God had chosen her to oppose the king's enemies not in spite of, but because of, her smallness: "Placuit Deo sic facere per unam simplicem puellam, pro repellendo adversarios Regis."[72] Associating her own name with the linked names "Jhesus Maria,"

Joan placed herself heroically at the side of Christ as His Helpmate, as another Mary, as someone instrumental (as Mary, the New Eve, had been) in restoring God's Kingdom on earth.

Joan wore armor, dressing herself in battle gear, even as the Virgin Mary was sometimes depicted (as Marina Warner has taught us) "in full armour, in her aspect as the Tower of David."[73] Warner points to "the Albrecht altar painted in Mary's honor before 1440, possibly while Joan was alive," where "the Virgin wears mailshirt and a breastplate, gauntlets and leg pieces of armour under a voluminous mantle" (figure 2.2)[74] According to Warner, this depiction of the Virgin Mary, inspired by Marian exegesis of Solomon's Song of Songs 4:4 and 6:10, was often misidentified as a portrait of Joan of Arc. In his monograph on the Albrechtsaltar, Wolfgang Huber similarly points to the panel painting of "Mary as Queen of Potestates [Powers]" and observes, "Unwillkürlich denkt man hier an Jeanne d'Arc, die Jungfrau von Orléans, die erst 1431 verbrannt worden war."[75] Although Huber finds a direct, Jehannine inspiration for the painting unlikely ("unwahrscheinlich"), he points to biblical sources for the image of Mary as a battle leader and shows that such an image was strongly evocative in fifteenth-century piety.

Joan herself may have regarded the masculine attire that she wore at God's command and as a protection for her virginity as a Marian dress, whereas her enemies, citing Deuteronomy 22:5, held it to be an abomination worthy of the death penalty. After the battle for Paris, according to the testimony of Perceval de Cagny, Joan left her white armor behind her as an offering at the altar of the Virgin Mary at Saint Denis.[76]

Two Marian Puzzles

There are two puzzling, little-known episodes in Joan's history that suggest the extent of Joan's identification with Mary. The first bears upon the suit of white armor that I have just mentioned. Joan attacked Paris on September 8, 1429. That day was the Feast of the Nativity of the Blessed Virgin. At the siege of Orléans, Joan had refused to fight on the Feast of the Ascension,[77] but in seeming contradiction of this principle, she led the Parisian attack on Mary's feastday. Her judges at Rouen asked her whether she knew that it was a feastday, and she replied that she did.[78] Later they asked her "whether it was right to attack the town of Paris on the day of the Festival of the Blessed Mary," and Joan gave a provocative answer, stating "that it was good to observe the Festival of the Blessed Mary; and it seemed to her in her conscience good to keep the Festival of our Lady from beginning to end" [*respondit quod est bene factum servare festa Beatae Mariae; et videtur ei in ejus conscientia, quod esset bene factum servare festa Beatae Mariae a principio usque ad finem*].[79]

What are we to make of this? Was the attack, then, a violation of Joan's conscience, something she undertook, against her better judgment, at the prodding of the other officers and her superiors [*ad requestam nobilium*]?[80] Or did Joan view the attack on Paris as an act of worship, a way of keeping "the Festival of our Lady from beginning to end"? Given that Joan laid down her white armor at the altar of Mary in the abbey church at Saint-Denis after her defeat at Paris,[81] it may well be that she had dedicated the assault on Paris to Mary and had fought it consciously in Mary's own armor, hoping to renew the mystery of Mary's birth in the miracle of the city's surrender to the king of France. When asked whether she had left her armor at Saint Denis in order for it to be worshipped there, she answered that she was only following a chivalric custom, whereby a warrior who had been wounded in battle would offer up his protective armor in thanks giving to God.[82] Understood in the larger context of Joan's *imitatio Mariae*, the same military action that her judges viewed as evidence of Joan's lack of Marian devotion may indeed have been a great, bittersweet proof of it.

About the second Marian puzzle in the trial records, Vita Sackville-West has written, "Several queer stories, not exactly legends, crop up in connexion with Jeanne, and this one certainly deserves to rank amongst them."[83] An article in the Act of Accusation brought against Joan asserts that on one occasion she told Robert Baudricourt, the governor of Vaucouleurs, that she would give birth to three sons: a pope, an emperor, and a king. In response to Baudricourt's gallant offer to father one of these illustrious offspring, Joan allegedly declined, saying, " 'Gentil Robert, nennil, nennil, il n'est pas temps; le Saint-Esperit y ouvrera' " [nay, nay, Master Robert, now is not the time; the Holy Spirit will see to it].[84] Baudricourt supposedly circulated the story of this conversation, zestfully relating it more than once in the presence of clergymen and nobles.

As Sackville-West notes, the passage gives rise to a host of questions:

> Did [Joan] really make this boast to Baudricourt, or did she not? Was she falsely accused of having made it, and, if so, why? What gave rise to it? Was it compatible with what we know of her character?. . .Finally, if she had really boasted thus to Baudricourt, would it have led him to a greater belief in her, or the reverse? Would the claim have appeared any more extravagant to his mediaeval credulity than the claim that she could redeem France? It is difficult to decide.[85]

Commenting on the same passage, Anatole France wonders instead about the mixture of different types of language in the recorded exchange between Baudricourt and Joan: direct and indirect discourse, Latin and French, literal and allegorical. The speech of the interlocutors, writes Anatole France, seems to come from opposite sources and to represent different semantic registers: the one (that of Baudricourt), simple, rustic, literal-minded, and rudely naïve; the other (that of Joan), sublime, mysterious, and allegorical.[86] Interpreting Joan's prophecy of her three sons—one a pope, one a king, and one an emperor—as an allegory, France suggests that Joan's hidden meaning is religio-political. That is to say, the accomplishment of her mission would renew the tripartite Christian social order, establishing peace and concord in Christendom.[87]

France's religio-political interpretation is a feasible one, given Joan's use of allegorical speech on other occasions. Joan, in fact, was using the imagery of pregnancy during the days in Vaucouleurs with reference to her salvific mission for her homeland. The testimony of Catherine le Royer, at whose home in Vaucouleurs Joan was staying, indicates that Joan grew impatient waiting for Baudricourt to send her to the dauphin at Chinon. Joan reminded an astonished Catherine of the prophecy that France would be "lost through a woman" and "redeemed by a virgin from the frontiers of Lorraine." Catherine reports that Jeanne's eagerness to be about the fulfillment of her mission was such "that the time seemed to her as long as to a woman great with child" [*ac si esset mulier praegnans*].[88]

Anatole France's analysis overlooks, however, the obvious Marian imagery in Joan's alleged boast to Baudricourt. In claiming that the Holy Spirit would bring about the conception of sons within her womb, the Joan of the dialogue figures herself boldly as an *altera Maria*. The words that Baudricourt understood to name an earthly pope, a king, and an emperor were also nouns used to refer to the three persons of the Trinity: the Father ("papa"); the Incarnate Son, who was crowned with thorns as king ("rex"), and the Holy Spirit, who is the ruler ("imperator") of hearts. In saying that she would give birth to these three sons through the working of the Holy Spirit—*le Saint-Esperit y ouvrera*—the Joan of the reported dialogue represents herself as a Shrine Madonna or *Vierge ouvrante*.

The medieval Shrine Madonnas were wooden statues of the Virgin Mary that opened up to display the persons of the Trinity literally contained within Mary's womb (or symbolically, as Barbara Newman explains, within her heart): "In the later Middle Ages it was commonplace to call Mary the bride or chamber of the Trinity so as to celebrate the fullness of the Godhead dwelling within her soul."[89] Drawing on the extensive research of Christoph Baumer, Newman reports: "By 1500 Shrine Madonnas could be found in churches and convents from Portugal to Poland, and as far north as England and Sweden. French kings owned priceless golden *Vierges* inlaid with jewels, with interior carvings of ivory. . . .Other statues belonged to confraternities or to highborn nuns who used them in their personal devotions. Some were later converted to Eucharistic tabernacles, with the actual Body of Christ in the Host

2.3 Shrine Madonna, Erzbischöfliches Dom- and Diözesanmuseum, Vienna. Courtesy of the Erzbischöfliches Dom- and Diözesanmuseum.

substituted for his representation on the Cross."[90] (Figure 2.3 shows one such Shrine Madonna.)[91]

Joan's self-representation in the reported dialogue matches the depictions of Mary in these Shrine Madonnas. It may be that a spunky Joan depicted herself thus in answer to the insulting offer of Baudricourt to make her an unwed mother, rather than a maid. Or it may be that Joan never spoke the words. In the trial records, she explicitly denies having ever made such a boast.[92] What then of the accusation? It would seem that someone else—cognizant of the close resemblance between Joan and Mary in the popular imagination of fifteenth-century France—fashioned this accusation as an illustration of her blasphemous presumption to imitate Mary to the point of identifying with her. Such a hypothesis of Marian presumption is supported by the accusation that immediately follows. Joan is asked whether her voices call to her using the Marian title, "daughter of God," and she replies that they do frequently address her thus.[93] In either case, then, whether true or false, the "queer story" of the reported dialogue between Baudricourt and Joan in the Articles of Accusation corroborates the historical evidence for Joan's Marian devotion and identification with Mary.

Deborah Fraioli has urged us to interpret the records of the trials of Joan of Arc within the larger context of the theological and pastoral concerns that occupied the participants in the Councils of Constance (1414–18) and Basel (1431–39), especially those related to the discernment of spirits [*discretio spirituum*]. It is worth noting that a Marian dogma, the dogma of the Immaculate Conception, was also under debate at Basel, the council to whose judgment Joan herself appealed.[94] If Joan's supporters regarded her as an *altera Maria*, whereas her enemies saw her as an unregenerate Eve, that contest cannot be unrelated to the theological questions concerning Mary herself and her place in the plan and work of salvation.

Earlier I quoted my colleague's spontaneous remark about the perceived difficulty of uniting Joan the virago with Mary the humble handmaid. Karen Sullivan similarly identifies two different characterizations of Joan of Arc. "The vast majority of authors on Joan," Sullivan writes, "have stressed either Joan's agency, as a captain-at-arms, or her mediation of an other's agency, as an envoy of God, in saving her country. . . .One can argue with equal conviction [both] that Joan was distinguished by an active, almost Blakean initiative in transforming herself into what she wanted to be and that she was marked by a more passive, almost Marian willingness to serve as the handmaid of the Lord. It is not clear that these two portraits of Joan are irreconcilable."[95]

Today, as during Joan's own lifetime, people find it hard to reconcile the two, to unite the "volo"—the resolute "I will" of the virago—with the equally courageous "fiat"—the "let it be" of the handmaid. Too often, and too easily, we see these features of determination and surrender as intrinsically opposed. Joan of Arc's life, action, and suffering, however, suggest the opposite. Indeed, as I have argued in this essay, Joan is likely to have seen these same polarities united in the person of the Virgin Mary, with whom she identified.

I began this study with Joan's childhood devotion to our Lady of Bermont. I end with a devotional image from present-day Domremy. A stained-glass window in the Basilica there shows Joan of Arc presenting France, personified as a kneeling maiden, to the Virgin Mary (figure 2.4). Joan's face is upturned toward Mary, who looks down, holding the Christ Child close to her heart. Joan's right hand clasps her down-pointed sword;

2.4 Stained-glass window, Basilica at Domremy. Courtesy of Jean Frisk, Marian Library, University of Dayton.

with it, and with her open left hand, she gestures toward France to make of her an offering to the Virgin-Mother above them. France's hands, too, are open in self-offering to Mary. The three women form a feminine trinity, with Christ at the heart and Mary at the head.[96] A modern representation of the medieval Joan's devotion to Mary, it captures more of the Maid's spirit and spirituality than has been supposed.

Notes

1. Renée Grisel, *Présence de Jeanne D'Arc* (Paris: Nouvelles Editions Latines, 1956), p. 167: "A ce culte de la Vierge, Jeanne participe dès l'enfance, si la

légende—on ne sait en vérité pourquoi—passe souvent ce détail sous silence." Quoted and trans. Lionel Carl Nadeau, "Mark Twain's Joan of Arc: An Analysis of the Background and Original Sources," unpub. Ph.D. diss. (Muncie, IN: Ball State University, 1979), p. 35.

2. Caroline Walker Bynum, *Holy Feast and Holy Fast: The Religious Significance of Food to Medieval Women* (Berkeley: University of California Press, 1987), p. 269.
3. Régine Pernoud, *Joan of Arc By Herself and Her Witnesses*, trans. Edward Hyams (Lanham: Scarborough House, 1994), pp. 15–16; *Procès de Condamnation et de Réhabilitation de Jeanne D'Arc*, ed. Jules Quicherat, 5 vols. (Paris: Jules Renouard, 1841; New York: Johnson reprint, 1965), 1:46–47. On Joan's devotion to our Lady of Bermont, see A. Michel, "Sainte Jeanne D'Arc et Notre-Dame de Bermont," in *Maria: Etudes sur La Sainte Vierge*, ed. D'Hubert du Manoir (Paris: Beauchesne, 1958), Vol. 5, pp. 511–18.
4. Pernoud, *Joan of Arc*, p. 19; Régine Pernoud, *The Retrial of Joan of Arc*, trans. J.M. Cohen (New York: Harcourt, Brace and Company, 1955), p. 71; *Procès* 2:439–40.
5. Pernoud, *Joan of Arc*, pp. 18, 20; *Retrial*, p. 71; *Procès* 2:28.
6. Pernoud, *Joan of Arc*, pp. 16–17; *Retrial*, p. 65; *Procès* 2:390–91; 3:193.
7. Pernoud, *Joan of Arc*, p. 22; *Procès* 1:67.
8. Pernoud, *Joan of Arc*, p. 22; *Procès* 1:67.
9. Pernoud, *Joan of Arc*, p. 22; *Procès* 1:67.
10. Pernoud, *Joan of Arc*, p. 37; *Procès* 2:461.
11. *Procès* 2:459. Translation mine.
12. *Procès* 1:165.
13. Pernoud, *Joan of Arc*, p. 187; *Procès* 1:86–87.
14. Pernoud, *Joan of Arc*, p. 177; *Procès* 1:185.
15. Pernoud, *Joan of Arc*, p. 186; *Procès* 1:83.
16. Pernoud, *Joan of Arc*, p. 62; *Procès* 1:78.
17. Pernoud, *Joan of Arc*, p. 60; *Retrial*, p. 162; *Procès* 3:104.
18. Pernoud, *Joan of Arc*, p. 60; *Retrial*, pp. 127, 162–63; *Procès* 3:14, 104.
19. Pernoud, *Joan of Arc*, p. 83; *Procès* 4:152.
20. Deborah Fraioli, *Joan of Arc: The Early Debate* (Woodbridge: Boydell Press, 2000), p. 206. In an appendix Fraioli provides a translation of the complete text of *The Poitiers Conclusions*.
21. Fraioli, *Joan of Arc: The Early Debate*, p. 206.
22. Fraioli, *Joan of Arc*, p. 208. In another appendix Fraioli provides a translation of the complete letter.
23. Fraioli, *Joan of Arc*, p. 208.
24. Marina Warner notes, "the recognition scene at Chinon has been depicted in paint and in words, as a secular equivalent of the Annunciation to Mary, with Joan as Gabriel announcing to Charles that he is himself France's Messiah" (*Joan of Arc: The Image of Female Heroism* [New York: Alfred A. Knopf, 1981], p. 57). See Warner's reproduction of an illustration of Chapelain's epic, *La Pucelle, ou La France delivrée* (plate 21).
25. *Procès* 5:99.

26. *Procès* 5:98.
27. *Procès* 5:98–99: "Audiat, quaeso, vestra reverendissima potestas, et exultet animus in dono puellari tam coelesti, quod temporibus nostris cunctipotens praestare dignatus est. Adaccessit coelestis Puella, et quod ipse pater cunctipotens virgini Mariae prae caeteris praestitit, scilicet ut eam tam pulchram aspicientes, quisque ille esset, qualiscumque et ex vita inmorali, dies duxit suos ab omni concupiscentia saeculi. Qui tamen diceretur eadem asseri et de virgine nobis missa, cujus nomen Joanna? Joanna, inquam, Puella, habitu pastorali induta, et quasi virili, de mandata Dei omnipotentis accessit ad regem per diversa formidabilia itinera, sine violentia, illaesa, illibata, associata cum personis; accessit ad regem, et. . .ex dispositione regalis consilii ordinatum fuit ut non illico regem alloqueretur, sed pluribus a viris et exquisitissimis clericis, doctoribus in sacra pagina, et aliis diligenter noscere[tur]. Sed evenit ut, non obstante illa proposita dispositione, sine mora ad reginam access[er]it Puella, et peteret regem quem Dalphinum appellabat. Non continuit rex, sed statim ad eam accessit." Translation mine.
28. For a Marian approach to Liberation Theology, see Leonardo Boff, O.F.M., *The Maternal Face of God: The Feminine and Its Religious Expressions*, trans. Robert R. Barr and John W. Diercksmeier (San Francisco: Harper and Row, 1987).
29. Fraioli, *Joan of Arc*, p. 59.
30. Quoted in Fraioli, *Joan of Arc*, p. 60.
31. Fraioli, *Joan of Arc*, p. 59.
32. *Procès* 5:87.
33. *Procès* 4:501.
34. Quoted in Fraioli, *Joan of Arc*, p. 93.
35. Fraioli, *Joan of Arc*, pp. 37, 90–91.
36. *Procès* 2:444.
37. Antonio Morosini, *La chronique d'Antonio Morosini: Extraits relatifs à l'histoire de France*, ed. and trans. Léon Dorez and Germain Lefèvre-Pontalis, 4 vols. (Paris: Société de l'Histoire de France, 1898–1902), 3:80–81; quoted and translated in Fraioli, *Joan of Arc*, p. 57.
38. *Procès* 4:310; quoted in Fraioli, *Joan of Arc*, p. 125. Notice the use of the word "pucelle" for both Mary and Joan.
39. Christine de Pisan, "Le Ditié de Jehanne D'Arc," ed. and trans. Angus J. Kennedy and Kenneth Varty, *Nottingham Medieval Studies* 18 (1974): 29–55; 19 (1975): 53–76. The quoted lines from stanza 22 appear on p. 68.
40. Pernoud, *Joan of Arc*, pp. 147–48; *Procès* 1:105.
41. Pernoud, *Joan of Arc*, p. 154; *Procès* 1:110.
42. Pernoud, *Joan of Arc*, p. 173; *Procès* 1:176.
43. See Friedrich Schiller, *Die Jungfrau von Orleans*, ed. Benno von Weise and Lieselotte Blumenthal. In *Schillers Werke (Nationalausgabe)*, Bd. 9 (Weimar: Hermann Böhlaus, 1948; *The Maiden of Orleans*, trans. John T. Krumpelmann, University of North Carolina Studies in the Germanic Languages and Literatures 24 (Chapel Hill: University of North Carolina Press, 1959).

44. Paul Claudel, *Jeanne d'Arc au Bûcher*, in *Théâtre de Paul Claudel*, 2 vols., ed. Jacques Madaule (Paris: Gallimard, 1956), 2:1199–226.
45. Karen Sullivan, *The Interrogation of Joan of Arc*, Medieval Cultures 20 (Minneapolis: University of Minnesota Press, 1999), p. 94. For the relevant passage in the *Miroir*, see *Procès* 4:268–69.
46. *Procès* 4:430.
47. *Procès* 4:430.
48. Karen Sullivan, " 'I Do Not Name to You the Voice of St. Michael': The Identification of Joan of Arc's Voices," in *Fresh Verdicts on Joan of Arc*, ed. Bonnie Wheeler and Charles T. Wood (New York: Garland, 1996), pp. 85–112.
49. See Pernoud, *Joan of Arc*, p. 206.
50. *Procès* 1:85.
51. *Procès* 1:93.
52. *Procès* 1:328.
53. *Procès* 1:282–83.
54. *Procès* 1:283.
55. *Procès* 1:400. The name Gabriel was regularly glossed in medieval hymns and in commentaries on the Annunciation as "Fortitudo Dei" [Strength of God]. The name was viewed as appropriate, given Christ's courage in accepting mortality and martyrdom. See Maria Elisabeth Güssmann, *Die Verkündigung an Maria im Dogmatischen Verstandnis des Mittelalters* (Munich: Max Hueber, 1957), p. 109.
56. Pernoud, *Joan of Arc*, p. 194; *Procès* 1:278–79.
57. Pernoud, *Joan of Arc*, p. 173; *Procès* 1:175.
58. *The Trial of Jeanne D'Arc*, trans. W.P. Barrett (London: Gotham House, 1932), p. 205; *Procès* 1:167–68.
59. See Marina Warner, *Alone of All Her Sex: The Myth and Cult of the Virgin Mary* (New York: Knopf, 1976).
60. See Donald Weinstein and Rudolph M. Bell, *Saints and Society: The Worlds of Western Christendom 1000–1700* (Chicago: University of Chicago Press, 1982), pp. 123–37.
61. Bynum, *Holy Feast and Holy Fast*, pp. 81–82. It must be noted, however, that while Bynum doubts the reliability of quantitative evidence with reference to medieval food practices, she (curiously) accepts it without question regarding female devotion to Mary. See note 57, p. 318; note 45, p. 409.
62. Julia Kristeva, "Stabat Mater," in *Tales of Love*, trans. Leon S. Roudiez (New York: Columbia University Press, 1987), p. 256.
63. Barbara Newman, "Intimate Pieties: Holy Trinity and Holy Family in the Late Middle Ages," *Religion and Literature* 31.1 (1999): 87. See also Pamela Sheingorn, "The Maternal Behavior of God: Divine Father as Fantasy Husband," in *Medieval Mothering*, ed. John Carmi Parsons and Bonnie Wheeler (New York: Garland, 1996), pp. 77–99.
64. Newman, "Intimate Pieties," p. 86.
65. See Newman, "Intimate Pieties," for a study of Saint Birgitta and Margery Kempe from the perspective of Marian identification. See also Rosemar

Hale, "*Imitatio Mariae*: Motherhood Motifs in Late Medieval German Spirituality," Ph.D. diss., Harvard University, 1992.

66. Pernoud, *Joan of Arc*, pp. 23–24; *Procès* 1:128.
67. See Don Denny, *The Annunciation from the Right: From Early Christian Times to the Sixteenth Century* (New York: Garland, 1977).
68. Pernoud, *Joan of Arc*, p. 182; *Procès* 1:61–62. See also the account of Joan's voices and the Angelus bells given by the fifteenth-century historian Thomas Basin in his *Histoire de Charles VII, Procès* 4:352.
69. Pernoud, *Joan of Arc*, p. 190; *Procès* 1:130.
70. Warner, *Joan of Arc: The Image of Female Heroism*, p. 22.
71. Caroline H. Ebertshäuser, Herbert Haag, Joe H. Kirchberger, Dorothee Sölle, *Mary: Art, Culture, and Religion Through the Ages*, trans. Peter Heinegg (New York: Crossroad, 1998), p. 159.
72. *Procès* 1:290.
73. Warner, *Joan of Arc*, p. 235.
74. Warner, *Joan of Arc*, p. 235.
75. Wolfgang Huber, *Der Albrechtsaltar und Sein Meister* (Wein: Tusch, 1981), p. 62. In a letter to me, Dr. Huber reports that the altar, originally commissioned by the Teutonic Knights, was reconstructed after the restoration that ended in 1980 and stands today in the Saint Sebastian's chapel of the abbey at the Stiftsmuseum, Klosterneuberg, Austria. I thank Dr. Huber for his assistance in obtaining a photo of the panel painting and permission from the Stiftsmuseum to reproduce it.
76. *Procès* 4:29.
77. Pernoud, *Joan of Arc*, p. 87.
78. *Procès* 1:57.
79. *Procès* 1:147–48.
80. *Procès* 1:146–47.
81. *Procès* 1:29.
82. Pernoud, *Joan of Arc*, p. 175; *Procès* 1:179.
83. Vita Sackville-West, *Saint Joan of Arc* (New York: Doubleday, 1991), p. 90.
84. *Procès* 1:219–20.
85. Sackville-West, *Saint Joan of Arc*, pp. 90–91.
86. Anatole France, *Vie de Jeanne D'Arc* (Paris: Calmann-Lévy, 1908), 1:90–91.
87. France, *Vie de Jeanne D'Arc*, p. 91.
88. Sackville-West, *Saint Joan of Arc*, p. 89. *Procès* 2:446.
89. Newman, "Intimate Pieties," p. 86.
90. Newman, "Intimate Pieties," p. 86. See Christoph Baumer, "Die Schreinmadonna," *Marian Library Studies* 9 (1977): 239–72. Baumer includes many photographic illustrations of *Vierges ouvrantes*. Cf. Bynum, *Holy Feast, Holy Fast*, p. 268.
91. I thank the director of the museum for the photographs and for permission to use them here.
92. *Procès* 1:220.
93. Pernoud, *Joan of Arc*, p. 190; *Procès* 1:220.

94. A conciliar decree of September 17, 1439 declared the doctrine of the Immaculate Conception to be dogma. That decree was, however, subsequently ruled invalid on procedural grounds. See Aeneas Sylvius Piccolominus (Pius II), *De Gestis Consilii Basiliensis Commentariorum, Libri II*, ed. and trans. Denys Hay and W.K. Smith (Oxford: Clarendon Press, 1967), note 2, p. 154.
95. Sullivan, *Interrogation*, p. 60.
96. For a study of the medieval feminine trinity in relation to the dogma of the Immaculate Conception, see Ann W. Astell, "Chaucer's 'St. Anne Trinity': Devotion, Dynasty, Dogma, and Debate," *Studies in Philology* 94.4 (1997): 395–416.

CHAPTER 3

SAINT JOAN AND CONFESSION: INTERNAL AND EXTERNAL FORUM

Henry Ansgar Kelly

This chapter analyzes Joan's experiences with the sacrament of confession (which were very positive) and the Church's judicial system (which were negative, in violation of canon law).

The Church's penitential system, as it had developed by the thirteenth century, embraced both the internal and external forum. The internal forum was the realm of sacramental confession, where there was strict confidentiality between confessor and penitent. The penalty for any priest who broke this sacramental seal was life imprisonment, a sanction imposed at the Fourth Lateran Council in 1215.[1] The external forum encompassed the various ecclesiastical courts under the jurisdiction of pope, bishop, archdeacon, and rural dean or archpriest. This forum, too, guaranteed rights of confidentiality for the defendant, which were established in the same Lateran Council when the rules of inquisitorial procedure were set forth. There was a principle that the Church did not judge secret crimes, so that Church courts (and secular courts as well) were not to bring charges *ex officio* (i.e., in an inquisition) against any person except for sins or crimes that were public. The judge's first step was to determine the existence of *fama publica*, which is the belief of reputable persons that the implicated person (defendant) was guilty of a specific public crime. The second step was to establish the truth or falsity of this suspicion.[2] If the actual guilt of the defendant could not be proved, the judge had the option of ordering compurgation, a process in which the defendant is required to back up his or her denial of guilt by producing a specified number of character witnesses.[3]

In Joan of Arc's trial before Bishop Cauchon, these rules of inquisitorial due process were flagrantly violated. In spite of all her implicit and explicit protests, no specific charges were leveled, no witnesses were produced to establish *fama publica*, and no proofs of any crimes were brought forward. She was convicted solely on responses that she made to enforced questioning. If she had known the law, or been advised about it, she could have remained silent, or, rather, formally interrupted the trial by an appeal to Cauchon's superiors, either his metropolitan, that is, Regnault de Chartres, archbishop of Rheims, or the pope. Even if Cauchon had rejected her appeal and refused to undo the grievance by following due process, she could have continued to maintain her refusal to answer, and, at the most, she could have been punished only for contempt of court (assuming, of course, that the bishop would have followed the rule of law in this matter).[4]

Cauchon's illegal strategy was one commonly used by heresy inquisitors, namely, to persuade or threaten Joan to make incriminating statements about herself, on the pretense that he was a representative of Church authority and had a right to explore her mind and conscience in this way. In fact, as a bishop, he had more jurisdiction than a heresy inquisitor did, in that he had the right to prosecute not only matters of faith, but also any other sin—including such offenses as stealing a bishop's horse!

When a defendant makes a private statement in open court, it immediately becomes "notorious," and fair game for prosecution. However, if a defendant makes such a statement only to the inquisitor and his recorder, by all rights it should not be prosecuted publicly but rather, at the most, liable only to secret abjuration and penance. This is the position stated by Thomas de Torquemada half a century after Joan's trial, in the Instructions of Seville in 1484.[5]

In addressing Joan at the very beginning, as part of his "charitable" exhortation, Cauchon told her that her truthful responses to questions in matters of the faith would serve not only to speed along "her process" but also to effect the clearing of her conscience ("la descharge de sa conscience," "exoneracio proprie consciencie").[6] Joan seemed to accept that he had at least some rights in this matter, and mainly balked when she felt that his questions would violate the oath of secrecy that she had taken about the revelations made to her.

She refused to take open-ended oaths in court because she was afraid that she would be forced to violate this previous commitment. In actual fact, her oath of secrecy would have been only a simple vow from which Cauchon, acting as her bishop, could have dispensed her, but this ploy does not seem to have occurred to him; or perhaps he realized that such an offer would not have been accepted by her. Joan asked her questioners repeatedly if a particular query pertained to their "process," perhaps indicating that if it did not, even though it might somehow deal with matters of faith, she did not consider herself obliged to answer it. Moreover, she frequently told the questioners to "pass on" to other matters. At times, this seems not to have been an outright refusal to respond, but only an unwillingness to answer "for now." At one point, when asked about the appearance of Saints Michael and Gabriel, she responded that her questioners would know nothing more than what she had already answered, for now ("pour le present"). To the next question, whether she knew by revelation if she would escape, she first said that that did not touch on their process, and then she asked, "Do you want me to speak against myself?"[7] By this she may have meant, not that she would be violating her sworn promise not to reveal what she had been told in her visions, but rather that she could not be expected to compromise herself and her rights as a prisoner of war.

It became quite clear at the very beginning of her interrogation that Joan fully understood the rule about the sacramental seal, when she was asked to recite the prayers she had learned from her mother. Different accounts of this scene are given in the French and Latin texts, the former based on the original transcript of her trial (though passed through a faulty scribe),[8] and the latter a doctored translation prepared by Thomas Courcelles for Bishop Cauchon four years after the trial. Neither text specifies who is asking the first questions about her early life, but when she is asked to recite the *Pater noster* and *Ave Maria*, Joan's response in the French text indicates that it was not Cauchon who made this request but someone else, probably the promoter, John d'Estivet. She said that she would do so willingly, provided that Monseigneur, the bishop of Beauvais, who was present, would hear her in confession ("Respond qu'elle le dira voluntiers, pourveu que monseigneur l'evesque de Beauvoys, que estoit present, la vouldroit oyr de confession"). The Latin has the bishop himself asking ("Item requisita per nos"), and only to say the *Pater noster*, and Joan responding to him directly to hear her confession ("Respondit quod audiremus eam in confessione, et ipsa nobis diceret libenter"). The Latin text has the bishop continue to ask for her recitation, whereas in the French the further requests are still anonymous ("elle fust plusieurs foys requise"), and the bishop only intervenes to offer her one or two notable persons from the gathered assembly to whom she could recite the prayers. The Latin text adds that these notable men would be French-speakers ("de lingua gallicana"). Her response is in keeping with her previous answers: she will not recite her prayers to any such persons unless they hear her in confession.[9]

However, although these responses of Joan had the effect of preventing her questioners from examining the accuracy of her prayers and her understanding of them, this may not have been her primary intention. It may be that she really did want to go to confession to Cauchon. Later on, when she was challenged about her refusal ("Why do you not willingly say the *Pater noster*, since you say you are a child of God?"), she replied, "I do say it willingly; and previously when I refused, it was with the intention of having Msgr. Beauvais hear my confession."[10] Perhaps she believed that by unburdening her conscience to her judge directly and privately, in the sacrament of confession, she would convince him of her innocence of any moral fault, since to lie to a confessor would be an extremely serious sin. This is the sort of explanation that Pierre Tisset favors.[11]

An earlier incident may lend weight to this interpretation. When Joan was in Vaucouleurs, according to a witness testifying in 1456, namely, Catherine, wife of Henry Le Royer (at whose house Joan stayed for three weeks), she liked to go the Church and to confession; Catherine in fact took her there herself and and saw her confess to the curate, John Fournier. Then, later on, Robert de Beaudricourt brought the curate to see Joan in the Le Royer house; there, wearing his stole around his neck, the priest adjured her, saying: "If you are an evil thing, depart from us, and, if good, come here next to us." Joan went up to him and knelt down; and then she rebuked him for doing such a thing, since he had heard her confession.[12] Clearly she believed that he should have known the truth about her from having heard her confession.

There is another factor to be considered here. We will see below that Joan's last confessor, Martin Ladvenu, said that she was very simple and barely knew her prayers: "Valde simplex mulier erat, ut pene solum sciens suum *Pater Noster, Ave Maria*, et *Credo*."[13] This response seems to echo the instructions confessors were given about monitoring the knowledge of these prayers when uneducated penitents came to them. Here is what John Burgh says in his *Pupilla oculi*, written in the 1380s: "If the priest sees that the penitent is simple or unlettered, he should inquire if he knows the Lord's Prayer, the Angelic Salutation, and the Symbol of Faith, and, if he does not, he should teach him, or admonish him to learn them."[14] Joan was clearly used to being asked to recite her prayers by confessors who did not know her, and she was doubtless most comfortable in saying them under these circumstances. Confessors were also to inquire whether their simple penitents had the right faith and knew the meaning of the articles contained in the creed.[15] Perhaps her past experience with confessors alerted Joan to expect similar questioning if she recited the creed to Cauchon in public.

The effort to have her expose her knowledge or lack of knowledge of her prayers on this first day of questioning, February 21, was abandoned for the time being. On the second day, February 22, Cauchon attempted to persuade her again to swear an absolute oath to tell the truth, assuring her (falsely) that not even a prince could or should refuse to take such an oath in matters of faith. She replied that she had sworn an oath yesterday; the Latin adds: "That should well suffice for you" (a canonically sound opinion). Then she told him, "You burden me too much" ("Vous me chargez trop," "Vos nimis oneratis me").[16] Cauchon had assured her the day before that such an oath would serve to unburden her conscience, but she clearly saw it as having the opposite effect. When Cauchon pressed her again on this matter, on February 24, she told him, "Mark you well when you say you are my judge, for you are taking on a great burden"; and she repeats that he is burdening her excessively.[17] Finally, she was threatened that if she refused to take the blanket oath, she would be attainted and convicted of what was charged against her ("admonnestee de ce faire sur peine de estre attaintte et convaincue des cas a elle imposez"). This outrageous statement, that she would be convicted of charges before any charges had even been made against her, was toned down a bit in Courcelles's translation: "sub pena essendi onerata de illo quod sibi imponebatur" ("under pain of being burdened by what was being alleged against her"). Joan simply responded, "I have sworn enough" (omitted by Courcelles), adding, "Pass on."[18] Later, one of the charges against her was that, in contempt of the precepts and sanctions of the Church, she had several times refused to swear to tell the truth in court, thus rendering herself suspect.[19]

Joan was certainly right in saying that she had sworn enough, for in fact she had sworn too much. Apart from the fact that defendants were not to be sworn in more than once, there was no excuse for being sworn at all until charges had not only been presented and explained but also justified by establishing probable cause, through the testimony of trustworthy witnesses, that the defendant was believed to be guilty of the charges.[20] However, the premature imposition of oaths had doubtless become so commonplace that by the fifteenth century even learned jurists may not have always recognized the violation of the *ordo juris* that the process entailed.[21]

On the second day, February 22, we are explicitly told that Cauchon handed the questioning over to Master John Beaupere, identified in the Latin version as an outstanding professor of theology. When he asked Joan if she went to confession every year ("si elle se confessoit tous les ans"), she responded, yes, to her own curate (i.e., her parish priest), or, if he was not available, to another priest with the curate's permission.[22] She added that when she was at Neufchatel (she had just said that she stayed there fifteen days or so when there was fear of a Burgundian attack), she went two or three times to religious mendicants (i.e., friars). Finally, she volunteered that she received communion every year ("tous les ans") at Easter; but, when asked if she received communion at any feastdays other than Easter, she gave the first of her "pass on" responses.[23]

We might be inclined to think that her first *tous les ans* meant the same thing as the second, and that she only went to confession once a year every year. But on the face of it, this would clearly be a mistake, since she went at least weekly to confession to friars during the brief time that she was away from her home parish, and we can readily assume that she also confessed frequently when she was at home. She also shows that she was aware of the regulation that one could confess to friars, at least Dominicans and Franciscans, without one's curate's permission or even the local bishop's license.[24]

She undoubtedly specified that she went to communion at Easter time in order to assure the court that she performed her Easter duty. Why she did not wish to divulge, at least at this time, her practice concerning communion on other occasions during the year is not clear. There is now, and was then, as common assumption that the Easter duty of receiving communion entailed a parallel duty of going to confession at that time, but that was not quite the case. The Lateran law specified that one must confess one's sins to one's proper priest at least once a year ("saltem semel in anno"), and to receive communion at least at Easter ("ad minus in Pascha"). Naturally, if one were guilty of any mortal sins, the confession would have to be made before receiving the Easter communion; but if one did not have any mortal sins, the confession could be made at any time.

Some authorities on confession, Raymund Pennafort tells us, insisted that venial sins as well as mortal sins had to be confessed, and Raymund believed that this was the safer course.[25] But others pointed out that it was only the deliberate omission of a mortal sin that would invalidate confession, and that there were other ways in which venial sins could be removed, like saying prayers or blessing oneself with holy water. However, everyone was encouraged to confess any venial sins that came to mind.[26]

Let us see what the record tells us about Joan's practice of confession before she came to trial, starting with her early years.[27]

In the preliminary inquisition or inquest that was ordered on December 20, 1455, for Lorraine, as part of the retrial of Joan's condemnation, the questions concerning her personal piety were these:

> VI. [In her adolescence, from the age of seven until she left home], did she willingly and often go to church and holy places?
> VIII. During the same time, did she willingly and often go to confession?[28]

We note that there is nothing here about going to communion, presumably because frequent communion was not much practiced at the time, even by the most pious of persons.

The first witness to testify was John Morel, who said that he saw her go to confession at Easter and other solemn feastdays, and that she confessed to her local curate, William Fronte.[29] Confession in those days, before the invention of the confessional, was very public in its privacy, and one could easily be seen going to confession. The nineteenth witness, Mengette Joyart, lets us know how it was done: she says that she saw her many times on her knees going to confession to the curate.[30]

The fifth witness, John Moen, believed that she went to confession many times through the year after she reached the age of reason ("dum habuit intellectum").[31] This, of course, was in keeping with the Lateran decree discussed earlier, which specifies that the obligation of yearly confession began when one reached the years of discretion. Some authorities set the limit at ten or eleven and linked the appropriate age with the ability not only to commit serious sins but also to receive the Eucharist with due reverence.[32] But others took the Council to mean the age of seven, and that was undoubtedly the intention of the formulators of the articles of inquiry, who specified Joan's adolescence as extending from her seventh year ("a septennio").[33] The twenty-ninth witness, Nicholas Bailly, heard it said by the residents of Domremy that Joan went to confession practically every month ("quasi quolibet mense").[34]

The sixth witness, a priest, testified that Joan's curate told him that she often confessed her sins to him, and that he had other praises for her piety: she went to daily Mass, and, whenever she had money, she would give it to him to say Masses (i.e., we are to understand, for her special intentions).[35] Another witness, the fourteenth, Hauviette de Syonne, and the fifteenth, John Waterin, also said that the curate remarked on Joan's frequent confessions.[36]

We saw earlier that when Joan was at Vaucouleurs she went to confession to the curate there. There was testimony from two other priests that she also went to them when she was in Vaucouleurs. She confessed two or three times to John Colin (who in 1456 was the curate of Domremy),[37] and four times to Henry Arnolin, three of the times during Lent, and once on a great feastday.[38] Esquire Bertrand de Poulengy saw her go to confession many times, both in Vaucouleurs and in battle, sometimes twice a week.[39]

In the inquest held at Orléans, conducted by the archbishop of Rheims in February of 1456, Ralph de Gaucourt reported that Joan often went to confession, prayed assiduously, heard mass daily, and frequently went to communion; similarly, Francis Garival, general counsel of the king, said that at Poitiers she often confessed and received communion frequently.[40] The priest Peter Compaing reported that she would exhort her troops to go to confession, and that La Hire and others of his company did so at her urging.[41]

The inquest held the previous January in Paris, by order of the bishop of Paris and inquisitor of France as well as the archbishop of Reims, gathered similar testimony. Simon Beaucroix, an esquire who was also a married cleric, recalled that she often urged the soldiers to be confessed, and she herself did so every other day, going to mass every day and communion every week.[42] The Augustinian friar, John Pasquerel, said that she had him gather all of the priests in the company for prayers twice a day, inviting the soldiers to attend as well, but only if they had confessed that day; and, of course, all the priests stood ready to hear the confessions. After the victory at Orléans, she lamented the soldiers who had died without confession. She went to confession to Pasquerel herself, and she ordered him to encourage the victorious soldiers to confess even now, and to thank God for the victory.[43] Theobald of Termes, the bailiff of Chartres, reported that a Dominican friar who had heard her confession many times, namely, Robert Baignart, declared her to be a true woman of God.[44]

The knight Aimon de Macy said that Nicholas d'Ecqueville, who had heard her confession when, like him, she was a prisoner at Crotoy, spoke of her similarly.[45] And William La Chambre, master of arts and medicine, who knew her only during her trial at Rouen, said that Peter Maurice, when he had heard her confession, was astounded by it; he had never heard such a confession before from anyone, not even a doctor (i.e., of theology), and he concluded that she was a truly holy person.[46] Thomas Courcelles, rector of the University of Paris at the time of Joan's condemnation, who was one of only three assessors at her trial to vote for torture (and who later, as noted earlier, produced the Latin record of her trial for Bishop Cauchon), testifying now in 1456, spoke of Maurice only as having told him that he had exhorted her to submit to the Church.[47] This tallies with the Latin record of the trial that Courcelles produced.

Courcelles also testified that Nicholas Loiselleur (one of the other assessors who voted for torture) had said that he had often spoken to Joan *in habitu dissimulato* (i.e., he pretended to be a countryman of hers and on the French side); he revealed to her that he was a priest, and Courcelles thought that he heard her in confession.[48] This was confirmed by William Manchon, the principal notary, testifying in Rouen on December 17, 1455. He said that Loiselleur often heard her in confession after deceiving her in the forementioned way, and she always consulted with him before being led out to continue the trial.[49] We can readily believe that Loiselleur would not be above revealing what he heard in Joan's confessions, but that was perhaps not even necessary, since, as Manchon testified here, Cauchon and the earl of Warwick had arranged it so that they could eavesdrop on Joan and their spy.[50] In his earlier testimony, in 1450, Manchon said that Loiselleur asked Joan if he could be her confessor, and he stated that other notaries were installed to overhear what was said; and, in addition, it seemed to Manchon, Loiselleur repeated to the notaries what was said.[51]

Let us now resume our examination of Joan's testimony in the trial before Cauchon and his assessors. On March 14, she was interrogated about her attempted escape from the tower of Beaurevoir. When asked if she made the daring leap at the behest of her voices, she freely admitted that Saint Catherine advised her daily against it, and after she went ahead and did it, the saint comforted her by telling her to confess what she had done and seek God's pardon for it. She was interrupted by the allegation that, according to witnesses, when she recovered her speech after her fall, she denied and cursed God and his saints, and would she be willing to submit herself to the testimony already obtained or to be obtained? She replied by denying any such outburst on her part, and by saying that she submitted herself only to God and to no one else, and to good confession.[52]

Later the same day she was asked, concerning the revelation that had been made to her—that she would be saved if she kept her promise of virginity—whether there was any need for her to go to confession. She replied that she was not conscious of having committed a mortal sin; if she had, she was certain that Saints Catherine and Margaret would have left her. Nevertheless, she added, one could not cleanse one's conscience too much.[53] In other words, Joan was saying, it is only mandatory to go to confession when one is in the state of mortal sin; but it is beneficial for one's soul to confess as often as possible.

Her questioners took this response as a cue to ask her about mortal sins that she may have committed. Was it a mortal sin to accept a prisoner for ransom and then have him put to death? Or to attack Paris on a feastday, or to take the bishop's horse, or to jump from the tower, or to wear male clothes, or to consent to the death of Franquet Darras? Out of all of these allegations, she admitted a sin only concerning the leap from the tower, in that she went against her saintly advisors, but she considered herself absolved of it after she confessed it, which Saint Catherine confirmed. Did she do great penance for it? "Yes," she responded, "in what I suffered from the fall." Was it a mortal sin? "I don't know, but I leave myself to God."[54]

When her testimony was incorporated into a set of seventy articles of accusation by the promotor Estivet,[55] the exchange resulted in the charge of boasting that the sinful leap that she had taken at the suggestion of the devil had been pardoned, contrary to Scripture, which says that we cannot be sure of pardon (article 64). Joan's response was simply to refer to her original answer, and, as for the conclusion of the article (i.e., the part about Scripture), she referred herself to God.[56] Her accusers were ignoring, of course, the doctrine of the sacrament of penance and the assurances that attended the devout practice of confession. Perhaps this was the reason that when her "confessions" were reduced to twelve articles, she was only said to claim knowledge by revelation that her sin was forgiven; but in this new formulation she was also said to have admitted that it was a great sin ("magnum peccatum") to offend her saints in this way (article 8). Then another charge was added: she did not think that she had ever committed a mortal sin, because, if she had, the two saints would not have visited her daily, as she claimed they did (article 9).[57] In the testimony just cited, she did not exactly say that she had never consciously committed a mortal sin in her life, but perhaps this was indeed what she meant.

On the basis of article 8, the theology faculty of the University of Paris declared her guilty of pusillanimity verging on despair (taking her leap not as an effort to escape but as attempted suicide); she was guilty also of a presumptuous and rash assertion of the remission of guilt; and of having a bad opinion of free will. The next article showed her guilty of a presumptuous and rash assertion and a pernicious lie: it contradicted her statement in the previous article (i.e., presumably, her alleged admission of a great sin); and she showed herself deficient in faith.[58] The canonists, for their part, found her erroneous in being certain that she would go to paradise as if she were already there, since, they said, when one was here on earth, only the supreme judge knew whether one deserved reward or punishment. The canonists also took up an assertion in the first article that Joan preferred wearing male clothes to going to mass and to receiving the Eucharist at the time ordained for it (Joan of course said no such thing), and they distorted it by saying that she preferred not to receive the body of Christ and not to go to confession at the time set for it by the Church (thus showing, in addition to their inability to read the articles accurately, their erroneous belief that confession was mandatory at Easter time); therefore she erred in the faith and was most vehemently suspect of heresy, and should be diligently examined on the articles of the faith.[59] They seemed to think that this latter procedure, of being interrogated on one's beliefs, was canonically regular, whereas it was in fact a clear violation of the *ordo juris* in the external forum.

Of course, Joan had evaded the trap of being asked to recite the *Pater noster* and then being tested on it, by insisting on saying it only in confession. She did something similar when required to respond to article 4 of the seventy articles on March 27. This article addressed the judges with the intention of informing them more fully about the defendant (*rea*), stating that she was born in the village of Grus, and so on. In other words, instead of presenting the testimony of witnesses, the promoter simply made assertions, which Joan was supposed to accept or reject. The article went on to assert that she was not instructed in the fundamentals of the faith in her youth ("Que Johanna in juventute non fuit edocta nec instructa in credulitate nec primitivis fidei"), but rather she was taught by old women who practiced sorcery, from many of whom, especially her godmother, she learned of visions of fates or fatal spirits, *fees* in French, and she confessed before the judges here that she did not know whether these fates were evil spirits. In her response Joan simply denied all this part of the article, adding that she knew nothing about fairies. As for her education, she was taught her belief ("creance") well. Thereupon she was asked to say the *Credo*, and she replied, "Ask the confessor to whom I have recited it" ("Demandez au confesseur a qui je l'ay dit"). Courcelles later translated this as, "Ask *my* confessor" ("Petatis a meo confessore cui dixi").[60]

Tisset takes her to be referring to a specific confessor, probably Loiselleur,[61] presumably since he was the one person we know of to whom she went to confession since the trial began. But because Loiselleur ostensibly approached her as a secret supporter and a secret priest, would she be willing to betray the confidences of her supposed friend? It seems more likely that she was telling them to ask any confessor to whom she had made her confession, indicating that she always recited the creed when she confessed, and that she was giving permission to her confessors to speak freely on this point. However, it may be that in such circumstances permission was not thought to be necessary. It is clear from the testimony in the retrial that her confessors seemed to have had no hesitation about revealing the contents of Joan's confessions during her lifetime, as long as it was not a matter of revealing her sins but only of telling what redounded to her praise.

One of these confessors reported as having praised Joan was, as we have seen, Peter Maurice. Let us look at what else the records have to say about him. According to Manchon, he was one of the two priests whom Cauchon appointed to counsel Joan near the end of the trial (the other was a Carmelite friar).[62] In the trial record we find him on May 23 in the position of explaining to Joan in French "certain points" on which she was found erroneous and deficient by the University of Paris.[63] As far as we know, the text of the twelve articles had never been shown to her, and it seems that Maurice only explained to her the portions that the theologians singled out for their adverse judgments.

Tisset asserts that Joan went to confession to Maurice at the end of the trial,[64] but this conclusion seems to be just an inference on his part. We must ask the question, was Joan allowed to go to confession during her trial? On April 18, when she felt so ill that she was afraid that she was dying, she asked Cauchon to be allowed to go to confession, receive communion, and be buried in consecrated ground. The bishop replied: "If you should wish to have the rights and sacraments of the Church, it would be necessary for you to confess as good Catholics ought to do and to submit to Holy Church" ("Se vouloies avoir les droittures et sacremens de l'Eglise, il fauldroit que vous feissiez comme les bons catholiques doyvent faire et vous submeissies a saincte Eglise").[65] Cauchon is presumably saying here that Joan would have to make a public submission to the "Church" (represented by him) before he would authorize a confessor for her. Perhaps he was using the analogy of a confessor denying absolution to a penitent thief until restitution was made. But on the face of it, his statement comes close to a denial of confession to a person in danger of death, which, of course, was inexcusable. This was probably the reason that in the Latin version his statement was emended to say that she could not receive the sacraments except for the sacrament of penance, which he was always prepared to grant.[66]

If Cauchon said four years after the trial that he was always ready to let Joan go to confession during the trial, can we believe him? Given her penchant for going to confession frequently, she would surely have desired it, but perhaps she would not have wished to confess to any of the priests who were sitting in judgment against her, apart from her offers of saying her prayers to them within the protected environment of the sacrament. At any rate, we do not hear anything else about the subject of confession until after her abjuration.

As mentioned earlier, Joan seems not to have been given the full text of the twelve articles sent to the University of Paris, but only Maurice's fairly accurate summary of the points singled out by the theologians. For instance, from the long first article, he told her only of her alleged assertion of visions of Saints Catherine and Margaret and the theologians' conclusion that they were mendacious communications from diabolical spirits.[67] He omitted the false charge in the article that Joan preferred wearing male gear to performing her Easter duty, and the canonists' doubly false inclusion of a mandatory Easter confession in the charge.

Maurice urged her especially to reconsider her response to the twelfth article, on submission to the Church, and he warned her that in his opinion only abjuration would redeem her soul and save her body from death. But she responded to all of the articles only by referring to her earlier statements.[68] One of the persons present at Maurice's instruction was the Dominican friar Isembart de La Pierre, who in the retrial said that Joan originally understood "submission to the Church" to mean submission to Cauchon's tribunal, until Maurice explained to her that it meant submission to the pope, and then Joan said that she readily agreed to it.[69]

After Joan's abjuration, on Thursday, May 24, Cauchon declared her absolved of the excommunication with which she had been bound, but only if she returned to the Church with true heart and faith not feigned, and observed the injunctions he had laid or would lay upon her.[70] However, there had been no decree of excommunication against her earlier in the trial. The only mention of excommunication in the record appears in the French text (not in the Latin), in the responses of the assessors to the question of Joan's taking an oath to answer the articles at the beginning of the so-called ordinary process, as a possible consequence of her refusal to swear.[71] Now Cauchon was asserting that she had been in an excommunicated state all along, and that she was hereby absolved of it, as long as her abjuration (which included a willingness to submit to the Church) was sincere. If it was not, she was still excommunicated. Furthermore, the bishop's statement clearly implies that if she were to violate any of the terms of her absolution, the excommunication would again take effect. But, as we will see below, Cauchon did not adhere to this position, since he allowed Joan to receive communion. True, this was after he was assured by Martin Ladvenu that she had made a good confession to him, but being absolved in the private forum would have had no effect upon a judgment of excommunication made in the public forum, without a formal lifting of the sanction by the judge.

The abjuration itself and the events of the next days are difficult to reconstruct exactly.[72] I will not attempt to give a complete picture of what occurred, but will concentrate on what pertains to confession. After Joan's reassumption of male clothes, the two judges, Cauchon and the deputy inquisitor, visited her in prison on Monday, May 28 (Courcelles in the Latin version says that he himself accompanied the judges, along with others, including La Pierre), and they told her that she had promised and sworn not to wear male clothes. She responded that she was not aware of having made such an oath. On further questioning, she said that Saints Catherine and Margaret told her of God's great "pity" over her betrayal, by which she was damning herself to save her life.[73] (In other words, she said she was being told by her voices that she had committed a mortal sin.) She now declared that she had never done anything against God or the faith, no matter what she had been told to revoke, and that she did not understand what was on the schedule of abjuration.[74]

Manchon in 1450 said that he too was present in the prison, to record the interview with Joan on the Monday, and afterward he finished recording the trial to the end; but he insisted he was not at the examination that others carried out with Joan on the side, like private persons. Cauchon tried to force him to sign their statements, but he refused.[75] Probably he was referring to the set of depositions made on June 7, of seven assessors who recounted their alleged interviews with Joan on the morning of Wednesday, May 30, before she was taken out to be sentenced and executed. This document appears at the end of the authorized record, after the affidavits of the scribes.[76] Among the seven deponents are the familiar figures of Courcelles and Loiselleur, but they also include the two priests who, we are assured, served as Joan's sincere confessors, namely, Peter Maurice, canon of Rouen, and the Dominican Martin Ladvenu, and also another Dominican, John Toutmoullié, who, we have on good evidence, accompanied Ladvenu to hear Joan's confession on that morning. All of these witnesses claimed that Joan admitted that she had been deceived by her voices because their promise of deliverance was not kept. Only two of them mentioned anything about confession. One was the treacherous Loiselleur, who said that he urged her to confess to the people that she had been deceived by her voices, and she responded by asking her confessor to remind her to do so when she was led out to judgment. He said that she seemed greatly penitent about the crimes perpetrated by her; and, with great contrition, both in prison and in the place of public judgment, she asked forgiveness of the English and Burgundians for causing them to be killed, exiled, and injured.[77]

We note that Loiselleur did not state positively that she went to confession, but James le Camus did; he allegedly testified that a little while after admitting that her voices were not good in deceiving her, she confessed her sins to Ladvenu, and he gave her communion after she declared her belief that the host was the body of Christ. Then, afterward, when Ladvenu asked her if she still retained any belief in the voices, she said no, because they had deceived her.[78]

Ladvenu himself allegedly testified only that Joan "said and confessed" that her voices deceived her; asked what brought her to that conclusion, she replied that it was Ladvenu himself and Peter Maurice and Nicholas Loiselleur (in other words, the three priests who are known to have heard her in confession), who exhorted her concerning the salvation of her soul; and that when they inquired whether she actually had such apparitions, she said that she did, and that she now agreed with the judgments of churchmen that they came from malign spirits, and she was no longer willing to believe in them. And though in her confessions and responses during the trial she had boasted about the angel bringing the crown, she now freely and without coercion stated and asserted that there was no such angel or crown.[79]

In the four authenticated depositions that Ladvenu gave two decades later (in a much different atmosphere, of course), his story was consistently contrary to this suspect deposition. In the 1450 interview, he is identified as Joan's "specialis confessor et director in extremis," though he himself does not mention his role as confessor. It was on this occasion that he said that she was very simple, and hardly knew anything but her prayers, as noted earlier. The only thing that he says she told him in prison after her abjuration was that she was raped by an English magnate ("fuit violenter multum infestata, et oppressione et ejus corruptione etiam a quodam magnate Anglicorum"), which she also stated publicly as the reason why she put on male dress.[80]

In the inquest at Rouen in 1452, Ladvenu was questioned twice. In the first session, his response to the sixth article (which stated that Joan was a simple girl, good and Catholic, frequently desiring to confess her sins and to hear mass, so that from the way she ended her life the bystanders could judge her to be faithful and Christian)[81] is a bit hard to decipher: he may be saying that he often heard her asking for confession, or, more likely, that he himself often heard her in confession ("audivit de confessione").[82] By the way, Manchon testified to this article that she asked to go to confession and hear mass; but he says nothing about whether she was allowed to do so.[83] In Ladvenu's second session, responding to new articles (not given in the record), he says that by order of the judges he administered the Body of Christ to Joan,[84] omitting reference to hearing her confession.

In 1455, Ladvenu repeated his testimony about the English lord, though this time he seemed to indicate that his attempt at rape was not successful ("eam temptavit vi opprimere"). As for his role on the last day, he said simply that by the license and order of the judges he heard her confession and administered to her the Body of Christ, which she humbly received with such great devotion and weeping that he could not describe it. And from that moment, he said, he never left her until she gave up her spirit. He added that while he was speaking with her about her salvation, Bishop Cauchon and some canons of Rouen came to see her, and she blamed him for her death, since he had promised to place her in the hands of the Church, but instead he abandoned her to the hands of her capital enemies. In response to a final question, Ladvenu said that she always up to the end maintained that her voices were from God, and that she was not deceived by them.[85]

Toutmouillié testified only in 1450. He accompanied Ladvenu, he said, who had been sent by Cauchon to tell Joan of her imminent death; he was to induce her to true patience, and to hear her confession ("et illam de confessione audiret"), all of which Ladvenu did with great sollicitude and charity.[86]

It is interesting that the theological and canonical implications of Joan's reception of penance and communion before her sentence of relapse were not raised with the more academic clerics in the retrial, but only with Manchon, who, though a priest, was not formally trained in the law. After testifying that communion was given to Joan before the final sentence was passed against her, he was asked, how was it that "they" had given communion to her, seeing that they had previously declared her excommunicate and heretical; and did they absolve her "in the form of the Church"? Manchon replied that "this was debated by the judges and their counsellors, whether she should be given the sacrament of the Eucharist if she should ask for it, and that she should be absolved in the penitential forum." He concluded by saying that he did not see any other absolution given to her.[87]

This exchange is difficult to interpret. Does *in forma ecclesie* refer to the Church's external forum? Does the clause, *et quod absolveretur in foro penitentiali*, mean, "they also debated whether she should be absolved in the forum of sacramental penance," or does it mean, "and they concluded that she should be absolved only in the sacrament of penance"? In either case, the debate would have had to occur before Joan received sacramental absolution from Ladvenu; and, furthermore, since there was no absolution in the external forum, her reception of communion would have been irregular.

Another reliable witness, namely, John Massieu, assures us that the debate over whether to give Joan communion occurred after she was confessed by Ladvenu. John Massieu in 1430 was dean of Christianity in Rouen, a position that was the urban equivalent of rural dean or rural archpriest, the lowest level of ecclesiastical judge; and it seems to have been a standard duty of all such deans to serve as the bishop's apparitor or summoner.[88] This at any rate was Massieu's function during Joan's trial.[89] In the 1452 inquest, he said that Joan received communion after a two-fold confession made to Ladvenu ("post binam confessionem ipsi fratri Martino factam"),[90] but nothing else in his three accounts indicates anything about a double confession. In 1456, he said that Ladvenu heard Joan in confession, and, once her confession was heard, Ladvenu sent Massieu to report to Cauchon how ("qualiter") she was heard in confession. He was also to report that she had asked for the Eucharist. The bishop thereupon gathered together some persons to deliberate upon the matter, and, after the deliberation, he told Massieu to tell Ladvenu to give her communion and whatever else she asked for.[91] In earlier testimony, Massieu said that the Eucharist was brought irreverently by a priest named Peter ("per quemdam dominum Petrum"),[92] and, still earlier, he said that Ladvenu was irritated at such lack of reverence and made the offending minister go back and put on a stole and bring candlebearers.[93]

Did Joan also go to confession to Peter Maurice that last morning? Apart from the unreliable testimony of the document that Manchon refused to sign, one later witness, namely, the priest John Riquier, did say that Maurice was present with her. Maurice told him that he visited her that morning, and Joan said to him, "Master Peter, where will I be later today?" He replied, "Don't you have good hope in the Lord?" She answered, "Yes, I do, and, God willing, I will be in paradise."[94]

Joan was finally taken by Ladvenu and Massieu to the place of sentence and execution, in the Old Market of Rouen. Before sentencing her, Cauchon urged her to take care for the salvation of her soul and to repent, and he appointed Isembart de La Pierre as well as Ladvenu to minister to her. In the course of his sentence, he declared her relapsed into the sentences of excommunication that she had previously incurred. He then asserted that he was casting her forth like a putrid limb from the body of the Church and committing her to secular justice, and then, using a standard formula, he requested the secular power not to impose the penalty of death or mutilation. Finally, he called for the sacrament of penance to be administered, if true signs of penitence should appear in her.[95]

We know from Ladvenu and many other witnesses that the secular judges failed in their obligation to pass a formal judgment; instead, they simply sat on their scaffold as spectators. We also know that, even though she was just now declared excommunicated and urged to repent and receive the sacrament of confession, no attempt was made to hear her confession again. Ladvenu doubtless considered her fully confessed and absolved and, being in the state of grace, ready for death. He was with her on the ambo or scaffold where she stood during Nicholas Midi's sermon before the sentence was delivered. She was led down from this scaffold and taken up to another, where the pyre was set. Ladvenu said that when she saw or felt the fire, she asked him to descend, presumably from the first scaffold, and to hold the crucifix up high so that she could see it.[96] But Massieu reported that Ladvenu descended from the scaffold with Joan and accompanied her to the place of punishment.[97]

As we saw earlier, according to the fraudulent document of June 7, Loiselleur claimed that before she died Joan begged forgiveness from the English and Burgundians for what she had done to them. Massieu, in contrast, testified that she forgave her enemies—and her allies—what they had done to her. Her pious lamentations and prayers lasted for almost half an hour before she was executed. Showing great signs "of her contrition, penitence, and fervor of faith," she "most humbly asked for mercy for all sort of people, of whatever condition they were, both of her party and the other, asking them to pray for her, as she forgave them the evil that they did to her."[98]

While it is believable that Joan would have asked forgiveness for everything she had ever done wrong, including in her campaigns against the English and Burgundians, it must have been in the spirit reported by Massieu rather than by Loiselleur.

We have seen that witnesses said that Joan frequently confessed "her sins" to her confessors. Of course, they would not have known what sort of thing she was telling them. We can be sure that she did lay out whatever she had done that seemed not right to her, but she must have told them other things as well. Perhaps she did recite her prayers to them, and ask them to explain what the Latin meant (for she would have said them in Latin, not French), and doubtless too she asked for advice on how to lead her life as sinlessly as possible, especially in the great matters that she had to deal with on her missions. If she was never, or rarely, aware of having seriously offended God, she was nevertheless concerned, as she herself said, to cleanse her conscience as much as possible, and that clearly meant frequent use of the sacrament that God had given for that purpose.

We can readily conclude that the internal forum of the Church as it functioned in Joan's life had a consistently beneficial effect on her, for it must have been the chief way in which she acquired her knowledge of Church doctrine and spiritual formation, apart from the teachings and maxims of maternal instruction and sermons and homilies in Church. Going to confession may have had a good psychological and spiritual effect on her even when it was being manipulated by her mortal enemies.

What about the external forum? It would seem, at first thought, that the opposite conclusion must be reached, that its effect on her was far from beneficial. It was, after all, her enemies' abuse of the ecclesiastical court system that brought her to her death. But, if we take the long view, *sub specie aeternitatis*, we should doubtless conclude that it was this very abuse that confirmed and demonstrated her saintliness. Clearly, she was an extraordinarily pious person throughout her military campaigns on behalf of her king. But would that have been enough for canonization, without the "martyrdom" that she suffered later, that is, the witness of heroic fortitude and faith that she manifested during her persecution at the hands of a wicked episcopal judge? This judge himself provided us, in effect, with her spiritual autobiography, in eliciting the responses that he did, and showing how she managed to persevere in her resolve, even though abandoned by her allies (who could have stripped Cauchon's court of its authority by appealing the case to Rome at any time during her trial in Rouen), and in the midst of overt foes, treacherous spies, reluctant collaborators, and sympathizers who were too timid or cowardly to help her. Furthermore, once the case was belatedly appealed to the pope, the retrial that he authorized, which overturned the first tainted verdict, supplied scores of external witnesses to describe her sanctity. And, centuries later, both trials provided an inestimably rich dossier for her final trial of canonization. In this last tribunal, her designated opponents, the "devil's advocates," though they acknowledged her as full of admirable qualities in the first phase of her career, found her sadly diminished at the end and very far from saintly virtue, and many members of the "jury" of consultors agreed with them. But the votes that counted, those of cardinals and pope, declared her heroically virtuous from beginning to end. It is only remarkable that, as the opposition was quick to point out, there was no groundswell of veneration for her as a saint from the very time of her death, but only 300 years after her "rehabilitation."[99]

Joan was denied the title of martyr, because it was decided that her death, though unjust on the part of her killers and holy on her part, was not inflicted because of her defense of the Christian faith. Her loyalty to her voices, which were accepted as genuine heavenly communications, did not qualify, for they were classified as private rather than public revelation. Moreover, she could not be called a confessor, as she would have been if she had not been female, since the word *confessor* in Latin can only be masculine, and, in consequence, it was never applied to women. Joan was instead declared a holy virgin. A female saint who was neither a virgin nor a martyr could only be defined in that negative way, as *nec virgo nec martyr.* However, when women were finally declared doctors of the Church, beginning in 1970 with Theresa of Avila and Catherine of Siena, the term used was the masculine *doctor,*[100] even though, unlike in the case of *confessor,* a feminine form was available, namely, *doctrix.* The time now seems ripe to break the sex barrier with *confessor* as well. It would be particularly appropriate to declare Joan of Arc a confessor of the faith, and to recognize that she became such in great measure because of her practice of frequent confession in the internal forum of penance and her stalwart confession of the truth in the external forum of the Church.

Notes

1. Innocent III, *Omnis utriusque sexus,* canon 21 of the Fourth Lateran Council, *Decretales Gregorii IX* (*Liber Extra* = *X*) 5.38.12, ed. Emil Friedberg, *Corpus iuris canonici* (Leipzig, 1879–81), 2:887–88.
2. Innocent III, *Qualiter et quando* no. 2, X 5.1.24, canon 8 of the Fourth Lateran Council (Friedberg 2:745–47); for the relevant text, see H. A. Kelly, *Inquisitions and Other Trial Procedures in the Medieval West,* Variorum Collected Studies Series (Aldershot 2001), chap. 2 ("Inquisitorial Due Process and the Status of Secret Crimes"), p. 410, n. 7.
3. Kelly, *Inquisitions,* Introduction, p. xii.
4. H.A. Kelly, "The Right to Remain Silent: Before and After Joan of Arc," *Speculum* 68 (1993): 992–1026, reprinted (and indexed) in *Inquisitions and Other Trial Procedures,* chap. 3. Joan was in fact asked at one point if she would submit herself to the archbishop of Rheims and others who she said witnessed the sign given to the king; she replied that she would only do so if they would give her a messenger and she could write to them about this entire trial. When queried again about the sign that she said was given to the archbishop and asked if she would submit to him, she replied, "Make him come here {and [hear?] what I intend to say}, and then I will answer you; but he would not dare to say anything contrary to what I have said." See Pierre Tisset, ed., with Yvonne Lanhers, *Procès de condamnation de Jeanne d'Arc,* 3 vols. (Paris, 1960–71), 1:345, 350 (original French text and Latin translation; in my translation of her response, I enclose in wavy brackets the

phrase omitted in the Latin; see Tisset's modern French translation, 2:302). Earlier, Joan was asked, if the pope and general council were here, would she submit to the council, she refused to entertain the speculation; then, asked if she would submit to the pope, she replied, "Take me to him, and I will reply to him" (ibid., 1:343). She gave a similar answer earlier still (1:175–76). At the end, just before the sentence was to be read, Joan responded to the question of her submission to the Church by saying that she asked for all she had done and said to be sent to the pope, to whom she submitted herself, after God; when she repeated this demand, she was told that it was too far, and that the ordinaries in their dioceses represented the Church (1:387–88). The sentence, which had obviously been written before these final appeals to Rome, stated that she had repeatedly refused to submit herself to our lord the pope and to a general council (1:414).

5. Kelly, "Inquisitorial Due Process," p. 419.
6. Tisset 1:37–38.
7. Tisset 1:92.
8. Tisset 1:xxi–xxvi; Kelly, "Right," p. 993, n. 3. The more accurate d'Urfé MS begins in the midst of the March 3 session (1:94). Tisset follows modern conventions for u/v in both the French and Latin text, but he does so for i/j only in the French; I extend this policy to the Latin text as well. He has unadvisedly rendered the ligature for "tt" as "ct" (as seems to have been done in the spelling of "Connecticut" for "Connetticut"), but I restore the proper spelling in all citations of the text.
9. Tisset 1:41.
10. Tisset 1:126: March 12: "Interroguee, puisqu'elle se dit fille de Dieu, pourquoy elle ne dist voulentiers *Pater noster*? Respond: Elle la dist voulentiers; et autrefois, quand elle recusa la dire, c'estoit en intencion que monseigneur de Beauves la confessast."
11. Tisset 3:79.
12. Pierre Duparc, ed., *Procès en nullité de la condamnation de Jeanne d'Arc*, 5 vols. (Paris 1977–88), 1:297–98. Fournier's actions are reported thus: "Ipse presbyter apportaverat stolam, et coram dicto capitaneo eam adjuraverat, dicendo sic, quod si esset mala res, quod recederet ab eis, et si bona, veniret juxta ipsos." In his translation, 3:285, Duparc overreads *eam adjuraverat* as "l'avait exorcisée." Joan's reaction: "Johanna se traxit juxta ipsum sacerdotem et erga sua genua; dicebat etiam ipsa Johanna quod presbyter non bene f[e]cerat, quia suam audierat confessionem."
13. Paul Doncoeur and Yvonne Lanhers, *La rehabilitation de Jeanne la Pucelle* [vol. 1]: *La enquête ordonnée par Charles VI en 1450* (Paris 1956), p. 43.
14. John Burgh, *Pupilla oculi* (Paris 1527) part 5, chap. 7, section A: "Et si videat sacerdos penitentem esse simplicem vel idiotam, inquirat ab eo an sciat orationem dominicam, salutationem angelicam, et simbolum fideil, et, si nescit, doceat eum, vel moneat ut addiscat."
15. Burgh V.8.B.
16. Tisset 1:45.

17. Tisset 1:55: "Advisez bien de ce que dictes, estre mon juge, car vous prenez une grande charge, et me chargez trop."
18. Tisset 1:57.
19. Tisset 1:272, article 60 of the 70 articles.
20. See Kelly, *Inquisitions*, Introduction, pp. xii–xiii.
21. See Adhémar Esmein, "Le serment des inculpés en droit canonique," *Bibliothèque de l'Ecole des Hautes Etudes, Sciences réligieuses* 7 (1896): 231–48; Kelly, "Right," p. 996.
22. In later Anglican use, the "curate" is the assistant pastor and the "vicar" is the pastor; in the Middle Ages, however, the "curate" is the head priest with the cure of souls, whether "rector" of the parish, or "perpetual vicar" in appropriated parishes, while subordinate priests are variously called "vicars" of "chaplains."
23. Tisset 1:45–47.
24. *Constitutiones clementinae* 3.7.2 (*Dudum*), renewing the decretal *Super cathedram* of Boniface VIII (Friedberg 2:1161–64, spec. 1163. commentators considered the privilege to apply to other friars as well, namely, Carmelites and Augustinians, by extension. See William Lyndwood, *Provinciale* (1432) 5,16,16 v. *proprio sacerdoti* (Oxford 1679, repr. Farnborough 1968), p. 344, n. b.
25. Raimundus de Pennafort, *Summa de paenitentia*, ed. Xaverio Ochoa and Aloisio Diez, Universa bibliotheca iuris, vol. 1 B (Rome: Commentarium pro religiosis, 1976), 3.34.21 (cols. 816–17).
26. See the Ordinary Gloss to *Omnis utriusque*, v. *omnia sua peccata* (*CJC* 2:1872): "Alias non esset fructuosa penitentia. . . .Non tamen venialia, quia illa tolluntur per orationem dominicam, vel per aquam benedictam. . . .Tamen si recolit, confiteatur illa" ("*all his or her sins*: Otherwise the penitence would not be fruitful. . . .Not however venial sins, because they are taken away by the Lord's Prayer or holy water. . . But if the confessant remembers them, let him or her confess them"). See Pennafort 3.34.60 (cols. 864–65) for other means of forgiving venial sins, namely, receiving communion, giving alms, participating in the general confession (i.e., the *confiteor*) at mass, and being blessed by a bishop or priest. Lyndwood, *Provinciale* 3.23.8 (p. 237, n. *a*), gives a dozen methods, listing canonical authorities for each. To Pennafort's list he adds fasting, devout beating of one's breast, confessing to someone not a priest, extreme unction, and, of course, baptism (for one not yet a Christian) and contrition of heart.
27. A brief summary of Joan's use of the sacrament of penance is given by Duparc, *Procès en nullité* 5:153–55. For the record of condemnation, see the index under "confession" in Tisset 3:260–61.
28. Duparc 1:250: All together, there are twelve articles of inquiry.
29. Duparc 1:254. The third witness, Beatrice Estellin, spoke similarly: she went to confession on appropriate days, especially Easter (1:258). So too the widow Jeannette de Vittel, 1:264. Others simply answered yes, she often and willingly went to confession. One witness, the eighteenth, Isabellette de

Spinal, said that she often went to church with Joan, who was the godmother of her son, and saw her go to confession to the curate: 1:282–83.

30. Duparc 1:285: "Confitebatur libenter; viditque eam pluries genibus flexis coram curato dicte ville."
31. Duparc 1:262.
32. See, e.g., John Burgh, citing Thomas Aquinas: *Pupilla oculi* IV.8.[F].
33. Duparc 1:250, article V: "Item, de conversatione ejus in adolescentia, a septennio usque ad egressum illius a domo paterna." In article VII, this period is referred to as "the aforesaid time of youth" ("predicto tempore juventutis").
34. Duparc 1:302.
35. Duparc 1:263.
36. Duparc 1:275–77.
37. Duparc 1:286.
38. Duparc 1:308.
39. Duparc 1:304.
40. Duparc 1:327–29.
41. Duparc 1:338.
42. Duparc 1:371, 373.
43. Duparc 1:391–92.
44. Duparc 1:403.
45. Duparc 1:405.
46. Duparc 1:350. La Chambre testified that he had examined Joan *quasi nuda* when tending to some infirmity, and, as far as he could tell *secundum artem medicine*, she was a virgin.
47. Duparc 1:358
48. Duparc 1:358.
49. Duparc 1:420–21.
50. Duparc 1:421.
51. Doncoeur and Lanhers, *La enquête. . .en 1450*, p. 48.
52. Tisset 1:144–46.
53. Tisset 1:149–50.
54. Tisset 1:150–53.
55. We know from the French text that the articles were explained to Joan by Courcelles, a point that Courcelles later omitted from the Latin text: Tisset, 1:190. On the question of oaths taken at this time, see Kelly, "Right to Remain Silent," pp. 1020–1021.
56. Tisset 1:282.
57. Tisset 1:294–95.
58. Tisset 1:362.
59. Tisset 1:363–64.
60. Tisset 1:196–97.
61. Tisset 3:79.
62. Duparc 1:217.
63. Tisset 1:375.
64. Tisset 3:79.

65. Tisset 1:329–30.
66. Tisset "Tunc fuit ei dictum quod, si vellet habere sacramenta Ecclesie, opportebat quod confiteretur tanquam bona catholica et eciam quod se submitteret Ecclesie, et quod, si perseveraret in illo proposito de non submittendo se Ecclesie, non poterant sibi ministrari sacramenta que petebat, excepta sacramento penitencie, quod semper eramus parati exhibere" ("Then it was said to her that, if she wished to have the sacraments of the Church, it was necessary for her to confess like a good Catholic and also that she submit to the Church, and that, if she persisted in her determination not to submit to the Church, the sacraments that she asked for could not be administered to her, except for the sacrament of penance, which we were always prepared to make available").
67. Tisset 1:375–76.
68. Tisset 1:380–84.
69. Duparc 1:223.
70. Tisset 1:393: "ab excommunicacionis vinculis quibus tenebaris adstricta te absolvimus per presentes, si tamen ad Ecclesiam vero corde et fide non ficta redieris, injunctaque tibi et injungenda per nos servaveris."
71. Tisset 1:187. See Kelly, "Right," pp. 1018–1019.
72. For a good assessment of the evidence, see Frances Gies, *Joan of Arc: The Legend and the Reality* (New York 1981), pp. 211–24.
73. Tisset 1:397.
74. Tisset 1:399.
75. Doncoeur and Lanhers, *La enquête. . .en 1450*, p. 51; cf. Jules Quicherat, *Procès de condamnation et de réhabilitation de Jeanne d'Arc*, 5 vols. (Paris 1841–49), 2:14.
76. Tisset 1:416–22; see Tisset's explanation of the untrustworthiness of this document, 3:43–44; but he does hold out the possibility that there are some elements of truth in it.
77. Tisset 1:421–22.
78. Tisset 1:420.
79. Tisset 1:417–18.
80. Doncoeur and Lanhers, pp. 43, 45.
81. Duparc 1:178.
82. Duparc 1:189. The whole statement reads, "Dicit quod plus [=pluries?] eamdem Johannam petentem et requirentem audivit de confessione." *Audire de confessione* is the idiom used for "hearing in confession," as in the testimony of Toutmouillié, later. Ladvenu goes on to say that he found her always to be faithful and devout, including at her death.
83. Duparc 1:182.
84. Duparc 1:236.
85. Duparc 1:442–44.
86. Doncoeur and Lanhers, p. 41.
87. Duparc 1:427: "Interrogatus insuper qualiter sibi tradiderunt eucharistie sacramentum, attento quod eam declaraverant excommunicatam et hereticam, et si eam absolverint in forma Ecclesie, dicit quod super hoc fuit

deliberatum per judices et consiliarios, an sibi petenti deberet dari eucharistie sacramentum, et quod absolveretur in foro penitentiali; non tamen vidit aliam absolutionem sibi exhiberi."

88. See H.A. Kelly, *Canon Law and the Archpriest of Hita* (Binghamton: MRTS, 1984), pp. 37, 52.
89. In the 1450 inquest, Massieu spoke of himself as the apparitor of the promotor, Estivet, but otherwise he referred to carrying out the bishop's orders (Doncoeur and Lanhers, pp. 52–56). The promotor, of course, was the bishop's assistant, and his orders would be considered the bishop's orders. See Kelly, "Right to Remain Silent," p. 1012.
90. Duparc 1:210.
91. Duparc 1:434–35.
92. Duparc 1:210.
93. Doncoeur and Lanhers, p. 55.
94. Duparc 1:461: "Cui ipsa Johanna dixit, 'Magister Petre, ubi ego ero hodie de sero?' Et ipse magister Petrus respondit, 'Nonne habetis vos bonam spem in Domino?' Que dixit quod sic, et quod, Deo favente, esset in paradiso."
95. Tisset 1:410–12.
96. Duparc 1:443.
97. Duparc 1:435.
98. Doncoeur and Lanhers, p. 55; cf, Quicherat 2:19: "en requerant aussi a toute maniere de gens, de quelque condition qu'ilz fussent, tant de son party que d'aultre, mercy tres humble, en requerant qu'ilz voulsissent prier pour elle, en leur pardonnant [*le mal qu'ilz lui avoint fait*]." The bracketed words, present in Quicherat, were mistakenly left out in the Doncoeur and Lanhers text. See Tisset 3:44.
99. For an account of her canonization process, see Kelly, "Joan of Arc's Last Trial: The Attack of the Devil's Advocates," *Fresh Verdicts on Joan of Arc*, ed. Bonnie Wheeler and Charles T. Wood (New York: Garland Publishing, Inc., 1996), pp. 205–236, repr. in *Inquisitions*, chap. 4.
100. Theresa was declared a Doctor on September 27 and Catherine on October 4. See *Acta Apostolicae Sedis* 62 (1970): 590: "Summus Pontifex Sanctam Theresiam de Avila, Virginem, Ecclesiae universalis Doctorem devlaravit"; p. 673: "Sancta Catharina, Virgo, Ecclesiae universalis Doctor declarata est."

CHAPTER 4

JOAN OF ARC AND *LEX PRIVATA*: A SPIRIT OF FREEDOM IN THE LAW

Jane Marie Pinzino

This essay demonstrates how the Christian principle that the Holy Spirit endows unique privileges gave rise to a fifteenth-century controversy that resulted in the legal decision of Joan of Arc's nullification trial (1450–57). This not only authorized the violations of biblical and canon law for which she had been condemned in 1431, but argued the validity of lex privata for all the faithful.

Qui privata lege ducuntur spiritu Dei aguntur, et non sunt sub lege communi et publica, quia ubi spiritus, ubi libertas.

[They who are led by the private law are moved by the spirit of God and are not under the communal and public law, because where the spirit is, there is liberty.]

—*Thomas Basin, The Nullification Trial of Joan of Arc, 1457**

Joan of Arc's spirituality, distinctively alive to the inward experience of divine encounter and its blessings, also bestowed upon her difficult and dangerous requirements that demanded radical forms of active service in the world. Joan's unique moral commission to transform the injustices of her society, a vocation of public leadership that she accepted through a private, spiritual endowment, persistently posed her with unique challenges regarding responsible choices for her personal conduct and actions. At times, her commitment to fulfill the profound and enduring command from God to lead her people out of oppression resulted, ironically, in her own tangible violations of ecclesiastical law—the medieval Church's legal traditions that supported both individual salvation and the proper ordering of Christian society, values that Joan herself firmly upheld. The history of *lex privata*, that is, an individual's spiritual freedom from the canon law that otherwise sustained Christian social order in medieval Europe, posed Church authorities with numerous challenges in interpretation and application over the centuries, challenges that reached their crisis point in the fifteenth-century legal cases of Joan of Arc. Joan of Arc's nullification trial of 1450–57 vigorously met the challenge of defining the authority of *lex privata* for not only its own but subsequent generations of Christians—obedience to divine revelation takes precedence over obedience to canon law.

Joan believed that she was justified to leave her parents without permission, to wear men's clothing, to bear arms although a woman, and most significantly, to make vows to heaven on the basis of her independent, spiritual authority—all actions otherwise considered violations of laws binding upon all Christians[1]—because she received direct inspiration from God to do so. Her binding obligation, according to the essence of her trial testimony, was service to a higher good appointed by heaven, the alleviation of her people's suffering.

Consequently, the two fifteenth-century inquisition trials pertaining to Joan's case gave rise to a vigorous discussion among prominent canonists concerning the rights of personal freedom from the law. This debate ultimately resulted in a major legal decision that reordered spiritual values in ways that profoundly humbled ecclesiastical authority, a striking chapter from religious history often overlooked. These legal reforms embodied a notable support of individual, moral initiative that reveals the far reach that Joan of Arc extended, well beyond even her own bold intentions, to root values of personal freedom in moral responsibility for the repair of worldly injustice. The net outcome for Western culture, the story that will be told here, was one Christian tribunal's pledge of allegiance to a law of spiritual freedom to define and sustain the spirit of the law.

While the medieval Church upheld the accountability of its faithful to the law for the sake of both the personal and the common good, the Church also acknowledged that this law might at times be suspended by a worthy Christian in obedience to a direct mandate issued by divine revelation. This principle of personal freedom from the law authorized through spiritual endowment was codified in medieval terms as *lex privata* ("private law"). Defending *lex privata* as a right endowed by natural law, medieval canonists determined that personal entitlements to renounce the law were defensibly grounded in the authority of private, mystical experience. The concept of *lex privata* recognized the liberty granted by the Holy Spirit to an individual for carrying out special commands that might violate *lex publica* or *lex communis* ("public law" or "common law"). This grant of freedom from the public law was explicitly inscribed by the medieval Church, a vital paradox that generated the internal crisis in values that potently erupted in the guilty verdicts imposed upon Joan of Arc in her condemnation trial of 1431, and that forcefully reemerged in the Church's judgment to reverse those verdicts in her posthumous "rehabilitation" or "nullification" trial of 1450–57.

Lex Privata in Western Thought from Its Origins to the Fifteenth Century

Lex privata's ancient origins in secular law and complex development in Western Christendom testify to a tumultuous and volatile history uniquely available to us through the legal opinions issued by leading fifteenth-century canonists (Basin, Berruyer, Montigny, and Bréhal) who supported the nullification trial that overturned Joan's heresy conviction, both redeeming her memory and honoring her Christian example. On Joan's behalf, four erudite churchmen, specialists in canon law and its enforcement, vigorously argued the authority of divine revelation over established legal codes in the obedience required of every Christian in meeting the demands of faith. The very fact that the most prominent canon lawyers in fifteenth-century France imposed strong restraints on the foundation of their own authority, that is, the Church's body of canon law, is a remarkable story that has been overlooked in histories of medieval inquisition. Following the generous leads provided by the nullification trial's collective record of *consilia* (legal opinions), the following analysis defines the history of the term *lex privata* itself, its occasions of application and controversy, and its celebration in the piety of late medieval France following the final departure of the English in the Hundred Years War, the cause for which Joan of Arc had fought.

The Christian sense of *lex privata* originated with Augustine who appropriated it from the language of Roman law. In the Roman context, *ius publicum* and *ius privatum* were contrasting domains of law, the former being the law concerned with the functioning of the state and the latter the law with the special interests of individuals addressing such matters as marriage and inheritance laws.[2] The term *lex* developed as a type of *ius, ius* being a law in the most general sense and *lex* being a written law, derived according to Isidore of Seville from the Latin word *legere*, "to read."[3] *Lex privata* eventually came to refer to the law "written" in one's heart by God.

Augustine cast *ius privatum* (private law) as well as a term synonymous in his usage, *licentia privata* (private freedom), in a Christian mold that denoted the special guardianship of angels over individual human beings.

> Omnis anima partim privati cuiusdam sui potestam gerit, partim universitatis legibus sicut publicis coercetur et regitur. . .{U}naquaque res visibilis in hoc

mundo habet potestatem angelicam sibi praepositam, sicut aliquot locis divina scriptura testatur. . .[4]

[Every soul carries in part its own power by virtue of a certain private{law}; in part it is restrained and ruled by laws of the universe or public laws. . .Every visible thing in this world has an angelic power set over it, just as is taught in several places in divine Scripture. . .]

While Augustine allowed that everyone abides by the authority of private law to a certain extent, he saw a potential danger in this, for by virtue of private law some individuals are tempted to become gods unto themselves. For Augustine, while both private and public law come from God, public or "universal" law is worthier of obedience.

Sed unaquaeque anima tanto est pietate purgatior, quanto privato suo minus delectata legem universitatis intuetur ei que devote ac libenter obtemperat. Est enim lex universitatis divina sapientia. . .Sed ubi divina tamquam publica lex iubet, vincit utique privatam licentiam, quamquam et ipsa privata licentia nisi universalis divinae potestatis permissione nulla esset.[5]

[But each and every soul is the purer in piety when, having received less pleasure in its own private domain, it contemplates all the more the universal law and obeys it willingly and devotedly, for the universal law is the divine Wisdom. . .But where the divine law commands in the manner of public law, it obviously prevails over private freedom, although even private freedom itself would be nothing apart from the permission of the universal divine power.][6]

Similarly in *De musica* [On Music], Augustine affirmed the superiority of universal law and yet acknowledged the place of private law in God's own plan for the world: "Attentio namque animae ad corporis partem inquieta negotia contrahit, et universali lege neglecta privati cuiusdam operis amor, quod ipsum tamen ab universitate quam deus regit not potest alienari"[7] [For the fixation of the soul on a part of the body produces troublesome affairs resulting in the universal laws being neglected for the love of some private concern; yet this private concern cannot be separated from the universe that God rules].

Further, in his letter *Contra Faustum* [Reply to Faustus the Manichaean], Augustine argued against the Manichaean denouncement of marriage, caustically referring to those who hold *lex privata* superior to the *lex publica* as mentally ill: "Et demens profecto ille, non tantum stultus putandus est, qui id existimet lege privata prohiberi posse, quod sit publica concessum"[8] [And indeed he is to be considered not only foolish but also truly insane, who thinks that a private law can prohibit what is allowed by the public]. Therefore, while Augustine affirmed *lex privata* to a certain extent, he viewed it as inferior to *lex publica* and cautioned against its abuse.

His view would give way to a more positive understanding of *lex privata* among thinkers later in the Middle Ages, and eventually to a claim for its conditional superiority over public law by a pope.

In the sixth century, Facundus Hermianensis († post 571) wrote a theological treatise about the Trinity that referred to its mystery of three persons in one as *lex privata*, a law unto itself found nowhere else in the universe.[9] *Lex privata* in his usage was a theological rather than a legal term denoting the *sui generis* quality of the Godhead. A century later, Isidore of Seville († 636) in his encyclopedia of knowledge, *Etymologiarum sive originum libri xx* [Of Etymologies or Origins in twenty books] identified the Church's legal term *privilegium*, "privilege," in its etymology as *privi* and *legi*, that is, "private law."[10] In Isidore's seventh-century definition *lex privata* and *privilegium* were roughly synonyms. *Privilegium*, the more common term in the law of the Church, derived its definition from Roman law. According to Adolf Berger, *privilegium* was "a legal enactment concerning a specific person or case and involving an exemption from common rules."[11] *Privilegium* and *lex privata* would evolve into distinctly different ideas later in the Middle Ages. *Lex privata* would refer specifically to a dispensation from God rooted in spiritual experience. While both terms implied a suspension of public law, *privilegium* was an official action taken by an ecclesiastical authority and *lex privata* taken by God directly in the inward consciousness of an individual of faith.

Lex privata in this sense dates to the contribution of Gratian, a Bolognese master of laws, who compiled the authoritative text of canon law referred to as the *Decretum* (1140) and implemented by the Roman Church in its legal judgments for seven centuries, from the twelfth century up to its official closure in 1917. In the chapter known as *Duae Sunt*, C. 19 q.2 c.2, Gratian cited a letter of Pope Urban II (1088–99) that authorized freedom for secular clergymen to renounce their diocesan responsibilities—that is, obligations to the Church for performing its liturgy and providing pastoral care to its laity—in answer to a religious calling of a different sort. A member of the secular clergy might abdicate the obligations publicly conferred upon him in the sacrament of ordination, to take instead the vows of a monk in response to a private call to lead a cloistered, rather than public, religious life. Accordingly, by virtue of Urban's decree, a diocesan priest or bishop might elect, as an obligation imposed by a unique divine revelation, to separate from the world and enter a monastery, taking vows of obedience to an abbot and submitting to a rule of discipline usually far more rigorous than that imposed upon the secular clergy. The letter attributed to Urban II appears in Gratian as follows:

> Duae sunt, inquit, leges: una publica, altera privata. Publica lex est, quae a sanctis Patribus scriptis est confirmata, ut est lex canonum, quae quidem propter transgressiones est tradita. . .Lex vero privata est, que instinctu Sancti

> Spiritus in corde scribitur, sicut de quibusdam dicit Apostolus. . .Dignior est enim lex privata quam publica. Spiritus quidem Dei lex est, et qui Spiritu Dei aguntur lege Dei ducuntur; et quis est, qui Spiritui sancto possit digne resistere? Quisquis igitur hoc Spiritu ducitur, etiam episcopo suo contradicente, eat liber nostra auctoritate. Justo enim lex non est posita, sed ubi Spiritus Dei, ibi libertas et si Spiritu Dei ducimini, non estis sub lege.[12]

> [There are two laws, he{Urban}said: one public and the other private. The public law, as established by the writings of the holy Fathers, is canon law that was given because of transgressions. . .But truly, the private law is written in the heart by the inspiration of the Holy Spirit, just as the Apostle says about certain people. . .The private law is worthier than the public. Indeed the Spirit of God is law, and they who act by the Spirit of God are led by the law of God; and who can fittingly resist the Holy spirit? Thus anyone led by this Spirit, even contradicting his bishop, may go free by our authority. For the law is not laid down for the just person, for where there is the Spirit of God, there is liberty, and if you are led by the Spirit of God, you are not under the law.]

An important qualification that developed in *lex privata*'s implementation, however, was that when a secular canon retreated to an enclosed community, he elected a way of life far more strenuous and austere than that of his previous vocation. *Lex privata* guaranteed the right to progress from a less difficult vocation to a more difficult one, but not the other way around.[13] The nature of chosenness endorsed by this concept of freedom, therefore, was a chosenness that increased one's personal responsibility rather than decreased it—a freedom *for* service to a greater mission rather than a freedom *from* the constraints of an onerous personal obligation. Kenneth Pennington has documented the origins of the *lex privata* controversy engendered by Gratian's *Decretum* in the twelfth and thirteenth centuries, a debate devoted in part to defining this principle of service to the "common good" presumed by Causa 19.[14]

Gerd Tellenbach refers to Causa 19's guarantee of freedom from the public law and its authorship attributed to Urban II as "a remarkable modification of the absoluteness of canon law."[15] It is indeed extraordinary that at a time when the medieval Church embraced significant increases in its purview of authority, the *Decretum* tempered that authority with a legal warrant that endowed the faithful with rights and privileges for developing their independent capacities of discernment and judgment. While the authenticity of Urban II's authorship cannot be adequately substantiated and Horst Fuhrmann considers it a forgery,[16] the principle of *lex privata* became, nevertheless, highly influential from the twelfth century onward with the papal force that it claimed. Moreover, a crucial point for the analysis offered here—a point offered in the discussion that follows about *lex privata*'s role in the legal cases of Joan of Arc—is the recognition of the vigorous spiritual individualism nurtured by Causa 19 in an influence that extended well beyond its original objectives supporting the rights of secular clergy to enter a monastery. *Lex privata* invigorated a broad cultural impulse that favored the authority of inward revelation and the rights endowed in the interiority of faith. Christian thinkers as prominent as Aquinas addressed the implications of *lex privata* for all the faithful.

Thomas Aquinas (1225–74), the prestigious Dominican scholar in residence at the University of Paris, took up *lex privata* in his *Summa theologiae*.[17] The nullification trial canonists honored the contributions of the "Holy Doctor" in support of *lex privata*. In Aquinas's schema, *lex privata*'s key point of contrast was with *lex humana*, "human law" (a term of contrast he chose over *lex publica*). For Aquinas, the essence of a law resided in its coercive power; its moral quality defined the force of its mandate for compliance. All laws do not merit an equal degree of compliance on the part of a "spiritual" or "just" individual, for forms of *lex humana* might be either just or unjust. Good Christians are obliged not to uphold unjust forms of *lex humana*. In its just forms, *lex humana* orders society toward the common good, mandating its compliance as a moral obligation for individuals in support of a just society for all. An unjust law, however, conflicts with divine law—making it not binding on individuals of conscience. Moreover, *lex privata* is superior to even the identifiable, just forms of *lex humana* for "spiritual" individuals, referred to also as "sons of God" by Aquinas, that is, those who reveal a divine law written in their hearts.

> Utrum omnes subiiciantur legi. . .Lege autem privata Spiritus sancti ducuntur omnes viri spirituales, qui sunt filii Dei; secundum illud Rom. (8.14), *Qui Spiritu Dei aguntur, hi filii Dei sunt*. Ergo non omnes homines legi humanae subiiciuntur. . .{L}ex Spiritus sancti est superior omni lege humanitus posita; et ideo viri spirituales, secundum hoc quod lege Spiritus sancti ducuntur non subduntur legi quantum ad ea quae repugnant ductioni Spiritus sancti.[18]
>
> [Whether all are subject to the law. . .Now all spiritual men are led by the private law of the Holy Spirit; they are the sons of God according to Rom. (8.14): "They who are led by the Spirit of God are sons of God." Therefore not all persons are subject to human law. . .The law of the Holy Spirit is superior to all law laid down humanly. And therefore spiritual men are guided by the law of the Holy Spirit and are not subject to the law in those things that oppose the guidance of the Holy Spirit.]

Aquinas's teaching shaped Christian values for centuries with a high regard for prayer and contemplation through which God reveals his will. Christian principles of moral discernment grounded in an individual's religious discipline and spiritual experience developed an even more profound authority in Roman Christendom by virtue of this charge issued by the Holy Doctor.

The impact of Urban's teaching also manifested itself in the legal literature that pertained to upholding the "common good" of society beyond the purview of the Church. Gaines Post has shown that in the later Middle Ages, "the commands of God for a private morality could. . .be compromised for the sake of a higher moral end, that of the State."[19] For example, an anonymous philosopher in the thirteenth century argued in *Questiones in libros ethicorum* [Questions on the Books of Ethics] that an act of adultery could be legitimate if it were undertaken for the sake of preserving the common good from tyranny or another great evil. In a hypothetical situation posited by the philosopher, a citizen might commit adultery with the wife of a man who has plans to tyrannize the public, and through this illicit liaison gain secret information useful for deterring the tyrant. The adultery would then be excused though its prohibition belonged to the Ten Commandments.[20] However, a superior moral purpose justifes an action normally considered immoral—a summary assessment representing the principle of *lex privata* that was applied across a range of medieval thought. Individual responsibility to a higher moral end was understood, with reliable consistency, as a matter of personal exemption from the public law in service to the common good.

The Church's precepts of *lex publica*, laid out in the Bible and canon law and promulgated primarily through pastoral care and preaching, were at times enforced more aggressively and coercively through inquisition proceedings, that is, trials devoted to the legal enforcement of Christian faith and conduct. Joan of Arc underwent such a set of proceedings at age nineteen, having left home two years earlier to lead battles against the supporters of the English crown who controlled parts of France. The story of the *lex privata* controversy in the fifteenth century begins with Joan's own account of her faith and conduct to a court of episcopal inquisition, a tribunal gathered in 1431 in the diocese of Rouen and presided over by its local bishop, Pierre Cauchon—a cleric overtly hostile to Joan's political cause. The tribunal charged her with numerous violations of Church law. Joan defended her illicit actions and behaviors as minor transgressions allowed by God himself for the sake of a greater cause, the liberation of the French kingdom. She explained that it was her primary obligation to obey the law directly mandated to her by heaven over the law of the Church, a law she normally upheld and obeyed. Joan's bold and perhaps naïve self-defense on this point, suggesting her implicit sense of moral empowerment akin to the principle of *lex privata*, sealed the tribunal's lethal decision to convict her of prideful transgressions of biblical and canon law, pronouncing upon her a verdict of heresy and sending her to the stake.

Joan's testimony in the trial record suggests that she indeed experienced a personal freedom from the public law as a spiritual endowment that supported her divine vocation to deliver France. In her view, the powers of heaven had inwardly imparted to her unique privileges, including autonomous decision-making authority regarding the moral courses of action that she undertook and also recommended to others—a privilege that, as she freely accepted it, bore the profound responsibility of transforming the fragmented and suffering world in which she lived. As the record of Joan's varied choices indicate—both the record of her testimony and the record of her choices in personal conduct—she believed that heaven had granted her exemptions from certain laws binding upon Christians, a personal freedom that bestowed profound obligations upon her and required her to put her own life on the line in service to the common good.

The unique freedoms that she appeared to enjoy (which, according to Cauchon and other judges in the condemnation trial, she pridefully abused to advance her own self-interest and personal gain), in fact obliged her to arduous demands and monumental tasks imposed upon her by God in her appointment as a prophet. Her privileges did not pertain to personal gain or antinomianism, but to God's own concrete forms of her empowerment for transforming the world. While the Latin term *lex privata* or any French equivalent appears to have been unknown to Joan, she carried out a prophetic calling emboldened by a strong sense of a moral responsibility that freed her from obedience to *lex publica* by virtue of her submission to a private law through direct divine revelation.

In the 1450s, Joan's supporters rallied at her memory and protested the injustices she had endured at the hands of Cauchon in 1431. Her supporters had by now witnessed the complete departure of the English from France, an event that Joan had once promised and predicted as the will of God. They recalled the potent efficacy of her unique spirituality to transform the harsh realities of an enduring political injustice; a public outcry rose up against the horrors and final fate she had suffered in her trial. At the initial behest of her surviving, beloved king, Charles VII, the Church undertook a legal investigation into the trial of 1431, a second trial that put the first trial on trial for alleged illegal procedures, violations of due process, and abuses of institutional power.

The nullification trial spanned a formidable seven years, 1450–57, resulting in a decision to clear the stain of heresy from the Church's memory of Joan, a bold decision rigorously supported by an extensive body of evidence and argumentation. Rome appointed responsibility for the case to a member of France's most esteemed clerical leadership, the Grand

Inquisitor of France, Jean Bréhal, a member of the Dominican order and a supporter of Joan's political cause. Bréhal conducted extensive eyewitness hearings and solicited the contributions of leading canonists, all of whom were also sympathetic to Joan's political cause, and who exhaustively documented the irregularities of the first trial and submitted detailed *consilia* (legal opinions) in support of the decision for nullifying the first trial. The outcome consisted of two legal decisions of a radical sort seldom found in ecclesiastical cases. Joan's rightful place in the memory of the Church as a holy woman was strongly promulgated, and Pierre Cauchon's excommunication was issued as a posthumous decree, the only accountability possible for the Church to enforce concerning the bishop's egregious abuses of power in the condemnation trial.

The *consilia* of the following contributors, each of whom applied *lex privata* to endorse the case to nullify Joan's condemnation, will be considered here: Thomas Basin (1412–91), a licentiate in both civil and canon law as well as bishop of Lisieux and author of *Histoire de Charles VII* [The History of Charles VII]; Jean de Montigny, Professor of Canon Law and dean of the University of Paris beginning in 1445; Martin Berruyer († 1465), a theologian trained at the University of Paris who served as Bishop of Le Mans; and Jean Bréhal († ca. 1478) already referred to earlier, a Dominican professor of theology and Grand Inquisitor of France. Bréhal himself decided which of the *consilia* offered by various canonists merited inclusion in the final trial record. Further, he synthesized the salient points among them in his own *consilium* entitled the *Recollectio* that concludes the trial record and pronounces the nullification. This cast of clerics, all individuals of prominent influence and prestige in the Church, shared a mission to right the wrong that Joan had suffered in her condemnation trial. While none of them had met her while she was alive, they studied her testimony in the condemnation trial record as well as the testimony of over one hundred surviving eyewitnesses to her life gathered for the new trial. Their verdict was unanimous: Joan had been wrongly convicted and executed.

The canonists took up their pens with great zeal to address the thorny point of contention over the obligations imposed by public law and the privileges granted by private law. The time had come to articulate a direct response to the *lex privata* controversy that had been mounting for centuries and had now crystallized dramatically in the case of Joan of Arc. Accordingly, the nullification trial's conclusions addressed not merely the unique challenges posed by Joan's case, but answered more significantly the demand for an authoritative legal precedent to serve all of Roman Christendom.

The nullification-trial canonists ardently defended the Christian authority of *lex privata*, consciously prescribing it for the Roman Church as endorsement of personal freedom from public law as a right of natural law, and moreover, documenting the right in a thorough historical sweep dating it back to biblical origins. The obligation imposed upon individuals to obey the directives of divine revelation, the sort of radical obedience that Joan of Arc modeled well in her time, necessitated a personal freedom that the Church itself must guarantee for the faithful, according to these canonists. *Lex privata* itself therefore represented the true spirit of Christian law—humble submission to the greater moral wisdom of God. Moreover, a vocation bestowed by *lex privata* demanded that an individual develop inward disciplines and capacities of moral discernment and sound judgment, forms of self-denial and strengths of Christian character that bear fruit in the form of judicious actions serving the repair of the world. *Lex privata* emerged from the nullification trial discussion scarcely as an antinomian warrant, and more substantially as a self-sacrificial commitment to a greater cause and the common good.

For the first time in Western Christian thought, as the historical record suggests in the nullification trial, a narration of the origins and development of *lex privata* was explicitly undertaken to promulgate its authenticity for the universal Church. The nullification-trial canonists justified its moral imperative for both spiritual formation and legal implementation to pertain to both the clergy and the laity, as discussed below. According to these fifteenth-century canonists, the earliest ideals of *lex privata* are embedded in narratives from the Old Testament, then further developed in Jesus's teachings and Paul's proclamations in the New Testament, followed then by its definitions and redefinitions by subsequent generations of Christian thinkers, including the provisions in canon law proffered by Gratian who attributed it to Pope Urban II, and pursued in the work of theologians as significant as Aquinas. In their discussions, *lex privata* refers to an individual's freedom from the public law granted as a spiritual endowment, a gift from heaven and an outpouring of grace—decidedly not a virtue belonging to the independence of a rational conscience, the type of secular individualism more familiar to us in the modern world. *Lex privata* always revealed itself as a theocentric principle in Western thought up to the fifteenth century.

Moreover, *lex privata*, though naturally superior to *lex publica*, was still a matter of law—divine law to be obeyed. It was a law encoded not in texts and common traditions but in the spiritual experience of the individual, properly belonging to the interior life. However, the nullification-trial canonists went to great lengths to argue that *lex privata* issued from an external source, God in heaven rather than the individual him/herself. That *lex privata* might result from an individual's fanciful imagination or demonic self-delusion was a challenge the nullification-trial canonists directly address, for those were the very judgments leveled against Joan in the condemnation trial.

A lasting achievement of the nullification trial however resides in this narrative defense of *lex privata*, a meticulously detailed theological and legal commentary, a summary of which follows here. The nullification trial canonists found a number of warrants for this principle in the Vulgate Bible, warrants that emerge in the Old Testament narratives and the values they implicitly espoused. The primary Old Testament prototype of *lex privata* was the story of the binding of Isaac in Genesis 22. In this account, Abraham was commanded by the Lord to sacrifice his only son Isaac, born to him and Sarah late in life, in fulfillment of a promise by God. The man of faith proceeded to carry out this killing, an apparent violation of moral law—the prohibition against murder belongs to the Ten Commandments—until the critical moment in which an angel from God replaced Isaac with a ram for the sacrifice. However, according to the canonists, had God actually required the killing of Isaac, Abraham would not have been guilty of murder since he had received a special command directly from heaven to perform the action. Accordingly, Abraham's freedom from the law was conferred by a unique revelation from God who exclusively claims the freedom to give and to take life, a point supported earlier in Genesis by the remarkable gift of a son that Abraham and Sarah received in joy when they were already well beyond their childbearing years.

Other Old Testament supports for *lex privata* included God's command to the Israelites to plunder the Egyptians upon fleeing their bondage (Exodus 12), an act that violated the prohibition against stealing in the Ten Commandments. In addition, God commanded the prophet Hosea to take a wife of harlotry (Hosea 1), a violation of the commandment against adultery, also one of the Ten Commandments. Among the host of other instances cited in the nullification trial are Abram's adultery in delivering his wife Sarai to Pharaoh (Genesis 12); Jacob's deception of his father to supplant the firstborn prerogative of his brother Esau by dressing in Esau's clothes (Genesis 27); Moses's killing of the Egyptian slavedriver who brutalized a fellow Israelite (Exodus 2); Phineas's murder of Zimri who had taken a foreign wife (Numbers 25); and multiple homicides committed by Samson in revenge for the death of his wife (Judges 15). Each of these Old Testament exempla was used in explicit support of Joan of Arc's *lex privata* in her nullification trial, although of course no equivalent to the Latin term itself presents itself in the Hebrew Scriptures.[21]

In the New Testament, according to the nullification trial's continuing narrative, Jesus's endorsement of *lex privata* appears in John 3.8, "Spiritus ubi vult spirat, et vocem eius audis, sed nescis unde veniat, aut quo vadat: sic est omnis qui natus ex spiritu" [The spirit blows where it will, and you hear its sound, but you do not know where it comes from or where it goes: likewise it is with everyone who is born of the spirit]. God moves and works his will in unseen ways like the wind whose effects are known by human beings in a form of direct experience outwardly invisible. Jesus called his followers to find their true life in the spirit rather than in the flesh: "Oportet vos nasci denuo," John 3.7b [You must be born anew]. God's truth, a transcendent reality beyond the limits of human comprehension, draws human beings into encounter through an irresistible power. Delivering oneself over to the action of the Holy Spirit is the authentic Christian response to the call of discipleship, a call to which Joan faithfully responded.

The nullification trial further cited John Chrysostom (ca. 347–407), Patriarch of Constantinople, in a homily: "Indeed since no one can restrain the wind, but it moves where it will, even more so are the laws of nature unable to restrain the working of the Holy Spirit."[22] Based on Chrysostom's point here, a key component of *lex privata* emerged in the nullification trial's assessment: special commands from God cannot ultimately be resisted, only accepted and lived in faith. In responding to her vocation to deliver France, Joan of Arc knew no alternative that would give her spirit rest.

Paul's teachings in the New Testament on law, grace, and freedom figure prominently in the nullification trial's treatment of *lex privata*. Giles Constable has quipped concerning Paul's teaching on freedom, that the Apostle put the genie in the bottle and medieval thinkers let it out.[23] Several Pauline texts are worthy of note according to the nullification trial, including one we know to have been commonly cited in medieval monastic literature—2 Corinthians 3.17: "Dominus autem Spiritus est: Ubi autem Spiritus Domini, ibi libertas" [For the Lord is Spirit: for where the Spirit of the Lord is, there is liberty].[24] *Libertas* developed in medieval Christian thought as a spiritual value akin to *lex privata*. *Libertas*, along with its cognates *libere* and *liberius*, were terms frequently used by medieval monks and nuns who had "liberated" themselves from the servitude of worldly concerns in order to serve the Lord unfettered.[25] Monastic liberty freed men and women from the demands of family, and women in particular from the rigors of childbearing and rearing. Having renounced family life, monks and nuns were free to choose another calling, to pursue a spiritual vocation—a vocation that, although it renounced the world, posed moral merit as service to the betterment of the world through prayer.

Other Pauline teachings in support of *lex privata* and cited by the nullification-trial canonists include segments of Galatians in which Paul castigates Christians who insist that Gentile converts to Christianity shall observe Jewish law including that of circumcision. In Paul's view, such adherence to law was a return to the bondage of sin that contrasted severely with a new life in faith that brought liberty of the spirit: "Itaque, fratres, non sumus ancillae filii, sed liberae: qua libertate Christus nos liberavit. State, et nolite iterum iugo servitutis contineri" (Galatians 4.31–5.1) [Therefore brothers, we are not sons of a servant woman but of a free woman: for liberty Christ liberated us. Stand and do not be constrained again by the yoke of slavery]. Later in the same letter Paul straightforwardly states, "Si spiritu ducimini, non estis sub lege" (Galatians 5.18) [If you are led by the spirit, you are not under the law]. Christians are to live with the assurance that the era of the law, an epoch of enslavement, has been brought to a close and the era of freedom in the Holy Spirit has been inaugurated through Christ. The law bears provisional and conditional authority, while the freedom of the Holy Spirit guarantees true empowerment.

An additional Pauline warrant for *lex privata* comes from 1 Timothy 1.9a, where Paul wrote, "Sciens hoc quia lex iusto non est posita, sed iniustis" [We know that the law is laid down not for the just person, but for the unjust ones]. The essence of Paul's teaching was that some people adhere to the public law of their own accord (referring to moral laws like the Ten Commandments rather than ceremonial laws like circumcision), without its being imposed upon them by an external authority such as the Torah. This idea is reinforced in another Pauline letter, Romans, in which the Apostle lays out a teaching identified as crucial in the nullification trial's view of *lex privata*: "Cum enim gentes, quae legem non habent, naturaliter ea, quae legis sunt, faciunt, eiusmodi legem non habentes, ipsi sibi sunt lex: qui ostendunt opus legis scriptum in cordibus suis, testimonium reddente illis conscientia ipsorum" (Romans 2.14–15a) [For when Gentiles, who do not have the law, naturally do the things that are of the law, though not having the law, they are a law unto themselves: they show that the work of the law is written in their hearts, their own conscience bearing witness]. This notion of a law written in the heart by God offers tangible legal privileges that the nullification-trial canonists seek to defend.

These canonists continue their *lex privata* narrative beyond its biblical beginnings to evaluate the contributions of those Christian thinkers whose views traditionally matter most in such concerns, most importantly Augustine, Aquinas, and Gratian, all of whom we have already considered. A significant accomplishment of the nullification trial, therefore, was to document the history of *lex privata* as a genuine Christian principle, establishing its Scriptural origins and pursuing its subsequent centuries of applications by the Church right up to the fifteenth century. Then, having set forth its validity for the Church, the canonists proceeded to build their argument on behalf of Joan of Arc.

Joan's mystical revelations, through which she received special commands from God that violated *lex publica*, are the starting point for the canonists' discussion of Joan and *lex privata* in the nullification trial. According to her condemnation trial testimony, Joan heard voices from heaven urging her to come to the aid of France in its war against the English crown, beginning at the mere age of thirteen. She reported to the inquisitors in 1431 that Saints Michael, Catherine, and Margaret appeared to her and instructed and comforted her. A verdict handed down by the trial judges pronounced these visions to be either lies on Joan's part or demonic in origin.[26] The nullification-trial canonists expressed a more generous view, consciously "assuming the best" about Joan and her visions. Jean Montigny, for example, defended Joan's mystical experience as a sign of the Holy Spirit that blows where it will, choosing a meek and humble servant upon whom to bestow its inward graces: "Assistit etiam Ecclesie semper ipsam dirigendo per occultos instinctus Spiritus Sancti, ut sic non deficiat fides"[27] [Also He assists the Church always by directing it through hidden impulses of the Holy Spirit, in order that faith does not weaken]. The Holy Spirit works in this way for the benefit of society (*propter utilitatem communitatis*) according to Montigny, endowing a woman like Joan with the gift of prophecy that brings deliverance for a people.[28]

We know from Joan's trial testimony that she vowed her virginity for "as long as it pleased God" in response to gifts of heavenly vision, a secret she kept between herself and the powers that visited her from above.[29] That she made a vow to heaven of her own accord, not consulting with her parish priest, shows that she experienced a degree of spiritual independence from the clerical hierarchy, though she faithfully attended Mass and frequently confessed to a priest, as ample eyewitness testimony in the nullification trial indicates.[30] Concerning the vow of virginity, however, the University of Paris censured her action in its statement on the case:

> Item, tu as dit, a ceulx que tu appelles sainct Michel, saincte Katherine et saincte Margueritte, tu as faict plusieurs reverences en te agenouillant, en baissant la terre sur laquelle ilz marchoyent, en leur {vouant} virginité. . .A quoy les clers disent que, supposé que tu ayes eu des revelacions et apparicions desquelles tu te vantes, en la maniere que tu le dys, tu es ydolastre, invocatrice des dyables, errante en la foy, et as faict temerement serment illicite.[31]
>
> [You have said that to those whom you call Saint Michael, Saint Catherine and Saint Margaret you made several reverences, kneeling and kissing the ground they walked on, and vowing your virginity to them. . .To which the clerks say that supposing you have had the revelations and apparitions of which you boast, in the way that you say, you are an idolater, an invoker of demons, a wanderer from the Faith, and have rashly taken an unlawful oath.][32]

The university clerics denounced her oath as an act of worship that must be made to God alone, as Thomas Aquinas taught.[33] The vows she had made to her angels and saints therefore made her suspect of idolatry. Her trial testimony suggests, however, that Joan herself did not distinguish between the authority of her communications with Saints Michael, Catherine, and Margaret, versus that of God directly; in fact, Joan appears to have been puzzled by the emphasis her judges placed on this: "Respond: Il debvoit bien suffire de le promettre a ceulx qui estoyent envoyez de par luy, c'est assavoir a saincte Katherine et saincte Margueritte"[34] [She answered: It ought to be sufficient to promise it to those who were sent by Him, that is to Saint Catherine and Saint Margaret].[35] Joan considered that by virtue of her visions from God and the vow she took, she obligated herself to fulfill a mission that God intended, however difficult it may prove to be.

A few years after pledging her virginity, Joan broke off her betrothal to a young man of her parents' choosing, answering to a call different from that of marriage and asserting freedom from the cares of the world similar to that of vowed religious.[36] Pursuing a plan for her life that contradicted her parents' plan was Joan's first public display of independence from authority, a commitment in public deed to a private law that was granted to her by heaven. She seemingly modeled herself after the behavior of holy women in Christian history such as Thecla in *The Acts of Paul*,[37] and Christina in *The Life of Christina of Markyate*,[38] both of whom rejected their parents' plan for them to marry.

For a number of years before leaving her parental home to fight for France, Joan had concealed from everyone around her, including her parish priest, the visions she experienced.

> Mais doubtoit moult le reveler, pour doubte des Bourguygnons, que ilz ne l'empeschassent de son voyage; et par especial doubtoit moult son pere, qu'il ne l'empeschast de fere son voyage.[39]
>
> [And she also said that she was greatly afraid of telling about them {the visions}, for fear of the Burgundians[40] preventing her making her journey; and especially was she afraid of her father, that he too might hinder the journey.][41]

In fulfillment of a divine command, Joan left home in 1429 at age seventeen without her parents' knowledge, seeking the miracle that would grant her an audience with the dauphin, the future king Charles VII. She wished him to authorize her to lead the French armies against the English and their Burgundian allies at the besieged city of Orléans. Among the verdicts in her condemnation trial was the judgment that in leaving her parents without warning she caused them "such anxiety that they went almost out of their minds,"[42]and thus violated the commandment to honor one's father and mother, one of the Ten Commandments (Exodus 20).[43] Joan replied in defense that her action had not been a matter for her to decide.

If she had been disobedient to her parents, she had nevertheless been obedient to a higher command. Joan thereby expressed a sense of personal empowerment with values closely akin to that of *lex privata*. Her trial testimony reads as follows:

> Interroguee se, quand elle partist de ses pere et mere, elle cuidoit point pecher, Respond: Puisque Dieu le commandoit, il le convenoit faire. Et dit oultre, Puisque Dieu le commandoit, se elle eust eu cent peres and cent meres, et si elle eust esté fille du roy, elle fut partye.[44]
>
> [Asked if when she left her father and mother she believed that she had not committed a sin, She answered: Since God so commanded, I had to obey. She added that since God so commanded, if she had had a hundred fathers and mothers, and if she had been a king's daughter, she would still have gone.][45]

Joan moreover reported to the court that she had later written her parents asking their forgiveness and they had granted it. Joan thus considered herself absolved from the suffering she caused her family in her service to alleviate the suffering of the entire people.

In his nullification-trial *Recollectio*, Jean Bréhal defended Joan's departure from her parental home based on the idea that reverence both for one's parents and for God are virtues, but obedience to God is the greater obligation. The responsibility for moral discernment resides in the individual, a remarkable humbling by the Grand Inquisitor of his own ecclesiastical authority. Bréhal cited as warrant Jesus's own example according to which, at age twelve, he stayed behind at the Temple in Jerusalem without his parents' knowledge as they journeyed back to Nazareth after a pilgrimage. When after a few days they found and reproached him, he replied, " 'Quid est quod me quaerebatis? nesciebatis quia in his quae Patris mei sunt, oportet me esse?' " (Luke 2. 49) ["Why were you searching for me? Did you not know that I must be in my Father's house?"]. Devotion to his Father in heaven took explicit precedence over obligation to his earthly parents. That Bréhal compared Joan's behavior favorably to that of Jesus suggests the very high regard in which he held her claim to divine revelation.

Bréhal found additional biblical support for Joan's conduct in a teaching of Peter and the Apostles: " 'Obedire oportet Deo magis quam hominibus' " (Acts 5.29) ["It is of greater necessity to obey God than human beings"]. Bréhal also drew upon Augustine who said: "Amandus est generator, sed preponendus est creator"[46] [The generator is to be loved, but the creator is to be preferred]. In essence, Bréhal justified Joan's action on the authority of her spiritual experience as she reported it, the inward conversations she held with heaven that the condemnation trial judges held suspect. The Inquisitor explicitly applied the principle of *lex privata* to her decision to leave home, emphasizing the inviolable freedom of the human mind. He thereby sounded a call for the sanctity of individual conscience and the authority of personal piety, which would become fundamental tenets in the early modern reforms of spirituality, Catholic as well as Protestant, beginning in the following century.[47]

> Cum itaque mens hominis, ultra predictam ejus naturalem libertatem, interiore divini spiritus motione agitur, jam quo ad illud ad quod prosequendum seu agendum impellitur a vinculo communis legis penitus absolvitur. Lex namque spiritus lex privata est, que maximam libertatem inducit. . .[48]
>
> [When therefore the mind of a person, beyond its natural liberty mentioned before, is moved interiorly by the motion of the divine spirit, impelled then to proceed or act for that reason, he/she is inwardly released from the fetters of the common law. For the law of the spirit is a private law that grants greatest liberty. . .]

Finally, Bréhal argued that had Joan told her parents about her plans to depart for France, they would likely have delayed her or even impeded her from going, and the suffering of the French people would not have been alleviated according to God's plan. Serving the public welfare was far more important than upholding the traditional relations prescribed for the family's household.

In addition to this matter of leaving home, Joan violated public law in wearing men's clothing and cutting her hair short. The condemnation trial judges pronounced her guilty of these transgressions, and while the nullification-trial canonists granted that those judges had ostensible legal warrants for their decision, they nevertheless argued against its moral merit. They defined a judge's moral responsibility in decision-making to be one that embraces the true spirit of the law rather than aggressively enforcing the letter of the law. In the traditions of scholastic argumentation, the nullification-trial canonists laid out first the case against Joan in this matter of her hair and dress. According to Deuteronomy 22.5, a woman may not dress as a man or a man as a woman. Gratian reiterated the point for women in the *Decretum* I. 30. 6: "Si qua mulier suo proposito utile judicans, ut virile veste utatur, propter hoc virilem habitum imitetur, anathema sit"[49] [If a woman judges it useful for her own purposes to wear male dress, and because of that she copies male clothing, let her be anathema]. In the New Testament, Paul taught that it was disgraceful for a woman to have her hair cut off (1 Corinthians 11.6). In the condemnation trial, when questioned several times about wearing men's dress, Joan responded that everything she had done including wearing men's clothing was, "at Our Lord's command, and if He had ordered Jeanne to take a different dress, she would have done so, since it would have been at God's command."[50] As in her decision to leave home, Joan believed she was answering to a higher authority in her choice of dress. She stated that wearing men's clothing allowed her to serve France most effectively on the battlefield. Her private law aimed to enhance the common good, her own argument implicitly sounding the keynote of *lex privata*. Consider her testimony on this point:

> Interroguee si, en prenant habit d'homme, elle pensoit mal faire, Respond que non; et encoires de present, si elle estoit en l'autre party et en cest habit d'homme, luy semble que se seroit un des grands biens de France, de faire comme elle faisoit au devant de sa prinse.[51]
>
> [Questioned whether in taking male dress she thought she had done wrong, She answered no; and that even at this moment if she were with her own people and wearing this male dress, it seemed to her it would be for the great good of France to do as she used to do before she was taken prisoner.][52]

In their verdicts, the judges of the University of Paris condemned her for transgressing divine law, the Holy Scriptures, and canon law in wearing men's clothing, and particularly for receiving the Eucharist dressed that way.[53]

In the nullification trial, Jean Bréhal laid down the greater principle by which Joan's dress ought to be considered: "Sed ubi ex opposito concurrunt humilitas, castitas et necessitas, nihil est penitus quod in hoc exteriore cultu prejudicet"[54] [But where on the other hand humility, chastity and necessity exist, there is nothing inwardly that adversely judges the exterior appearance]. Bréhal shifted the legal focus from outward appearances to interior qualities of faith and inward disciplines of moral character. This shift of attention from the outward to the inward defined the legal criteria that the nullification trial upheld as its underlying principle, a principle owing its force to traditions of *lex privata*.

Bishop Martin Berruyer defended Joan's cross-dressing in his nullification trial *consilium* to accord with the *exempla* of holy women celebrated by the Church, women of faith who by virtue of a private law, lived among men disguised as men:

> Ad hoc enim videbatur lege privata Spiritus Sancti duci, sicut et sancte Tecla, Eugenia, Pelagia, Marina et alie que habitum viri detulerunt et comam inciderunt et sic inter viros conversate sunt, ut recitat Vincentius in *Speculo*.[55]
>
> [Concerning this it seemed she was led by a private law of the Holy Spirit, just as in the cases of Saints Thecla, Eugenia, Pelagia, Marina and others who wore a man's dress and cut their hair and lived thus among men, as Vincent relates in *Speculum*.]

In his *consilium*, the bishop of Lisieux, Thomas Basin, assessed the significance of the Old Testament injunction against women wearing men's clothing for the purposes of curtailing temptations either to fornicate (disguised as a man, a woman might more easily gain access to men's quarters) or to worship pagan deities (certain ancient rituals of polytheistic peoples involved the cross-dressing of the sexes). Moreover, the greater good that defined Joan's *lex privata*, her defense of the French kingdom, superseded her obligations to biblical law. For Basin, Scripture itself and the divine revelations that it embodied, must properly be submitted to the authority of God's ongoing revelation in the world.

> Nam illud *Deuteronomii* XXII et canones allegati intelliguntur, ubi mulier virili veste uteretur, aut comam sibi amputaret ad lasciviam, aut ob superstitionem, secundum ritum veterem Gentilium, ut dictum est, non autem ubi, vel propter aliquam rationabilem causam et honestam, vel lege privata ducta que dignior est publica, mulier propter aliquod magnum bonum tali habitu uteretur, ut in facto Johanne fuisse creditur.[56]
>
> [For Deuteronomy 22 and the canons mentioned are understood in the situation in which a woman wears male dress or cuts her hair for lasciviousness, or out of superstition, according to the rite of the old Gentiles, as was said, but not because of any rational or honest reason, or because she was led by the private law which is more worthy than the public; a woman may wear such dress for the purpose of any great good, as Joan is believed in fact to have done.]

Closely related to this matter of wearing male clothing was the issue of bearing arms. In the condemnation-trial verdicts, the judges put these two points together: "{E}t si as dit que pour nulles choses tu ne feroys serment de ne porter point ledit habit et les armes; et en toutes lesdictes choses tu dis avoir bien faict et du commandement de Dieu. Quand a ses pointz les clers dyent que tu blasmes Dieu. . .etc."[57] [You have said that not for anything would you take an oath not to wear this dress or carry arms; and concerning all these matters you have said that you did well, and obediently to God's command. As for these points, the clerks say that you blaspheme God. . .etc.].[58] Joan stated in the trial that when her voices first told her that she must go to the aid of France in war, she excused herself saying that she was only a poor woman who knew neither how to ride nor wage war.[59] She took pains to demonstrate to the court that her inspiration in the conduct of war came from heaven and not from her own schemes. The sword she used itself occasioned a miracle, for it was found buried in the ground in a certain church, in a location revealed to her by her Voices and known to no one else.[60] She testified further that in battle she carried the standard, and though she carried the sword for self-defense, she never killed anyone.[61] In essence, Joan appeared to believe that she was not authorized by heaven to be a combatant, at least in part because she was a woman.

In this realm of action therefore, the realm of physical violence, Joan did not claim the privileges of *lex privata*, but consciously drew a line that circumscribed her liberties even as she served the common good on the battlefield.

According to Jean Bréhal's *Recollectio*, there existed no law in the Church prohibiting women to bear arms, though he conceded it was a widely accepted social norm that developed from the teaching in Deuteronomy 22.5. The biblical precept that prohibited a woman putting on men's clothing was made in response to pagan rites dedicated to Mars, the god of war. In these ritual celebrations, women donned men's military garb and carried weapons. The prohibition of Israelite participation in these rites resulted in the belief among succeeding generations that women may not bear arms. Bréhal argued however that the real issue at stake in the Bible was the elimination of worship of false gods and not the prohibition of women in military action.[62] Nevertheless, Bréhal acknowledged that under normal circumstances women did not serve as soldiers in Christian society. Consequently, Bréhal did not stress the fact that Joan was a *woman* waging war, but that she waged a *just war* in accordance with the traditional Christian definition attributed to Augustine, a war justified according to the principles of legitimate authority, just cause, and right intention.[63] Thus, Bréhal allowed a higher moral end to prevail over a social norm, the customary principle of *lex privata*. He cited Augustine's *Contra Faustum* in support of Joan's moral conduct in war:

> Nocendi cupiditas, ulciscendi crudelitas, impacatus atque implacabilis animus, feritas rebellandi, libido dominandi, et si qua similia, hec sunt que in bellis jure culpantur; que plerumque ut etiam inde puniantur publice justitie repugnantes, sive Deo sive aliquo legitimo imperio jubente, gerenda ipsa bella suscipiuntur a bonis, cum in eo rerum humanarum ordine inveniuntur, ubi eos vel jubere tale aliquid, vel in talibus obedire, juste ordo constringit.[64]
>
> [The real evils in war are love of violence, revengeful cruelty, fierce and implacable enmity, wild resistance, and the lust of power, and such like; and it is generally to punish these things, when force is required to inflict the punishment, that, in obedience to God or some lawful authority, good men undertake wars, when they find themselves in such a position as regards the conduct of human affairs, that right conduct requires them to act, or to make others act in this way.][65]

The net outcome of Joan of Arc's condemnation and nullification trials, most simply put, was the latter's profound reassertion of religious values that favored the authority of personal discernment in experiences of divine encounter. These values endorsed the autonomy of personal choice over public law as a privilege granted to the faithful through a private, spiritual endowment in service to a higher end, the common good. We have amply considered the ways in which *lex privata* conditionally allowed individuals, including Joan of Arc, freedoms to perform technically illicit actions. We conclude with an insight from the Grand Inquisitor Bréhal's *Recollectio* into another dimension of this freedom, an empowerment that issues as a gift from God to support one's unique call to the realm of action. Bréhal celebrated the grace that is experienced inwardly, by virtue of *lex privata*, as an individual's grant of freedom from the weight of moral guilt for having broken the public law. The Grand Inquisitor wrote, "Porro, extante ipsa lege privata divine inspirationis, ab omni lege communi eximebatur et ab omni culpa penitus expers reddebatur. . ."[66] [Furthermore, in the private law itself emerging from divine inspiration, one is released from all common law and one is rendered inwardly free from all guilt]. *Lex privata* thus endowed the Lord's chosen not only with an authority to act in ways contrary to the public law, but with inner provisions of comfort and joy that they may sustain their difficult mission to transform the world, strengthened from within by the Holy Spirit.

The resolution of the *lex privata* crisis in fifteenth-century France provided Roman Christendom with a thoroughly defended, legal precedent in favor of personal freedom from the public law, a freedom that an individual enjoyed not as a release from responsibility, but as an empowerment that increased responsibility and obliged personal accountability to a more rigorous moral standard. According to the conclusions proffered in the nullification trial's *consilia*, the Church itself must guarantee this freedom to the faithful and submit its own exercise of power to the authority of God who freely acts in the world for the work of redemption. *Lex privata* charged the faithful to abide by a freedom in the spirit of the law that repaired the world as heaven intended.

Notes

I would like to extend my thanks to Prof. Ann Astell whose thoughtful feedback and scholarly networking as coeditor of this volume connected me to Kenneth Pennington at Catholic University of America. Prof. Pennington's work on *lex privata* is an important foundation for this chapter and he graciously provided vital feedback on an early draft of this essay, generously sharing with me his own work-in-progress.

* Pierre Duparc, ed., *Procès en nullité de la condamnation de Jeanne D'Arc*, 5 vols. (Paris: Librairie C. Klincksieck, 1977–88), 2:208. All translations are mine unless otherwise noted.

1. For a useful source of the legal documentation citing the twelve principal transgressions for which Joan of Arc was convicted in her inquisition trial in 1431, see W.S. Scott, *The Trial of Joan of Arc*, "The Reading of the Censures of the University [of Paris]" (Westport, Conn.: Associated Booksellers, 1956), pp. 154–62.

2. Adolf Berger, *Encyclopedic Dictionary of Roman Law* (Philadelphia: The American Philosophical Society, 1953), p. 532.
3. Isidore of Seville, *Etymologiarum sive originum libri xx*, 5.3.2, ed. W.M. Lindsay (New York: Oxford University Press, 1911).
4. Augustine of Hippo, *De diversis questionibus octoginta tribus*, q. 79.1, ed. Almut Mutzenbecher, Corpus Christianorum Series Latina (Turnholt: Brepols, 1975), 44A:225.
5. Augustine of Hippo, *De diversis questionibus octoginta tribus*, q. 79.1, SL 44A:226.
6. Augustine of Hippo, *St. Augustine: Eighty-three Different Questions*, q. 79.1, trans. David L. Mosher, The Fathers of the Church (Washington, D.C.: The Catholic University of America Press, 1982), 70:200–01.
7. Augustine of Hippo, *De musica* 6, PL 32:1188.
8. Augustine of Hippo, *Contra Faustum* 30.4, CSEL 25:752.
9. Facundus Hermianensis, *Pro defensione trium cap. lib. xii ad Iustinianum*, 1.3.5, ed. Clement and Plaetse, Corpus Christianorum Series Latina (Turnholt: Brepols, 1975), 90A:12.
10. Isidore of Seville, *Etymologiarum sive originum libri xx* 5.18.
11. Berger, *Encyclopedic Dictionary of Roman Law*, p. 651.
12. PL 187:1093–94.
13. For an excellent analysis as well as critical review of the recent scholarship on Causa 19, and the implications of its "radical doctrine" for religious orders, see Kenneth Pennington's article, "Gratian, Causa 19, and the Birth of Jurisprudence," in *Ius ecclesiae: Rivista internazionale di diritto canonico*, 2003. Also useful is Pennington's earlier treatment on Causa 19's earliest controversies in *Popes and Bishops* (see n. 15 below), pp. 102–110.
14. Kenneth Pennington, *Popes and Bishops: The Papal Monarchy in the Twelfth and Thirteenth Centuries* (Philadelphia: University of Pennsylvania Press, 1984), p. 105.
15. Gerd Tellenbach, *The Church in Western Europe from the Tenth to the Early Twelfth Century*, trans. Timothy Reuter (Cambridge: Cambridge University Press, 1993), p. 317.
16. See Horst Fuhrmann, *Papst Urban II. Und der Stand der Regularkanoniker* (Munich: 1984), pp. 17–21.
17. Thomas Aquinas, *Summa theologiae*, 1–2, q. 96, ed. and trans. Thomas Gilby O.P. (New York: Blackfriars, 1963), 28:118–41.
18. Aquinas, *Summa theologiae*, 1–2, q. 96.5, 28:132, 134.
19. Gaines Post, *Studies in Medieval Legal Thought, Public Law and the State, 1100–1322* (Princeton: Princeton University Press, 1964), p. 305.
20. Paris, Bibliothèque Nationale MS lat. 14698, fol. 146, as cited in Post, *Medieval Legal Thought*, p. 305, n. 136.
21. Duparc, *Procès en nullité de la condamnation*, 2:441, 464.
22. John Chrysostom, *Homilies on St. John 1–47*, my translation adapted from: trans. Sister Thomas Aquinas Goggin, S.C.H., The Fathers of the Church (Washington D.C.: The Catholic University of America Press, 1957), 1:254.
23. Giles Constable, "Liberty and Free Choice in Monastic Thought and Life, especially in the Eleventh and Twelfth Centuries," in *La notion de liberté au*

Moyen Age: Byzance, Islam, Occident, ed. Janine Sourdel-Thomine, Dominique Sourdel, and George Makdisi, Paris-Penn-Dumbarton Oaks Colloquia IV (Paris, 1985), p. 112.

24. The freedom that the Apostle had in mind may not compare to the concept of *lex privata* in the nullification trial, however, i.e., the freedom of an individual's special dispensation from heaven, but humankind's freedom from the wages of sin and the weight of divine judgment. According to interpretations of Paul more common in Christian thought than *lex privata*, the Apostle taught that Christian freedom meant release from the burden of sin that Adam and Eve's disobedience had produced to the sorrow of the human condition. The law of Moses, the original covenant given by God in response to the sin of the first human parents, had the effect of demonstrating the grim reality concerning humanity's propensity to sin, for everyone fell short in striving to abide by it. While the law was necessary to show human beings the path of righteousness, the effect of the law was to underscore the sinfulness of humanity. The freedom of Christian faith meant however that the believer was no longer subject to judgment by God according to the law, but according to the grace freely given by Christ in choosing death on the cross as a pledge of his love for humankind.
25. Constable, "Liberty and Free Choice in Monastic Thought and Life," pp. 101–02.
26. W.S. Scott, ed., *The Trial of Joan of Arc* (Westport, Conn.: Associated Booksellers, 1956), p. 155. P. Paul Doncoeur, ed., *La minute française des interrogatoires de Jeanne la Pucelle* (Melun: Librairie D'Argences, 1952), p. 255.
27. Duparc, *Procès*, 2:269.
28. Duparc, *Procès*, 2:276.
29. Her testimony on this matter is as follows: "*Item*, dit que la premiere foys qu'elle ouyt sa voix, elle voua sa virginité, tant qu'il plairoit a Dieu. Et estoit en l'aage de XIII ans, ou environ," *La minute française*, p. 157. [Further, she said that the first time that she heard the voice, she vowed her virginity for as long as it pleased God. And she was thirteen years old, or thereabouts].
30. Duparc, *Procès*, 1:253–54, 256, 258, 260, 261, 263, etc.
31. Doncoeur, *La minute française*, p. 261.
32. Scott, *The Trial of Joan of Arc*, pp. 158–59.
33. Thomas Aquinas, *Summa theologiae*, 2–2, q. 88.5, ed. and trans. Kevin D. O'Rourke O.P. (New York: Blackfriars, 1963), 39:172–75. Thomas did allow that a "promise," *promissio*, (in contrast to a "vow," *votum*) may be made to saints and prelates. For example, one might promise a saint or prelate that one would fulfill a vow that had been made to God. In the nullification trial, Thomas Basin argued on behalf of the legitimacy of Joan's vow based on Aquinas' distinction between vow and promise. See Duparc, *Procès en nullité de la condamnation*, 2:205.
34. Doncoeur, *La minute française*, p. 157.
35. Scott, *The Trial of Joan of Arc*, p. 103.
36. Scott, *The Trial of Joan of Arc*, p. 104.

37. "The Acts of Paul and Thecla," in *The Apocryphal New Testament*, trans. J. K. Elliott (New York: Clarendon Oxford Press, 1994), pp. 364–89.
38. *The Life of Christina of Markyate: A Twelfth Century Recluse*, ed. and trans. C. H. Talbot (New York: Oxford University Press, 1959).
39. Doncoeur, *La minute française*, p. 159.
40. Burgundians were French supporters of the English crown in France.
41. Scott, *The Trial of Joan of Arc*, p. 104.
42. Scott, *The Trial of Joan of Arc*, p. 157. "[I]lz en ont esté si desplaisans qu'ilz en sont tombez presque en demence," Doncoeur, *La minute française*, p. 259.
43. Scott, *The Trial of Joan of Arc*, p. 157.
44. Doncoeur, *La minute française*, p. 159.
45. Scott, *The Trial of Joan of Arc*, pp. 104–105.
46. Duparc, *Procès*, 2:454. Augustine of Hippo, *Sermo 100*, PL 38:603.
47. For example, in the Protestant movement of the sixteenth century, the former monk Martin Luther of Germany preached a piety of direct encounter with God through prayer and Scripture study. In Catholic circles, the Society of Jesus under the leadership of Ignatius of Loyola also brought into focus the inner life of prayer, meditation, and examination of the conscience. While these trends were not altogether new in the history of Christian spirituality, they did represent a renewal of piety as lived by the individual.
48. Duparc, *Procès*, 2:455.
49. PL 187:165.
50. Scott, *The Trial of Joan of Arc*, pp. 79–80. "[H]oc est per preceptum Domini nostri; et, si alium habitum preciperet eidem Johanne accipere, illum acciperet, ex quo hoc faceret per preceptum Dei," Doncoeur, *La minute Française*, p. 114.
51. Doncoeur, *La minute française*, p. 161.
52. Scott, *The Trial of Joan of Arc*, p. 106.
53. Scott, *The Trial of Joan of Arc*, p. 156.
54. Duparc, *Procès*, 2:465.
55. Duparc, *Procès*, 2:249.
56. Duparc, *Procès*, 2:208.
57. Doncoeur, *La minute française*, p. 257.
58. Scott, *The Trial of Joan of Arc*, p. 156.
59. Doncoeur, *La minute française*, p. 93; Scott, *The Trial of Joan of Arc*, p. 67.
60. Doncoeur, *La minute française*, p. 118; Scott, *The Trial of Joan of Arc*, p. 81.
61. Doncoeur, *La minute française*, p. 120; Scott, *The Trial of Joan of Arc*, p. 82.
62. Duparc, *Procès*, 2:468.
63. Duparc, *Procès*, 2:459, 467–68.
64. Duparc, *Procès*, 2:468. Augustine of Hippo, *Contra Faustum* 22.74, CSEL 25:672.
65. Augustine of Hippo, *Reply to Faustus the Manichaean* 12.75, The Nicene and Post-Nicene Fathers (Grand Rapids: Wm. B Eerdmans Publishing Company, repr. 1989), 4:301.
66. Duparc, *Procès*, 2:464.

CHAPTER 5

JOAN OF ARC'S CALL TO CRUSADE

Kelly DeVries

This chapter proposes that Joan of Arc, like other medieval warriors, made Calls to Crusade that showed her awareness of historical and political events.

From 1099 to the end of the Middle Ages medieval warriors often displayed their spirituality by participating in a crusade, and medieval military leaders went further by also making Calls for those same crusades. Even after 1291, with the loss of the Holy Land in the Middle East, Calls for Crusades persisted, with almost every military leader insisting that as soon as they had completed their bellicose task, they would depart for the more spiritual endeavor of fighting against the infidel; and they would ask their enemy to make peace with them so that they, too, would join in that endeavor. Thus it would seem strange if Joan of Arc, as a military leader who claimed direct guidance from God, would not also have made a Call for Crusade. In fact, this most spiritual late medieval warrior made at least three of them.

Of course, Joan of Arc's military priority was the Hundred Years War. If one follows closely the two self-proclaimed goals of Joan's mission, the two that she achieved, to raise the siege of Orléans and to lead Charles the dauphin to Reims for his coronation and consecration,[1] or even her four goals, which Seguin Seguin, her confessor at Poitiers revealed in her rehabilitation trial, adding two which she did not achieve—that the city of Paris would return to French rule and that the duke of Orléans would be returned from England[2]—it is evident that her military thoughts first and foremost dwelt on the Anglo-Franco-Burgundian conflict then being fought in her homeland. Before she was executed, on May 30, 1431 in Rouen, she would play a decisive role in that war. But, during the early fifteenth century in which she lived it would have been strange for Joan not to have thought beyond the boundaries of her own conflict, toward the Middle East, eastern Mediterranean, and southeastern Europe.

One of the salient features of late medieval military society was the remembrance of the crusaders' failure at Acre in 1291. Throughout the next two centuries Calls to Crusade to the Holy Land and eastern Mediterranean were frequent. Indeed, almost all military, diplomatic, and spiritual rhetoric of the period contained a Call to Crusade. Thus it should come as no surprise that Joan of Arc too made her own Calls to Crusade. As was shown both by her actions and later trial testimony, Joan was certainly aware of historical and political events. The critical evidence in this inquiry are two letters that Joan wrote: the first, written to Philip the Good, duke of Burgundy, on July 17, 1429, after she had enabled the crowning of King Charles VII of France; the second is her letter to the Hussites, written on March 23, 1430. In this chapter, reference will be made to these two Calls to Crusade, as well as to her famous Letter to the English, written on March 22, 1429, which, while not as direct in its Call to Crusade as the other two Letters, can also be considered such a Call.[3]

In 1291, the last major stronghold of the Latin Crusade Kingdoms in the Holy Land, Acre, fell to the Mamluks. It was a hard-fought battle, one of the most violent and bloody of the entire crusades, which largely pitted the undermanned Knights Templars and Knights Hospitallers against more numerous Middle Eastern Islamic soldiers. A generation later this defeat would haunt the Templars to their order's dissolution and leaders' deaths; the Hospitallers survived chiefly because of their isolation on the island of Rhodes.[4]

From then on, the urge for western Europeans to return to the Holy Land seemed to be ever present, although rarely were any steps taken to do so. Most often this urge was seen in times of war, sometimes as a propaganda ploy to divert attention from defeat. This can be seen, for example, in 1302, following the defeat of his army to the Flemish rebels at the battle of Courtrai, when French King Philip IV (the Fair) invoked a Call to Crusade. In an effort to rally his people, especially his churchmen, who he hoped would pay for military revenge against the rebels of his northern county, Philip and his advisors sent letters and gave sermons throughout the kingdom. Their theme was simple: finish off the Flemish rebellion so that a crusade might be waged; the longer the rebellion, the longer the wait before a return to the Middle East. For example, in a *sermo* given to "those about to proceed to war" against the Flemings, Philip remarks that the expedition has a further purpose:

> Even this contains the highest piety, which is thus shown: the peace of the king is the peace of the kingdom: the peace of the kingdom is the peace of the church, of knowledge, virtue and justice, and it is the acquisition of the Holy Land. Therefore, he who goes against the king, labors against the entire church, against the Catholic doctrine, against sanctity and justice and the Holy Land.[5]

Other French royal Calls to Crusade followed during the reigns of Philip V, Philip VI, and Charles VI.[6] Indeed, it was during the reign of Charles VI that the disastrous Nicopolis Crusade was undertaken, called such because of the defeat of the western and central European forces near that town by the Ottoman Turks in 1396.[7] By the time of the last fourteenth-century Call to Crusade the enemy had shifted to the Ottoman Turks, but these and future Calls for crusading action were the same.

One of the obvious impediments to a crusade against Islamic forces, perhaps the most important one, was war between Christian powers in the west, especially the various wars of the Hundred Years War,[8] which ranged from the early fourteenth century until the late fifteenth century. From the very beginning of these wars, the popes had tried to use the Call to Crusade to bring peace between these warring states. In 1345, Pope Clement VI wrote separate letters to both Philip VI and Edward III asking them to stop their conflict and to unite to go on crusade. "Oh, how much better a crusade against the Turk enemies of our faith, than the present fratricidal strife," the pontiff wrote to the English king.[9] And in 1370, a new pope, Urban V, repeated a Call to Crusade to the kings of France and England, hoping that the peace brought about with the Treaty of Brétigny, signed ten years previously, might encourage them to unite against the Turks.[10] Even after Joan of Arc's appearance these Calls would continue. In 1451, Pope Nicholas V wrote to Kings Henry VI and Charles VII to plead with them for peace so that they might help to avert the fall of Constantinople. No peace was made and no help was forthcoming.[11] And in 1456 and again in 1459, Pope Pius II called on western leaders, primarily Duke Philip the Good of Burgundy and King Charles VII of France, to carry out a crusade against the Ottomans whose capture of Byzantium a few years before meant that these Islamic armies might ultimately turn their attacks against the west.[12]

But one did not have to be a pope to recognize the need for peace between warring Christian states in the Hundred Years War before a crusade against the Turks could be undertaken. In the early fourteenth century, French "travel writer" Burcard warned Philip VI that the Turks were so powerful that should there not be a peaceful, unified effort by all western nations against them, a crusade would fail.[13] In ca. 1380, the Englishman John Gower also recognized this need for western European peace, writing:

> The lineal descent by right of his mother proclaims Christ as the heir of the land in which he was born. . .But a pagan interloper holds it now. . .we do not carry on war against these men by attacking either their persons or their property. . .Instead we are fighting open battles over worldly possessions with our brothers.[14]

And in 1420, Emmanuel Piloti would devote the first few pages of his *Traité sur le Passage en Terre Sainte* to a plea for the Venetians to solve their problems with the German emperor and with the duke of Burgundy to stop his fighting on the side of the English against the French king. Only then could Christians deliver Jerusalem from the hands of Turkish pagans.[15] Others who called for an end of warfare in western Europe so that a crusade against the Turks could be undertaken include Pierre de Thomas,[16] John Mandeville,[17] Eustace Deschamps,[18] Christine de Pisan,[19] the anonymous author of the *Tractatus de Regimine Principum* written for King Henry VI,[20] and Saint Bridget of Sweden.[21] (Saint Bridget even asked her cousin, King Magnus, to intervene in the Hundred Years War because the French and English were behaving as "beasts.")

Perhaps the most influential of these late medieval instigators of peace between England and France as a means of crusade was Philippe de Mézières. Mézières, who was so critical of the crusaders after their defeat at Nicopolis, had been tireless in his efforts to get the crusade underway. In almost all of his writings and sermons, he asked for peace between the warring western kingdoms. In his *Letter to King Richard II*, written in 1395, he is especially eloquent in his pleas for peace between England and France. Praising the English king, Mézières compares him to a lodestone who is not only loved by his own subjects,

> but, what is more, has attracted his enemies, accepted by long habit as natural enemies, namely, the good men of France, and indeed, our much loved King Charles himself.

This lodestone has odd powers, but one of the greatest is that it was able to stop the flow of blood, especially that which had been lost in the war between France and England. This will allow the two kings, now at peace, to take their subjects on a "Holy Passage" to regain the Christian lands acquired by Mézières's so-called King Vigilant, the sultan of Babylon.[22]

Therefore, it is not out of the question for Joan of Arc also to be concerned that the warfare in her own lands between Christian princes meant that no crusade would be undertaken, especially if she was the internationally "informed" girl that most biographers, including myself, would have her be. Indeed, it would be extremely unusual for Joan not to be concerned over what had occurred and what would continue to occur in the Middle East, eastern Mediterranean, and southeastern Europe.

But what proof is there of this? Her vocalized mission never included any mention of a crusade. According to the president of the Chamber of Accounts in the dauphin's court, Simon Charles, Joan "said that she had two commissions for which she had been sent by the King of Heaven: one to raise the siege of Orléans, the other to lead the King to Reims for his coronation and consecration,"[23] while her confessor, Seguin Seguin, claimed that when interviewed by him at Poitiers, she added two other military achievements that would also come about, although not necessarily to be achieved by her:

> . . .she said to me and others present four things which were then still to come, and which afterwards occurred. First, she said that the English would be defeated, that the siege before Orléans would be raised, and the town of Orléans would be freed of the English; however, she would first send them a summons. Second, she said that the King would be anointed at Reims. Third, that the city of Paris would return to the King's rule, and that the Duke of Orléans would return from England.[24]

Still, despite the extension of her purported mission in this remembrance, again Joan did not mention a crusade, either toward the Middle East, against the Ottomans, or in opposition to any heretical group.

But is that sufficient evidence to affirm that Joan of Arc was unaware of the situation in the Middle East, central Europe, and the eastern Mediterranean and unconcerned with a crusade? Her detailed knowledge of what was happening between the English and French along the Loire River, despite being miles away from that action, certainly gives an indication of a young woman quite aware of the events of her world. It may also decry the notion of medieval peasants ignorant of anything outside of their small world.[25] She surely must have known about, and was concerned with, the need for a crusade, and her way of doing this was by ending the conflict in France between the Anglo-Burgundians and France.

This becomes initially evident in Joan's Letter to the English dictated around March 22, 1429, at the conclusion of her trial at Poitiers and sent from Blois to the English besiegers of Orléans between April 24 and 27. This letter makes clear Joan's confidence and her defiance of all who opposed her, and therefore also opposed God:

> *Jesus-Maria,*
>
> King of England, and you, duke of Bedford, who call yourself regent of the kingdom of France, you, William de la Pole, Sir John Talbot, and you, Sir Thomas Scales, who call yourself lieutenant of the aforesaid duke of Bedford, render your account to the King of Heaven. Surrender to the Maid, who is sent here from God, the King of Heaven, the keys to all of the good cities that you have taken and violated in France. She has come here from God to proclaim the blood royal. She is entirely ready to make peace, if you are willing to settle accounts with her, provided that you give up France and pay for having occupied her. And those among you, archers, companions-at-arms, gentlemen, and others who are before the city of Orléans, go back to your own countries, for God's sake. And if you do not do so, wait for the word of the Maid who will come visit you briefly, to your great damage. If you do not do so, I am commander of the armies, and in whatever place I shall meet your French allies, I shall make them leave it, whether they wish to or not; and if they will not obey, I shall have them all killed. I am sent from God, the King of Heaven, to chase you out of all of France, body for body [every last one of you]. And if they wish to obey, I shall have mercy on them. And have no other opinion, for you shall never hold the kingdom of France from God, the King of Heaven, the son of St. Mary; but King Charles, the true heir, will hold it; for God, the King of Heaven, wishes it so and has revealed through the Maid, and he will enter Paris with a goodly company. If you do not wish to believe this message from God through the Maid, then wherever we find you we will strike you there, and make a great uproar greater than any made in France for a thousand years, if you do not come to terms. And believe firmly that the King of Heaven will send the Maid more force than you will ever know how to achieve with all of your assaults on her and on her good men-at-arms; and in the exchange of blows we shall see who has better right from the King of Heaven. You, duke of Bedford, the Maid prays you and requests that you cause no more destruction. If you will settle your account, you can join her company, in which the French will achieve the finest feat ever accomplished in Christendom. And give answer, if you wish to make peace in the city of Orléans; and if indeed you do not do so, be mindful soon of your great damages.[26]

Of course, the primary purpose of this letter was for Joan of Arc to introduce herself to and to declare war against the English. However, this should not be interpreted as a formal declaration of war in the manner of those required by legal and military theorists earlier in the Middle Ages.[27] Although it certainly can be said that at the time of her appearance Joan meant to open a new phase of the war, the tradition of such declarations had long since fallen out of custom; the Hundred Years War had not been so begun, nor had any new phase of it.

So Joan of Arc must have meant something else with this Letter. As Joan honestly and earnestly believed that she was sent from God, the Letter to the English must be seen in that light. She invokes the name of God a number of times, calling the English military leaders "to render your account to the King of Heaven," and "to surrender to the Maid, who is sent here from God, the King of Heaven, the keys to all of the good cities that you have taken and violated in France," that they should "go back to your own countries, for God's sake." Did she sincerely believe that such a call for surrender, even attached as it was to God's name, would bring the desired result? Probably not, although she wanted to give the English a chance to retreat without loss of life before she would "come visit you briefly, to your great damage." If they did not leave France, Joan would "make them leave it, whether they wish to or not; and if they will not obey, [she would] have them all killed." Joan was confident that the English would never conquer France, as God had given it to the dauphin, Charles; and she was equally confident that she would be the one to drive them from France, sending her "more force than you will ever know how to achieve with all of your assaults on her and on her good men-at-arms."

At this point in the Letter to the English, Joan changes her approach and somewhat softens her tone for the answer as to why this retreat (or defeat) of the English was necessary: "If you will settle your account, you can join her [Joan's] company, in which the French will achieve the finest feat ever accomplished in Christendom." This feat was unquestionably the recapture of the Holy Land, although by this time that meant conquering the Ottoman Turks along the way. Joan of Arc had made her first Call to Crusade.

Her second Call came on July 17, 1429, in a letter written from Joan to Duke Philip the Good of Burgundy. Much had happened in the short time since she had written her Letter to the English. The English military leadership in occupied France, naturally, had not surrendered. And Joan of Arc, true to her promise, had brought "great damage" to the English cause. She initially focused on raising the siege of Orléans, relieving the city through a mixture of enthusiasm and some tactical bravado: her frontal assaults cost her many French soldiers, but they also defeated the English besiegers established in the several boulevards, including Saint Loup and the Augustins, and the masonry-fortified bridgehead of the Tourelles.[28] A month after raising the siege of Orléans, she won victories over the English at Jargeau, Beaugency, and Meung, and she was at Patay, where the remainder of the English soldiers who had been along the Loire River were quickly defeated in battle.[29] From there Joan had led a French coronation army to crown the dauphin as Charles VII at Reims. This force faced little resistance along the route, with the large Burgundian-held sites of Auxerre, Troyes, and Reims all surrendering without conflict.[30] On July 17, 1429, she stood by the new king's side as he was crowned at the Cathedral of Notre-Dame at Reims.[31] It had been a very good few months for the Maid.

Sometime on the very day of Charles VII's coronation, Joan of Arc wrote the new king's cousin, Philip the Good. She was concerned that this duke of Burgundy would continue to fight on the side of the English against the French. She wrote:

> *Jhesus Maria*
> High and dread prince, duke of Burgundy, the Maid calls upon you by the King of Heaven, my rightful and sovereign Lord, to make a firm and lasting peace with the king of France. You two must pardon one another fully with a sincere heart, as loyal Christians should; and if it pleases you to make war, go and wage it on the Saracens. Prince of Burgundy, I pray you, supplicate, and humbly request rather than require you, make war no more on the holy kingdom of France. Withdraw at once and swiftly those of your men who are in certain places and fortresses of the aforesaid holy kingdom. As for the gentle king of France, he is ready to make peace with you, saving his honor, if it has to do with you alone. And I must make known to you from the King of Heaven, my rightful and sovereign Lord, for your good and for your honor and upon your life, that you will win no more battles against loyal Frenchmen and that all those who wage war against the aforesaid holy kingdom of France are warring against King Jesus, King of Heaven and of all earth, my rightful and sovereign Lord. And I pray you and call upon you with hands joined not to seek any battle nor war against us, neither you nor your men nor subjects, and believe firmly that no number of men that you bring against us will win, and that there will be great pity for the battle and the bloodshed there of those who come against us.[32]

This letter is much more direct in its Call to Crusade. But, at the same time, Joan also shows that she knew why the ducal cousin was at odds with his royal cousin. In 1419, in an action all too typical of the civil war known as the Armagnac–Burgundian conflict, Philip's father, John the Fearless, was assassinated at the bridge of Montereau by arrangement of the then dauphin. This event threw Philip into the English camp, first in alliance with King Henry V and then with the duke of Bedford, regent of the very young Henry VI, and commander of all English forces in occupied France (one of the men to whom Joan of Arc directed her Letter to the English). This had not always been a fruitful relationship for Philip, but he had stayed with the English rather than side with the assassin of his father.[33]

In writing this Letter to Philip the Good, Joan was reminding him of the reasons for his separation from French allegiance, while pleading with him to recognize that there were injustices done on both sides of the Armagnac–Burgundian civil war/dispute—John the Fearless had, after all, assassinated the dauphin's uncle, Louis of Orléans, in 1407, an act that essentially began the dispute.[34] It would be best for both sides to "pardon one another fully with a sincere heart, as loyal Christians should," especially as the direction of the war had suddenly changed, and Joan obviously believed that the English were on their way off the Continent, in particular if she could get the Burgundians also to pull out of the war. The reason for this mutual forgiveness was to "go and wage [war] on the Saracens."

Joan of Arc presses the point further: "Prince of Burgundy, I pray you, supplicate, and humbly request rather than require you, make war no more on the holy kingdom of France. Withdraw at once and swiftly those of your men who are in certain places and fortresses of the aforesaid holy kingdom." Clearly, in Joan's mind, it is up to the duke to initiate peace with France, although Charles would reciprocate: "he is ready to make peace with you." Again, she invokes the name of God, telling Philip that he cannot win when fighting "against loyal Frenchmen." As shown in the Letter to the English, Joan firmly believes that whoever fights against the Kingdom of France, battles "against King Jesus, King of Heaven and of all earth, my rightful and sovereign Lord," resulting in a "great pity for the battle and the bloodshed there of those who come against us." Such warfare means that a crusade, God's chosen form of warfare, cannot go forward. Philip the Good needed to forgive Charles VII and vice versa. Joan had issued her second Call to Crusade.

Joan of Arc's third Call to Crusade was a letter specifically directed at a heretical group, the Hussites, written on March 23, 1430. In this letter Joan retained her customary self-confidence—God was still using her for His purposes—but she no longer was as happy with her situation either when she initially addressed the English or when she pled with the duke of Burgundy for an end to the Armagnac–Burgundian civil war. Disappointments with the French king and his advisors had helped Joan of Arc develop a distrust of her (and her God's) own chosen allegiance. After the coronation, which in turn led to the surrender of more formerly occupied French towns, Charles VII had failed to support Joan's attack on Paris, forcing a withdrawal of French troops after only one day of fighting and the wounding of the Maid.[35] Once she had recovered, as the end of 1429 approached, and despite Joan's former military leader colleagues, Jean, the duke of Alençon, and Arthur de Richemont, asking for her attendance in their military theaters, she was shipped off to the upper Loire, under-prepared, undermanned, and under-provisioned, to fight against the mercenary captain, Perrinet Gressart. She would be successful in capturing Saint-Pierre-le-Moûtier, but failed against Gressart's fortified headquarters at La Charité-sur-Loire.[36] On Christmas day 1429, Joan had returned in despair to the king's court; even being ennobled did not encourage her. There followed three months of inaction, which frustrated the French general, so that by March 1430 she was looking for other venues for her military leadership. One of those was to join the crusade against the Hussites, already in progress in Central Europe. Announcing this possibility, she wrote to "the Hussites":

> *Jesus-Maria*
> For some time now, rumor and public information have reported to me, Joan the Maid, that from true Christians you have become heretics and that, like the Saracens, you have destroyed true religion and worship; embracing a shameful and criminal superstition and wishing to protect and propagate it, there is no shameful deed of belief you do not dare. You ruin the sacraments of the Church, you rend the articles of Faith, you destroy churches, you smash and burn the statues which have been erected as memorable monuments, you massacre Christians simply because they have kept the true Faith.
>
> What is this frenzy? What rage or madness drives you? This Faith, which Almighty God, which is the Son, which the Holy Spirit have revealed, established, given sway and glorified a thousandfold through miracles is the faith which you persecute, which you wish to overturn and obliterate. You are blind, not because you lack foresight. Do you think that you will not be punished for this? Or do you not realize that God will block your criminal efforts? Do you think He will allow you to remain in darkness and error? The more you give yourselves over to criminal sacrilege, the more He will ready great punishment and torment for you.
>
> As for myself, I tell you frankly that if I were not kept busy with these English wars I would have come to see you a long time ago. But if I do not hear that you have corrected yourselves, I may well leave these English and set off against you, so that, by the sword if I cannot otherwise, I may remove your madness and foul superstition, taking either your heresy or your lives. But if you choose instead to return to the Catholic faith and to the original source of light, send me your ambassadors and I shall tell them what you must do. If you do not wish to do so and persist in resisting the spur, recall how much criminal harm you have done and wait for me, who will deal with you comparably with the aid of divine and human force.[37]

There is some question about the validity of this letter. Joan of Arc had written letters to the citizens of Reims both a week before and a few days after the Letter to the Hussites. In these she promised that she would come running to them if they were attacked, which naturally would be a bit difficult if she was fighting in Central Europe against the Hussites.[38] On the other hand, in the months of inactivity Joan had been counseling a militarily idle Charles VII to pursue war against his enemies in the north of France. However, this advice was met with deaf ears, and Joan, it seemed, sought to find a new divine "purpose," which might very well have included the possibility of leaving from France and fulfilling what she had already called others to do, fight a crusade.

The Letter to the Hussites has several of the *topoi* of Joan's other two Calls to Crusade. She defends her belief in God and the Church and the divinity of her military mission: "This Faith, which Almighty God, which is the Son, which the Holy Spirit have revealed, established, given sway and glorified a thousand-fold through miracles is the faith which you persecute, which you wish to overturn and obliterate." Joan felt certain that her victories were some of these "miracles." And she calls on the Hussites to stop their heresy, which she characterizes not just as "a shameful and criminal superstition and wishing to protect and propagate it," but also in more violent terms, terms which, because of her own military activity, she is quite accustomed to: "there is no shameful deed of belief you do not dare. You ruin the sacraments of the Church, you rend the articles of Faith, you destroy churches, you smash and burn the statues which have been erected as memorable monuments, you massacre Christians simply because they have kept the true Faith." Like the English, Joan was giving the Hussites a chance to give up their "sinful" ways on their own, recognizing that they would be punished if they did not: "Do you think that you will not be punished for this? Or do you not realize that God will block your criminal efforts? Do you think He will allow you to remain in darkness and error? The more you give yourselves over to criminal sacrilege, the more He will ready great punishment and torment for you." Indeed, Joan of Arc would not mind being the agent of that punishment "were [she] not kept busy with these English wars." In this letter, this is where Joan shows her frustration with her current situation, combining this frustration with a threat to the Hussites: "But if I do not hear that you have corrected yourselves, I may well leave these English and set off against you, so that, by the sword if I cannot otherwise, I may remove your madness and foul superstition, taking either your heresy or your lives." If, on the other hand, they did return to God's Church, she would counsel them; if they did not, "wait for me, who will deal with you comparably with the aid of divine and human force." Joan had issued her third, and most open Call to Crusade.

But there are two distinct differences between this Call to Crusade and her other two. First, she had changed her target from the "Saracens," so named in the letter to Philip the Good and justifiably assumed in the "finest feat ever accomplished in Christendom" referred to in her Letter to the English. She, of course, provided her own rationale for this change in the beginning of the Letter to the Hussites: "For some time now, rumor and public information have reported to me, Joan the Maid, that from true Christians you have become heretics." Obviously, she had learned of this heretical group only during the time of her own military activity. Yet, this should not be taken as evidence of Joan of Arc's ignorance of international affairs, as the crusade against the Hussites had only been called a decade before, when Pope Martin V had issued a bull against them, and that it was even later that non-local crusading forces, never large in number, engaged them in warfare.[39] It is also apparent that, after hearing of the outrageous and violent atrocities of the Hussites, from "rumor and public information," Joan had placed them above the "Saracens" in her pecking order of groups needing a crusade.

Second, in the Letter to the Hussites Joan did not call on anyone in particular to go on crusade. The English had not surrendered, as she had asked for in her Letter to them; so they would not be joining her. Philip the Good and the Burgundians had also not made peace with the French, as Joan had requested from him; so they would not be joining her. Finally, due to their lack of activities over the last few months, Joan had lost faith in the French political and military leadership; so she did not think that they would be joining her. Still, she had over the past year discovered her own drawing power among soldiers,[40] and she was confident that she and they could carry on a crusade on their own. Hence, the final paragraph of her Letter to the Hussites promises them that should she "not hear that you have corrected yourselves," she, with her faithful soldiers and her God, would lead a crusade against them: "wait for me, who will deal with you comparably with the aid of divine and human force."

Joan of Arc did not live to carry out a crusade. Two months to the day after she had written her Letter to the Hussites she was captured by the Burgundian forces besieging Compiègne. Instead of going on a crusade against the Hussites, she had chosen to escape from her Loire palatial "prison" to assist her beloved loyal Frenchmen in that northern town who were resisting Philip the Good's forces. On May 30, 1431, she would be burned at Rouen. Her unanswered Call to Crusade thus joined all of those other late medieval Calls to Crusade which also went unanswered.

Notes

1. As expressed by Simon Charles in Joan of Arc's rehabilitation trial, in Pierre Duparc, ed., *Procès en nullité de la condamnation de Jeanne d'Arc* (Paris: Klincksieck, 1977–89), I:399–400.
2. Seguin Seguin, in Duparc I:472–73. See also Alençon's testimony, in Duparc I:382.
3. While writing this essay, I happened upon Norman Housley's "*Pro deo et patria mori*: Sanctified Patriotism in Europe, 1400–1600," in *War and Competition Between States*, ed. Philippe Contamine (Oxford: Clarendon Press,

2000), pp. 233–34, which also sees Joan's letters to Philip the Good and the Hussites as Calls to Crusade, but does not elaborate on this nor does he include the Letter to the English among Joan of Arc's Calls to Crusade.

4. Almost every general history of the crusades covers this last major engagement. See especially Steven Runciman, *A History of the Crusades*, Vol. III: *The Kingdom of Acre* (New York: Harper and Row, Publishers, 1967); Hans Eberhard Mayer, *The Crusades* (Oxford: Oxford University Press, 1972); Jean Richard, *The Crusades, c.1071–c.1291*, trans. Jean Birrell (Cambridge: Cambridge University Press, 1999); and Carole Hillenbrand, *The Crusades: Islamic Perspectives* (New York: Routledge, 2000). See also Donald P. Little, "The Fall of 'Akkā in 690/1291: The Muslim Version," in *Studies in Islamic History and Civilization in Honour of Professor David Ayalon*, ed. Moshe Sharon (Leiden: E. J. Brill, 1986).
5. An edition of this *sermo* was made by Jean Leclerq and entitled "Un sermon prononcé pendant la guerre de Flandre sous Philippe le Bel," *Revue du moyen âge latin* 1 (1945): 165–72.
6. On these "Calls" see C.J. Tyerman, "Philip V of France, the Assemblies of 1319–20 and the crusade," *Bulletin of the Institute of Historical Research* 57 (1984): 15–34; C.J. Tyerman, "Philip VI and the Recovery of the Holy Land," *English Historical Review* 100 (1985): 25–52; and James Magee, "Crusading at the Court of Charles VI, 1388–1396," *French History* 12 (1998): 367–83.
7. For a concise account of this crusade and its modern historiography see Kelly DeVries, "The Lack of a Western European Military Response to the Ottoman Invasions of Eastern Europe from Nicopolis (1396) to Mohács (1526)," *Journal of Military History* 63 (1999): 539–59; reprinted in *Guns and Men in Medieval Europe, 1200–1500: Studies in Military History and Technology* (Aldershot: Ashgate Variorum, 2002), essay VII.
8. The customary view of the Hundred Years War as the Anglo-French conflict dated from 1337 to 1453 is, in my opinion, too narrowly focused for the number of conflicts that make up what I call "The Hundred Years Wars." See Kelly DeVries, *The Hundred Years Wars, 1302–1485* (London: Longmans, forthcoming).
9. The text of this letter is in Robert of Avesbury, *De gestis mirabilibus Edwardi III*, ed. E.M. Thompson (London: Her Majesty's Stationery Office, 1889), pp. 394–95. See also Norman Housley, *The Later Crusades, 1274–1580: From Lyons to Alcazar* (Oxford: Oxford University Press, 1992), pp. 38–39; Michael R. Powicke, "War as a Means of Peace: Some Late Medieval Themes," in *Documenting the Past: Essays in Medieval History Presented to George Peddy Cuttino*, ed. J.S. Hamilton and P.J. Bradley (Woodbridge: Boydell and Brewer, 1989), p. 218; Aziz Suryal Atiya, "The Crusade in the Fourteenth Century," in *A History of the Crusades*, ed. K.M. Setton, Vol. II: *The Later Crusades*, ed. R.L. Wolff and H.W. Hazard (Madison: University of Wisconsin Press, 1969), p. 12; and Peter Topping, "The Morea, 1311–1364," in *A History of the Crusades*, ed. K. M. Setton, Vol. II: *The Later Crusades*, ed. R.L. Wolff and H.W. Hazard (Madison: University of Wisconsin Press, 1969), p. 133.

10. Deno Geanakoplos, "Byzantium and the Crusades, 1354–1453," in *A History of the Crusades*, ed. K.M. Setton, vol. 2: *The Later Crusades*, ed. R.L.Wolff and H.W. Hazard (Madison: University of Wisconsin Press, 1969), p. 79.
11. Powicke, p. 219. See also the letter from Henry VI to the ambassadors of Philip the Good of Burgundy in Anne F. Sutton, "The Contents of the Manuscript," in *The Politics of Fifteenth-Century England: John Vale's Book* (Stroud: Sutton, 1995), pp. 140–41.
12. See DeVries, "The Lack of a Western European Military Response," pp. 539–59.
13. Atiya Aziz Suryal, *The Crusade in the Later Middle Ages* (London: Methuen, 1938), pp. 95–113, and Powicke, p. 222.
14. John Gower, "Vox clamantis," in *Complete Works*, ed. G.C. Macauley (Oxford: Clarendon Press, 1899–1902), III.9.650–70, V.5.307–10. See also Elizabeth Siberry, "Criticism of Crusading in Fourteenth-Century England," in *Crusade and Settlement*, ed. P. W. Edbury (Cardiff: University College Cardiff Press, 1985), p. 130.
15. Emmanuel Piloti, *Traité d'Emmanuel Piloti sur le passage en Terre Sainte (1420)*, ed. P. -H. Dopp (Leuven: E. Nauwelaerts, 1958), pp. 9–10.
16. Atiya, *Crusade*, pp. 128–36 and Powicke, pp. 222–23.
17. Sir John Mandeville, *Travels*, ed. M. Letts (London: Hakluyt Society, 1953), I:2. See also Siberry, p. 131.
18. Eustace Deschamps, *Œuvres complètes*, ed. Q. de Saint Hilaire and G. Raynaud (Paris: Firmin Didot et cie., 1878–1903), I:138–39.
19. Christine de Pisan, *Ditié de Jehanne d'Arc*, ed. A.J. Kennedy and K. Varty (Oxford: Society for the Study of Mediaeval Languages and Literature, 1977).
20. *Tractatus de regimine principum ad regem Henricum sextum*, in *Four English Political Tracts of the Later Middle Ages*, ed. J.P. Genêt (London: Royal Historical Society, 1977), p. 70. See also Powicke, p. 224.
21. J. Jorgensen, *Saint Bridget of Sweden* (London: Longmans, Green, 1954), pp. 270–73. See also Powicke, p. 222.
22. This letter can be found both in its original Old French and in an English translation in Philippe de Mézières, *Letter to King Richard II: A Plea Made in 1395 for Peace Between England and France*, ed. and trans. G.W. Coopland (Liverpool: Liverpool University Press, 1975). The quotations appear on pp. 12–13. Similar messages appear in all of Mézières's writings. See N. Jorga, *Philippe de Mézières (1327–1405) et la croisade au XIVe siècle* (Paris: E. Bouillon, 1896).
23. See note 1 above. This was remembered by Simon Charles in Joan of Arc's rehabilitation trial.
24. See note 2 above. See also Alençon's testimony, in Duparc I:382. These were also testimonies in the rehabilitation trial.
25. This notion has unfortunately been perpetuated since at least Eileen Power's *Medieval People* (London: Methuen, 1932; repr., 1963). Judging from the history of Joan of Arc, at least, the presumption of ignorance on the part of medieval peasants should be revised.

26. Although the original letter has long disappeared, there were several copies made of it, many of which survive. The French text can be found in Régine Pernoud and Marie-Véronique Clin, *Joan of Arc: Her Story*, trans. and rev. J.duQ. Adams (New York: St. Martin's Press, 1998), pp. 249–50, and Jules Quicherat, ed., *Procès de condamnation et de réhabilitation de Jeanne d'Arc dite la Pucelle* (Paris: Jules Renouard et Cie., 1841–49), 5:95–98. I have used the English translation in *Joan of Arc: Her Story*, pp. 33–34. See also Marina Warner, *Joan of Arc: The Image of Female Heroism* (Harmondsworth: Penguin, 1981), pp. 82–83, and Deborah A. Fraioli, *Joan of Arc: The Early Debate* (Woodbridge: The Boydell Press, 2000), pp. 69–87, although neither work regards it as a Call to Crusade.
27. See Frederick H. Russell, *The Just War in the Middle Ages* (Cambridge: Cambridge University Press, 1975). For an example of this, see Kelly DeVries, "Medieval Declarations of War: An Example from 1212," *Scintilla* 4 (1987): 20–37; reprinted in *Guns and Men in Medieval Europe*, essay II.
28. See Kelly DeVries, *Joan of Arc: A Military Leader* (Stroud: Sutton, 1999), pp. 77–94.
29. See DeVries, *Joan of Arc*, pp. 97–121.
30. See DeVries, *Joan of Arc*, pp. 122–34.
31. See DeVries, *Joan of Arc*, pp. 133–34.
32. This Letter is preserved in the Archives du Nord in Lille. It is edited in Quicherat 5:126–27, and *Joan of Arc: Her Story*, pp. 253–54. I have used the translation found in *Joan of Arc: Her Story*, pp. 67–68. See also Warner, pp. 180–81; Régine Pernoud, *Joan of Arc by Herself and Her Witnesses*, trans. E. Hyams (New York: Dorset Press, 1964), p. 128; and Ferdinand de Liocourt, *La mission de Jeanne d'Arc* (Paris: Nouvelle Éditions Latines, 1974–76), II:198.
33. An analysis of this period in Philip the Good's military career can be found in Richard Vaughan, *Philip the Good: The Apogee of Burgundy* (London: Longmans, 1970), pp. 1–60, and in Kelly DeVries and Robert D. Smith, *A History of Gunpowder Weaponry during the Fourteenth and Fifteenth Centuries: The Artillery of the Valois Dukes of Burgundy* (forthcoming 2004).
34. See Edouard Perroy, *The Hundred Years War*, trans. W.B. Wells (New York: Oxford University Press, 1951), pp. 226–27; Richard Vaughan, *John the Fearless: The Growth of Burgundian Power* (London: Longmans, 1966), pp. 43–48; Bertrand Schnerb, *Les Armagnacs et les Bourguignons: La maudite guerre* (Paris: Librairie Académique Perrin, 1988), pp. 67–76; and Bernard Guenée, *Un meurtre, une société: L'assassinat du Duc d'Orléans, 23 novembre 1407* (Paris: Gallimard, 1992).
35. See DeVries, *Joan of Arc*, pp. 141–55.
36. See DeVries, *Joan of Arc*, pp. 156–65.
37. This Letter, originally written in Latin, is found in a German translation in the Vienna *Reichsregister* D. f. 236 r. I have used the translation in *Joan of Arc: Her Story*, p. 259.
38. In *Joan of Arc: Her Story*, Pernoud and Clin (pp. 158–59) are direct in their opinion that Joan did not write this letter: "this letter was not dictated by

Joan; it is the work of Pasquerel, her confessor." Liocourt (II:267) and Warner (p. 181) accept the letter as hers.

39. There are several histories of the Hussites and the wars fought against them. The best general surveys are Frederick G. Heymann, "The Crusades against the Hussites," in *A History of the Crusades*, Vol. 3: *The Fourteenth and Fifteenth Centuries*, ed. Harry W. Hazard (Madison: University of Wisconsin Press, 1975), pp. 586–646, and Frederick G. Heymann, *John Zizka and the Hussite Revolution* (Princeton: Princeton University Press, 1955), with the best military history being Silvia Petrin, *Der österreichische Hussitenkrieg, 1420–1434*, Militärhistorische Schriftenreihe 44 (Vienna: Heeresgeschichtlichen Museum; Militärwissenschaftliches Institut, 1994).
40. On this see Kelly DeVries, "A Woman as Leader of Men: A Reassessment of Joan of Arc's Military Career," in *Fresh Verdicts on Joan of Arc*, ed. Bonnie Wheeler and Charles Wood (New York: Garland Publishing, Inc., 1996), pp. 3–18; reprinted in *Guns and Men in Medieval Europe*, essay VI.

PART TWO

CLERICAL PERCEPTIONS OF JOAN'S SPIRITUALITY IN HER OWN TIME

CHAPTER 6

JEANNE AND THE CLERGY

George H. Tavard

This chapter surveys Joan's relations with the clergy, before and during her trial in Rouen. These clergy represented different spiritual traditions, and this helps to explain their varying responses to the Maid.

The picture one draws of Jeanne d'Arc depends on which aspect of her character or career one has chosen to place at the center. While she herself was as straightforward as could be, the historical setting of her time and place have given her picture a complexity in which disparate strands need to be sorted out. Here I attempt to understand her relation with the priests, both diocesan and religious, whom she met at the various stages of her life. In this survey, however, I will abstain from considering her ambiguous relationship with the archbishop of Reims, Regnault de Chartres, a lukewarm actor in her plan to lead the dauphin to his coronation, and reluctant to encourage her in her military projects, or with the bishop of Beauvais, Pierre Cauchon, an open adversary of Charles VII and therefore of Jeanne's claim to have received a mission from God. On opposite sides of the dynastic divide in the Hundred Years War, they both were political bishops, who must have understood each other much better than they could understand the young woman mystic from the marches of Lorraine.

Jeanne was familiar with the clergy. Although she said that her mother had taught her all she knew in religion, she must have learned something from the long-time pastor of the small parish of Greux-Domremy,[1] where she heard mass often and to whom she confessed her sins frequently.[2] Her rebuke of the priest who wanted to exorcise her in Vaucouleurs shows that she recognized proper pastoral behavior, and she was not afraid to reprove a priest who behaved differently.

Ecclesiastically Jeanne was born in the diocese of Toul, the largest of the three bishoprics of Lorraine. She met with diocesan officials when she was summoned, at a date that has not been determined, to answer a charge of refusing to marry a man to whom she was apparently engaged. The ecclesiastical tribunal found her not guilty, for she herself had not consented to her engagement, which presumably had been made by her father. On that occasion she saw the unfinished cathedral of Toul, that she must have seen a second time when she traveled to Nancy to meet the duke of Lorraine, Charles II (1365–1431), called *le Hardi*, "the Bold," for his military feats in German lands.[3]

★

The Church in which Jeanne *la Pucelle* lived and prayed was also the home of the clerics who confronted her in the ecclesiastical tribunal of Rouen, just as it was the home also of those who cautiously supported her in Poitiers. A word should be said about these clerics before we look at the ecclesiastics in Rouen.

Unlike the team gathered by Cauchon, the eighteen or so churchmen in Poitiers were not hostile, even if they seem to have been hesitant before what must have been a new problem for most of them. How were they to judge the claims of a mystic? From what can be gathered about this inquiry in the absence of the acts, most of the participants were from religious orders.[4] In fact the Dominican Seguin Seguin, when he testified at the nullity investigation in May of 1456, named two other Dominicans who had taken part with himself in the examination of Jeanne at Poitiers: Guillaume Aymerie and Pierre Turlure. He even reported that *la Pucelle* had made fun of his provincial pronunciation when she said that her voices spoke French with a better accent than his.[5] It was Guillaume Aymerie who provoked Jeanne's famous retort: "In God's name, the soldiers will fight, and God will give the victory."[6]

The task of the churchmen in Poitiers was strictly theological. In fact, three short documents, all composed, it would seem, by secular clergy, may be said to reflect the mind of the team in Poitiers, even though only the first may have been composed in view of the question that the dauphin had asked: is Jeanne truly sent by God? This is a *dissertatio* by Jacques Gelu, bishop of Embrun. It is addressed to the dauphin. It urges him to accept God's wisdom as it comes to him, even if it be through a young woman dressed in male clothes.[7] The second, and in my estimation the most important of the three documents, is a *De quadam puella* that is included in the works of the theologian Jean Gerson (1363–1429).[8] Although Gerson's authorship has been questioned, I see no persuasive reason to reject it. The value of these pages lies in their argument that Jeanne is a living example of *pietas fidei*. This placed her squarely in the spiritual tradition of Franciscanism, for "piety of faith" was prominent in the works of Saint Bonaventure.[9] Briefly, it meant that her life and her actions promote devotion and pious affection toward God and the things of God. Because of this she ought to be trusted. The third document to be mentioned is a longer treatise attributed to a theologian at the University of Cologne, Henri de Gorcum. This stated the pros and cons regarding *la Pucelle's* divine mission without reaching a personal conclusion.[10]

While the text that Jeanne during her trial called "the book" of Poitiers has disappeared, a short list of conclusions, written in French, has remained. It is not certain that this was actually composed in Poitiers at the end of the examination of Jeanne. It could be a later summary of the conclusion. The text, however, adequately reflects what took place. The clergy in Poitiers asserted that since no one could find anything else in her than "goodness, humility, virginity, devotion, honesty, simplicity,"[11] the king ought to give her a chance to show what she said would be the divine sign of her mission, the lifting of the siege of Orléans.

*

If the theologians in Poitiers may have been biased in favor of a positive recommendation, which they could believe was the dauphin's wish, three years later in Rouen the shadow of the politicians at the service of the English monarchy loomed much larger, along with that of the military men that Jeanne had defeated on the field of battle. With the connivance of the bishop of Beauvais, Pierre Cauchon de Sommièvre (ca. 1371–1442), a few bishops of French sees and many priests were involved in her trial as actors or as witnesses, and some presumably as merely curious visitors.

Pierre Cauchon had personal reasons to oppose Jeanne. With a licentiate in *Decretum* (canon law), this canon of the cathedral of Reims was rector of the University of Paris when the duke of Burgundy Jean *sans Peur* (1371–1419) named him to his advisory council, in 1409. A notorious collector of ecclesiastical benefices, canon of several cathedrals, he was in the pay of both the duke of Burgundy and the king of England. After he attended the council of Constance (1414–18) as a delegate from Burgundy, he took part on behalf of Queen Isabeau in the negotiations that led to the Treaty of Troyes (May 21, 1420), by which an Anglo-French-Burgundian agreement decreed that the yet unborn son of Henry V of England would inherit the crown of France at the death of Charles VI (d. 1422). Bishop of Beauvais in 1420, executor of the will of the late Charles VI, a counselor of Henry VI in 1423, he had a personal stake in frustrating the aims of the discarded dauphin and the Armagnac party. In 1429 he abandoned his episcopal see before the advance of Charles VII, recently crowned in Reims. He then took refuge in Rouen with the prospect of becoming the archbishop, since he was the choice of the duke of Bedford, regent of France for Henry VI.[12] Pope Eugene IV (1431–47), however, only made him bishop of Evreux, in 1432.

Though Cauchon was in his way a clever canonist, his direction of the trial went from bad to worse. The "beautiful trial" he promised began with a legal fiction, the temporary transfer of the castle of Rouen to the diocese of Beauvais, and it ended in a miserable subterfuge when the court declared Jeanne guilty of heresy for wearing male vestments, and of relapse after maneuvering her into an apparent abjuration.

In spite of his high position in the eyes of the duke of Bedford Cauchon had the visible support of very few bishops in his hostility to Jeanne *la Pucelle*. Those who are mentioned in the minutes of the trial were all connected with England, Burgundy, or Normandy. Two were English. Cardinal Henry Beaufort (d. 1447), great uncle of the young King Henry VI, bishop of Winchester and chancellor of England, was in Rouen through the trial. There is no doubt that he kept an eye on the proceedings, and that he was bent on protecting and promoting the interests of his nephew. He came in person to the cemetery of St.-Ouen on May 24, along with William Alnwick (d. 1449), then bishop of Norwich, guardian of the king's private seal. Given the alliance of Church and State, they presumably interpreted the service of the king of England as included in their episcopal duties. One may assume that they were invited to witness the abjuration that was necessary to the condemnation to death of the accused as relapse. Beaufort was also present at the burning.

Like his brother Jean de Luxembourg, by one of whose soldiers Jeanne was captured, Louis de Luxembourg, bishop of Thérouanne, was of the Burgundian party and an active partisan of the double monarchy. On May 23 he attended the reading of the twelve articles of accusation together with another Burgundian, the bishop of Noyon, Jean de Mailly. Both were also present in the cemetery of St.-Ouen and at the burning of Jeanne. By contrast, the absence of Norman bishops is striking. The duke of Bedford ruled Normandy with an iron fist, and it cannot be accident that the native bishops shunned the trial. The two bishops of Normandy who are cited as giving their opinion on the articles of accusation were not native. Zanon of Castiglione, bishop of Lisieux, was Italian, and Philibert de Montjeu, bishop of Coutances, was Burgundian.

★

Secular priests, canonists, or theologians, acted as judges, assessors, or secretaries at the trial. The exact number is not certain, since the acts record no effort to identify every participant and visitor completely. Taking secular and regular clergy together, Vita Sackville-West counted "one cardinal, six bishops, thirty-two doctors of theology, sixteen bachelors of theology, seven doctors of medicine, and one hundred and three other associates. . ."[13] Some attended one or more sessions, out of professional interest, or desire to please the authorities, or simple curiosity. Priests of the diocese of Rouen were understandably in the majority, numbering at least thirty-five. From other dioceses in Normandy there were four priests from Coutances, three from Lisieux, one from Evreux. Five priests were from England, eight from Paris, connected with the university, two from Beauvais, and one each from Reims and Châlons, cities in Burgundian territory. In addition, nine are not clearly identified. Most of those who acted as judges or assessors showed various degrees of hostility through their questions or admonitions. Surely Jeanne was intuitive enough to sense this. The worst case, however, she never detected. She never suspected that Nicolas Loyseleur lied when he pretended to be from Lorraine, and still less that he arranged for two notaries—Guillaume Manchon, who reported the fact at the nullity inquiry,[14] and Boisguillaume—to hear what she said to him in confession.

In assessing the meaning of these numbers one should distinguish between the lower clergy of rural parishes, close to ordinary people, and graduates of the university, learned in law or in theology. Rural clergy would have been the most qualified to understand her demeanor and her reactions, but there is no indication that any such pastor came to see the goings on in Rouen. In terms of human culture, those who were assiduous in attendance had little in common with the young woman from the borders of Lorraine. Whether they truly believed that she was a tool of the devil must have been relatively unimportant to them, as long as they could find some reason for her condemnation. As to those who visited the trial only once, hardly anything can be said. They may have been repelled by what they saw and heard or they were not interested in the doings of the Inquisition and the opinion of the University of Paris.

In fact the canonists who lived in France under English rule were not unanimous in their opinion. When Pierre Cauchon asked Jean Lohier and Nicolas de Houppeville for a judgment, they declared the trial uncanonical and the proceedings improper, and they refused to have anything to do with the court. Lohier left the area, and de Houppeville was imprisoned for a while.[15] Several others asserted later, at the nullity investigation, that they had been subjected to undue pressure to conform to the views of Pierre Cauchon.

That there was uncertainty and some disarray about the trial of Jeanne among the Norman clergy seems undeniable. Outside of the immediate area around Rouen there could have been no exact knowledge of the proceedings. Sympathy or hostility toward the prisoner was inspired by national or dynastic feeling about her cause and career, rather than from an objective acquaintance with her character, her piety, her spiritual experience, the conditions of her detention, and the march of the trial.

★

The religious orders that were represented among the assessors, witnesses, and occasional visitors to the tribunal form a more variegated picture than the diocesan clergy. The crowd of canon lawyers and theologians that Cauchon gathered around him included monks, friars, and a few canons regular.

Jeanne's experience before going to Chinon had given her scant knowledge of monks. Benedictine abbeys were numerous in Lorraine, and especially powerful in the southern part of the duchy, in the Vosges Mountains, where they rejected the authority of the bishop of Toul. There were no monasteries of either men or women, however, in the vicinity of Domremy. On the way to Chinon the soldiers who guided Jeanne elected to spend the first night at St-Urbain-de-Joinville, an old Benedictine monastery founded in the ninth century. This must have been the first time she visited such an institution, in which, according to the Rule of Saint Benedict, "all the guests who arrive must be received like Christ" [*Omnes supervenientes hospites tanquam Christus suscipiantur*].[16] The history of her campaigns does not record other connections with abbeys. Monasticism, female or male, hardly figured in Jeanne's horizon, though admittedly she had met with ecclesiastical judges at the investigation of Poitiers, when the dauphin had her examined theologically by theologians and canonists, under the presidency of the archbishop of Reims, Regnault de Chartres.

In Rouen seven Benedictine abbots and one Cistercian took part in the trial. One of the Benedictines, the abbot of Mont-St-Michel, Robert Jolivet de Montpinchon (d. 1444), presents an intriguing figure.[17] Although his attendance is mentioned only once in the acts, on May 24, he was a determined partisan of the English king. Elected abbot in 1411, he abandoned his abbey in 1419. Mont-St-Michel was in fact a sharp thorn in the English side. Close to the coast near St. Malo, but surrounded by water, heavily fortified, and defended by a small but determined garrison, it was never conquered by the English military. Both friends and foes of Charles VII therefore regarded it as a symbol of resistance, and the people could see it as a sign that Saint Michael, traditional patron saint of the French monarchy since the time of Charlemagne, was opposed to the English cause, a claim that could be supported by Jeanne's designation of the archangel Michael as the chief of her celestial voices. That Montpinchon fled from Mont-St-Michel to English-held Normandy points him out as a determined partisan of the double monarchy. In fact he soon entered the service of the duke of Bedford, who frequently sent him on diplomatic and military missions. All this was done in disregard of major principles of the Rule of Saint Benedict: The abbot is bound to his monastery and its monks (ch. 3); the monks should "make themselves alien to the affairs of the world" (ch. 4); and their "workshop" should be what the rule calls "stability in the community" (*stabilitas in congregatione*, ch. 4).

The abbot of the monastery of the Holy Trinity in Fécamp, Gilles de Duremort (d. 1444), attended most of the time, and he played a dominant role when, on May 29, he answered the question whether Jeanne had relapsed: Indeed she had relapsed, but the articles (*la cédule*) ought to be explained again to her, along with an exhortation based on the word of God, and the officers of secular justice should be invited to treat her with kindness [*. . . ladite Jeanne doit être abandonnée à la justice séculière en priant celle-ci de vouloir agir doucement avec elle*].[18] No fewer than thirty-five lawyers declared themselves in agreement with the abbot.[19] Secretary Jean Massieu declared at the nullity investigation that Duremort "acted from hatred of Jeanne and love of the English more than concern for justice."[20] Pierre Miget, prior of Longueville, is said to have been "most assiduous" in attendance.[21] The abbot of Jumièges, Nicolas Le Roux, was present nine times. One wonders if all these Benedictine monks ever compared the actions and words of the accused with the seventy-four "instruments of good works" that are listed in chapter 4 of the Rule of Saint Benedict.

⋆

From her experience before she was captured near Compiègne, Jeanne had more familiarity with friars than with monks. The preachers who from time to time came to her village from the city of Neufchâteau were *Cordeliers*, a branch of the Franciscans. In fact the *Cordeliers* had a considerable influence in spreading knowledge of the spirituality of the Rhineland mystics. Nunneries were numerous on both sides of the Rhine, and as the cloistered sisters did not normally engage in outward works of mercy, their chaplains nurtured their meditations and prayers with explanations of the spiritual ways of imitation and contemplation of Christ. This was the context of the great Dominican mystics, Meister Eckhart, Johann Tauler, Heinrich Suso, Nicholas of Strasbourg. Eckhart, Tauler, and Suso often preached in convents, promoting a christocentric spirituality that was at the same time simple and oriented to the mystical life.

What happened along the Rhine could have a quick impact in Lorraine, since commercial and cultural exchanges between the duchy and the German lands were just about equal to those with France. Most of Lorraine was still part of the Holy Roman Germanic Empire. The promotion of German or French contacts was largely tied to the marriages of the dukes with German or with French princesses.[22] The duchy itself, French-speaking in its capital city of Nancy and to the West and South, was also German-speaking along its northern border. And it had an extension in Alsace through the Vosges Mountains, around the small town of St-Hippolyte, between Strasbourg and Colmar. These geographic and cultural conditions favored the impact of ideas and devotions coming from the German lands. While Vaucouleurs and Domremy belonged in Jeanne's time to the kingdom of France, the influence of the duchy was considerable. The captain of Vaucouleurs himself, Jean de Baudricourt, though he was at the service of the dauphin, came from the nobility of the duchy.

It was a *Cordelier* of Neufchâteau who, in 1399, translated into French the *Horologium sapientiae*, Suso's Latin version of his major writing, *The Little Book of Eternal Wisdom*. Suso's emphasis on the sufferings of Christ, and Tauler's sermons on the familiarity of the Christian soul with the Eternal Wisdom of God, happened to converge with a central aspect of the Franciscan tradition, to which the preaching of Bernardino of Siena (1380–1444) was, during Jeanne's own life, giving a popular version centered on devotion to the Name of Jesus. The *Cordeliers* of Neufchâteau may well have put some of this emphasis in their sermons. This is the most likely source for Jeanne's wish to have the names of Jesus and Mary inscribed on her standard. That Jeanne gave primary importance to the kingship of Jesus Christ in "the kingdom of Paradise" and on earth came from the same source, her profound conviction of the universal kingship of Christ. It followed that the kingship of Christ must be the sole source of the legitimacy of human kings. And if Charles VII, rather than the English child Henry VI, was the legitimate king intended by God, this simply reflected the view that the recent treaty of Troyes, that had been made possible by the madness of Charles VI, was illegitimate. This was Jeannes's whole case against the duke of Bedford, so-called regent of France.

It was also a *Cordelier* that the city of Troyes sent to Jeanne when the dauphin and his army arrived before its walls on the way to the coronation. Friar Richard "made the sign of the cross and threw holy water." Jeanne's response, "Approach boldly; I will not fly away!" [*Répond que ceux de la ville de Troyes, comme elle pense, l'envoièrent devers elle, disans que ils doubtaient que ce ne feust pas chose de par Dieu. Et quand il vint devers elle, en apprchant, il faisoit signe de la croix et gectait eaue benoicte. Et elle lui dist: Approuchez hardiment, je ne m'envouleray pas*][23] is indicative both of her understanding that he feared she might be a witch and of her sense of humor. It also denotes a certain tolerance of the friar's antics, though, as she testified, she had never met him before.

In the trial itself five Franciscans attended in part or in whole. Jacques Guesdon, guardian of the friary in Rouen, doctor in theology, was assiduously present, the only one from his house. One may presume that the regulars in Rouen were under a certain amount of pressure from the chapter and from Pierre Cauchon to send delegates to the castle during the trial. That only the guardian attended may denote some reluctance on their part to collaborate with the domination of the duke of Bedford. A few other Franciscans are mentioned in the minutes. Gérard Feuillet, also a doctor in theology, was part of the delegation of the University of Paris; his name does not recur after April 18. Jean Fouchier, doctor in theology, himself a Norman, was present several times in May. Neither one took an active part in the interrogations. Jacques le Tessier asked a few questions, and he worked with Nicolas Midi at the redaction of the twelve articles of indictment. Jean de Nibat, who had come from Paris, was present about fifteen times, and at the end he voted to abandon Jeanne to the secular arm. In addition, an Italian, Giovanni da Fano, came only on one day, February 27, presumably out of curiosity. On the whole, therefore, the Franciscans had little to do with the trial. One cannot rule out that Jeanne's familiarity with the *Cordeliers* of Neufchâteau was known in Rouen. And in any case there was little in the Franciscan outlook and way of life that could have prompted them to give any weight to a strict adherence to the rules of canon law as these were interpreted by Bishop Cauchon.

⋆

The Dominicans were more prominent at the trial of Jeanne, be it only because the Order of Preachers was heavily involved in the Inquisition. Their presence, however, was notoriously ambiguous. The Grand Inquisitor of France, Jean Graverent, chose not to attend. Instead, he delegated his colleague, Jean Le Maistre, Inquisitor in Rouen. Le Maistre followed orders; but he attended reluctantly and he took no part in the questioning. His assistant, Jean Duval, was present only once. Admittedly, on the feast of Saint Martin in 1431 Graverent preached a sermon that disparaged Jeanne in the church of St-Martin-des-Champs in Paris.[24] Saint Martin of Tours was, at the time, popularly treated as a "patron saint" of the French nation. The irony, which of course no one in the fifteenth century could foresee, is that in 1920 Jeanne was given the same title and function by the pope who canonized her, Benedict XV.

The most noted Dominicans at the trial were Martin Ladvenu and Isambart de la Pierre, not only because they were frequently present, especially Isambart, but also because they assisted Jeanne on her last day, when Ladvenu was authorized to hear her confession and bring her holy communion. Given the sympathy with Jeanne that seems implied in their assistance of her, it remains surprising that the two of them generally followed the general trend of the participants. When all seemed lost for the accused, they voted in favor of abandoning Jeanne to the secular arm, which was equivalent to death by fire.

Another Dominican, Jean Toutmouillé, who never attended the sessions of the tribunal, accompanied Ladvenu when Jeanne received communion on the morning of her death. Guillaume Adélie, master regent of theology in Paris, came on April 18, halfway through the proceedings, and he was among those who, on that day, exhorted Jeanne to submit to the Church Militant.[25] Jean or Raoul Sylvestris (rendered in French as Le Sauvage), bachelor in theology, also a Friar preacher, is mentioned on April 21 as having spoken in favor of sending the acts of the trial, and the decision, to the Apostolic See "for the peace of the greater number of consciences,"[26] although, on May 19, he was willing to trust the judges "as to the way to proceed ulteriorly."

Marie-Dominique Chapotin was undoubtedly correct when he argued against the contention that Dominicans plotted the downfall of Jeanne d'Arc with Bishop Cauchon.[27] The one Dominican who testified at the nullity trial was precisely Seguin Seguin, who had previously examined her orthodoxy in Poitiers. If the Friars–preachers were clearly not eager to support the condemnation of Jeanne, they may have been influenced in this by the spiritual freedom that was one of their characteristics. Unlike most religious communities, and notably the Benedictine monasteries, the Dominican Order did not center its spirituality on following a Rule or a set of Constitutions. The Rule was that of Saint Augustine, which puts the stress on "unanimity of hearts." And the vows were reduced to one: obedience to the prior, that is, to the successor of Saint Dominic. Precisely, the main concern of Dominic de Guzman, when he founded the Order in 1216, was to orient the struggle against the Albigensians away from coercion by force toward persuasion by preaching. In Rouen, except for the attempts of Cauchon to have Jeanne wear feminine clothing, there was scant effort to be persuasive in talking with Jeanne. Coercion was the rule in the prison where she was kept in chains.[28]

It should be noted, though there is no need to dwell on the point, that Friars–preachers were active in the nullity investigation. The Dominican Jean Bréhal, Grand Inquisitor of France, was in the cathedral of Paris in 1455 when the mother of Jeanne *la Pucelle* presented her petition against the condemnation of her daughter.

★

Besides Friars-preachers and Friars minor, two Carmelites attended the proceedings in Rouen. Pierre Houdenc, the prior of the local Carmelite friary, for which the duke of Bedford had a special liking,[29] came ten times and was present at the burning of Jeanne. Guillaume Le Boucher, from the same community, attended most of the sessions, took part in the questioning, and he adhered to the opinion of the abbot of Fécamp.

Of the Hermits of Saint Augustine, there were only two. Jean Lefèvre, a professor in Paris, attended the trial from February 21 to May 29. Though he had been a devoted partisan of Henry VI, he became active in the nullity investigation. Jean Le Vautier was present twice, February 27 and March 1. Another Augustinian was Guillaume Le Bourg, prior of the Canons Regular of Saint Lô in Rouen. He came only a few times, and he was at the cemetery of St.-Ouen on March 23. It may not be accidental that there were so few Augustinians, for it was known that Jeanne's chaplain, Jean Pasquerel, was attached to the Hermits' house in Tours. Pasquerel had met Jeanne's mother at the pilgrimage of Notre-Dame du Puy-en-Velay, where she had traveled to invoke the Virgin. He became Jeanne's chaplain and confessor when the expedition to lift the siege of Orléans was being prepared in Tours. He was to testify about the holiness of Jeanne and the authenticity of her mission, when the nullity enquiry was under way.

It is reasonable to assume that Isabelle Romée was no stranger to the interest that Pasquerel took in her daughter. He accompanied her through her career, from Chinon to Orléans and to Reims, and in her subsequent expeditions. That he was captured with her near Compiègne shows that he did not hesitate to stay by her side in battle. It would have been easy for the bishop of Beauvais to have Jean Pasquerel summoned to Rouen as a witness if he was looking for the truth about Jeanne. Given the purpose of the trial, however, it was politically correct not to secure the chaplain's testimony. The Augustinian communities in Normandy, which mostly stood away from the proceedings in Rouen, must have detected the real intentions of the bishop of Beauvais.

That there was curiosity about the trial is evident, and it is likely that some of the religious communities in Rouen were pressured into sending in a few of their members. All the friars were preachers, familiar with the quality of Christian life in the lower classes, but better trained than the rural diocesan clergy, while the wealth of the abbeys forced the abbots to frequent the lay and military authorities in their areas. Jeanne belonged only to the ordinary peasantry, and, furthermore, she came from the margins of the Kingdom. (Journeying to Chinon meant, for her, "going into France.") In the aristocratic circles around the duke of Bedford, "regent of France" for Henry VI, such a person was of little value. And the clergy in high positions could presumably control their conscience if they could find an objective reason to please the duke and have Jeanne burnt. The bishop of Beauvais tried hard to provide such a reason.

★

The attitude of the clergy before Jeanne d'Arc's claims to angelic visions and a divine mission should be seen against the backdrop of the spiritual movements of the fifteenth century. This was the time when the *béguines*, lay women inspired by *devotio moderna*, began to live in loose communities;[30] while they were not established in Lorraine they were numerous down the Rhine in the Netherlands. The Friends of God, an informal and chiefly lay movement in the Rhineland dedicated to spiritual friendship with God and with one another, had long been dominated by a merchant of Strasbourg, Rulman Merswin (1307–82), whose successor, Nicholas of Basle, had been burnt as a heretic in 1410. In small conventicles designated as the Brethren of the Free Spirit[31] there was a resurgence of the standard medieval heresy, which tended to oppose the institutional church to a spiritual church that could be experienced in small like-minded groups. Lorraine was not immune to such influences.[32] Flagellants had crisscrossed the area during the plagues of 1348 and 1369. In 1374 the city of Metz was agitated by the Saint Vitus dance, a hysterical reaction to the plague. Several heretics called Turlupins were burnt under Duke Jean I (d. 1390), who, however, was lenient toward the Waldensians, since he ordered a French translation of the Bible to be made for their use. In 1425 an Augustinian, Jean Chatelin, was burnt as a heretic in Metz, though his heresy has not been identified.

When her judges interrogated Jeanne about "the article *Unam sanctam*" and the Church Militant, they were testing her kinship with the Free Spirits. There is in fact a certain kinship between her and Marguerite Porete (ca. 1250–1310), a *béguine* from the Lowlands, who made a distinction between *Sainte-Eglise-la Petite*, governed by reason, and *Sainte-Eglise-la Grande*, governed by the theological virtues, though she also affirmed their identity.[33] Jeanne, when her time came, was in a similar predicament. She could not express herself scholastically. Like Marguerite she always stood by what she said. But she was not interested in explaining how the Church Militant differs from the Church Triumphant. As proof of her obedience to the Church Militant she appealed to the pope. Jeanne's answers, however, counted for little when they could not be used against her. The nature of the Church Militant provided the twelfth topic of accusation. Canon Pierre Maurice told her, on May 23, in the last "charitable exhortation" before sentencing: "As to this article, the learned clerks esteem that you are schismatic, evil-thinking concerning the unity and authority of the Church, apostate and, until this day in which we are, heretic in the faith with obstinacy."[34]

★

The influence of the clergy, and especially of the Friars, on Jeanne *la Pucelle* and her spirituality is evidently inseparable from the spiritual movements that were agitating the church of her time, notably in the wide valley of the Rhine, that is, the Rhine itself and the rivers that flow into it. The Meuse, on whose left bank Jeanne was born and raised, is one of the most prominent of these. The flow of the waters from South to North presents a reverse image of the flow of ideas from North to South. The spread of *devotio moderna*, born in the Netherlands at the end of the fourteenth century, is well documented. The modern devotion, and its emphasis on nonclerical holiness, reached the lands of Lorraine in the course of the fifteenth century.[35] The highlights of Jeanne's spiritual life are in harmony with the simplicity that is recommended in the *Imitatio*. Desire for heaven (bk. III, 48.1), purity of intention and simplicity of affection (bk. III, 54), an exclusive devotion to the will of God (bk. III, 10), all of this nourished by frequent interior dialogues with the Lord (bk. II, 1), were precisely the chief marks of Jeanne's life and prayer.

The *Imitation of Christ* does not encourage pilgrimages since it says explicitly: "They who travel a lot seldom become holy" [*Qui multum peregrinantur raro sanctificantur*].[36] Jeanne, however, whose sense of pilgrimage came from her mother, was a pilgrim in more senses than one. She began as a child with regular visits to the small chapel of Notre-Dame de Bermont, in the woods, some two kilometers north of Domremy. On the way to Nancy she made a sizable detour to the shrine of Ste-Nicolas-de-Port. As she went to Chinon she stopped at Ste-Catherine de Fierbois. In addition, the piety that Jeanne promoted in the army, especially on the way to Orléans, had recognizable features of a pilgrim's piety. Pasquerel testified that she ordered the priests to gather "twice a day, morning and evening" in order to sing "antiphons and hymns of Our Lady," along with "soldiers who had been to confession."[37] A procession is itself a form of pilgrimage, adapted to the possibilities of those who cannot afford a long journey to a distant shrine. Indeed, that the occupants of the English forts refrained from attacking the Armagnac soldiery on the way to Orléans could be due in part to their astonishment at the sight of the priestly procession that passed within striking distance.

Another symbol of Jeanne's involvement with the spiritual hierarchy was her significant gesture in the church of the abbey of St-Denis, where, on September 11 or 12, 1429, after the failure of the assault on the capital city, Jeanne left a suit of armor and a sword. She did so, as she said, "out of devotion, as is customary with soldiers when they have been wounded" [*Respond que ce fust par dévocion; ainsi que il est accoustumé par les gens d'armes, quant ils sont bleciés*].[38] The action was also homage to Saint Denis, the first bishop of Paris, who was presumed to be the Areopagyte, and the patron saint, along with the archangel Michael, of the French monarchy. Jeanne added: *et pour ce qu'elle avait été blecée devant Paris, les offrit à Saint Denis, pour ce que c'est le cry de France*.[39] The traditional war cry of the French soldiers under the monarchy—*Montjoie Saint-Denis*—was at the same time an acclamation and an invocation.[40] Because Jeanne was aware of the king's reluctance to pursue the fighting, it may have also been for her a prayer for assistance. And since Jeanne had already fulfilled her central mission, it also expressed thanksgiving, and possibly a reluctant admission that her career was practically over. As he declared at the nullity trial, the duke of Alençon heard "Jeanne tell the king, I shall last one year, not much more" [*Audivitque aliquando dictam Johannam dicentem regi quod ipsa Johanna duraret per annum et non multum plus*].[41] In September 1429, more than halfway through the foreseen year of her availability, Jeanne's recent wound reminding her of her mortality, her gift to the church of St-Denis could also be symbolic of the coming end of her endeavors for the king.

Rouen, where Jeanne was led as a prisoner of the duke of Bedford, was not notable as a place of pilgrimage. It became one as that was where Jeanne made her final pilgrimage to Calvary, ultimately a more awesome and more inspiring event than any pilgrimage she could have made to the holy shrines of Christendom.

★

Jeanne's relations with the institutional hierarchy of bishops, priests, and deacons were ambiguous since many in the secular and regular clergy were hostile to her cause and to her, though others admired and supported her. There has always been in the Church, however, besides the magisterial hierarchy, a charismatic hierarchy of holiness, a sort of "invisible monastery" composed of all the saints and holy figures of a given period. Jeanne was of course familiar with the archangel Michael and the saints Catherine and Margaret as she could see their pictures and statues. She heard their voices; she saw their lights. And she also found comfort in the knowledge that, as she assured the dauphin, the former sovereigns "St. Louis and Charlemagne are kneeling before Him and saying a prayer for you" ["*Je vous dis que Dieu a pitié de vous, de vostre royaume, et de vostre peuple; car saict Louys et Charlemagne sont à genoux devant luy, en faisant une prière pour vous*"].[42]

★

This survey confirms what I have described elsewhere as Jeanne's spiritual way.[43] The girl from Domremy is unique, not only because of the originality of her life's work,[44] but also because her spiritual way cannot be adequately explained by precedents she might have known, teachings she might have received, examples she might have followed, or convictions she might have absorbed from her background and her family. All attempts to classify her fail. She was neither a witch, nor a sick or mentally disturbed young woman. She did not fit the conventional image of a seer. That shepherds and shepherdesses have been prone to visions is irrelevant in her case, since, despite her iconography and some of her biographers, she herself denied being a shepherdess. All that emerges from her well-documented childhood is that she was an illiterate girl helping her mother with the house chores, playing with other children, assiduous in church, and often seeking solitude for prayer. She became a warrior, but a most unusual one, who did not use her sword or her hatchet in battle, who prayed for her enemies, and who tried to help the wounded among them.[45] As a prisoner she complained about the conditions of her incarceration, but the only person she got impatient with in the court proceedings was the bishop who was paid to build a canonical case so that he could bring her to death by fire.

In the spiritual milieu of the fifteenth century Jeanne stands out against the background of a lay holiness that was promoted in various ways by the friars, the *béguines*, and the adepts of the modern devotion. No one else approaches her conjunction of total devotion to God and the King of Paradise with total self-sacrifice in the cause of justice and of the proper order of society as it was conceived in her time. While she had the devoted support of some priests, and her chaplain Jean Pasquerel was exemplary in his ministry to her, she mainly suffered from the suspicions of the clergy, especially in the last year of her life. The official acknowledgment of her holiness, when it finally came, was long overdue.

Notes

1. Domremy should be spelled with no accent; this fits the standard local pronunciation and the spelling of the classics, Quicherat, Tisset; the accent (Domrémy) derives from mapmakers who have ignored the local pronunciation and made the wrong choice between two accepted forms of the name, Remy or Rémy.
2. According to Françoise Meltzer, Jeanne d'Arc "never took catechism" (*For Fear of the Fire. Joan of Arc and the Limits of Subjectivity* [Chicago: University of Chicago Press, 2001], p. 80); there is no way to know for certain if some sort of catechism was taught to children in her parish, but one cannot assume there was no such teaching; in any case an elementary catechism would not contradict Jeanne's statement that her mother taught her what she knew of religion.

3. Jeanne was accompanied by the soldier Jean de Nouillonpont (alias, de Metz) as far as Toul; they must have crossed into the duchy east of Vaucouleurs going toward Blénod, and then turned north toward Toul; she then went east toward Nancy, possibly with her cousin Durand Laxard; since on the way she visited the shrine of Saint Nicolas, the patron of Lorraine, at St-Nicolas-de-Port, which is on the east of Nancy, she must have followed the Moselle river to Pont-St-Vincent and then passed through the villages of Lupcourt and Ville-en-Vermois on the way to St-Nicolas-de-Port.
4. Deborah A. Fraioli, *Joan of Arc: The Early Debate* (Woodbridge: Boydell Press, 2000), p. 47.
5. Jules Quicherat, *Procès de condamnation et de réhabilitation de Jeanne d'Arc dite la Pucelle*, 5 vols. (Paris, 1849), 3:202–204.
6. Quicherat 3:204.
7. For an extensive discussion of this text see Fraioli, *Joan of Arc*, pp. 87–102.
8. Quicherat 3:298–306.
9. Quicherat 3:300; on the piety of faith, see Tavard, *Transiency and Permanence. The Nature of Theology According to St. Bonaventure* (St. Bonaventure: Franciscan Institute, 1974), pp. 203–211.
10. Quicherat 3:411–21.
11. Quicherat 3:302; English translation in Fraioli, *Joan of Arc*, pp. 206–207.
12. Tisset 2:388–91.
13. V. Sackville West, *Saint Joan of Arc* (New York: Literary Guild, 1931), pp. 288–89.
14. Quicherat 2:10–11.
15. Quicherat, *Procès*, on Lohier, 2:138; 3:50; on de Houppeville, 2:354; 3:50, 139, 163, 183, etc.
16. Rule of Saint Benedict, ch. 53.
17. Tisset 2:383–425.
18. Tisset 2:350.
19. Tisset 3:322.
20. Tisset 2:398.
21. Miget is said to have been "*très assidu au procès*" (Tisset 2:418).
22. Since Duke Raoul had been killed at the battle of Crécy (1346) the dukes of Lorraine kept their distance from the quarrels between the French and the English, and they entertained good relations with the dukes of Burgundy, who had to cross the duchy to reach their possessions in the Lowlands. In 1407 at Champigneulles near Nancy, Charles II had repelled Louis d'Orléans who was trying to gain territories in Lorraine and Luxemburg; in 1412 he had rejected a judgment of the Parliament of Paris that interfered with his sovereignty over Neufchâteau; in 1418 he had been made *connétable* by the duke of Burgundy Jean *sans Peur* (1371–1419). Being himself half-German (his mother was Sophia von Wurtemberg), he had fought in Lithuania, and also in Hungary against the Turks, by the side of his German relatives. In spite of his ties with Germany and his friendship with Burgundy, he requested the governor of Vaucouleurs to have Jeanne visit Nancy before going into France.

23. Tisset 1:98.
24. *Journal d'un bourgeois de Paris*, 1405–49, ed. Alexandre Tuetey (Paris, 1881), pp. 270–71; in this sermon Graverent also alluded to Catherine de la Rochelle, Péronne, and Friar Richard.
25. Tisset 1:332.
26. Quicherat 1:370–74.
27. Marie-Dominique Chapotin, *La Guerre de cent ans, Jeanne d'Arc, et les Dominicains* (Paris, 1889), pp. 124–59.
28. As he defended the friars–preachers, Chapotin put a large part of the blame on some of the friars minor; he thus contradicted the revisionist view of *la Pucelle*, according to which the girl who was putatively from Domremy, but was really Claude des Armoises (her married name), had been trained for her mission by high-ranking members of the Poor Clares (Saint Colette) and of the Third Order.
29. Tisset 2:405.
30. Jill Raitt, ed., *Christian Spirituality. High Middle Ages and Reformation* (New York: Crossroad, 1987), p. 124; the *béguines*' male counterparts were called *bėghards*.
31. Ronald Knox, *Enthusiasm* (Oxford: Clarendon Press, 1950), pp. 92–116; Leszek Kolakowski, *Chrétiens sans églises. La conscience religieuse et le lien confessionnel au XVIIe siècle* (Paris: Gallimard, 1969).
32. Michel Parisse, ed., *Histoire de la Lorraine* (Paris: Privat, 1978), pp. 220–23.
33. She wrote *The Mirror of Simple Souls* around 1290: Max Huot de Longchamp, ed., *Marguerite Porete. Le Miroir des âmes simples et anéanties* (Paris: Albin Michel, 1997); Marguerite, who was not trained in the scholastic language, stood by what she had written, and she died by fire on June 1, 1310, even though three theologians, among whom a former regent at the faculty of theology of Paris, Godefroid de Fontaines (d. 1306), had testified to her orthodoxy.
34. Tisset 2:380.
35. A copy of *Imitatio Christi* was acquired for a library in the city of Verdun toward the end of the century (Parisse, *Histoire*, p. 223).
36. *Imitatio Christi*, part I, ch. 23, n. 24.
37. Quicherat 3:104–105.
38. Tisset 1:170; according to Georges Bordonove, the armor she offered to Saint Denis had been taken from a prisoner (*Jeanne d'Arc et la guerre de cent ans* [Paris: Pygmalion, 1994], p. 185).
39. Tisset 1:171.
40. A *montjoie* is an informal heap of stones, erected as a signpost or in commemoration of some happening; *Montjoie Saint-Denis* would connote a celebration of Saint-Denis, the first bishop of Paris, as a heavenly protector of France.
41. Quicherat 3:. 99.
42. *Chronique de la Pucelle. . .Réimpression de l'édition de Vallet de Viriville* (Caen: Paradigmes, 1992), p. 274.

43. Tavard, "The Spirituality of St. Joan" in *Joan of Arc at the University*, ed. Mary Elizabeth Tallon (Milwaukee: Marquette University Press, 1997), pp. 43–58; *The Spiritual Way of St. Jeanne d'Arc* (Collegeville: Liturgical Press, 1998).
44. The poet Villon, in 1461, summed up a simple, nontheological view of Jeanne that must have been common among the people as he evoked the passing of time in his *Ballade des dames du temps jadis*: "And Jeanne the good Lorrainer / Whom English burnt in Rouen, / Where are the snows of former times?" (*Et Jeanne la bonne Lorraine / Qu'Anglais brulèrent à Rouen, / Mais où sont les neiges d'antan?*).
45. Tavard, "St. Jeanne d'Arc as Peacemaker" (*Dialogue and Alliance* [Spring/Summer 1998]: 2.1, 75–89).

CHAPTER 7

GERSON JUDGING WOMEN OF SPIRIT: FROM FEMALE MYSTICS TO JOAN OF ARC

Deborah Fraioli

This chapter proposes that the cliché that Gerson was hostile to high-profile female mystics but made a significant exception for Joan of Arc is inaccurate on both counts.

By reexamining the prevailing opinion that Gerson was hostile or skeptical toward female visionaries but made an unusual exception for Joan of Arc, I hope to challenge the legitimacy of this view and show in what ways it can be found wanting.[1] The extremely shaky foundations on which this two-part notion is based, which have gone largely unexamined by purveyors of the cliché, will be explored in what follows. It is principally the first part of the proposition that will be examined here. My purpose is to argue that the practice of discernment, in which Gerson was a renowned expert, and perhaps our own errors in interpreting the documents, not hatred either of women or of direct spiritual inspiration, are responsible for his alleged intolerance of the female visionary experience. Logically, scholars have deduced Gerson's hostility to lay and feminine spiritual inspiration from his works on the discernment of spirits, since the very object of the process of discernment is to make pronouncements, either of fraudulence or genuine inspiration, in cases where direct experience of God is claimed. Thus my remarks address the four principal works on discernment by the chancellor: *De distinctione verarum visionum a falsis* (1401), *Letter to Jean Morel* or *Judicium de vita sanctae Erminae* (pre-1401?),

De probatione spirituum (1415), and *De examinatione doctrinarum* (1423), although I will briefly comment on the plausibility of Gerson's endorsement of Joan of Arc by reference to these tracts.

Already in *De distinctione verarum visionum a falsis*, Gerson's first formal treatise on the discernment of spirits, he appears to veer from the gender neutral tradition of discernment literature by including two scathing critiques of female mystics, the woman from Arras and Marie de Valenciennes.[2] Few who read this treatise will forget either the vivid depiction of the Arras woman's frantic cycle of fasting and gorging, or the cold assessment of her "arrogance" and "obstinacy," which prompted Gerson's brusque departure from her. Nor does he hide his contempt for Marie de Valenciennes on whom he places the stiff charge of confusing carnal and divine love. Gerson derides her erroneous belief that a person in a high state of devotion was "released from all the precepts of the law" and might follow the precept: "Have charity, and do what you want."[3] He condemns her for "[thinking] she would always enjoy God. . .however far she was from following God's precepts."[4] This, for Gerson, is the lethal snare for virtue engendered by passionate feeling, dangerously documented in the Beghard and Beguine movements.[5] Gerson includes in his series of deluded women a contemporary whom he deems "out of her mind," and women known as *agapetae*, already made memorable by the satire of Jerome, who were misguided religious living in unsafe familiarity with men.[6]

But the very treatise that displays these female *exempla in malo*, in descriptions permeated with the glib misogynist rhetoric of the church fathers, more importantly gives an intricate and sophisticated justification of the *need*, as well as a careful demonstration of the *method*, for distinguishing true inspiration from false. To Gerson, the scandal of the charlatan seer endangers the spiritual well-being of individual believers.[7] Thus it is not cruelty, prejudice, or the desire to oppress, which drives the process of the discernment of spirits, but the need to try to recognize what God means (or has done) for man. The hand of God is not shortened that it cannot save (Isaiah 59:1), but the true must be distinguished from the false (1 John 4:1). Those who intentionally deceive, as well as the merely deluded, must be dismissed in order to provide better recognition of genuine exemplars.

For Gerson the women described in this treatise, who fail to fulfill discernment imperatives by not seeking counsel, not controlling impetuosity and temptation, or not establishing the necessity of their callings, are removed from genuine exemplarity. This rejection, based on legitimate principle, must be separated from the offense felt by the modern observer at Gerson's ridicule of female asceticism, especially inasmuch as Jerome, a possible model, used antifeminist satire to encourage (male) asceticism, not to discourage it.[8] In *De distinctione verarum visionum a falsis*, Gerson's debunking of several false cases of female mysticism sets the stage for demonstrating the difficulty of skillfully handling discernment cases, given that in the exercise of their pastoral responsibility the examining clergy must require of the visionary "something. . .beyond the normal course of nature," or something supernatural.[9] Gerson recognizes that priests can ultimately not have absolute certitude regarding their own pronouncements since that would obviate man's need for faith.[10] Thus the necessity of beginning any case with an appreciable measure of doubt regarding the candidate is wholly appropriate. Despite focus by modern critics on the number of female mystics seemingly discredited by Gerson in this treatise, the errors of *men* are not shielded from exposure. In fact, Gerson points a finger at the delusions of two men, each of whom believed he was to become pope, and perhaps also at himself.[11] The satiric portrait of the theology student—neither lay nor female—who carouses, and believes religious devotion to be "a fable or a bore," is every bit as caustic as that of the woman from Arras.[12] Finally, Gerson does not omit female *exempla in bono*. In addition to the prominent example of the Virgin Mary, he includes a female counterexample to the *agapetae*, the devout Angela of Foligno, who knew to mistrust love.[13]

Thus in *De distinctione verarum visionum a falsis*, Gerson justifies the severity of the discernment procedure (which might be mistaken for hostility) in view of the remarkably exacting nature of evaluating self-proclaimed inspiration. But he also uses this treatise of 1401, originally a set of university lectures on the gospel of Mark,[14] to uphold the legitimacy of individual (including female) spiritual experience. Implicit in the winnowing of the false from the true is the affirmation that genuine inspiration exists. In thinking that there is "no valid basis for hope in holy revelations," he avers, the cleric commits a worse fault than in being overconfident of his own intellectual powers of discernment.[15] According to Gerson, the certainty of the mystical experience is known to the individual who encounters it. This is the scattering of the darkness of doubt of which Gerson speaks. The chancellor states that the recipient "in no way can be in doubt about it" and it must "be perceived as something clearly coming from God," that is, to the person himself.[16] Struggling to describe the ineffability of the genuine prophetic revelation, Gerson speaks of a taste, a "kind of breath and odor within [one]self,"[17] and later in the treatise of "a great calm," a kind of humble surrender.[18] The audacity of Gerson's acceptance of private inspiration is marked by his avowal that "perhaps the worldly wise will not believe that such illuminations take place."[19] This is very favorable material for female mystics and lay spirituality in general, given the experiential nature of such revelations.[20] And indeed, Gerson reports that Augustine's mother Monica was able to distinguish truth from falsehood among her own visions, adding: "Why then should someone be surprised if a universal rule or certain and infallible teaching cannot be handed over on this matter. . . .This is more a matter of experience. . .than a question of some technique."[21] Based on the favorable climate established in these remarks, the modern reader might even be led to wonder to what degree this treatise could have opened the floodgates to female mysticism, rather than the reverse.

A third and final point about *De distinctione verarum visionum a falsis* further removes the label "hostile to women" from the treatise. This is its similarity to the *Poitiers Conclusions*, the official document by which Joan of Arc was granted provisional authorization to embark on her mission.[22] Nothing places Gerson at the hearings held at Poitiers in March 1429, but his friends and colleagues, who gathered at the dauphin's request to probe the case of the Maid, appear to have drawn on (or made decisions consonant with) at least four principles from this work of 1401: first, that the prelates not reject a claim out of hand ("ought not to turn away nor reject the Maid who says she is sent by God");[23] second, that they not believe too readily ("nor should he believe in her immediately or lightly");[24] third, that the revelations serve a useful purpose ("given [Charles's] necessity and that of his kingdom [and]. . .the Maid. . .sent. . .for his succor");[25] and finally, that one should await the outcome before passing final judgment ("the king. . . .must not prevent her from going to Orléans. . . .For doubting or dismissing her [before she could show her sign]. . .would be to repel the Holy Spirit").[26] In this instance, Gerson's treatise, which has been identified as hostile to women, appears to have provided substance and surety for the initial approval of the Maid.

The second work under discussion here, but likely to have been Gerson's first writing on the discernment of spirits, is Gerson's *Letter to Jean Morel or Judicium*,[27] written roughly contemporaneously with *De distinctione verarum visionum a falsis*.[28] It was composed as a letter rather than a formal treatise, and although invoking broad principles, it addresses the specific case of the visions of the widow Ermine of Reims. The recipient is Jean Morel, a prior of Reims, a locale from which Gerson drew his modest origins and had maintained close ties. The letter's purpose is circumscribed and fairly personal. Gerson is finally submitting to Morel's persistent requests, over an unspecified period of time, that he examine and pronounce upon the visions of the simple and pious Ermine. She had died in Reims in 1396 and her confessor had subsequently transcribed her visions.

The date of the letter has been disputed, but the editor and translator of the book of Ermine's visions, Claude Arnaud-Gillet, convincingly overturns Palémon Glorieux's speculative dating of 1408,[29] suggesting a date of approximately 1401.[30] On the basis of doctrine, the letter aligns itself naturally with Gerson's period of concern with popular devotion, the era of much of his writing addressed to his sisters on the virtues of *les simples gens*,[31] for it validates the visions of an ordinary woman, and seeks "to close the mouths of those who want to undermine the faith of the simple."[32] Moreover, in the *Letter to Jean Morel* Gerson's discernment criteria are not supported by the full array of traditional biblical citations, perhaps suggesting a lack of familiarity at this time with other discernment literature, nor is his doctrine fully developed. In *De distinctione verarum visionum a falsis*, Gerson seems conversant with other works on discernment,[33] but this is not generally verifiable in the Morel letter.[34] By the time he wrote *De probatione spirituum*, at the Council of Constance in 1415, he had largely mastered the literature yet regretted not having at hand "several works" on discernment, which he had previously read. But he may have begun studying the tracts of Henry of Langenstein, Pierre d'Ailly, and Alfonso of Jaén as early as the late 1390s, as well as a number of works by the church fathers, of whom Cassian was currently very popular. By 1401 Gerson would cite the bedrock biblical citations 1 John 4:1 and 2 Cor. 11:14, so essential to the discernment tracts of Alphonso of Jaén (or Pecha) and Henry of Langenstein (or Hesse). But the *Letter to Jean Morel* offers no hint as yet of the influence of men like Henry of Langenstein, to whom he directly alludes in *De probatione spirituum*, and whom he had discovered at least by the time of the Council of Constance in 1415.[35] Reference is lacking in the *Letter to Jean Morel* to such basic tenets of discernment as looking at the end to which a vision tends, or requiring an aspect of necessity of a revelation. And rather than support his premises primarily with theological arguments, Gerson invokes a "natural sense of equity" [*naturalis aequitas*], the norms of political discourse [*politica conversatio*], natural law [*juris naturalis*], and civil conduct [*civiliter vivens*] as reasons why Ermine can be believed.[36] Moreover, Gerson never refers Jean Morel to *De distinctione verarum visionum a falsis*, plausibly suggesting that the treatise had not yet been composed. In fact, the treatise of 1401 may be the fulfillment of a half-promise made by Gerson at the end of the *Letter to Jean Morel* to write on discernment at greater length at a future date.[37] A close examination of the differences between these nearly contemporary texts could conceivably substantiate the chronological priority of the *Letter to Jean Morel.*

Gerson displayed an understandable reticence toward Ermine's phantasmagoric visions, as seen by his admonition that the book not be generally distributed, but only to "those who it is likely will be edified by it."[38] In other words, Gerson is apt to have approved the book, both as a favor to a friend and to avert the scandal of overturning the ostensibly harmless cult of a pious local citizen. Admitting these circumstances, it is nonetheless true that Gerson here fully acknowledges the spiritual experience of a simple person and a woman, a clear precedent, if this opinion was not later retracted, for the commissioners who faced a similar question about Joan of Arc in 1429.[39] The letter conforms to Gerson's understanding of a basic principle of discernment but in Ermine's case marshals only rudimentary doctrinal evidence—that the spirit can reside in the most unlikely people and that direct spiritual experience is not just the prerogative of the clergy.[40] He has also scrutinized the book "without any rash attachment" and has subjected it to examination "as long and as much as I thought required."[41] Allusion is even made to "submitting the matter to the judgment of the Holy See."[42] This is evidence of typically Gersonian caution, which nonetheless affirms the miraculous, a heedfulness also subscribed to by the commission at Poitiers. As noted by Alexandra Barratt, Gerson "regarded the mystical way as an option to all. . .in spite of the possible hazards of heresy and delusion."[43] The hazards were precisely what made scrupulous examination in such cases compulsory.

Gerson takes the case of Ermine to be worthy of pious belief, but not a requirement for salvation. Nor must all of the facts written down have necessarily occurred as recounted.[44] But he criticizes any instant dissenter against Ermine's visions as "rash and crude."[45] We cannot, he asserts, doggedly attack "someone who wants to be believed in his [or her] assertions, especially when. . .strengthened by an oath."[46] To do so is to violate both divine and natural law: divine law by breaking the "golden rule" (Tobit 4:16), and natural law because "no one who lives in a civilized manner should stubbornly refuse to believe what another person says when no falsity or clear breach of truth is apparent."[47] This injunction to believe someone who wants to be believed, in the absence of apparent evil, finds near duplication in the recommendation of the *Poitiers Conclusions* that the king believe Joan of Arc rather than "[doubt] her without appearance of evil."[48] Furthermore, several biblical principles affirmed in this letter (Isaiah 59:1; 1 Cor. 12:11; 1 Cor. 1:27) link it directly to arguments Gerson made (and never retracted) in other discernment works, and to the tract on Joan of Arc known as *De quadam puella* (1429?), of which Gerson is possibly the author.[49] In particular, the verse 1 Cor. 1:27, which acknowledges the power of weakness, was used to authorize Joan of Arc in *De quadam puella*. What a fine trick, Gerson exclaims in the *Letter to Jean Morel*, to conquer by means of such an insignificant woman, thus reiterating a biblical point already used to validate Hildegard of Bingen and others,[50] and anticipating by a number of years Christine de Pizan's *Ditié de Jeanne D'Arc*, as well as other Johannic sources.[51]

Gerson has proceeded with so much caution in the *Letter to Jean Morel*, advising against widespread dissemination of her visions and noting that not everything in the book of visions need be believed exactly as stated, that it seems unlikely he would have needed to foreswear this qualified but favorable opinion. Only one statement seems to lack the severe attitude toward discernment so evident in later works, the statement that when in doubt it honors God and the Christian religion more to attribute an event piously to a miracle than stubbornly to deny the miraculous.[52] With the passage of time and the profusion of mystics, this statement may later have seemed naïve to Gerson. But its openness to divine solicitude strikes a note similar to the *Poitiers Conclusions* in that Joan's authenticity was at first largely authorized by divine *possibility*. This receptivity to miraculous occurrence is aligned with several of Gerson's deeply held beliefs, also expressed in this letter: first, that God can still create a miracle (Isaiah 59:1);[53] second, that the same events that frequently occur naturally can also occur miraculously;[54] and finally, that Ermine's female simplicity does not prevent the possibility of a miracle.[55] Based on the *Letter to Jean Morel*, whatever the eventual status of Gerson's judgment, one cannot doubt his conviction that God chose even simple women to work his miracles.

The charge of Gerson's hostility toward female mystics is leveled particularly at *De probatione spirituum*, written in 1415 while the Council of Constance was in session. More specifically, the tract is considered to be anti-Brigittine, in the sense of denying the authenticity of her divine calling.[56] It has sometimes been asserted erroneously that Gerson composed *De probatione spirituum* to dissuade against the confirmation of Bridget's canonization, during the council at Constance in early February 1415.[57] By introducing Bridget's case at the council, the Swedes sought broader recognition for her canonization of 1391 and the authority of the general council. Her initial canonization by the Roman Pope Boniface IX held limited authority in light of the rival Avignon papacy of Clement VII during the schism.[58] Gerson's *De probatione spirtuum* does indeed raise specific doubts "during the Sacred Council in which the canonization of saints and the examination of their teachings are being discussed," about the nature of Bridget's visions.[59] But by the date of Gerson's arrival at Constance on February 21, 1415, the official confirmation of Bridget was already three weeks old.[60] The *De probatione spirituum* was not written until August 1415, making the supposition that its purpose was to oppose Bridget's canonization confirmation chronologically impossible.[61]

Judging by Gerson's remarks in *De probatione spirituum*, however, there is little question that he held misgivings, and may have been entirely skeptical, of Bridget's inspiration. Nevertheless, he does not condemn or even openly oppose her canonization.[62] The canonization had been unanimously endorsed by the council and Gerson would not have favored the potential for scandal of his own dissenting pronouncement, even after the fact.[63] It is conceivable that Gerson primarily objected to the ease with which Bridget had received confirmation by John XXIII and the council,[64] and for that matter by Boniface IX before him.[65] Moreover, it is likely that Bridget is not as pivotal to *De probatione spirituum* as some scholars have assumed. Paschal Boland seems to have assimilated into his translation of *De probatione spirituum* an apparent scribal annotation, heightening by this personal emphasis the importance of the Brigittine question.[66] Separating this annotation from the treatise proper allows us to perceive more clearly that Gerson's growing concern was less specifically about Bridget, than about lax discernment examinations, false doctrine purveyed by other alleged prophets and heretics, and the undue proliferation of saints. Henry of Langenstein, named by Gerson in *De probatione spirituum*, had apparently influenced Gerson on the need to contain the number of saints.[67]

In fact, the specific cases for which *De probatione spirituum* was written were those of three additional Swedish candidates, eagerly put forward by the Swedish delegation to John XXIII, an effort undoubtedly encouraged by Bridget's recent swift confirmation.[68] According to Jacques Lenfant's *History of the Council of Constance*, the authority of John XXIII was already weakened by the time the letter for the additional three candidates was received.[69] The outcome was that their cases were not quickly decided by an amenable pope but were instead entrusted to the stringency of a commission of the council, of which Gerson was a member. Lenfant states that the commission wanted to "inquire into the saints, their life and miracles, and to see if in general it were not more proper to lessen the number of saints than to increase it."[70] The validity of these three Swedish cases, then, not Bridget, constituted Gerson's immediate purpose in writing *De probatione spirituum*. But an underlying factor must have been Gerson's objection to soft papal criteria of approval and generally careless discernment procedures, especially in the recent case of Bridget.

Gerson would instinctively have had political objections to Bridget. She articulated overtly anti-French revelations, campaigned against the Avignon papacy, and differently from a visionary like Ermine of Reims, tried to intervene globally with popes, kings, and emperors, rather than locally. The larger a mystic's profile, the more Gerson had reason to worry. Yet in the final analysis, Gerson's *De probatione spirituum* is primarily directed at theologians and their responsibility (here undoubtedly referring to the Constance commission itself) for rendering more careful decisions in discernment cases. Thus he cites biblical passages from which to draw guidance, now significant among them Matt. 7:16: "By their fruits you will know them." He enumerates the interrogatory precepts of: Who? What? Why? To whom? What kind? Whence? needed to probe the life of the visionary. He warns against the passionate, the young, and the female. He insists on the detailed examination of the individual, his (or her) education, habits, likes, and associates, as well as the candidate's wealth or poverty, the one associated with pride and sensuality, the other with deception.[71] He emphasizes that the individual must present something supernatural and that the character of the visions must be examined in every detail for the presence of a single falsehood.[72] Gerson further decries the general curiosity toward mystics, which distracts the faithful from the needs of their own salvation, and causes them to put too great faith in the uncanonized.[73] Additionally, he rails against those who refuse to work out their salvation in ordinary ways.[74] Gerson's remarks often imply that he had women, and perhaps chiefly Bridget, in mind. Indeed Eric Colledge claims that Gerson rearranges Alphonso of Jaén's *Epistola solitarii*, a theological tract arguing the Swedish mystic's divine inspiration, in order "to throw the onus of proof back on to the supporters of St. Bridget."[75] But before pleading Bridget's case, the *Epistola* presents a rich and useful synthesis of discernment criteria, which may have simply proved irresistible to Gerson for his own writing.[76]

One of Gerson's salient points in *De probation spirituum* is to determine why a given revelation takes place, not just in view of its "proximate end" [*fine. . .proximo*] but for its "unexpressed and ultimate objective" [*(fine). . .occulto et longinquo*).[77] Gerson argues: "The first effect may seem to be good, beneficial, worthy. . .which in fact becomes a scandal. . .either because the ultimate end does not correspond to the first, or because something false and erroneous was discovered. . .which previously had been reported as a sign of holiness and piety."[78] Importantly, he does not support this point with Brigittine error, but with the controversial careers of Jean de Varennes of Saint-Lié and John Hus, the former jailed in 1396, the latter condemned to death and burned at the stake in July 1415, during the Council of Constance.[79] The attack on these two men warns specifically that initial enthusiasm for a doctrine may be misplaced, and that errors may be uncovered with the passage of time, which necessitate retraction, and even condemnation, of views originally deemed pious.

When Gerson shifts his focus in *De probatione spirituum* several paragraphs later to visionary women, it is only to deliver conventional misogynist platitudes, with no real indication that he has the prominent and influential career of Bridget in mind. Women, with their long-winded prattle, he states, were the bane of Saints Augustine and Bonaventure, and if time alone was wasted, such a fault pleases the devil.[80] Gerson is thus reverting to the timeless rhetoric of his classical and patristic sources, which he had already exploited in *De distinctione verarum visionum a falsis*.

The conventional notion that *De probatione spirituum* was directed against female mystics found seeming reinforcement in two points made in Gerson's *De examinatione doctrinarum* of 1423. First, Gerson alleges that on his deathbed Gregory XI "exhorted all around him to beware of certain persons, whether men or women, who, under the pretext of religion, published visions, which only proceeded from their own brain."[81] Although this reference has generally been seen as a reference to Saints Bridget and Catherine, the words "whether men or women," distinctly include male prophets in the criticism. In fact, Georges Peyronnet numbers Peter of Aragon among those alluded to here by Gerson.[82] Second, *De examinatione doctrinarum* contains an apparent retraction of Gerson's endorsement of Ermine of Reims in the *Letter to Jean Morel*.

The retraction question rests on whether the original reading in *De examinatione doctrinarum* was "de quadam Hermina, Remensi" (Paris BNF 3126 and Glorieux edition) and hence refers to Ermine, or "de *quo*dam Er*emita* Remensi" (Du Pin edition) and refers to "a certain hermit of Reims," undoubtedly Jean de Varennes.[83] Claude Arnaud-Gillet argues reasonably that Du Pin imitated the misreading "eremita," which he found in the 1606 edition of Gerson's works by E. Richer, and ignored the reading "Hermina," which he found in Paris manuscript B.N. 3126.[84] Nevertheless, from a historical and psychological viewpoint it is difficult to renounce the "eremita" reading entirely, especially given the limited manuscript evidence in favor of the Ermine reading. If the view is admitted that sees Gerson less as anti-Bridget and antiwoman than as simply an advocate of exacting discernment examinations, and if the relative insignificance and local nature of Ermine's case is taken into account, Gerson's continued endorsement of Ermine's visions stands as compelling and logical, if not documentable.[85] Moreover, Gerson emphatically insisted on the genuineness of his signature at the end of the *Letter to Jean Morel* and thus of his sincere and considered conviction as he delivered a positive opinion of Ermine. Furthermore, one is at a loss to think of any new knowledge about Ermine that could have emerged causing Gerson to reverse himself on the case, since her visions had already been collected and set in writing for several years by the time he endorsed her. Such is not the case, however, with Jean de Varennes. As previously mentioned, *De probatione spirituum* cites Jean de Varennes in the context of those about whom something false or erroneous had gradually come to light.[86] Varennes was a once familiar face at the court of Avignon, a man whose popularity had extended to King Charles VI, but who withdrew suddenly to Reims to continue life as a hermit, there to become a potent accuser and adversary of Archbishop Guy de Roye. The archbishop, who was eventually responsible for Varennes's imprisonment, could potentially have influenced Gerson against this formerly popular hermit.[87] There is, then, an ongoing temptation to see Jean de Varennes rather than Ermine as the target of Gerson's retraction.

It appears that if Gerson did indeed retract his endorsement of the visions of Ermine, the fact was not well known. It is not inconceivable that the commissioners at Poitiers knew of Gerson's letter on Ermine, in which he affirmed the principle of female revelation, which found authority in the biblical precept of the weak overcoming the strong.[88] Moreover, the manuscript tradition offers no evidence of the letter's suppression in later transcriptions of Gerson's works. The *Letter to Jean Morel* is found in Paris BNF fr. 25213, executed for Marguerite de Bavière (d. 1441), sister of John the Fearless, following a transcription of the book of Ermine's visions, yet apparently devoid of any sign of retraction.[89] A manuscript of Gerson's works from the fifteenth century (between 1436? and 1448), Paris BNF lat 14903, also contains a transcription of the Morel letter added to previously blank pages by the knowledgeable Gerson admirer Guillaume Tuysselet, as if in confirmation of Gerson's unchanged opinion on Ermine.[90] A third manuscript, Paris BNF fr. 25552, announces the Morel letter (without recording it) after the transcription of the book of Ermine's visions.[91]

The question that remains to be addressed is the manner in which the foregoing examination of Gerson's attitude toward female mystics might have bearing on his convictions about Joan of Arc in 1429. In fact, pronouncements by Gerson on individual female mystics in the four discernment treatises, at times seemingly contradictory or heavily influenced by historical circumstances, have little predictive value as to whether Joan of Arc would have won his approval. The case of Joan of Arc, despite being legitimized by earlier female mystics, was so entirely *sui generis*, not involving papal politics, not offering written works for ecclesiastical scrutiny, and not confined to a local cult like her closest Gersonian exemplar Ermine, that no previously written statement by Gerson could forecast his understanding of Joan's case. Furthermore, no depiction of Gerson as either moderate or headstrong, sympathetic to women or hostile—each image supported by details of the chancellor's life and career—validly predicts what he might have thought about the Maid.

But the ambiguity of this shifting evidence must yield to an even greater ambiguity, in fact, uncertainty, as to whether Gerson ever endorsed the Maid. One can only argue the point by reference to the unsigned tract known as *De mirabili victoria* (*DMV*), alternately titled *De puella aurelianensi* or *Super facto Puelle*, attributed to Gerson. This work vigorously proclaims the certainty of the divine origins of Joan's mission but lacks a manuscript tradition conclusively verifying Gersonian authorship. A great deal turns on the authorship question, since appended to *DMV* are three justifications for the Maid's male dress, which prove, if the treatise is genuine, that Gerson had declared the grounds for her condemnation to be false in advance of Joan's trial. However, despite the hollow promise in certain manuscripts of *DMV* that the author will address "the Maid and the faith she is due," the tract shows only a faint similarity to the criteria and scriptural bases for the testing of prophets. This is true whether one compares *DMV* to Gerson's works, those of Henry of Langenstein, Alphonso of Jaén, or even the early architect of discernment John Cassian. The treatise is a harangue rather than a discernment discourse, a blend of royalist polemic and academic dispute, which was definitely not written for the Poitiers investigation. It alludes to a time of diminishing miracles, an era not even suitable for the traditional (but questionable) May 14 date of the treatise, since one could hardly speak of a dearth of miracles only six days after the victory at Orléans.

It is additionally confusing that the first extant references to *DMV* occur in Anglo-Burgundian lands. The earliest evidence is from a partial transcription of *DMV* followed by a rebuttal, copied in 1435 but presumably composed at the University of Paris in late September 1429.[92] Gerson is not named as the author. The second reference occurs in a letter, dated November 20, 1429, from an Italian merchant in Bruges to his father in Venice. The merchant applauds Gerson's approval of the Maid, vowing to include in his letter a copy of *DMV*, which does not survive.[93] With Paris under Burgundian rule since 1418, and Flanders a Burgundian fief, the extant evidence suggests that the initial milieu in which *DMV* circulated was that of the Anglo-Burgundian double monarchy, not lands held by the partisans of Dauphin Charles.[94] Had *DMV* circulated in Burgundian territory through royalist propaganda channels, the well-informed Christine de Pizan, who knew Gerson but knows nothing of *DMV*, might be expected to have seen this ardently pro-Joan document. One might hypothesize, based on the tenor and certain details of *DMV*, that its author was participating in a volatile controversy between pro- and anti-Joan factions, the latter most likely the University of Paris.[95] But whether one might look somewhere in Burgundian-held France for *DMV*'s defensively royalist author is a question of sheer speculation. By and large, however, the author is so partisan, and introduces justifications of the Maid so uncharacteristic of both Gerson and discernment in general, that the treatise invites challenge to its authority (and authorship). Particularly atypical of Gerson's well-known restraint in discernment is the declaration in *DMV* of the author's absolute certainty [*ex certis signis*] of the divinity of Joan of Arc's mission. In discernment, Gerson believed, one never dealt with certainties.

A competing treatise, *De quadam puella*, in many ways more Gersonian in its caution toward female revelation than *DMV*, and diametrically opposed to it in spirit, raises additional questions about the Gersonian authorship of *DMV*. This second tract, unlike *DMV*, is mindful of arguments on both sides of the Maid's controversial mission, including the potential transgression of her cross-dressing. In laying out contradictory arguments, it is reminiscent of the closing lines of Gerson's *Letter to Jean Morel*, in which, imbued with scholastic rigor, he reminds his addressee: "there is no doubt that objections can be made in almost all matters, even those that are most true."[96] Printed in the first edition of Gerson's works in Cologne in 1484, *De quadam puella* was rejected in the next edition of 1501, as "seem[ing] rather to be the style of Heinrich of Gorckum."[97] *DMV* was then transcribed in the 1501 edition as Gerson's *genuine* work, perhaps due to publicity from Joan's nullification trial of 1456, where DMV was annexed as an extra-judicial treatise. Given the difficulties, a satisfactory resolution of the authorship question has yet to be written. The ascription of *De quadam puella* to Gorckum, however, may simply deepen the mystery of *DMV*. A devoted disciple of Gerson, the putative author Gorckum exhibits a restrained and attentive approach to discernment in *De quadam puella*, which more resembles *De distinctione verarum visionum a falsis* and *De probatione spirituum* in tone and tendency than *DMV*. But, like Gerson's, this author's apparent mistrust of female prophets does not exclude the possibility of their divine election. One is left to wonder why Gorckum, if the author of *De quadam puella*, would be more soberly Gersonian than Gerson himself, if the author of *DMV*.

In the final analysis, there is ample evidence that Gerson's works on discernment show signal reserve toward the female mystical experience. Obviously, he was not as sanguine toward female prophecy as the promoters of Bridget's canonization, and he was surely led to still greater reserve by the exhortations of Henry of Langenstein over the burgeoning problem of self-proclaimed prophets. However, the root of the problem was not the prideful charlatans allowed into the ranks of the blessed, but the lax standards of judgment and the ignorance or incompetence of the examining clergy. Nonetheless, despite the dangers, Gerson never disavowed the lesson of 1 Cor. 12:11 allowing inspiration to anyone. With his winnowing of the ranks of female mystics, he reserved a place for those who passed the test of the probing of the spirit. But in the self-assurance of *DMV*'s positive identification of the hand of God in Joan's case, one finds little that is familiar. No one knows whether Gerson jettisoned his scruples and stifled his skepticism for the cause of France. But based on the uncertainty of the evidence, there is room, for those who are so inclined, to argue not only that Gerson may have remained neutral on the Maid, but also that he may never have written on her case at all.

Notes

1. Representative of part or all of this view, sometimes with qualifications, in otherwise very useful works are: Caroline Walker Bynum, *Holy Feast and Holy Fast: The Religious Significance of Food to Medieval Women* (Berkeley: University of California Press, 1987), pp. 22 and 315, n. 43; D. Catherine Brown,

Pastor and Laity in the Theology of Jean Gerson (Cambridge: Cambridge University Press, 1987), pp. 222–24; André Vauchez, *The Laity in the Middle Ages: Religious Beliefs and Devotional Practices*, ed. and intro. Daniel E. Bornstein, trans. Margery J. Schneider (Notre Dame: University of Notre Dame Press, 1993), p. 263; Jo Ann McNamara, "The Rhetoric of Orthodoxy: Clerical Authority and Female Innovation in the Struggle with Heresy," in *Maps of Flesh and Light: The Religious Experience of Medieval Women Mystics*, ed. Ulrike Wiethaus (Syracuse: Syracuse University Press, 1993), p. 26; James L. Connolly, *Jean Gerson: Reformer and Mystic* (Louvain: Librairie Universitaire, 1928), p. 240; Ann Llewellyn Barstow, *Joan of Arc: Heretic, Mystic, Shaman* (Lewiston, N.Y.: Mellen Press, 1986), p. 41; and Claire L. Sahlin, *Birgitta of Sweden and the Voice of Prophecy* (Woodbridge, Suffolk: Boydell Press, 2001), p. 168.

2. Marie de Valenciennes is thought to be Margaret Porete. See Brian Patrick McGuire, trans., *Jean Gerson: Early Works* (New York: Paulist Press, 1998), p. 459, note 56.
3. McGuire, *Early Works*, p. 356; Palémon Glorieux, *Oeuvres Complètes [de] Jean Gerson* (Paris: Desclée, 1960–73), 3:51.
4. McGuire, *Early Works*, p. 357; Glorieux, *Oeuvres* 3:52.
5. McGuire, *Early Works*, pp. 356 and 358; Glorieux, *Oeuvres* 3:51 and 3:52.
6. McGuire, *Early Works*, pp. 356 and 459, n. 50; Glorieux, *Oeuvres* 3:51.
7. B. J. Caiger, "Doctrine and Discipline in the Church of Jean Gerson," *Journal of Ecclesiastical History* 41.3 (1990): 389–407 (p. 393).
8. David S. Wiesen, *St. Jerome as a Satirist: A Study in Christian Latin Thought and Letters* (Ithaca, N.Y.: Cornell University Press, 1964), pp. 115–16. Gerson's satire is less humorous than that of Jerome and may therefore appear merely misogynist.
9. McGuire, *Early Works*, p. 335; Glorieux, *Oeuvres* 3:37.
10. McGuire, *Early Works*, p. 335; Glorieux, *Oeuvres* 3:37.
11. McGuire, *Early Works*, pp. 336 and 357 (see p. 460, n. 60); Glorieux, *Oeuvres* 3:38 and 3:52.
12. McGuire, *Early Works*, pp. 337–38; Glorieux, *Oeuvres* 3:38–39.
13. McGuire, *Early Works*, pp. 356 and 459, n. 53; Glorieux, *Oeuvres* 3:51.
14. McGuire, *Early Works*, p. 455, n. 1.
15. McGuire, *Early Works*, p. 359; Glorieux, *Oeuvres* 3:53.
16. McGuire, *Early Works*, p. 350; Glorieux, *Oeuvres* 3:47.
17. McGuire, *Early Works*, p. 350; Glorieux, *Oeuvres* 3:47.
18. McGuire, *Early Works*, p. 360; Glorieux, *Oeuvres* 3:54.
19. McGuire, *Early Works*, p. 360; Glorieux, *Oeuvres* 3:54.
20. Gerson requires that these revelations be subjected to testing as well. Although they are harder to judge, they are not exempt from the requirement of 1 John 4:1 that the spirit be probed.
21. McGuire, *Early Works*, p. 351; Glorieux, *Oeuvres* 3:48.
22. For an English translation of the *Poitiers Conclusions*, see Deborah Fraioli, *Joan of Arc: The Early Debate* (Woodbridge, Suffolk: Boydell Press, 2000), appendix II, pp. 206–207.

23. For Gerson's point see McGuire, *Early Works*, p. 337; Glorieux, *Oeuvres* 3:38. The quotations in parentheses are from the *Poitiers Conclusions*.
24. McGuire, *Early Works*, p. 337; Glorieux, *Oeuvres* 3:38.
25. McGuire, *Early Works*, pp. 341 and 355; Glorieux, *Oeuvres* 3:41 and 3:51.
26. McGuire, *Early Works*, p. 363; Glorieux, *Oeuvres* 3:56.
27. McGuire, *Early Works*, pp. 244–49; Glorieux, *Oeuvres* 2:93–96.
28. Claude Arnaud-Gillet, *Entre Dieu et Satan: Les visions d'Ermine de Reims († 1396) recueillies et transcrites par Jean Le Graveur* (préface d'André Vauchez) (Florence: Sismel: Edizioni del Galluzzo, 1997), p. 21.
29. Palémon Glorieux, "La vie et les oeuvres de Gerson: essai chronologique," *Archives d'histoire doctrinale et littéraire* 18 (1950): 172.
30. Arnaud-Gillet, *Entre Dieu et Satan*, p. 21.
31. McGuire, "Late Medieval Care and Control of Women: Jean Gerson and His Sisters," *Revue d'histoire ecclésiastique* 92.1 (1997): 29, identifies this as Gerson's time in Bruges (1399–1400).
32. McGuire, *Early Works*, p. 244; Glorieux, *Oeuvres* 2:93.
33. The main metaphor of testing metals, for instance, did not originate with Gerson. See Dyan Elliott, "Seeing Double: John Gerson, the Discernment of Spirits, and Joan of Arc," *American Historical Review* 107.1 (2002): 26–54 (p. 41, n. 69). I wish to thank Prof. Elliott for a copy of her informative article.
34. The *Letter to Jean Morel* and *De distinctione verarum visionum a falsis* both cite 1 Cor. 12:11 and Isaiah 59:1 but the Morel letter lacks 1 John 4:1 and 2 Cor. 11:14.
35. Paschal Boland, *The Concept of* Discretio Spirituum *in John Gerson's* "De Probatione Spirituum" *and* "De Distinctione Verarum Visionum A Falsis," Studies in Sacred Theology, 112 (Washington: Catholic University of America Press, 1959), p. 32; Glorieux, *Oeuvres* 9:181.
36. McGuire, *Early Works*, p. 245; Glorieux, *Oeuvres* 2:94.
37. McGuire, *Early Works*, p. 248; Glorieux, *Oeuvres* 2:96.
38. McGuire, *Early Works*, p. 246; Glorieux, *Oeuvres* 2:95. Françoise Bonney omits these last words when quoting from the letter, potentially promoting the misconception that Gerson forbade distribution of Ermine's book. See Bonney, "Jugement de Gerson sur deux expériences de la vie mystique de son époque: les visions d'Ermine et de Jeanne d'Arc," in *Actes du 95e congrès national des sociétés savantes, Reims, 1970, Champagne et Pays de la Meuse: Questions d'histoire et de philologie: Philologie et Histoire jusqu'à 1610,* Vol. 2 (Paris, 1975), p. 194.
39. The retraction question is treated in the discussion of *De examinatione doctrinarum* later.
40. Caiger, "Doctrine," pp. 396 and 402.
41. McGuire, *Early Works*, p. 245; Glorieux, *Oeuvres* 2:93.
42. McGuire, *Early Works*, p. 245; Glorieux, *Oeuvres* 2:93.
43. Alexandra Barratt, review of D. Catherine Brown, *Pastor and Laity in the Theology of Jean Gerson in Journal of Theological Studies* n.s. 39 (1988): 294.
44. See Caiger, "Doctrine," p. 400. Gerson's affirmation of the right not to believe every word a saint or holy woman wrote or uttered has sometimes

been taken as a denunciation of female inspiration. Here, however, he nevertheless approves a case of feminine illumination.

45. McGuire, *Early Works*, p. 245; Glorieux, *Oeuvres* 2:94.
46. McGuire, *Early Works*, p. 245; Glorieux, *Oeuvres* 2:94.
47. McGuire, *Early Works*, pp. 245–46; Glorieux, *Oeuvres* 2:94.
48. Fraioli, *Early Debate*, p. 207.
49. Fraioli, *Early Debate*, pp. 24–44.
50. Barbara Newman, "Divine Power Made Perfect in Weakness: St. Hildegard on the Frail Sex," in *Medieval Religious Women*, Vol. 2: *Peaceweavers*, ed. Lillian Thomas Shank and John A. Nichols (Kalamazoo: Cistercian Publications, 1987), pp. 103–22.
51. Deborah Fraioli, "Why Joan of Arc Never Became an Amazon," in *Fresh Verdicts on Joan of Arc*, ed. Bonnie Wheeler and Charles T. Wood (New York: Garland, 1996), pp. 189–204.
52. McGuire, *Early Works*, p. 246; Glorieux, *Oeuvres* 2:94.
53. McGuire, *Early Works*, p. 246; Glorieux, *Oeuvres* 2:94.
54. McGuire, *Early Works*, p. 246; Glorieux, *Oeuvres* 2:94.
55. McGuire, *Early Works*, p. 246; Glorieux, *Oeuvres* 2:95.
56. Eric Colledge, "Epistola solitarii ad reges: Alphonse of Pecha as Organizer of Birgittine and Urbanist Propaganda," *Mediaeval Studies* 18 (1956): 44; Dyan Elliott, "Authorizing a Life: The Collaboration of Dorothea of Montau and John Marienwerder," in *Gendered Voices: Medieval Saints and Their Interpreters*, ed. Catherine M. Mooney, foreword Caroline Walker Bynum (Philadelphia: University of Pennsylvania, 1999), p. 190.
57. Glorieux, "La vie," p. 181.
58. James [Jacques] Lenfant, *The History of the Council of Constance*, trans. Stephen Whatley (London: A. Bettesworth, etc., 1730), p. 106; Kari Elisabeth Børresen, "Birgitta's godlanguage: Exemplary Intention, Inapplicable Content," in *Birgitta, hendes vaerk og hendes klostre I Norden*, ed. Tore Nyberg (Odense University Studies in History and Social Sciences, 150) (Odense: Odense Universitetsforlag, 1991), p. 57.
59. The treatise makes only one specific reference to Bridget: "Of special interest is the case of Bridget, who claims to have enjoyed visions not only of angels, but also of Jesus Christ, Mary, Agnes, and other saints, who talk to her with the familiarity of friends, or as a bridegroom to his bride," Boland, *Concept*, p. 28; Glorieux, *Oeuvres* 9:179.
60. Glorieux, "La vie," p. 180. See Ulrichs von Richtental, *Chronik des Constanzer Concils, 1414 bis 1418* (Tübingen: Litterarischen Vereins in Stuttgart, 1882), p. 53, cited by F.R. Johnston, "English Defenders of St. Bridget" (Studies in St. Birgitta and the Brigittine Order, 1), *Analecta Cartusiana* 35,19 (1995): 268, n. 32.
61. Glorieux, "La vie," p. 181.
62. Boland, *Concept*, p. 51; Johnston, "English Defenders," p. 269.
63. It seems unlikely that Gerson, had he participated in the canonization confirmation process, would have voted against Bridget even if he were personally opposed. He was averse to overturning well-established cults of

venerated people, such as that of Bridget, since it put the integrity of the church in question. Moreover, any reversal of practices already in effect risked causing the faith of ordinary people to be undermined.

64. The description in Lenfant, *Council*, p. 106, makes the procedure of 1415 appear ceremonial rather than theological, hasty rather than painstaking; in short, a perfunctory procedure not in keeping with the scrutiny Gerson advocated in all his discernment tracts.
65. Only two people came forward in 1391 with objections to Bridget's canonization, and the one who asked for a more thorough examination of the candidate was soundly ridiculed. See Bridget Morris, *St Birgitta of Sweden* (Woodbridge, Suffolk: Boydell Press, 1999), p. 152.
66. Boland, *Concept*, p. 38: "Here ends the treatise of John Gerson. . .published because of some matters that arose in the aforesaid council about the canonization of Bridget (of Sweden)." See Glorieux, *Oeuvre* 9:185, where this final paragraph is not given. Du Pin, from whose text Boland worked, signals the non-treatise status of this final paragraph by setting it off in italics. See *Johannes Gerson, Opera Omnia*, ed. Louis Ellies Du Pin (Antwerp, 1706; repr. Hildesheim: Georg Olms Verlag, 1987), 1:43. In Danièle Calvot and Gilbert Ouy's *L'Oeuvre de Gerson à Saint-Victor de Paris: Catalogue des manuscrits* (Paris: Editions du CNRS, 1990), two out of three manuscripts of *De probatione spirituum* lack this postscript (see pp. 105 and 129). Only BNF lat. 14903 continues with "Et sic est finis huius tractatuli. . ." (p. 86).
67. See reference to Langenstein's *Concilium pacis* in Sahlin, *Birgitta*, p. 154, n. 67.
68. The three new Scandinavian candidates were Nicholas, bishop of Lincopin, Brynolphus, bishop of Scarren, and Nigris, monk of the order of Saint Austin; Lenfant, *Council*, p. 469. But see Sahlin, *Birgitta*, p. 163, who substitutes different candidates for two of the three names.
69. Lenfant, *Council*, p. 469.
70. Lenfant, *Council*, p. 469 (capitalization modernized).
71. Boland, *Concept*, pp. 30–31; Glorieux, *Oeuvres* 9:180.
72. Boland, *Concept*, p. 31; Glorieux, *Oeuvres* 9:181.
73. Boland, *Concept*, pp. 32 and 34; Glorieux, *Oeuvres* 9:181 and 9:182.
74. Boland, *Concept*, p. 33; Glorieux, *Oeuvres* 9:181.
75. Colledge, "Epistola," p. 45; see similarly Elliott, "Seeing Double," p. 36.
76. Arne Jönsson, *Alfonso of Jaén: His Life and Works with Critical Editions of the* Epistola Solitarii, *the* Informaciones *and the* Epistola Serui Christi (Studia Graeca et Latina Lundensia, 1) (Lund, Sweden: Lund University Press, 1989). See also Rosalynn Voaden, *God's Words, Women's Voices: The Discernment of Spirits in the Writing of Late-Medieval Women Visionaries* (York: York Medieval Press, 1999), esp. chapters 2 and 3.
77. Boland, *Concept*, p. 34; Glorieux, *Oeuvres* 9:182.
78. Boland, *Concept*, pp. 34–35; Glorieux, *Oeuvres* 9:182–83.
79. For the most complete study of Varennes see André Vauchez, "Un réformateur religieux dans la France de Charles VI: Jean de Varennes," *Académie des Inscriptions et Belles-Lettres* (Comptes rendus des séances de l'année 1998, novembre–décembre) (Paris, 1998): 1111–30. I wish to

express my gratitude to the author for the offprint of this useful article. See also Noël Valois, *La France et le Grand Schisme d'Occident* (Paris, 1901; repr. Hildesheim: Georg Olms Verlag, 1967), 3:28–29 and 3:84–86; Henri Jadart, *Jean de Gerson (1363–1429): Recherches sur son origine, son village natal et sa famille* (Reims: Deligne et Renart, 1881), pp. 177–96.

80. Boland, *Concept*, p. 36; Glorieux, *Oeuvres* 9:184.
81. I cite the English translation by Campbell Mackenzie of Emile de Bonnechose, *The Reformers before the Reformation: The Fifteenth Century: John Huss and the Council of Constance* (New York: Harper and Brothers, 1844), p. 10.
82. Georges Peyronnet, "Gerson, Charles VII et Jeanne d'Arc: La propagande au service de la guerre," *Revue d'Histoire Ecclésiastique* 84.2 (1989): 338.
83. Glorieux, *Oeuvres* 9:474; Du Pin, *Opera* 1:20.
84. Arnaud-Gillet, *Entre Dieu et Satan*, pp. 24–25. Based on Arnaud-Gillet, Vauchez, "Varennes," p. 1122, n. 50, states that *quodam eremita Remensi* "is not attested in any medieval manuscript" and that a reference to Ermine must therefore be the preferred reading. No further evidence is given.
85. The obvious weakness of this view is its dependence on the unverifiable existence of lost manuscripts providing the "eremita" reading.
86. Gerson also wrote unfavorably about Varennes in a letter to Pierre d'Ailly. See Du Pin, *Opera*, 3:430–32, cited by Arnaud-Gillet.
87. Arnaud-Gillet, *Entre Dieu et Satan*, p. 20, finds it likely that the clergy of Reims initially approved of Varennes. Du Pin, *Opera* 1:905–44, publishes Jean de Varennes's self-defense from prison to accuser Guy de Roye in the *Responsiones ad capita accusationum quibus impetebatur*.
88. According to Pope Pius II, *Memoirs of a Renaissance Pope: The Commentaries of Pius II, An Abridgment*, ed. Leona C. Gabel, trans. Florence A. Gragg (New York: Putnam, 1962), p. 203, this biblical principle was introduced at Poitiers relating to Joan. The *De quadam puella*, which seems quite likely to have been composed for the Poitiers commission, specifically cites 1 Cor. 1:27.
89. Calvot and Ouy, *Saint-Victor*, pp. 187–88.
90. Calvot and Ouy, *Saint-Victor*, pp. 86–87.
91. Calvot and Ouy, *Saint-Victor*, pp. 66 and 188.
92. Noël Valois, ed., "Un nouveau témoignage sur Jeanne d'Arc: Réponse d'un clerc parisien à l'apologie de la Pucelle par Jean Gerson (1429)," *Annuaire-Bulletin de la Société de l'Histoire de France* (Seconde partie, Documents et notices historiques) 43 (1906):161–79.
93. *Chronique d'Antonio Morosini: Extraits relatifs à l'histoire de France*, ed. and trans. Léon Dorez, 4 vols. (Paris: Librairie Renouard, 1898–1902), 2:232–35.
94. Peyronnet, "Gerson," p. 351.
95. An inconclusive coincidence links the abbey of Saint-Victor to an unusual line, "non patitur ludum fama, fides, oculus," found in *DMV*. According to Fourier Bonnard, *Histoire de l'Abbaye royale et de l'ordre des chanoines réguliers de St. Victor de Paris*, etc. (Paris: A. Savaète, 1904–08), 1:414–15, a tombstone inscription at Saint-Victor contained the same adage. According to Calvot and Ouy, *Saint-Victor*, p. 93, Saint-Victor also possessed a manuscript of

DMV (Paris BNF lat. 14904), composed of texts that the authors believe entered Paris after the end of the occupation or post-1436.

96. McGuire, *Early Works*, p. 248; Glorieux, *Oeuvres* 2:96.
97. Dorothy G. Wayman, "The Chancellor and Jeanne d'Arc," *Franciscan Studies* 17 (1957): 273–305 (p. 284). Scholars who have accepted Gerson's authorship of *De quadam puella* include Cynthia J. Brown, "Allegorical Design and Image-Making in Fifteenth-Century France: Alain Chartier's Joan of Arc," *French Studies* 53.4(1999): 385–404 (p. 385); Barstow, *Joan of Arc*, p. 134. Those who see Gerson's authorship of *De quadam puella* as possible include William A. Christian, Jr., *Apparitions in Late Medieval and Renaissance Spain* (Princeton: Princeton University Press, 1981), p. 240; Nicole Pons, "La propagande de guerre française avant l'apparition de Jeanne d'Arc," *Journal des savants* (1982): 191–214 (p. 210), and myself.

CHAPTER 8

A RECONSIDERATION OF JEAN GERSON'S ATTITUDE TOWARD JOAN OF ARC IN LIGHT OF HIS VIEWS ON POPULAR DEVOTION

Yelena Mazour-Matusevich

This chapter examines Gerson's often-disputed support of Joan of Arc's mission and his hypothetical opinion about her spirituality in the context of his general attitude toward popular devotional practices.

The goal of this chapter is not to prove whether Gerson was or was not a zealous supporter of Joan of Arc, but rather to develop arguments supporting two main points. First, one cannot speak about Gerson's general mistrust of women or feminine spirituality but rather about his doubts concerning institutionalized feminine religiosity and extreme, improvised, and bizarre religious practices.[1] Second, an analysis of Gerson's attitude toward forms of popular piety suggests that the Chancellor's positive judgment of Joan of Arc's visions and voices does not represent an exception to his presumed "almost universal antipathy" toward women, but reveals instead the continuity of Gerson's thought.[2]

Indeed, when placed in the context of Gerson's general attitude toward popular devotion, the terms and conditions of his judgment of Joan of Arc's mystical experience reveal several consistent elements. These elements are found in the texts written well before both of the two documents concerning Joan—*De mirabili victoria* (hereafter, *DMV*) and *De quadam puella* (hereafter, *DQP*)—sometimes attributed to his authorship.[3] The attribution of *DMV* to Gerson has been contested, among other reasons, on the grounds of its atypical style, which stands in contrast to Gerson's other theological treatises. The far more prudent *DQP*, attributed to Heinrich von Gorckum, seems more fully reflective of Gerson's style. The lifelong Gersonian scholar Gilbert Ouy supports Gerson's authorship of *De mirabili victoria/De puella Aurelianensi*, although he believes the document to be a combination of two different texts put together by Glorieux. Gilbert Ouy's main argument is that this text had been copied by Guillaume Tuysselet, Gerson's admirer and an intelligent copyist who could even recognize his longhand writing. Even though Tuysselet does not warranty the authenticity of the manuscript, the fact he copied it constitutes a solid argument in favor of Gersonian authorship.[4] A leading authority on Gerson, Brian Patrick McGuire, also supports the authenticity of *De mirabili victoria/De puella Aurelianensi* on the grounds of topical and scriptural correspondences between this text and Gerson's work *Super Cantica Canticorum*, written, according to his brother Jean the Celestine, three days before his death on July 12, 1429.[5] Without attempting to resolve the long debate about the authenticity of either document, I focus on elements that these two documents share and that are consistent with Gerson's treatment of individual mystical experiences in texts mentioned above. These texts are *The Mountain of Contemplation* (1400), *De distinctione verarum visionum a falsis* (1401), *The Spiritual Dialogue* (1407),[6] the letter concerning Ermine's case (1408), and *Letter to the Carthusians of Bâle* (1413).[7] Due to the controversy surrounding the authorship of *DMV* and *DQP*, these texts will be analyzed and compared in the second part of this chapter.

All the writings just mentioned deal, although to a different degree and from different perspectives, with issues concerning contemplative religious experiences. By definition mystical experience is an improvisation that supposes a certain amount of internal freedom. It is a form of "spiritual creativity," different for each individual, that can be observed and evaluated by an outsider only to a limited degree. Gerson is particularly aware of this, often emphasizing the diversity of spiritual experiences due to the variety of human temperaments and conditions: "For people are made in different ways, just as there are different callings by God."[8] The nature of mystical experience both fascinates and worries the prudent chancellor, which explains his constant hesitations and sometimes seemingly contradictory treatment of spiritual phenomena. Thus, on one hand it was Gerson who explicitly invited women to explore contemplation, on the other it was also he who warned against female visionaries. What may be a plausible explanation of such dissimilar treatment of feminine spirituality? I argue that the same criteria, appearing in all the aforementioned writings, determines

Gerson's judgment. These criteria are, in order of importance, humility, the spiritual profit to the community of believers or society, discrete behavior, independent status, and popular origins of the mystic. The sex of the mystic appears to be of lesser importance. All these factors are present in the evaluation of Joan of Arc's mission in *DMV* and *DQP*, as well as in *The Poitiers Conclusions*. Consequently, it is very important to trace these determining factors in earlier Gersonian texts.

Catherine Brown rightly remarks that Gerson's attitude toward women seems rather sympathetic everywhere except in his writings concerning visionaries,[9] who seem to provoke mistrust in the prudent chancellor.[10] Understanding motivations of Gerson's reticence might provide a key for the possible explanation of his choice in supporting Joan of Arc, a solitary female visionary of popular origin.[11]

Apparently the chancellor himself never experienced the state of mystical trance and had no visions. Whether or not he did, he insisted that one could never be quite sure of the nature of the supernatural. How can we know if this or that vision is truly inspired by God? How to be certain that the visionary is not the victim of sickness? In his treatise *De distinctione* Gerson asked himself precisely these questions. In order to distinguish the true revelations from the false, Gerson suggested some rules. First, the physical, mental, and moral health of the visionary (man or woman) has to be examined so that it can be firmly established that the visions were not provoked by trauma or by psychic anomaly.[12] Then the temperament of the person must be studied as well as his/her education, environment, and customs. The capstone of the truth lies however in the humility of the presumable "holy person": "For pride and humility are sufficient to distinguish the coin of spiritual operations."[13] As a true Christian, Gerson put humility above miracles: "[. . .] miraculous deeds and humility are two signs that are sufficient to show the sanctity of a person. Miracles themselves are not enough."[14]

Another sure sign of true revelations is discretion. "By this trait I understand a readiness to believe in that counsel which is the daughter of humility," explained Gerson in *De distinctione*.[15] Theologically speaking, discretion designates a moral moderation, "the middle way," a sort of opposition to excessive austerity, whether moral or physical.[16] Gerson seemed always to feel uneasy about extreme forms of asceticism: deprivations, exhausting fasting, flagellation, mortification of the flesh, and in general, physical, external manifestations of religiosity and mysticism that he judged contrary to discretion and humility. His attitude toward certain religious practices of which he disapproved in either sex is clearly expressed in the following: "Quaeris exercere zelum contra peccatores, queris eos de terra perdere, dabo tibi antidotum sine verborum strepiti, sine virga, sine carcere, sine flagellis aut vulnere, sine tuo periculo" [I will give you the cure without dazzling words, without birch, prison, flagellation or wounds, without putting yourself in peril].[17] He also believed that these practices were mainly responsible for the supernatural "visions and revelations" of female mystics of whom, as it is well known, he was particularly suspicious:

> Excessive abstinence and drunken overeating both lead to a similar end, except that excessive abstinence is harder to remedy, for it brings incurable illness from brain damage and mental disorder. It happens then through mania or rage or other melancholy passions that phantasms become so deeply rooted and buried in the brain that they are thought to be true objects that appear outside the mind.[18]

This attitude is visible in the case of the married woman from Arras whom Gerson met personally. This woman frequently imposed on herself complete fasting, sometimes for four and more days. By questioning this woman at length Gerson discovered her total ignorance in religious matters and lack or even refusal of spiritual direction. According to Gerson's account she was unable to explain why she was exhausting herself with fasting.[19] To him her fasting appeared to be senseless and indiscreet, because it brought her the admiration of many simple people in her community without any spiritual profit either for her or for them.[20] What was crucial for Gerson was that this woman lacked the most important proof of spiritual authenticity: "humility was missing in her."[21] Although Gerson completely disagreed with this woman's "foolish obstinacy," however, he did not employ any sanctions: "Finally I insisted, in good faith and in view of the greatest danger for her soul and body, that she give up this foolish obstinacy in fasting. She did not respond to these concerns. I then left, and I do not know what afterward happened."[22]

Gerson's leeriness toward female visionaries might also be explained by several other factors. One of them might have been the bitter souvenir of "holy ladies," including Saint Catherine, who advised Gregory XI to return to Rome, thus (in his view) causing the Great Schism.[23] Another factor is Gerson's skepticism about the state of religious houses for women in his time. His misgiving is evident from his letter to his sisters whom he did not encourage to take the veil: "because, to tell you the truth, and without blaming the religious house, I did not have great inclination, for several reasons that influenced me, to put you in any religious order that I knew."[24]

His reserve might be partly influenced by his fear of the "Beguine contamination" in the female religious congregations. The chancellor's disapprobation of Beguines could be motivated, among others, by typically Gersonian dislike of elitist tendencies in mysticism. Indeed, Marguerite Porete's pronounced "aristocratic" spirit definitely conflicts with Gerson's rather "democratic" inclinations and his understanding of Christian humility.[25] Also, the fact that Porete was not just a solitary visionary but a spiritual leader of a religious movement contributed to the chancellor's negative attitude. As a convinced guardian of the Catholic orthodoxy he regarded any religious group competing with the established order as a potential threat to his beloved Church. Here it seems appropriate to compare Porete's case to Joan of Arc's. In contrast to Porete, Joan of Arc was a solitary mystic, acting alone and not associated with any particular spiritual movement. She did not represent a menace to the orthodoxy, for her agenda was political rather than spiritual. Joan did not challenge the Catholic dogma or tradition in any way. Her meekness and simple faith, combined with her love for the Church, must have spoken directly in her favor in Gerson's eyes. However, even Gerson's apprehension of the Beguines should not be exaggerated or taken out of context, for *De distinctione* does not represent a particularly antifeminine text. Gerson himself prevents us from this assumption. Thus, while asserting the danger of confusing spiritual love with carnal love, he took care not to create the impression of accusing only women of this common error. If he spoke about Marguerite Porete as an example of such confusion, he also produced an example of a man guilty of the same error just before and right after he discussed Porete.[26]

At the same time the chancellor is sometimes explicitly critical of male intellectual authorities, as, for example, in his letter to Pierre d'Ailly:

> They have turned into lions or the most rapacious swine, atrocious in their fury, in word, example, and deed. I speak of the clergy and, above all else, of cathedral chapters. [. . .] Where, I ask, have you seen a theologian who has been appointed in order to minister to spiritual needs, to sow good seed and to preserve it, and for whom, in accord with papal decree, temporal goods even sparingly have been given?[27]

It seems to me that Gerson's infamous antipathy toward women should be regarded as a cliché or a historical misunderstanding. As Gilbert Ouy put it, "in a good number of Gerson's writings one finds the mark if not of 'feminism'—a term really too anachronous—at least of respect toward the woman that is opposite to the old misogyny of the clerical milieu as well as to the equivocal courtly love of the nobility."[28] His rather benign attitude toward women is manifest, for example, during the controversy of *The Romance of the Rose* when Gerson praised Christine de Pizan in his epistle *Talia de me* for having replied well to the misogynic feuds of Pierre Col. In his treatise *Against The Romance of the Rose* Gerson demanded reverence and respect for ladies at least because there are "the glorious virgin saints and others without number who even suffered most harsh torments and cruel deaths in order to guard their chastity or the temple of their hearts" and because of "the saint of saints."[29] Gerson's defense of women and his reverence of "virgin saints" certainly echo Christine de Pizan's arguments in her famous book *La cité des dames* and her poem devoted to Joan of Arc.

Furthermore, Gerson openly admitted that in general humility was more often found in women than in men. Humility is the most perfect means for salvation, and thus the spirituality of women, who excel in humility, is a depository of Christian wisdom and a source of contemplative experience. His focus on humility deserves special attention for it represents a leitmotiv in Gerson's writings. As André Combes, the famous scholar of Gerson's theology, justly remarked, the key word for the Chancellor's spirituality is humility. Humility is the beginning and the apogee of the contemplative quest, the means and the goal of every mystic. "For it is clearly impossible to reach true contemplation except through humility, as the Apostle teaches (1 Cor. 3:18)," Gerson declared in *The Mountain of Contemplation*.[30] More importantly, the chancellor regarded humble behavior and attitude as essential signs of genuine spirituality and even reliable proofs of the authenticity of the individual mystical experience. Indeed, it was mainly humility that determined Gerson's opinion concerning cases of feminine mystical experiences analyzed in this study and particularly his deliberation on Joan of Arc's mission. It was also for the lack of humility that he bitterly reproached his fellow religious clerks and university professors, who despised women instead of learning crucial spiritual lessons from them:

> And so it is that if a man walks with his head erect, that is, with a great conviction of his understanding and knowledge, and does not wish to lower himself in the manner of a small child or a simple woman, he will never be able to enter a gate so humble. That is why many great scholars have wished at times that they had remained in a state of simplicity, like their mothers, without knowing Latin.[31]

It is women's humility and devout nature ("ex hac radice dicitur sexus femineus devotus" [On this basis the feminine sex is said to be devout][32]) that allow them, according to Gerson, to comprehend even the highest Christian truths. The following passage from *The Mountain of Contemplation*, the treatise explicitly addressed to his sisters, introduces this new perspective on female spiritual potentials: "Some persons will wonder and ask why, in a matter so lofty as that of the contemplative life, I choose to write in French rather than in Latin, and more to women than to men."[33] Gerson's tone in this text is defensive, not only illustrating the apparent novelty of his enterprise of teaching women about theology but also showing the resistance of the scholarly milieu toward such an initiative. Nevertheless, he displays a remarkable confidence in his sisters' abilities: "The lack of learning of my sisters cannot keep me from going ahead, for I intend to speak only what they can fully grasp according to the understanding that I have seen in them."[34] His sisters' humility will be the main reason for the chancellor's confidence not only in their capabilities to gain theological knowledge but also in their readiness to lead an independent and self-sufficient contemplative life outside both marriage and monastery.[35] Although Gerson offered himself as a guide to his sisters, he trusted them to explore the Christian contemplation on their own. Except for the influence of their illustrious brother, his sisters' education and psychological profile were probably not very different from the upbringing of Joan of Arc herself. Therefore, the trust that he displayed in his sisters bears, in my opinion, the potential for his future endorsement of Joan's credibility.

The chancellor always sought lessons and examples of humility and found them in his parents, brothers, and, of course, his sisters. Gerson looked for these lessons not only in the writings of church fathers, saints, and mystics but also, as we will see, in conversations with different people about their spiritual experiences.[36] The example of such an interaction between Gerson and a woman parishioner is found in *The Mountain of Contemplation*:

> [As] I learned from a woman who because of her illness was forced for a long time to keep to one room. Once in speaking to me, she said: "I don't know what I will do when I lose this little room, for there is no other place where I can concentrate on my thoughts about God and myself."

One of these contemplative experiences is of particular importance because it became the source of one of the most important concepts in Gerson's spirituality: his idea of spiritual mendicancy. This idea is found in several of his works: *The Mountain of Contemplation*, *The Spiritual Dialogue*, and many sermons. It is most fully developed, however, in his vernacular tract *The Spiritual Mendicancy*. According to the chancellor himself, his ideas about spiritual mendicancy were inspired by a real laywoman named Agnes:

> Je parloye naguerez a une devote femme, nommee Agnes, demourant a Assoire, a l'occasion de laquelle je fis jadis le livre de mendicité espirituelle, pour ce que on m'avoit recité qu'elle queroit ses aumosnes de grace et faisoit sa procession de saint a saint tres diligenment et ardenment pour soy et pour les aultres, et en especial quant elle se doubtoit estre elongee de Dieu; et se mettoit devant Dieu comme condempnee devant le juge, comme povre mendiente devant ung riche seigneur.

> [I spoke lately to one devout woman named Agnes living in Aussoire. Thanks to this woman I wrote heretofore the book of spiritual mendicancy. For I had been told that she sought her alms of grace and made her procession from saint to saint very diligently and zealously for herself and for others, especially when she felt remote from God. She would put herself before God like the condemned before his judge, like a poor beggar before some wealthy lord.][37]

The episode demonstrates the chancellor's enthusiasm and joy inspired by this meeting with Agnes. It appears clear that Gerson authenticated and approved Agnes's religious inventiveness by recognizing her as "ceste devote femme qui des son enffance sert Dieu en estat de virginite sans reproche jusquues a son anciennete" [one who served God irreproachably in her virginity from her childhood to her old age].[38] Agnes's virginity, humility, simple life, and modest origin constitute reassuring elements for the chancellor. The same elements are later mentioned in *The Poitiers Conclusions*: "But in her is found no evil, only goodness, humility, virginity, piety, honesty, and simplicity."[39] Furthermore, Gerson does not seem to have been in the least fearful of independent, "direct" communication with God, such as he discovered in Agnes's spiritual mendicancy. On the contrary, he gave Agnes as an example to his sisters, thus showing that he would like them to be not only as devout as Agnes but also as original in their own devotion as she was. Therefore, we can see once more that Gerson was supportive of isolated female mystics while apprehensive of any organized forms of feminine devotion.

The chancellor employed the same goodwill when he expressed his opinion on the case of the supernatural visions of a certain Ermine, the simple woman who died in Reims in 1395.[40] Ermine's case is really abstruse: her visions are sometimes celestial, sometimes demonic. At times they represent satanic visions that appear under a celestial garment. Thus, Satan appeared to Ermine not only in his "habitual" form of the black cat, raven, or "classical and natural" look of the tailed "red-haired monster" with piggy feet but also under the form of three holy women: Saint Catherine, Saint Agnes, and Saint Mary-Madeleine. Once the Evil One even appeared to Ermine disguised as Saint Augustine himself! In spite of the confusion of Ermine's visions, however, Gerson did not judge her harshly.[41] Indeed, he did not believe himself to be in the position of condemning Ermine's visions: "Thus no one who lives in a civilized manner should stubbornly refuse to believe what another person says when no falsity or clear breach of truth is apparent."[42] He found a formulaic compromise by declaring her visions to be "truth of a secondary order": the one "in which if you do not believe, you will not be damned."[43] Thus Gerson wrote about Ermine's case to Jean Morel: "In the said book there is nothing that should be considered contrary to the Catholic faith or any of its articles of belief."[44] Therefore, if in the case of the married woman from Arras it was her lack of humility that awoke Gerson's suspicion, the main argument in Agnes's and Ermine's favor was, as he already stated in the *Mountain of Contemplation* and in *De distinctione*, the presence of their humility. Ermine also was an independent, isolated female mystic of popular origin. The same characteristics seem to determine Gerson's support in Joan's case.

Gerson nevertheless decided to avoid the distribution of the book relating Ermine's visions. His reasoning was the same as in his criticism of Jean Roesbroeck: he feared the effect that the exuberance of religious language might have on gross people, those whom he called *idiota* and *rustica*.

Ermine's visions belong to popular devotion, toward which Gerson always seemed indulgent. Popular superstitions, the adoration of "images," the too-ardent cult of local saints—in short, all the manifestations of surviving paganism—did not (in contrast to later reformers) worry Gerson excessively. Although the invented rituals of ignorant common people were regrettable and it was certainly commendable to correct them, one should not hasten to condemn or ridicule them, as long as they were not ill intentioned, but rather expressed genuine and deep-rooted religiosity and humility before the divine. In the chancellor's view, humility, the most distinctive Christian quality, made the forms of popular devotion tolerable and sometimes even desirable. Indeed, his letter to the Carthusians of Bâle displays his intimate knowledge of the terrain and his earnest sympathy toward simple people:

> [. . .] quod populus rudis dimittatur in simplicitate et consuetudine sua. . .nec sunt palam et expresse ita de se mala quin bene possint fieri cum intentione debita saltem generali conformandi se. . .etiam ecclesiae in hujusmodi ritibus, ceremoniis, cultibus, oratione et adoratione. . .salvantur tamen implicita fide vel intentione ; et hoc in explicita fide majorum.
>
> [It is better to leave the gross people in their simplicity and customs. . .as long they are not manifestly and openly bad in themselves, or can be made good by the intention, at least general, to be conform to. . .the Church in its rites, ceremonies, cults, prayers and worships. In this manner many simple souls. . .are nevertheless saved by the implicit faith or the intention that makes them join the explicit faith of more enlightened people.][45]

His tolerant attitude toward popular devotional practices contrasts with his absolute rejection of "sacrilegious rites of pagans" when practiced by the clergy: "Neither the place of prayer nor the presence of the holy Body of Christ, nor the celebration of the divine office, keep churchmen from acting in the most vile dissoluteness and performing such acts about which it is a horror either to write or even to think."[46] According to Gerson, what is admissible for the simple people is often criminal when practiced by the learned ones. Therefore, here we are dealing with one of main features of Gerson's thought: a remarkably indulgent approach toward forms of popular devotion contrasts to a prudent and even suspicious attitude to manifestations of more sophisticated and learned varieties of mysticism. This peculiarity of Gersonian thinking fully expresses itself in his dealing with feminine devotion. Clement and sympathetic when dealing with popular forms of feminine devotion as in cases of Agnes, the woman from Arras, his sisters, and Ermine, Gerson was distrustful and categorical in his attitude toward institutionalized female mystics often endorsed by male supporters.

Approached from this angle, Gerson's positive judgment of Joan of Arc's visions and voices appear consistent with his ideas about feminine popular devotion. Indeed, the Maiden's situation, social status, and character correspond exactly to the contemplative type likely to be approved by the chancellor. The birth status of the Pucelle could only reassure the chancellor, who tended, as I argued earlier, to be particularly indulgent toward popular forms of devotion. Agnès, Ermine, Gerson's sisters, and the woman from Arras were all of humble origin. The sex of the messenger of the supposedly divine mission did not exceedingly worry Gerson. As we have tried to demonstrate, he revealed a remarkable trust in female abilities and virtues in several of his earlier works. In order to justify the fact that God chose a young woman as his missionary, the author used the same argument as the reasoning he employed in *Against the Romance of the Rose*: references to the example of female saints and biblical figures. These references appear both in *DMV* and *DQP*. In *DMV* the author cites examples of Deborah, Saint Catherine, and Judith.[47] The author of *DQP* elaborates on the same topic:

> It is in harmony with the Holy Scriptures that God made use of the weak sex and of the age of innocence to offer peoples and kingdoms the happiness of salvation. [. . .] From there, proceeding with examples, one can read about Deborah, Hester, and Judith, how they obtained salvation for the people of God.[48]

In neither the *DMV* nor *DQP*, nor in Gerson's writings concerning Ermine, the woman from Arras, his sisters, or Agnes, does the author expatiate about particularities of female nature and temperament, or the specific character of feminine sanctity. The author's reservations in *DQP* are based on the general difficulty of telling the true prophet from the false, regardless of sex.[49] He even cites the cases of "the real prophets" who "from time to time prophesied a few events which did not occur," like Isaiah and Jonah.[50] Even considering the *DQP*'s author's serious misgivings concerning Joan's male attire, there is nothing in his judgment that reveals particular animosity toward women and feminine spirituality. His expressed aversions do not exceed the usual theological prudence and practice of discernment. The author takes special care not to judge Joan too harshly or too hastily, as was also the case in Gerson's handling of Ermine and Agnes. Indeed, Gerson's judgments in the separate cases of Ermine, Agnes, and (possibly) Joan of Arc reveal the chancellor as a keen observer and independent arbiter.

The author's opinion about Joan's mission suggests a similarity to Gerson's judgment of Ermine's case, where the chancellor describes criteria that mark the true visionary. According to Gerson's own rules, the circumstances of her life, her environment, family, and childhood, based on the testimonies of those who knew Joan, must first be examined carefully: "what is needed is the preliminary and clear knowledge of the mores of this young girl, of her words, her feats and acts, those which characterize her as a private person" (*DQP*, 200); and "[t]hey [i.e., the circumstances of her life] were submitted to research and through investigations which have been carried on by numerous investigators" (*DMV*, 210).

The same reasoning appears in *The Poitiers Conclusions*: "the said Maid to be tested as to her life, birth, moral comportment, and her purpose."[51] Such examinations of Joan of Arc provided evidence of her normalcy.[52] The results of these investigations are reflected in *The Poitiers Conclusions*: "and of her birth and life marvelous things are related as true."[53] Both *DMV* and *DQP* praise her for the Christian virtues and humility: "It is reported that she lives in chastity, sobriety and continence" (*DQP*, 199); and "these documents [The Maid's four official warnings] tend to the same end: to bring one to live in righteousness, in pity toward God, in justice toward other people, in sobriety which is in virtue and temperance toward oneself" (*DMV*, 210).

Both *DMV* and *DQP* insist on the fact that there is nothing in Joan's actions that speaks of sorcery or bizarre religious activities. Her loyalty to the Catholic Church is underlined: "in her practices, this Maid does not appear to resort to spells forbidden by the Church, not to disapproved superstitions" (*DMV*, 209); "on the contrary, she encourages people to acts of virtue and to other achievements of honesty in which God is glorified" (*DQP*, 202). Both texts highlight the disinterested character of the Maid's actions, which speaks in favor of her divine mission: "likewise the present young person, whom it is not inopportune to count among the good people especially sent by God, the more so since she is not in quest of presents and since she works with fervor to establish this good: peace" (*DQP*, 202); "Neither is she trying to secure her own interest, since she exposes her body to supreme peril, in evidence of her mission" (*DMV*, 209).

The typical Gersonian prudence regarding miracles as a sure proof of sanctity is manifest in both documents: "A first miracle does not always produce all the effect men expect of it. So. . .one should not conclude that what has been accomplished is not God's achievement" (*DMV*, 210). "Besides, because God, even nowadays, has not ceased to make use, in our favor [and] on purpose, of supernatural gifts, it is not abnormal for God to take an innocent girl" (*DQP*, 202).

In both texts the author attempts to justify the fact that the Maid was reported to wear men's cloth and armor, even if in *DQP* this attempt is timid: "Then, one should not be surprised that, as a rider, she [the Maid] is more enlightened by a second light than in her usual feminine condition because even David, when he wanted to consult the Lord, would wear the ephod, and used to take his psalterio" (*DQP*, 203). The author makes the point that in some exceptional cases external attributes might be necessary for extraordinary spiritual accomplishments to take place: "The Holy Spirit settles inwardly according to conditions found externally" (*DQP*, 203). In *DMV* the author's effort to justify Joan is far more pronounced: wearing of men's clothes does not constitute a misdeed because it could be a simple practical necessity of the war.[54]

Both *DMV* and *DQP* consider the historical circumstances supporting the Maid's case. The benefits of her mission to the community are emphasized in both documents. Concerning this matter, the arguments are similar: "On the opposite side, her adversaries, filled with fear, are as if they had lost their strength" (*DQP*, 199). "These enemies, it is assured, even their chiefs, hide, overtaken by a thousand fears" (*DMV*, 210). Yet again, the same arguments appear in *The Poitiers Conclusions*: "The king, given his necessity and that of his kingdom. . .ought not to turn away not reject the Maid who says she is sent by God for his succor."[55]

Put in the context of Gerson's attitude toward popular devotional practices, his opinion about feminine spirituality reveals a certain consistency that is easily traced throughout his works. This consistency allows us to think that Gerson's positive judgment of the Maid in one or both documents (*DMV* and *DQP*) attributed to him represents the natural fulfillment of Gerson's evolving thought on the subject. Indeed, *The Mountain of Contemplation* (1400), *De distinctione* (1401), *The Spiritual Dialogue* (1407),[56] the letter concerning Ermine's case (1408), and *Letter to the Carthusians of Bâle* (1413) had all been written well before both *DQP* and *DMV* and illustrate stages of this evolution. Thus, Gerson's tolerant attitude toward forms of popular devotion and particular attention to women's spiritual capacities prepared him for this crucial moment in his life and in our history.

Notes

1. Here this study echoes Deborah Fraioli's paper "Scattering the Darkness of Doubt" (presented at the 36th Congress of Medieval Studies in Kalamazoo, Michigan, May 2001): "[. . .] not hatred either of women or of mystical inspiration, are responsible for what we have often taken to be his [Gerson's] criticism of the female mystical experience."
2. Fraioli, "Scattering the Darkness of Doubt."
3. The texts of *De quadam puella* and *De mirabili victoria* are cited from Deborah A. Fraioli, *Joan of Arc: The Early Debate* (Woodbridge: The Boydell Press, 2000). The translations of *De quadam puella* and *De mirabili victoria* belong to H.G. Francq, in "Jean Gerson's Theological Treatise and Other Memoirs in Defence of Joan of Arc," *Revue de l'Université d'Ottawa* 41 (1971): 58–80. The titles are abridged for the sake of brevity as *DMV* and *DQP* (see D. Fraioli's preface to *Joan of Arc: The Early Debate*, p. ix). For convenience the references to *DMV* and *DQP* will be given in the text when two documents are being directly compared.
4. For the latest developments of this debate see Dorothy G. Wayman, "The Chancellor and Jeanne d'Arc, February–July," *Franciscan Studies* 17 (1957): 272–305. The text that we call, after Dorothy Wayman and Deborah Fraioli, *De mirabili victoria*, is found in Glorieux, *Oeuvres complètes* (Paris: Desclée, 1971), 9:661–65, where it is entitled *De puella Aurelianensi*, and in *Traité de Jean Gerson sur la Pucelle* (ed. and trans., J. -B. Monnoyeur, Paris, 1930).
5. *Super Cantica Canticorum* in Glorieux, *Oeuvres* 8:565–639, with a note at the end by Gerson's brother. See McGuire's article "Jean Gerson, the Shulammite, and the Maid" in this collection
6. This date is suggested by Glorieux
7. This essay emphasizes the similarities between these *DMV* and *DQP*, whereas Deborah Fraioli's paper mentioned earlier, as well as her article published in the present collection, both center on the differences between them
8. Brian Patrick McGuire, trans., *Jean Gerson: Early Works* (New York: Paulist Press, 1998), p. 239.
9. Catherine Brown, *Pastor and Laity in the Theology of Jean Gerson* (London: Cambridge University Press, 1987), p. 222 : "The charge of misogyny, it seems, cannot be brought against Gerson. Certainly he did not express any bitterness against women in those works intended for the eyes and ears of the laity. However, some of his Latin works do betray a critical attitude towards the female sex. Almost all the strictures occur in his writings about visionaries. . ."
10. A young scholar, Nancy McLoughlin, has recently offered yet another explanation of Gerson's mistrust of female visionaries. In her paper "Gerson's Anti-Mendicant Polemic in *De Probatione Spirituum*," presented at the 36th Congress of Medieval Studies in Kalamazoo (Michigan, May 2001), McLoughlin suggested that the severity of the chancellor could have been directed against the friars, the confessors of the women visionaries,

rather than against the women themselves. For example, Catherine of Siena was chiefly promoted by the Dominican friars who initiated her canonization. Indeed, Gerson's attitude toward the mendicants is rather clear. In his *Discours sur le fait des mendiants*, Gerson vigorously denounced mendicants as "faux Chrétiens" and one of the major evils from which the Church suffered: "Et nous le veons es persecutions de saincte eglise; la premiere fut mal, par tirans, la seconde pire par les heretiques, la tierce tes male par les fasulx crestiens que l'apostre appelle faulx freres ; la quatre sera incomparable par Antecrist." In the same document Gerson compared the mendicants to the devil himself: "Appeert que s'aucun homme ou aucun estat veult sans raison ou necessite troubler ceste ordre, on luy doit resister car ainsi fut fait ou ciel quant Lucifer ou les anges mauvais voulurent par orgueil passer leur ranc, leur order ou hierarchi" (Glorieux, *Oeuvres* 7.2:979 and 7.2:987).

Jo Ann McNamara also argues that Gerson's reaction against the visions of Birgitta of Sweden could have been influenced by the hostility of the university policy toward the mendicants ("Rhetoric of Orthodoxy," in *Maps of Flesh and Light: The Religious Experience of Medieval Women Mystics*, ed. Ulrike Wiethaus [New York: Syracuse University Press, 1993]). John Coakley shares this opinion in his article "Friars as the Confidents of Holy Women in Medieval Dominican Hagiography," *Images of Sainthood in Medieval Europe*, ed. Renate Blumenfeld-Kosinski (Ithaca and London: Cornell University Press, 1994).

11. Concerning Gerson's attitude toward women mystics see James Connolly, *John Gerson, Reformer and Mystic* (Louvain: Librairie Universitaire, 1928); B. P. McGuire, "Late Medieval Care and Control of Women: Jean Gerson and His Sisters," *Révue de l'Histoire Ecclésiastique* 92.1 (1997): 5–37, and Yelena Matusevich, "From Monastic to Individual Spirituality: Another perspective on Jean Gerson's Attitude toward Women," *Magistra* 6.1 (2000): 61–88.
12. McGuire, *Early Works*, p. 346: "Medical books are full of such monstrous apparitions and disturbances in the power of judgment resulting from injury to the interior powers."
13. McGuire, *Early Works*, p. 354.
14. McGuire, *Early Works*, p. 342.
15. McGuire, *Early Works*, p. 343.
16. McGuire, *Early Works*, p. 338: "You are safest if you take the middle way." About the idea of *discretio* in Gerson's writings see Paschal Boland, *The Concept of* Discretio Spirituum *in Jean Gerson's* "De Probatione Spirituum" *and* "De distinctione verarum visionem a falsis," in *Studies in Sacred Theology* (Washington, D. C.: Catholic University of America Press, 1959, 2nd ed.), p. 112.
17. Glorieux, *Oeuvres* 5: 225. My translation.
18. McGuire, *Early Works*, p. 345.
19. McGuire, *Early Works*, p. 344: "The woman could not produce any convincing reason why she acted in this way, except to say that she was unworthy to eat food."
20. McGuire, *Early Works*, pp. 343–44.

21. McGuire, *Early Works*, p. 344.
22. McGuire, *Early Works*, p. 344.
23. Françoise Bonney, "Jugement de Gerson sur deux expériences de la vie mystique de son époque: visions d'Ermine et de Jeanne d'Arc," in *Actes du 95e Congrès National des sociétés savantes, Reims, 1970, Champagne et Pays de la Meuse: Questions d'Histoire et de Philologie: Philologie et Histoire jusqu'à 1610* (Paris: 1975), vol. 2: 187–95, 189.
24. McGuire, "Late Medieval Care and Control of Women: Jean Gerson and His Sisters," p. 12. See Johannes Gerson, *Opera omnia*, ed. Louis Ellies Du Pin, 4 vols. (Antwerp, 1706), 8:830A: "...car a vray dire—et sans blasme de religion je n'avoie pas inclination grande que vous feüssiez mises en religion que je ne congneüsse, pour causes plusieurs qui a ce me mouvoient."
25. The examples of Porete's teachings that display her aristocratic way of thinking are abundant in *The Mirror of Simple Souls* (Ellen L. Babinsky, *Marguerite Porete: The Mirror of Simple Souls*, trans. [New York: Paulist Press, 1993]). Indeed, the title of chapter 63 "How Love calls those peasants for whom it is sufficient only to be saved" would be enough to put the prudent Gerson on guard. In this chapter Porete develops her idea about gentlemen of spirit who "are saved much more courteously than are the others" (p. 140).
26. McGuire, *Early Works*, pp. 356–57.
27. McGuire, *Early Works*, pp. 170–71.
28. Gilbert Ouy and Claude Gauvard, "Gerson et l'infanticide: défense des femmes et critique de la pénitence publique," in *Festschrift offert au Prof. Eric Hicks* (Genève: Slatkine, 2001), pp. 45–66, 45: "On trouve, d'ailleurs, dans bon nombre d'œuvres de Gerson la marque, sinon d'un féminisme—terme vraiment trop anachronique—du moins d'un respect de la femme qui s' oppose à la vieille misogynie du milieu clérical comme a la courtoisie équivoque du monde de la noblesse." My translation.
29. McGuire, *Early Works*, pp. 390–91.
30. McGuire, *Early Works*, p. 76.
31. McGuire, *Early Works*, p. 97.
32. McGuire, *Early Works*, p. 147.
33. McGuire, *Early Works*, p. 75. The French text in Glorieux, *Oeuvres* 7.1:16–55.
34. McGuire, *Early Works*, p. 75.
35. His sisters formed a tiny informal religious community where they chose to remain freely and which they could leave any time (as one of the sisters did).
36. McGuire, *Early Works*, p. 97.
37. Gerson, *Dialogue Spirituel*; Glorieux, *Oeuvres* 7.1: 72. My translation.
38. Glorieux, *Oeuvres* 7.1:172. My translation.
39. *The Poitiers Conclusions*, trans., D. Fraioli, *Joan of Arc: The Early Debate*, appendix II, p. 206.
40. The account of the visions of Ermine was addressed to the chancellor by Jean Morel, preacher of Saint-Denis de Reims, in about 1408. The manuscript is now found in Bibliothèque Nationale (BnP MS. Français 25552,

fol. 142–309). In the eighteenth century Ermine inspired the book by Fr.-J de Foigny, *Les merveilles de la vie, des combats et victoire d'Ermine, citoyenne de Reims* (Reims: 1648).

41. There is much debate about Gerson's possible retraction of his formal approval of Ermine's visions. The question was whether *De examination edoctrinarum* (1423) says "de quadam Herimina, Remensi" (Glorieux, *Oeuvres* 9:458–75) or "de quodam Eremita Remensi" (Du Pin, vol. 1, col. 7–22, thus referring to Jean de Varennes and his "heretical" views). After long deliberations, Gilbert Ouy, Deborah Fraioli, and I came to the conclusion that from a textual point of view, Gerson either never retracted his approval of Ermine's visions or, if he did, it was known by no one. Gilbert Ouy believes that Gerson had contacts with Jean de Varennes. An important dossier written by the latter is found in the collection of Saint Victor (BNF lat. 14907). According to Ouy, this dossier had been stolen from Gerson, along with other documents, by Adam de Baudribosc, friend of Simon de Plumetot (Gilbert Ouy, *L'oeuvre de Gerson à Saint-Victor de Paris* [Paris: Editions du CNRS, 1990], p. 125).
42. McGuire, *Early Works*, p. 246.
43. McGuire, *Early Works*, p.193.
44. McGuire, *Early Works*, p. 245.
45. Glorieux, *Oeuvres* 2:152. My translation.
46. McGuire, *Early Works*, p. 170.
47. Fraioli, *Early Debate* (*DMV*, 210).
48. Fraioli, *Early Debate* (*DQP*, 201–02).
49. Fraioli, *Early Debate* (*DQP*, 203): "Judging from external appearances and signs, the distinction is not easy to make between a true and a false prophet."
50. Fraioli, *Early Debate* (*DQP*, 204).
51. Fraioli, *Early Debate*, appendix II, p. 206.
52. Fraioli, *Early Debate* (*DQP*, 202): "Such a girl, a true individual among mankind, was sent on purpose by God for works which are accomplished not by human but by divine means, and one must grant her credit for it." *DMV*, 210: "The Maid and the men at arms, her followers, do not neglect the means of human prudence. . ."
53. Fraioli, *Early Debate*, appendix II, p. 206.
54. *DMV*, 211: "[. . .] conditions required to keep one's virtue, which command us to weight all circumstances and to consider what time, necessity, purpose, manner and other similar conditions demand, which are taken into account in the judgment of the wise."
55. Fraioli, *Early Debate*, appendix II, p. 206.
56. This date is suggested by P. Glorieux.

CHAPTER 9

JEAN GERSON, THE SHULAMMITE, AND THE MAID

Brian Patrick McGuire

This chapter asks how Joan of Arc was perceived by churchmen in her own time, and it suggests that we consider the model of the Shulammite woman described in Jean Gerson's last work, his Commentary on the Song of Songs.

The experts are in profound disagreement about the authorship of the two fifteenth-century evaluations on Joan of Arc known as *De mirabili victoria* and *De quadam puella.*[1] In an attempt to look at Gerson's understanding of Joan of Arc without getting bogged down in what has been called "a morass of scholarly debate,"[2] I will begin with a work that there is no doubt comes from his pen, his commentary on the Song of Songs, *Super Cantica Canticorum*, which according to his brother Jean the Celestine was completed three days before his death on July 12, 1429.[3] This is not an easy work to interpret, and I will be looking only at its final section. But I hope to convince the reader that in it Gerson revealed a yearning for a strong figure to bring peace, not only of a spiritual kind, but also in the physical world around him. Here Gerson, practically on his deathbed, may have expressed belief in the mission of Joan of Arc.

In what follows here, I do not expect my interpretation to provide any 'smoking gun' arguments, but I will draw on a decade of reading Gerson and thinking about him in terms of his life and times. My goal is to link him with Joan of Arc in their common love of the French monarchy. This approach might be called 'associative', bringing together as many cultural contexts as possible in order to place Gerson and Joan in a community of shared sympathies.[4]

Gerson had already written many treatises on the contemplative life, but he held himself back until the end from making a commentary on the Song of Songs in terms of spiritual love.[5] In his last years he obliged requests made by members of the Carthusian Order, especially at the Grande Chartreuse, that he provide his comments on various subjects.[6] In April of 1429 he gave way to a request from this quarter that he provide his own interpretation of the Song. He started by promising to consider the Old Testament book in terms of love in all its different forms. In his running commentary he managed, with a discipline typical for him, to get through all eight chapters of what for most modern readers appears to be a declaration of physical love, while for most medieval interpreters, the Song of Songs was an allegory of the love between Christ and his Church.[7]

In the tenth section of his exposition Gerson described purgative love, as seen in the young Shulammite, a mysterious woman in the text whom Gerson identified with the Old Testament figure Abishag.[8] The love here is *amor purgativus*, the purgative love that cleanses the soul and prepares it for the meeting with Christ the bridegroom. This love is also called *amor novitius*, novice love, which Gerson insists is available for all Christians, learned and unlettered, whatever their state of perfection or imperfection.[9] They can express this love through simple prayers of interjection, in which they cast up a few heartfelt words to God, rather than speculating over subtleties.

Gerson briefly considered here how the devout unlearned pray to God before images of the crucified or those of Christ lying in the manger or being adored by the Magi or presented in the temple. He praised the faith of the uneducated as expressed in simple, concrete prayers: "responses of this kind that are most brief and which conform to piety's affectivity, such as the one saying, 'Where Jesus, there is Mary' " [*ubi Jesus ibi Maria*].[10] Other examples are given, and then Gerson defended the use of images and pictures to represent the divine "under sense forms."

Gerson's *amor novitius* seeks out the kisses of the Christ child and is understood on the basis of the image of the young Shulammite girl [*sub typo dilectae Sunamitis adolescentulae*].[11] It is this girl who spoke out in the Song: "Place me as a seal on your heart, as a seal on your arm, for love is strong as death. . ." (Song 8:6). This love is seen first as the killing of carnal desires, but it can also be understood as the zeal many martyrs had shown in the love of Christ. Neither people nor tyrants could extinguish such love.

This *amor novitius* is not to be looked down on. In fact it is something we must learn: *ne contemnendus sed erudiendus videretur*.[12] At the end of the last chapter of the Song, Gerson saw Christ as the bridegroom commending the humility, sagacity, and power of such love "against empty fear and harmful lukewarmness." Christ speaks to the daughters of the heavenly Jerusalem and asks what is to be done with "our sister in the day of temptation, when she is to be addressed by the cleverness of heretics and the frequent insults of other enemies." This "little sister" is seen as the figure in the poem who is apparently so young that she lacks breasts. She will be given the protection she needs, the gifts necessary to guard her.

But here it turns out that the little sister has grown up and can defend herself. The freely given love of our Shulammite Abishag acknowledges that in her has been done what was intended to be done. "I," she says, "am the enclosed wall, everywhere as a powerful defense, so that the enemy's invasion does not get through, and my breasts are like towers, in keeping off the persistent and clever assault against them by these same enemies." The woman can then rejoice that because of her virtue in resisting, "I am made before my beloved as someone who finds peace." She does not give way to worldly, diabolical, or human fear. This is not because of her own power but thanks to the power of him who guards her and hands her over to her guardians [*non quidem propria virtute sed illius qui custodit et custodibus tradit*].

A further section adds another allegorical dimension to these images: the Shulammite is like a vineyard. Christ the peacemaker has handed this place over to angelic guardians and to doctors or prelates [*tradidit pacificus Christus eam custodibus angelicis et doctoribus seu praelatis*]. He has confirmed his custody of the young girl under the image of the vineyard and says, "My vineyard is with me, through its pleasingness and its guardianship." The Shulammite will be rewarded: Christ calls her a peacemaker, and she and all who cooperate with her are to be compensated, "they who guard the fruits of the same vineyard so that they not be lost or destroyed."

Here Gerson has been following the last verses of the eighth book of the Song of Songs, but he has reshaped them in his own reading, emphasizing a heroic girl, her guardians, and their defense of all that is good and virtuous against enemies who try to break in and destroy them. The Shulammite has become a tower of strength, but also the one who finds peace, *quasi pacem reperiens*. Gerson has completed his explication of the tenth verse of Song 8, where the Shulammite "became as one who finds peace." In the last lines of the treatise, Gerson, like the lover in the poem, asked that his beloved make haste and come. He in the end returns to the Song's opening and asks that "he kiss me with the kiss of his mouth."[13]

There is no final proof here that Gerson in writing these lines was specifically thinking of Joan of Arc, but there is much that points in that direction. The love that is as strong as death hints at Joan's dedication to fight to the death for the end of the English dominion in France. The many references to the faith of ordinary, uneducated people may have been a reminder that her simple faith was worthy of respect and belief. It is otherwise hard to understand why Gerson would have included this theme in an exposition of a biblical work he otherwise saw as dealing with the contemplative life. The inclusion of an interjectory prayer repeating the names of Jesus and Mary recalls the prayerful opening words in Joan's defiant March 1429 letter to the English.[14]

The Shulammite woman is seen in the Song as one whose brothers think of her as very young and immature, with no breasts. In reality she is "a wall" with breasts "like towers." Most importantly, she is able to bring peace, but only through the guardians that surround her. These are not armies: they are angels, theologians [*doctoribus*], or priests and bishops [*praelatis*]. Here is the closest we can come to Gerson's apparent use of what had recently happened at Poitiers, where theologians and prelates gathered together to debate the meaning of Joan's message and her claim to divine inspiration.[15] She had long been convinced that angels guarded and guided her, and here the angel of whom she later spoke to her inquisitors apparently gave her protection.

Gerson's statement that the Shulammite through her enormous strength and courage makes certain that "the enemy attack does not enter by stealth" [*ne subintret hostilis invasio*] could have been his way of describing how the Maid's strength had stopped the English from swindling or tricking their way into Orléans. It is not necessary to read every line, however, as a symbolic reference to an actual event. What is important here is to see Gerson making use of the last chapter of the Song in order to describe how a young girl with guts becomes a central figure in bringing peace. For him the Shulammite woman and those who helped or protected her were the instruments of Jesus in bringing deliverance to his people.

If Gerson in fact was seeing Joan in terms of the Song as a strong woman who brings peace to a great conflict, he was not the first medieval commentator to provide such a contemporary and political reading of the Song. In the early 1080s, an otherwise unknown figure, John of Mantua, saw Countess Matilda of Tuscany as the bride in his commentary on the Song. He described her as a woman who combined the active and the contemplative lives, and who now was defending the interests of the Church. John of Mantua wanted Matilda to use armed force to oppose Henry IV of Germany.[16] Later Shakespeare himself saw Joan of Arc in language reminiscent of the "black but beautiful bride" of the Song of Songs.[17] It would be a fascinating task, beyond the limits of this essay, to look more closely at the representations of the Song's bride from the eleventh to the seventeenth centuries and thus perhaps to see Gerson's Joan as belonging to a literary tradition.

The figure of Joan of Arc in Gerson's consciousness in the last months of his life needs also to be seen together with that of the French King

Charles VII and his son, the future Louis XI. The former had been in Gerson's Lyon already in 1420 and had seen to it that Gerson was compensated financially for the losses of his home and possessions in Paris.[18] Now, probably in the late spring or summer of 1429, Gerson wrote to the dauphin's teacher and described how he was to instruct his important pupil.[19] Gerson had earlier written a similar treatise, which is much longer and so detailed that its contents seem quite impractical.[20] His new attempt betrays a changed attitude. Instead of listing all the books that the dauphin should read, Gerson made it clear that what mattered was to teach the boy with gentleness and even tenderness.[21] He was to be instructed not in isolation but together with his friends [*familiarium*], and they are to be shown "grave affability and affable gravity." The teacher is not to make himself hateful to his pupil. He is to show gentleness [*mansuetudo*], but not in being sycophantic. Whatever "childhood imperfection" the dauphin shows, he is not to be treated harshly, and accusations made against him by others are not to be listened to. The teacher's function is to nurture, not to torture his pupil. He is to encourage him with exemplary stories and moral tales; he is to teach him the names and attributes of different saints, and to tell them about their lives and legends. Finally the teacher is to encourage his pupil to have "special devotion to some of the saints, and especially to his own good angel who protects him from evil."[22]

Once again we have Gerson's emphasis on the guardian angel, and in general we also see his profound sensitivity to forms of religious belief that can encourage those who are not theologically learned. What is surprising here, however, is the gentleness of Gerson's tone. He does not ask that the dauphin be treated with kid gloves, but there is nothing here of the usual harsh attitude toward formation of the young that characterized classical and early medieval treatments of the subject.[23]

Why did Gerson encourage such a gentle, understanding regime? He must have hoped that such an approach would create a person who in experiencing human love and tenderness was eager to learn about the religion that recommended such love. Just as Joan of Arc would save the monarchy by being a tough woman, the dauphin would continue the monarchy by being a gentle man.

If we consider these two treatises as manifestations of Gerson's concerns in his last year of life, then he sought peace through a female figure that would be Christ's instrument and planned continuity through a dauphin whose enlightened Christian way of life would strengthen the monarchy. The fact that Louis XI did not turn out in this manner does not detract from Gerson's great ambition.[24] What matters here is to see how much he loved the monarchy as an institution and thus was willing to summon the learning and experiences of a lifetime in order to secure its future.

In this context it seems apparent that Gerson, in spite of earlier hesitations about visionaries, would have welcomed the appearance of a young woman who provided hope for the French monarchy. I thus see the *De mirabili victoria*, which I would prefer to call, on the basis of its own first words, *Super facto puellae* [On the Maid's Deed], as written by the same Gerson who in his commentary on the Song of Songs visualized a woman who would make it possible to find peace. Here, after a careful section dealing in general with what can be believed in piety but is not an article of faith,[25] Gerson made a point on which he had spent endless effort at the Council of Constance: a local church or bishopric, as represented by its "prelates and doctors [of theology]," could make a judgment about a question of faith. This is what the council of Paris had done in 1414 concerning the question of the defense of tyrannicide, a matter that was dear to Gerson's heart and mind.[26] The *Super facto puellae* notes that questions concerning Mary's immaculate conception, indulgences, or the veneration of relics could also be decided by such authorities. It mentions a specific case in which Gerson had been closely involved: the relics of Saint-Denis, the patron of France, which were found both at Notre Dame and at the abbey of Saint-Denis.[27]

This review of what the official Church can do through a regional gathering of prelates and theologians ends with the conclusion that in terms of matters concerning "the piety of faith and devotion," then "the deed of this Maid" can be "supported" [*sustineri factum illius puellae*].[28] In other words, the claim of Joan of Arc to be the mouthpiece of divine revelation can be accepted as theologically valid, "especially because of its final cause, which is most just: the restitution of the king to his kingdom and the most just driving out and defeat of his most stubborn enemies."

The final cause in Aristotelian terms means the result or outcome of a phenomenon. The *factum* or phenomenon of Joan of Arc was in the spring of 1429 creating a new situation; for the first time in years it looked as if the king could get back his kingdom. Joan was clearing the path to Reims so Charles could be anointed and crowned. Through his careful initial arguments about pious phenomena, Gerson was opening the way for theological acceptance of Joan as the instrument of God's will. He was telescoping the complex arguments of his three earlier treatises on discernment of spirits and applying them to a single case.

Gerson may not have completed the treatise in the detail that he intended. Cryptically he offered four "civil and theological proofs" [*documenta*] to support the case for Joan: the king and those of the royal blood; the king's and the kingdom's army; churchmen with the people; and the girl herself. He did not explain what he meant, only adding that all these 'proofs' had the same content: "living well, piously for God, justly for one's neighbor, soberly, that is virtuously and temperately towards oneself."

The argument here seems to have been that the fact or phenomenon of Joan of Arc encouraged everyone from the king on down to live according to God's law. She was an example to all in her simplicity and trust in God's will and his goodness. Thus the results of her presence at court, in the army, and among the people indicated that she was speaking the truth. She was in her way of life her own proof (a common argument for sainthood in hagiography). What she did was not for material gain, nor to create more ill will, hatred, or revenge. Here Gerson may have been thinking in terms of the hateful attitude that had persisted in France since the killing of the king's brother Charles of Orléans in 1407. Joan was there to see "that peace comes" [*quatenus pax veniat*], a phrase from Isaiah (57:2) that Gerson years before had used as the theme of a sermon seeking reconciliation in the kingdom after the murder of Charles.[29]

The peace Joan brought would assure that "freed from the hand of our enemies by a gracious God we may serve him in holiness and justice before him for all our days. Amen." Gerson thus ended this section with a prayer, the words of Zachary in his joyful *Benedictus* in rejoicing at the birth of his son John the Baptist, who would herald the coming of the Messiah (Luke 1:74–75).

As if these lines were not sufficient, Gerson added a fragment of a line from Psalm 117 (118): 23, a song of joy in victory over one's enemies: "This has been done by the Lord" [*A domino factum est istud*]. Again we have the word *factum* as the point of departure for his considerations: the Maid's deed or fact comes from God and not from anywhere else.

There follows a section dealing with the question of Joan's male attire, and I am not at all certain that it belonged to the treatise as Gerson originally composed it. It is possible that the marginal note dating this treatise as May 14, 1429 and the deliverance of Orléans, as well as this statement about the acceptability of Joan's dress, were added later: by Gerson himself or by his brother Jean the Celestine, who functioned as his literary executor.[30]

What matters here, however, is not the precise dating of the treatise nor its possible incompleteness or fragmentary composition. My point is that Gerson in defending the Maid because of her exemplary way of life and the results of her efforts saw her as the peacemaker that he visualized at the end of his commentary on the Song of Songs. He accepted that a new Shulammite woman had arrived on the scene to make peace, and for those who might challenge the veracity of her claims, Gerson was willing to point to her *factum*, the fact or reality of what she was doing in restoring the king to his kingdom.

Gerson had shown in many great court sermons how much he loved the French monarchy and believed in its continuation.[31] In such sermons he also revealed concern for the poor and wretched of the kingdom and the victims of its civil and international conflicts. Time and again Gerson asked that peace come to suffering France and its troubled monarchy, and in the last year of his life, he saw Joan of Arc as the one who could bring that peace. She was the virtuous Shulammite woman.

This treatise may be the result of a question formally put to Gerson by a skeptical observer, and so it would fit into the genre of brief theological statements with which he communicated with the world during his last years. If this hypothesis is correct, then we have lost an initial section that would provide information about who requested Gerson's point of view. Gerson, living in relative isolation at Lyon, only knew what others told him about Joan. What mattered for him, however, was the fact that she both lived a good life and contributed to the restoration of the monarchy that Gerson loved.

And where is Joan herself in this discussion? She is present in her belief that God wanted the king to take back his kingdom. We find her in her letter to the English, with its heading "Jesus Maria," indicating a simple pious invocation of a type that Gerson commended in the common people. Joan expressed a direct, unswerving faith that did not need intellectual explanation. Gerson never stopped being impressed by such a faith, even though in the years after the Council of Constance, he would have his doubts. In his treatise *On the Examination of Doctrines* from 1423, Gerson backed away from some of his earlier belief in visionary people and even showed some regrets.[32] But Joan of Arc revived his faith in the possibility that one visionary, with the help of angelic and human guardians, could be God's instrument.

Jean Gerson and the Maid of Orléans were thus in agreement, the Lord did the deed for her: *A Domino factum est istud*. As Gerson lay dying, Joan and her king were on their way to his anointing at Reims. We can imagine Gerson following them in his mind, seeing in this unique alliance between the weak and the powerful the fulfillment of God's will. He could leave this world in the belief that his France would be saved, and so he could turn in the last lines of his treatise on the Song of Songs to the embraces of the Christ whom he loved. In the language of his brother, "he devoutly handed over his spirit to God and now, as it can be piously believed, enjoys the embraces and kisses of his beloved groom."[33] His soul was at peace, while his Shulammite maid rejoiced in the belief that peace for her beloved king was at hand.

Notes

1. For example, Deborah A. Fraioli, *Joan of Arc: The Early Debate* (Woodbridge: The Boydell Press, 2002), pp. 24–44 and 126–49, as well as her chaper in this volume. Fraioli's thesis that *De mirabili victoria* was not authored by

Gerson is a modification of the conclusions of Dorothy G. Wayman, "The Chancellor and Jeanne d'Arc: February–July A.D. 1429," *Franciscan Studies* 17 (1957): 273–305. The *De mirabili* is accepted as Gersonian in Dyan Elliott, "Seeing Double: Jean Gerson, the Discernment of Spirits, and Joan of Arc," *American Historical Review* 107 (2002): 26–54, esp. 44–47, where it is referred to as *De puella aurelianensi*, the title given to it in the edition by Palemon Glorieux, *Oeuvres complètes* 9 (Paris: Desclée, 1973), pp. 661–65. This is also the view of the leading Gersonian scholar, Gilbert Ouy, as confirmed in a recent telephone interview (January 15, 2003), and is to be found in an important recent treatment of the discernment of spirits: Cornelius Roth, *Discretio spirituum. Kriterien geistlicher Unterscheidung bei Johannes Gerson* (Würzburg: Echter Verlag, 2001), pp. 209–13.

2. Wendy Love Anderson, "Free Spirits, Presumptuous Women, and False Prophets: The Discernment of Spirits in the Late Middle Ages," Ph.D. diss. (University of Chicago, 2002), p. 290. This significant contribution to our understanding of the development of the discernment of spirits tradition deserves publication.
3. *Super Cantica Canticorum* in Glorieux, *Oeuvres complètes* 8 (Paris: Desclée, 1971), pp. 565–639, with a note at the end by Gerson's brother.
4. I am thankful to Ann Astell and Bonnie Wheeler for their criticisms of an earlier draft of this chapter and for suggesting that I be more specific about my methodology and approach.
5. I have translated some of these treatises in *Jean Gerson. Early Works* (New York: Paulist, 1998). I consider *The Mountain of Contemplation*, written in French for Gerson's sisters and other women, to be one of his central works, indicating an opening to women in their contemplative lives.
6. For this correspondence, see Glorieux, *Oeuvres complètes* 2 (1960), pp. 232–326. I have dealt with it in my forthcoming biography, "A World Reborn. Jean Gerson and the Last Medieval Reformation 1350–1450," chapter 10.
7. See, e.g., Denys Turner, *Eros and Allegory. Medieval Exegesis of the Song of Songs* (Kalamazoo: Cistercian, 1995).
8. Glorieux, *Oeuvres* 8:638. Abisac or Abishag the Shulammite was a beautiful girl brought to David. After his death one of his sons asked Solomon if he could marry her. See 1 Kings 1:3 and 2:17–24.
9. Glorieux, *Oeuvres* 8:633.
10. Glorieux, *Oeuvres* 8:634.
11. Glorieux, *Oeuvres* 8:637.
12. Glorieux, *Oeuvres* 8:638. The remainder of my analysis of Gerson's treatise is taken from this page, so there will be no further references.
13. Glorieux, *Oeuvres* 8:639.
14. Fraioli, *The Early Debate, Lettre aux Anglais*, trans. p. 208.
15. See Fraioli, *The Early Debate*, "The Poitiers Conclusions," pp. 206–207.
16. See Jean Leclercq, *Monks and Love in Twelfth-Century France* (Oxford: Clarendon Press, 1979), pp. 47–48. Also Ann W. Astell, *The Song of Songs in*

the Middle Ages (Ithaca: Cornell University Press, 1991), pp. 42–43. I am grateful to Ann Astell for these references.

17. *King Henry VI. Part One*, where Joan says, "... whereas I was black and swart before / With those clear rays which she (Our Lady) infus'd on me / That beauty am I bless'd with which you see." Again I am most grateful to Ann Astell for this reference.
18. Glorieux, *Oeuvres* 10:553, where the date is mistakenly given as 1419.
19. For dating, Max Lieberman, "Chronologie gersonienne," *Romania* 73 (1952): 487–96 and 75 (1954): 289–337, in answering Antoine Thomas, *Jean de Gerson et l'education des dauphins de France. Etude critique* (Paris: Droz, 1930).
20. Glorieux, *Oeuvres* 2:203–15.
21. Glorieux, *Oeuvres* 2:335–38.
22. Glorieux, *Oeuvres* 2:338.
23. See McGuire, "Education, Confession and Pious Fraud: Jean Gerson and a Late Medieval Change," *American Benedictine Review* 47 (1996): 310–38.
24. See the fascinating biography by Paul Murray Kendal, *Louis XI* (London: Allen and Unwin, 1971), where Louis's problematic relationship to his father is emphasized.
25. This section is not translated in Fraioli, *The Early Debate*, appendix IV, pp. 209–12.
26. For background, Alfred Coville, *Jean Petit. La question du tyrannicide au commencement du quinzième siècle* (Paris: Picard, 1932), as well as my forthcoming biography of Gerson. Also the chronology in Glorieux, *Oeuvres* 10:164–70.
27. Glorieux, *Oeuvres* 2:103–05; trans. McGuire, *Early Works*, pp. 256–58.
28. Glorieux, *Oeuvres* 9:663.
29. Glorieux, *Oeuvres* 7.2:1100–23, calls the sermon "Discours au roi pour la réconciliation" and gives a provisional dating of November 1408.
30. Here we are finally beginning to see the importance of Jean the Celestine in his brother's literary inheritance, as shown by Gilbert Ouy in a forthcoming article.
31. As *Vivat rex. Vive le roy*, from November 7, 1405. Glorieux, *Oeuvres* 7.2:1137–85.
32. Glorieux, *Oeuvres* 9:458–75. I agree with Deborah Fraioli and Yelena Matusevitch in their contributions to this volume (chapters 7 and 8) that Gerson's antifeminism in the discernment of spirits has been exaggerated.
33. Glorieux, *Oeuvres* 8:639.

PART THREE

JOAN'S SECULAR CONTEMPORARIES

CHAPTER 10

CHRISTINE DE PIZAN'S *DITIÉ DE JEHANNE D'ARC*: HISTORY, FEMINISM, AND GOD'S GRACE

Heather M. Arden

This chapter explores the underlying spirituality of Christine de Pizan's Ditié de Jehanne d'Arc *by examining anomalous aspects of her patriotism, feminism, and personal exultation.*

If Christine de Pizan's *Ditié de Jehanne d'Arc* has received less scholarly attention than her other major works, in particular the allegories, the love poetry, and her letters on the *Roman de la rose*, this lack of scholarly interest belies the significance of the *Ditié*.[1] Angus J. Kennedy and Kenneth Varty, the poem's modern editors, sum up its importance in these words: "the first poem to have been composed—in any language—on Joan of Arc, the only major one to have been written while Joan was still alive, and the last from the pen of a distinguished poetess, the *Ditié de Jehanne d'Arc* has unique claims to fame."[2] While the *Ditié* is important as a historical document—Harry F. Williams argues that Christine's "main intent was to record for posterity the historical importance of events in the year 1429"—it records not only memorable events but the optimism and joy of pro-French people at the time of Joan's first victories.[3] Furthermore, scholars have praised the *Ditié* as the culmination of Christine's thinking about women and their place in God's design. According to Jay Ruud, "Christine sees Joan as. . .a divine vindication of the female sex, including the author herself," while Alan P. Barr argues that the "poem's 'cast of characters' and structure similarly work to support Christine's basically feminist tale or parable."[4]

Thus scholars recognize that the *Ditié* interweaves the major political and feminist strands of Christine's earlier works.[5] This much is clear. There are, however, some peculiar elements in the *Ditié* that have not been recognized but that must be examined before we can understand the *Ditié*'s significance for Christine. The *Ditié* frames its most important arguments in hyperbolic language that suggests a new interpretation of the poem's meaning for Christine. When describing what Joan has accomplished for Charles and for France, Christine exclaims repeatedly that this was the greatest miracle of all time; when celebrating what Joan has accomplished as a woman, Christine is amazed that God would bestow such great honor on the weaker sex; and when speaking of her own feelings about Joan's accomplishments, Christine pours out her joy in a long, intense opening section. These anomalies—the surprising distance between Christine's subject and her response to it—suggest that for Christine Joan has a personal meaning beyond the political restitution of the French king, that Christine sees Joan as the unique recipient in her time of the mystery of God's truth. What I hope to show in this essay is that ultimately the *Ditié* reveals an intense spiritual connection between Christine and Joan, a real connection that surpasses and fulfills the author's earlier imagined relationship with God's emissaries.

"Je, Christine, qui ay plouré / XI ans en abbaye close. . ."—thus begins the *Ditié*, a short work of sixty-one eight-line stanzas, totaling 488 octosyllabic lines, plus a one-line explicit: "Explicit ung tresbel *Ditié* fait par Christine" [I, Christine, who have wept for eleven years in a walled abbey. . .Explicit a very beautiful poem composed by Christine].[6] Complete versions of the *Ditié* are found in two fifteenth-century manuscripts; a fragment is found in a third, which is probably a late fifteenth- or sixteenth-century copy of a manuscript dating from 1456.[7] It is dated internally twice by the author: the beginning of stanza 3 gives the year, "L'an mil CCCCXXIX," while the final stanza gives also the day: "L'an dessusdit mil CCCC / Et XXIX, le jour où fine / Le mois de juillet" [In 1429; in the above-mentioned year, 1429, on the last day of July].[8] Thus the *Ditié* was apparently composed largely in the ten days following the coronation of Charles VII at Rheims. The first twelve stanzas express Christine's joy and wonder at the miraculous victories of La Pucelle, followed by eight stanzas addressed to the king, expressing optimism about his great destiny and reminding him of his duty to his people. Stanzas 21–36 celebrate Joan's coming, her military triumphs, and her special meaning for France, for women, and for Christine. The following stanzas are addressed first to the French troops, to whom Christine promises "gloire ou ciel et los!" [glory and praise in heaven], since they are fighting for "le droit" [what is right].[9] Changing her epic tone, Christine then harangues the English and their

Burgundian allies in "concrete, violent, abusive" language.[10] After Christine urges Paris and the rebellious towns to be loyal to their king, she concludes with a prayer for peace and a final challenge to those who will not listen to her. Throughout the *Ditié* Christine reiterates the miraculous achievements of La Pucelle—"Par miracle fut envoiée"—and her special relationship to God [l.225; she was miraculously sent].

The First Anomaly: The Miracle of Miracles

Christine received the news about Joan while living "en abbaye close" [l.2; in a walled abbey]. This was probably the royal Dominican abbey of Poissy, where her daughter was a nun and where the king's sister also resided.[11] Thus she has heard about Joan's presentation to the king and her examination by the Parlement at Poitiers (March–April 1429):

> Car bien a esté esprouvée
> Par conseil (en conclusion,
> A l'effect la chose est prouvée),
> Et bien esté examinée
> A, ains que l'on l'ait voulu croire,
> Devant clers et sages menée
> Pour ensercher se chose voire
> Disoit, ainçois qu'il fust notoire
> Que Dieu l'eust vers le roy tramise. (ll.230–38)

> [For she was carefully put to the test in council (in short, a thing is proved by its effect) and well examined, before people were prepared to believe her; before it became common knowledge that God had sent her to the King, she was brought before clerks and wise men so that they could find out if she was telling the truth.]

Christine is aware that Joan was also tested by the king's council when God's angel led her to Charles (see ll.228–31), but she does not mention any of the doubts or questions concerning Joan that occupied the minds of her contemporaries. Instead Christine offers three kinds of proof of Joan's election: the prophecies that foretold her coming; her virtuous, pious life; and her military victories.

Christine accepts without question prophetic messages from widely disparate sources: in addition to a Christian writer (the Venerable Bede), she refers to the legendary characters Merlin and the Sybil.

> Car Merlin et Sebile et Bede. . .
> . . .leur[s] prophecies en firent,
> Disans qu'el pourteroit baniere
> Es guerres françoises, et dirent

De son fait toute la maniere. (ll.241, 245–48)

[Merlin, the Sibyl and Bede. . .made prophecies about her, saying that she would carry the banner in the French wars and describing all that she would achieve.]

By repeating the widespread belief that certain prophecies foretold Joan's coming. Christine indicates that she accepts the prophecies as proof of Joan's divine election.[12] The Sibyls in particular held special meaning for Christine, for she had devoted the opening sections of Book II of *Le Livre de la Cité des Dames* to the Sibyls, whom she had Christianized, and she is guided by a Sibyl in the *Livre du Chemin de Long Estude* (see later, p. 294).[13]

Second, Christine points to Joan's virtuous life as proof of her divine calling: "Et sa belle vie, par foy, / Monstre qu'elle est de Dieu en grace" [ll.249–50; the beauty of her life proves that she has been blessed with God's grace]. The virginity and piety of La Pucelle, "une vierge tendre" [l.86; a young virgin], implicitly confound suspicions of diabolical association and orient the *Ditié* toward hagiography.[14] Finally, Joan's military feats speak eloquently for the divine source of her power, which was made manifest when she besieged Orléans:

O! Comment lors bien y paru
Quant le siege ert devant Orliens,
Où premier sa force apparu!
Onc miracle, si com je tiens,
Ne fut plus cler, car Dieu aux siens
Aida telement. . .(ll.257–62)

[Oh, how clear this was at the siege of Orléans where her power was first made manifest! It is my belief that no miracle was ever more evident, for God so came to the help of his people. . .]

Christine suggests repeatedly that only God could have accomplished such astonishing feats through a young girl as the intermediary.

It is evident, then, that Christine, unlike many of her contemporaries, does not need to be convinced of the God-given nature of Joan's mission, that she already believes fervently in Joan's special relationship with God.[15] She is the "Pucelle de Dieu ordonnée" (l.171) [Maiden sent from God], and it is through La Pucelle that God has worked his grace for Charles (see ll.111–12). But here we encounter the first of the surprising elements, the first "anomaly" in the *Ditié* that this essay will attempt to understand—Christine's hyperbolic estimation of the importance of Joan's achievement. God has not worked an ordinary miracle, so to speak, through Joan's intervention but the greatest miracle in human history: "Chose *sur toute* merveillable!" (l.58, my italics) [something which is more wonderful than anything else!]. Her use of the word "merveillable" expresses the astonishment and wonder that she and her contemporaries must have felt when witnessing Joan's deeds. Beyond simple acceptance of Joan's usefulness to the French monarchy, Christine stresses the miraculous nature of Joan's accomplishments: the words "miracle," "merveille," or a synonym occur nine times in the poem.[16] Christine asks further whether anyone has ever seen an event "Plus hors de toute opinion" (l.74) [quite so extraordinary]: "Il n'est homs qui le peüst croire?" (l.84) [nobody would ever believe it]. It is noteworthy that this hyperbolic praise of Joan's deeds *precedes* the discussion of the proofs of her divine mission, suggesting that Christine wants to believe in the miracle even before proof is offered.

After emphasizing the amazement that she and others have felt, Christine searches for words to convey the enormity of this miracle: "Que puet-il d'autre estre dit plus. . ." (l.177) [And what more can be said. . .]. But how can she describe what, she repeatedly argues, is "chose oultre nature!" (l.192) [something quite extraordinary!]? Since the ineffable can only be expressed through what it is not, it is through a series of negative comparisons that Christine continually stresses how Joan's deeds are the most miraculous ever accomplished. First Christine argues that no man could accomplish what Joan has done, not even the great biblical heroes Moses, Joshua, and Gideon or the classical heroes, Hector and Achilles (ll.179, 193, 209, and 287). A simple woman is "Plus preux qu'onc homs ne fut à Romme!" (l.199) [braver than any man ever was in Rome!]. All the brave warriors who have ever lived cannot equal this little maiden (ll.203–06). Even the remarkable women of the past who received God's favor—Esther, Judith, and Deborah—achieved less than Joan (l.217).[17] The repetition of adverbs of temporal lack, "onc" and "jamais," in this section of the *Ditié*, reveals both the wondrous uniqueness of Joan and Christine's difficulty in describing her achievement: "Onc miracle, si com je tiens, ne fut plus cler" (ll.260–61) [it is my belief that no miracle was ever more evident]; see also ll.201–02, 215, and 283. Finally, Christine's intense praise of Joan reaches a paroxysm in her exclamation that she has done what "C^m hommes [fait] n'eussent" (l.270) [5000 men could not have done].

Is the reason for this hyperbole simply Christine's desire to see France and Charles as the recipients of God's favor? That Christine deeply loved her adopted country has been shown by Josette A. Wisman: "Christine de Pisan prouve que le sentiment national existait à l'aube du XVe siècle; les jugements de la poétesse sur la France et les Français sont la preuve de l'amour profond qu'elle ressentait pour sa patrie d'adoption."[18] She also believed that France was especially favored by God.[19] But does Christine's patriotism explain her hyperbolic claims on Joan's behalf? While accepting Charles as the ruler of the French, God's latest chosen people, Christine also sees weaknesses in the king. For example, she hopes that Charles will be "bon. . ./ droiturier et amant justice" [ll.137–38; good and upright, and a lover of justice] and that his pride will not shame him, as if those qualities could not be taken for granted. Christine praises God for performing miracles for Charles and his people, whether or not they are worthy. Thus the simple fact of France's special relation to God does not explain why Christine lifts Joan's achievement to the highest degree of miraculousness. To understand this first anomaly, to which I will return, we need to look at the second anomaly, the contradictory nature of Christine's view of Joan as a woman.

The Second Anomaly: The Miracle of Women

Scholars have often pointed out that the *Ditié* celebrates Joan as reflecting honor on womankind: "Hee! quel honneur au femenin / Sexe!" Christine exclaims in stanza 34 (l.265–66) [Oh! What honour for the female sex!]. Joan seems to prove the validity of Christine's lifelong defense of women's worth and abilities, a defense that motivated some of her earliest writings, such as *L'Epistre au dieu d'Amours*, her letters on the *Roman de la rose*, and of course *Le Livre de la Cité des Dames*.[20] In these writings almost all examples of women's worth were based on historical or fictional women, rather than living ones. After decades of arguing on behalf of her sex, Christine must have been overjoyed to see her arguments vindicated by a real woman, one who could accomplish what no man had been able to do. Joan is the king's "champion," to whom God has given "force et povoir" (ll.187–88; strength and power). Thus many scholars have stressed Joan's significance for Christine's feminism. The editors of the *Ditié*, for example, find it "easy to understand the particular sense of triumph she must have felt at the news of Joan's victories," and Alan P. Barr argues that for Christine, "Joan's timely arrival. . .provided a made-to-order elaboration of the major contention in *Le Livre de la Cité des Dames*: that women were at least the equal of men."[21]

But herein lies the second anomaly, for there is an unresolvable contradiction in Christine's praise of Joan as a woman. While it is true that she achieved military triumphs beyond the capabilities of her male contemporaries, she also achieved what no woman could have accomplished. In fact, Christine suggests that God chose a woman to reach his ends specifically in order to show His power. Christine had argued in previous works that women are naturally weaker and more cowardly than men. In *Le Livre de la Cité des Dames*, for example, Christine had several times remarked on women's "corps femenin et foyble," and their "paour femenine" [feminine and weak body; feminine fear].[22] The biblical heroine, Judith, mentioned earlier in l.217, is described in the *Cité des Dames* in a way that strikingly foreshadows the paradoxical nature of Joan's accomplishments: "et la bonne dame se mist en oroysons, priant tousjours Dieu qu'a son cuer fememin et paoureux donnast hardement et force de delivrer son peupple" [and the good lady began to pray, praying God continuously that to her feminine and fearful heart he would give the courage and force to deliver her people].[23] Thus Joan, like Judith, joins a timid woman's heart to divinely inspired courage and force.

But the miraculous nature of Joan's accomplishments is even more remarkable than those of her predecessors. In order to magnify the miracle of Joan's military exploits, Christine stresses three aspects of Joan's identity that make her unsuitable for this job: femaleness, age, and social class. Descriptive epithets for Joan combine these elements in various ways: "une vierge tendre" [a young virgin], "une jeune pucelle" [a young maiden], "Une femme—simple bergiere" [a *woman*—a simple shepherdess; translators' emphasis], "une fillete de XVI ans" [a little girl of sixteen], "la Pucellette" [the little Maid] (ll.86, 186, 198, 273, 393). She also stresses that Joan is "oultre nature"—beyond or outside of nature, thereby suggesting again that it is not in woman's nature to undertake such exploits (l.192; see also l.274). Christine repeatedly gives all of the credit to God, who is acting through Joan: "ce fait Dieu," "tout ce fait Dieu," "Plus a fait par ceste Pucelle" (ll.207, 224, 288) [this is God's doing, all this is God's doing; He has accomplished more through this Maid]. Joan is frequently described by means of past participles that make her the passive channel through which God's power is directed: she is "Pucelle de Dieu *ordonnée*" [Maiden sent from God]; "Pucelle *eslite*" [literally "chosen Maiden"]; "Par miracle fut *envoiée* / Et divine amonition / De l'ange de Dieu *convoiée*" [miraculously sent by divine command and conducted by the angel of the Lord] (ll.171, 184, 225–27; my emphasis). She is the direct object of God's will: he leads her, he counsels her. Since God's power flows into Joan, she can become so strong and hard (l.277) ["fort et dure"] that she puts France's enemies to flight, thereby ridding the country of them and recovering castles and villages: "Jamais force ne fu si grant" (l.283) [never did anyone see greater strength].

This is ambiguous praise of women's worth, to see women as so lowly that God chose one of them, rather than a man, in order to increase the splendor of his miraculous intervention: "quant à Dieu, c'est chose legiere" (l.200) [As far as God is concerned, this was easily accomplished]. While a few scholars have recognized the ambiguity of Christine's praise, most have focused solely on the honor to the feminine sex. Deborah Fraioli, however, points out that Joan's "glory lay in her weakness rather than a near-virile strength, for by her weakness she proved herself to be the instrument of

God."[24] Rosalind Brown-Grant makes the strongest case for Christine's "depiction of the Maid as an atypical woman whose actions are determined by her role as instrument of God."[25] This Christian belief that "low equals high" underlies the same conundrum that medieval theologians faced when trying to understand the Virgin Mary: was she simply a woman who was better than other women, while remaining a woman, or was she essentially different from other women through the grace of God?[26]

Rather than attempting to resolve this anomaly, Christine sublimated it in her glorification of Joan as God's handmaiden. The "honneur" that Joan receives is simply a function of God's grace, not of her personal worth. "Honneur" is the same word that we find used in reference to the divine favor that France has received: "O quel honneur à la couronne / De France par divine preuve!" [ll.89–90; And what honor for the French crown, this proof of divine intervention!]. In both cases, that of France and Joan, God's grace is not dependent on the virtues of the recipient. Thus, by emphasizing the miracle of God's grace, Christine leaves unresolved the question of Joan's function as a role model for other women. What she stresses is Joan's special relation to God. In a beautiful passage Christine describes Joan's steadfast faith:

> . . . Car, quoy qu'elle face,
> Tousjours a Dieu devant la face,
> Qu'elle appelle, sert et deprie
> En fait, en dit; ne va en place
> Où sa devotion detrie. (ll.252–56)
>
> [whatever she does, she always has her eyes fixed on God, to whom she prays and whom she invokes and serves in word and deed; nowhere does her devotion ever falter.]

Whether besieging the walls of Orléans or crowning Charles king of France, Joan always has the vision of God before her. And God in return bestows on all women, through Joan, not only honor but love (l.266).

The Third Anomaly: The Miracle of Joy

In the opening stanzas of the *Ditié* we find the third significant passage relating to Christine's view of La Pucelle. The *Ditié* begins with a surprising first-person pronoun and the author's name: "Je, Christine"—surprising in a poem that celebrates God's intervention on behalf of France by means of a remarkable heroine. This seemingly anomalous emphasis on the author and her feelings, rather than on the historical events to be recounted, continues through the first seven stanzas, which incorporate twenty-one first-person pronouns and verbs (there are only six first-person grammatical forms in the remaining fifty-four stanzas). When scholars have remarked on this rhetorical use of the first person, they have attributed it to Christine's happiness at seeing the French victories, the coronation of Charles VII, and the possibility of peace at last: "it is her main intention to relate how God brought back the sun and spring into her own life by miraculously restoring the fortunes of France and the French Crown"; "the cause of her deeply personal joy is a political event."[27] While these political developments are undoubtedly part of Christine's response, the number and intensity of the first-person forms, as well as her use of metaphors in this passage, suggest there may be a deeper source of Christine's need for emotional self-expression, a source linked to the first two anomalies discussed earlier. Again, it is a question of degree. Although it is expected that she will be happy at the news of French victories, the intensity of her joy points to a deeper motivation.

Christine's lyric opening of the *Ditié* expresses her joy as she sees winter change to spring, as she changes her language "De pleur en chant" (l.14) [From one of tears to one of song], as the doors of her cage open and she enters the good season again (stanza 2). She stresses the change in her situation: she has wept, now she begins to laugh; she used to stay sadly in her cage, now she will sing. Several verbs of desire and volition reveal her joyous feelings:

> Mais plus de rien je ne me dueil,
> Quant ores voy ce que [je] veulx. (ll.23–24)
>
> [But I no longer grieve over anything, now that I can see what I desire.]
>
> . . .la tresbelle
> Saison, que printemps on appelle,
> La Dieu mercy, qu'ay desirée,
> Où toute rien se renouvelle. . .(ll.28–31)
>
> [Thanks be to God, the lovely season called Spring, which I have longed for and in which every creature / thing is renewed.]

In addition to the exultant first-person verbs, we find most of the *Ditiés* few metaphors in this opening section. The repeated references to the earth's rebirth in springtime, to the door of her cage opening, and especially to the sun—all have a mystical connotation through the implied theme of light. The good, new season (l. 19) ["le bon temps neuf"], in which everything is green and renewed, echoes the common springtime opening of many medieval love songs. Christine gives this metaphor, however, a spiritual connotation by suggesting the world's rebirth through God's mercy. The image of the cage alludes to the Boethian metaphor of the soul that, like the caged bird, seeks to escape its imprisonment and to return to the light of God. In *The Consolation of Philosophy*, Book Three, Meter Two, Nature describes the longing of the caged bird for its natural home: "Now for the wood alone she sadly longs, / For the woods alone she sings her whispered songs."[28] This example, which Philosophy first cites as illustrating the power of Nature, she reinterprets as an image of how earthly creatures dream of their origin, however faint the vision: they instinctively seek the "true good", which is found only in God. This metaphor of the caged bird is reinterpreted by La Vieille in Jean de Meun's *Roman de la rose*, in a famous passage justifying free love, a passage that Christine undoubtedly knew. Her use of the metaphor at the beginning of the *Ditié* restores to it the spiritual meaning that it had in the *Consolation of Philosophy*. Thus by this brief reference to the caged bird Christine is able to suggest her release from earthly doubts and her joy at glimpsing the True Good through La Pucelle.

The third metaphor of the opening section centers on the sun, which has begun to shine again (l. 18) ["Reprint à luire li soleil"]. And the final word of the *Ditié* is "lumiere," when Christine argues that those whose heads are bent and their eyes heavy cannot see the light. Christine has lifted her eyes to the Sun, the source of her intense joy. Since medieval writers often associate light with God, the *Ditié*'s opening metaphors, which revolve around the image of light, point to Christine's intense spiritual feelings in response to Joan's coming.[29]

When we look now at the first two anomalies in light of the third, Christine's spiritual response to Joan of Arc, we can see how all three passages point in the same direction. First, Christine describes Joan's miraculous deeds in hyperbolic terms in order to suggest Joan's special relationship to God, for the greatest miracles are performed by God's special emissaries. Furthermore, the great honor bestowed by God on a little shepherd-girl suggests that she has a special place in his plan. Finally, it is because of Joan's numinous status that Christine feels the intense joy that she expresses in the beginning of the poem. Christine had imagined herself, in earlier works, in contact with divine handmaidens. In *Le Livre de la Cité des Dames*, for example, the three allegorical ladies who come to instruct and guide Christine are the daughters of God, while the female saints of Book III, such as Saint Christine, proclaim that God is their true father.[30] Christine gives us a more unusual divine handmaiden in the Sybil who guides the narrator on her journey in *Le Livre du Chemin de Long Estude* (thus replacing the male guide, Virgil, who accompanies Dante in the *Divine Comedy*), unusual because she and her nine sisters become Christian prophets and prophesy Christ's coming: "par grace de Dieu prophetes / Furent et du secret haultiesme / Parlerent" [through God we were prophets and spoke of the highest secret].[31] However, with the coming of Joan, Christine is in contact, not with a mythic, imaginary, or long-dead messenger from God, but with a living emissary, a being through whom Christine can feel herself in touch with the divine. This spiritual joy and wonder at the miracle of Joan of Arc is the underlying motivation of Christine's hyperbolic praise of Joan, her wonder at the honor bestowed on La Pucelle, and her joyous feelings of release from her cage, of soaring toward the light of God's presence.

This analysis of the three anomalies in the *Ditié de Jehanne d'Arc* suggests an important interpretive tool for understanding Joan's deeper significance for Christine. Each of the three rhetorical structures—the hyperbolic estimation of Joan's historical importance, the ambiguous praise of her as both a great warrior and frail woman, and finally Christine's focus on her own feelings—each considered in isolation allows for several interpretations. When considered together, however, they point toward the spiritual meaning for Christine of Joan's miraculous status. While this is not to deny the presence of political objectives that motivated the writing of the *Ditié*, as described by the scholars referred to in this essay and others, the anomalous elements in the poem point to a spiritual meaning that has gone unrecognized. Above all, an analysis of these anomalies defines more clearly the religious meaning of the *Ditié*: the intensity, exaggeration, and repetitiveness of these three passages are symptoms of Christine's intense feeling of connection to and participation in the divine events she recounts. It is this participation that allows her also to become a prophet, revealing the highest secrets of the divine: she proclaims, for example, that Joan "will cast down the English for good, for this is God's will" (ll.321–23), "she will restore harmony in Christendom and the Church. She will destroy the unbelievers. . ." (ll.329–30), she will even lead Charles to the Holy Land, to destroy the Saracens (ll.337–39). Through her inspired vision of Divine Providence, Christine has become a witness to God's plan.[32]

Yet Christine wrote the *Ditié* while living in a convent, far from the divine emissary she praises. In such circumstances how could she express her intense, personal connection to the miracle of Joan of Arc? I believe that it is through her poem itself, the *Ditié de Jehanne d'Arc*, that Christine realizes her personal connection to Joan and becomes a spiritual companion to this miraculous emissary. This then is the deeper significance of the *Ditié*: more than an historical document or a feminist treatise, it is the moving record of a spiritual rebirth.

Notes

My thanks to Angus J. Kennedy and Connie Scarborough for their helpful suggestions with this article.

1. For a bibliography of Christine de Pizan's prolific output, see Angus J. Kennedy, *Christine de Pizan: A Bibliographical Guide* (London: Grant and Cutler, 1984), and *Supplement 1* (London: Grant and Cutler, 1994); also Edith Yenal, *Christine de Pisan: A Bibliography of Writings by Her and about Her*, 2nd ed. (Metuchen, N. J.: Scarecrow Press, 1989). Little is added to these bibliographies in Jean-François Kosta-Théfaine's "Bibliographic du *Ditié de Jehanne d'Arc* (1429) de Christine de Pizan," *Ariane* 16 (1999–2000): 213–21. Charity Cannon Willard's critical biography, *Christine de Pizan: Her Life and Works* (New York: Persea Books, 1984), offers an excellent overview of Christine de Pizan's works in the context of her life and times.
2. Angus J. Kennedy and Kenneth Varty, eds. and trans., *Ditié de Jehanne d'Arc* (Oxford: Society for the Study of Mediæval Languages and Literature, 1977), p. 1. All citations are from this edition and translation. Available online at http://www.ijas.smu.edu.
3. Harry F. Williams, "Joan of Arc, Christine de Pizan, and Martin le Franc," *Fifteenth-Century Studies* 16 (1990): 233–37 (citation from p. 234).
4. Jay Ruud, "Medieval Woman Writing Medieval Woman: Christine de Pizan's *Ditié de Jehanne d'Arc*," in *Proceedings of the Eighth Annual Northern Plains Conference on Earlier British Literature*, ed. Robert J. De Smith (Sioux Center, Iowa: Dordt College, 2001), pp. 73–88 (citation from p. 86); Alan P. Barr, "Christine de Pisan's *Ditié de Jehanne d'Arc*: A Feminist Exemplum for the *Querelle des Femmes*," *Fifteenth-Century Studies* 14 (1988): 1–12 (citation from p. 6).
5. For editions of Christine's earlier political interventions, see *"The Epistle of the Prison of Human Life" with "An Epistle to the Queen of France" and "Lament on the Evils of the Civil War,"* ed. and trans. Josette A. Wisman (New York: Garland, 1984); and "L'Epistre à la reine," ed. Angus J. Kennedy, in *Revue des Langues Romanes* 92 (1988): 253–64. Kate Langdon Forhan analyzes Christine's political thought in *The Political Theory of Christine de Pizan* (Hampshire, England: Ashgate Publishing, 2002). For a discussion of feminism in the *Ditié* see later.
6. *Ditié* l.1 and after l.488. Line numbers for the *Ditié* will generally be given in the text of the essay.
7. The manuscripts are described in the Introduction to the *Ditié*, pp. 2–6.
8. *Ditié* ll.17 and 482–83. For a discussion of the accuracy of this date, see Anne D. Lutkus and Julia M. Walker, "PR pas PC: Christine de Pizan's Pro-Joan Propaganda," in *Fresh Verdicts on Joan of Arc*, ed. Bonnie Wheeler and Charles T. Wood (New York: Garland, 1996), pp. 145–60. But see also Angus J. Kennedy's reply, "La date du *Ditié de Jehanne d'Arc*: réponse à Anne D. Lutkus et Julia M. Walker," in *Au champ des escriptures: Actes du III*[e] *colloque international sur Christine de Pizan*, ed. Eric Hicks (Paris: Honoré Champion, 2000), pp. 749–70. The historical background of the *Ditié*, however, is less important to my argument than is Christine's intellectual and emotional response to Joan as an emissary of God. For a thoughtful overview of responses to Joan of Arc in different periods, see Ann W. Astell, "Seeing Double: Reflections In (and On) the Mirrors of Joan of Arc," *Studies in Medieval and Renaissance Teaching* 7.2 (1999): 5–15.

9. *Ditié* ll.298 and 302; see also l.303: "se combat pour droiture" [fights for justice].
10. Introduction to the *Ditié*, p. 15.
11. Introduction to the *Ditié*, pp. 1–2. For a detailed personal account of Christine's visit to her daughter in the abbey of Poissy, see "Le Livre du Dit de Poissy," in *The Love Debate Poems of Christine de Pizan*, ed. Barbara K. Altmann (Gainesville: University Press of Florida, 1998), pp. 203–74.
12. For more on the prophecies, see Deborah Fraioli, "The Literary Image of Joan of Arc: Prior Influences," *Speculum* 56.4 (1981): 811–30; Jean-François Kosta-Théfaine, "Entre poésie et prophétie: les sources du *Ditié de Jehanne d'Arc* de Christine de Pizan" *Romanistische Zeitschrift für Literaturgeschichte* 1–2 (1998); 41–56.
13. For the Sibyls in *Le Livre de la Cité des Dames*, see Maureen C. Curnow, *The "Livre de la Cité des Dames" of Christine de Pisan: A Critical Edition* (Ann Arbor, Mich. University Microfilms International, 1975), pp. 786–94. For a modern French translation, see *Le Livre de la Cité des Dames*, ed. Eric Hicks and Thérèse Moreau (Paris: Stock, 1996), p. 127 ff.
14. For an analysis of the role of the name "La Pucelle" in the elaboration of Joan's legend, see Carmelle Mira, "Les dénominations dans le *Ditié de Jeanne d'Arc* de Christine de Pizan et dans quelques oeuvres contemporaines: l'élaboration d'un mythe," in *Images de Jeanne d'Arc: Actes du colloque de Rouen (25, 26, 27 mai 1999)*, ed. Jean Maurice et Daniel Coty (Paris: Presses Universitaires de France, 2000), pp. 89–97.
15. In "La spiritualité de Jeanne d'Arc," reprinted in *La piété populaire au Moyen Age* (Turin: Bottega d'Erasmo, 1975), pp. 355–80, Etienne Delaruelle suggests other characteristics of Joan that may have influenced Christine's opinion of her, such as her banner ("il fait. . .figure de bannière sainte"; see *Ditié* l.246) and her "simplisme évangélique" (p. 369), characteristics that may have led Christine to see "en l'âme de Jeanne un chef-d'oeuvre de la grâce" (370).
16. For these terms, see the following lines: miracle, ll.194, 214, 223, 225, 260; merveille, l.202, merveillable, l.58; oultre/fors nature, ll.192, 274. Christine is only refering to human miracles, of course, not to the greatest miracle of all, the Incarnation.
17. Fraioli discusses these biblical heroines in "Literary Image" and in "Why Joan of Arc Never Became an Amazon," in *Fresh Verdicts* (see n. 8 earlier), pp. 189–204; see in particular pp. 194–96.
18. Josette A. Wisman, "L'éveil du sentiment national au Moyen Age: la pensée politique de Christine de Pisan," *Revue Historique* 257 (1977): 289–97 (citation from p. 297). On the concept of France as God's chosen people, see also Joseph R. Strayer, *Medieval Statecraft and the Perspectives of History* (Princeton: Princeton University Press, 1971), pp. 300–314.
19. Wisman, "L'éveil," p. 293.
20. "L'Epistre au dieu d'Amours" can be found in *Poems of Cupid, God of Love*, ed. Thelma S. Fenster and Mary Carpenter Erler (Leiden: E. J. Brill, 1990). For Christine's letters on the *Roman de la Rose*, see *La Querelle de la Rose*,

ed. J.L. Baird and John R. Kane (Chapel Hill: University of North Carolina Press, 1978).

21. Kennedy and Varty, *Ditié*, p. 15; Barr, "Feminist Exemplum," p. 4; see also p. 8.
22. Curnow, *Cité des Dames*, pp. 675 and 713 (my translation); Hicks and Moreau, *Cité des Dames*, pp. 68 and 87.
23. Curnow, *Cité des Dames*, p. 859; Hicks and Moreau, *Cité des Dames*, p. 170.
24. Fraioli, "Why Joan of Arc Never Became an Amazon," p. 189; see also p. 196.
25. Rosalind Brown-Grant, " 'Hée! Quel Honneur au Femenin Sexe!': Female Heroism in Christine de Pizan's *Ditié de Jehanne d'Arc*," in *Writers and Heroines: Essays on Women in French Literature* (Bern: Peter Lang, 1999), pp. 15–30 (citation from p. 18). See also Kevin Brownlee, "Structures of Authority in Christine de Pizan's *Ditié de Jehanne d'Arc*," in *Discourses of Authority in Medieval and Renaissance Literature*, ed. Kevin Brownlee and Walter Stephens (Hanover: University Press of New England for Dartmouth College, 1989), pp. 131–50, especially p. 136.
26. See, e.g., the discussion of whether the Virgin menstruated in Charles T. Wood, "The Doctors' Dilemma: Sin, Salvation, and the Menstrual Cycle in Medieval Thought," *Speculum* 56.4 (1981): 710–27. In this volume, Chapter 2, see Ann Astell's, "The Virgin Mary and the 'Voices' of Joan of Arc."
27. Kennedy and Varty, *Ditié*, p. 9; Brownlee, "Structures," p. 134. See also Jean Maurice, "La naissance d'une légende: la 'presence sensible' de la Pucelle dans le *Ditié de Jehanne d'Arc* de Christine de Pizan," in *Images de Jehanne d'Arc* (see n. 14 earlier), pp. 79–88.
28. Boethius, *The Consolation of Philosophy*, trans. V.E. Watts (London: Penguin Books, 1969), pp. 81–82. For a discussion of the caged bird metaphor in the *Roman de la Rose*, see Chauncey Wood, "La Vieille, Free Love, and Boethius in the *Roman de la Rose*," *Revue de Littérature Comparée* 51 (1977): 336–42.
29. Umberto Eco, *Art and Beauty in the Middle Ages*, trans. Hugh Bredin (New Haven: Yale University Press, 1986); in particular chap. IV: The Aesthetics of Light.
30. Curnow, *Cité des Dames*, pp. 627 (allegorical ladies) and 1001–10 (Saint Christine). The image of the dryness of the earth giving way to greenery in the opening section of the *Ditié* echoes the way Christine thanks the allegorical ladies in the *Cité des Dames*, whose words have vivified "la secheresce de mon entendement" (638). Hicks and Moreau, *Cité des Dames*, pp. 41, 47, and 255–61.
31. *Le Chemin de longue étude*, ed. and trans. Andrea Tarnowski (Paris: Livre de Poche, 2000), ll.524–26 (my translation).
32. Since the *Ditié* is the last work we have from Christine, she apparently stopped writing after Joan's death, which must have affected her deeply. Because of Joan's trial and execution, Christine may have come to see her as Charles Péguy did, centuries later—not only as "le trésor de la grâce," but also as "un trésor de la souffrance," which was "le prix de tout un people d'âmes" ("Le mystère de la charité de Jeanne d'Arc," in *Oeuvres poétiques complètes* [Paris: Gallimard, 1975], pp. 519 and 521).

CHAPTER 11

EN L'HONNEUR DE LA PUCELLE: RITUALIZING JOAN THE MAID IN FIFTEENTH-CENTURY ORLÉANS

Vicki L. Hamblin

This chapter discusses documents composed in Orléans in the wake of Joan the Maid's passing that reveal an evolving relationship between the heroine's spirituality and civic needs.

In 1428 and 1429, a nine-month long siege opposed French loyalists defending the city of Orléans for Charles VII and English troops intent on winning this key city in the name of their own king. That protracted siege came to a swift and definitive end with the arrival of Joan the Maid and French reinforcements. The apparently miraculous victory won by the French, and inspired by the Maid, was not to be forgotten in the hearts and minds of the Orléans population; documents produced locally in the fifteenth century all recount, to varying degrees and for different purposes, the significance of those events.

Given their varying intentions, it is no surprise that these documents also exhibit diverging perceptions of Joan's presence in their city. In some cases, such as in the local chronicles, personal recollections and rehabilitation records combined to constitute a popular veneration of the Maid. In other documents, like the official *Comptes de ville et de forteresse*, Joan is only incidentally present and only belatedly honored. Finally, in the *Mistère du siège d'Orléans*, a fifteenth-century mystery play that reenacts the long siege, Joan fulfills a carefully orchestrated public mandate.

In all cases, the historical Joan has been reincarnated ritualistically as part of a uniquely local tradition. Viewed collectively, these recreations reveal a local preoccupation with fashioning a Joan who was uniquely responsive to Orleans's social, political, and spiritual needs. In these recreations, rather than in the historical Joan, can be found the personage who earned the title of the "Maid of Orléans." This chapter focuses on how the chronicles, the *comptes*, and the mystery play characterized Joan's spirituality in response to these uniquely local preoccupations.

The Local Chronicles

Three chronicles were written in Orléans either during the 1428–29 siege or several decades after the French victory. The authority afforded these chronicles emanates from their status as firsthand narratives that in two cases, at least, have been supplemented by later, equally authoritative witnesses to various aspects of the siege, and therefore, to Joan's participation therein. They all feature, for example, repeated incidents of reported speech, such as witnesses' recollections of the Maid having said, en route to Poitiers, that she would have much to endure there.[1]

The *Petit traicté*, otherwise called the *Journal du siège d'Orléans*,[2] is based on a daily register of events that was written during the siege itself. This register was then amended or supplemented by Rehabilitation-era witnesses. According to city records, the amended journal was commissioned by municipal leaders in order to codify the events for local archives.[3] A second chronicle, also produced during the events of the siege and entitled the *Geste des nobles francoys*, was, according to historian Jules Quicherat, conceived as an informed document destined for a single, unidentified reader.[4] The *Geste* was later amplified to become the *Chronique de la Pucelle*, drawing from both the *Journal du siège d'Orléans* and the Rehabilitation record. A third chronicle, known as the *Chronique de l'établissement de la fête du 8 mai*, was not composed until after 1452 but is also the voice of a firsthand witness to the siege who recalls his own testimony, as well as that of others in the community.[5] Each of these works reflects both individual perceptions of Joan's role in the events and an evolving community involvement in recreating the Maid.

The anonymous author of the *Geste des nobles francoys* revels in the *émerveillement* that Joan's presence prompted among all those who encountered her in Orléans.[6] When, for example, Joan awakens with a premonition of the skirmish underway at the fortress of Saint Loup, she straddles her horse and rides away "comme si elle sceu le chemin par avant et toutesfois onques n'y avoit entr[é]" [as if she knew the way beforehand, although she had never been there].[7] A voice, according to the author, had warned Joan of that skirmish. As this episode illustrates, the *Geste*'s Joan is an active warrior responding to God's command; otherwise simple and uninformed, this Maid becomes an insistent, argumentative, and undaunted military leader when called upon to do so.

Unlike the contemporary *Geste*, the *Chronique de l'établissement de la fête du 8 mai* was conceived nostalgically as a reminder to citizens who had forgotten the significance of local traditions that commemorated the siege.[8] The reverent language of this chronicle has prompted scholars to assume that its author was religiously trained.[9] All references to Joan in this short account center on the miraculous nature of her actions, wherein "tout procédait de Dieu" [all things came from God].[10] Accordingly, this author does not transfer any authority to the Maid in his description of the victory celebration, despite his obvious bias in exhorting the forgetful citizens to participate in those activities.[11]

Finally, in the revised *Journal du siège d'Orléans* local citizens react to seeing Joan arrive in Orléans as if "ilz veissent Dieu descendre entre eulx" [they saw God descend among them].[12] Everyone marvels as a virtuous and courageous Joan accomplishes the signs that had been announced to her by God. In this very detailed chronicle, which incorporates Joan's biography as if part of its narration of local events, the Maid is an answer to prayers. This author defers especially to public opinion that held that Joan had been sent to the people of Orléans to relieve their suffering.

In all three of these locally produced chronicles, God's authority and the Court's judgment are seen as defining factors in favor of the Maid. Rather than arguing the case, all three chronicles underscore Joan's religious orthodoxy by stating quite simply that she was informed "par grâce divine" [by divine grace][13] and that she attended Mass.[14] All three narratives likewise accept the fact that Joan's difference lay only in the existence of *revelacions* or voices that were, from their perspective, necessarily divine. All three works repeatedly employ the word *émerveillé* or *merveille* to recall their collective response to the young woman who had not only liberated them, but who had lived among them for a short while. The heavy incidence of reported speech in all three works also lends credence to this collective memory that would be, or had been, justified by the Rehabilitation record in the 1450s.

Likewise, these chronicles revel in recalling popular rumors that had circulated about Joan's personal spirituality. For instance, the *Chronique de la fête* repeats Rehabilitation testimony to the effect that the wind suddenly changed direction when the Maid and French troops needed to cross the Loire river, as if this were a supernatural event.[15] The *Journal du siège* too includes an episode in which Joan saved a soldier's life by warning him to move from the spot where he was standing seconds before a cannonball lands there.[16] In the narration of these and other popular beliefs, the local chronicles relive Joan's spirituality as incidental and personal, thus extending her faith to miraculous arenas that fueled a more mystical, if simplistic, recollection of her divine mission. For the collective memory of those who had lived through the siege, these spiritual manifestations were no more in conflict with Joan's orthodox behavior than was her simplicity in areas not related to her mission. In fact, these manifestations gave to Joan the familiarity necessary to assign her a place within the community.

The *Comptes de ville et de forteresse*

While the three chronicles made of Joan a venerated member of the local community by recalling their contacts with her via the collective and the individual voices of its citizens, a distinctly different impression may be gleaned from the city's official records. Throughout the fifteenth century, the city leaders, called the *bourgeois*, maintained registers of city expenses. Essentially tallies, or lists, of how monies and materials were allocated in the defense and management of Orléans, the *Comptes* are abbreviated in their intent and in their content. For obvious reasons, then, while they do catalogue municipal efforts to meet the Maid's material needs, the entries do not acknowledge Joan's spiritual mission. They do, however, include numerous references to the city's annual celebration to commemorate the French victory. Beginning in 1429, the *Comptes* characterized that celebration as a civil procession, in which the city leaders, clergy, military leaders, and citizens participated, followed by at least one public sermon to praise God for the victory. Obviously, the historical Joan participated only in the celebration that took place in 1429. The *Comptes*, however, do not mention that participation; nor, as Pierre Mantellier has pointed out, is Joan's role in the victory given any particular status in subsequent references to the annual celebrations.[17] Moreover, it was not until the Rehabilitation era that the yearly celebration was afforded a measure of ecclesiastical status,[18] and decades still before the Maid was singled out from among the other military leaders who had fought beside her. Only in verses composed for the 1483 celebration may it be said that the Maid was honored individually,[19] despite claims that the city's *fêtes* honored the Maid from their inception.[20]

Unlike the local chronicles that reflected in their post-Rehabilitation revisions the evolving image of a venerable Joan, the official documents of Orléans, responded only slightly, and belatedly, to that image. Even tangentially, in financing the poem composed in 1483, the city's officials constructed for the Maid an image set only superficially in any spiritual context.[21] There are, of course, other signs that the city was responding to public opinion concerning the Maid. The *Comptes* remind us that the municipality supported Joan's mother, Isabelle Romée, until her death, and was equally magnanimous to Joan's brothers, Pierre and Jean. Further, in 1456, the city hosted the officials who had been commissioned to revise Joan's condemnation trial. The celebratory procession that led from Sainte Croix cathedral to Saint-Samson church was followed that year by a gala dinner for those all-important commissioners.[22] And, of course, the city did commission the *Journal du siège d'Orléans*, as already noted. Finally, and significantly, some years later, a monument was erected in Joan's honor on the bridge that connected the city to the Tourelles fortress.[23] However, this monument, which featured Joan and Charles VII in kneeling positions before Christ on the cross and an attentive Virgin Mary, was not sponsored by the city itself.[24]

The *Mistère du siège d'Orléans*

While the local chronicles fueled a popular veneration of the Maid that justified the collective memory of its citizens and that has become a prominent portrayal even in modern times, the city's official records refrained from recreating her image. Instead, they reacted to an evolving public opinion about the Maid by characteristically recording municipal activities that became increasingly Joan-centered in the decades after the Rehabilitation trial. A third document, also dating from the fifteenth century and compiled in Orléans, provides, for the purposes of this chapter, a glimpse into how popular recollections and official reserve combined in that city to create a local Joan.

The *Mistère du siège d'Orléans* reenacts for a local audience the 1428–29 battle between English invaders and French loyalists. In so doing, this work became the only French mystery play to perform contemporary history. Nonetheless, the play's reliance on local, authoritative documents,[25] its historical rather than allegorical scenario, and its God-centered message were standard features of the mystery genre.[26] Furthermore, the *Mistère du siège* linked the reality of the Orléans siege to a national debate and to God's role in determining the outcome of that debate.[27] In the folios of the *Mistère du siège*, three elements revolve around the central figure of Joan the Maid: as divine messenger, as military leader, and as local heroine. This triple role even assigns to her the role of exhorting the people of Orléans to take part in the city's commemorative processions and masses. In assigning that role to the Maid, the play's *fatiste*, or compiler, reiterated, for local citizens, the traditions instituted by municipal leaders in the years following the victory. In so doing, he also deviated from the personal experience that had been Joan's in Orléans in 1429.

The evolution from a personal Joan to the public Joan found in the folios of the *Mistère du siège* stems, no doubt, from a desire to assign to Joan's experience the authority that it needed in order to become part of the collective record. For example, the *Mistère du siège* includes, in the form of a dramatic monologue, the Maid's letter to the English written in late March 1429.[28] This letter's inclusion in a play dependent on written authority is in no way surprising. However, in this spectacle, the Maid asks an anonymous cleric to write and then to read the letter as per her dictates.[29] It is the cleric who pronounces this urgent message in the form of a monologue. It is the cleric who alternates, while reading verbatim from the letter, between third person references to the Maid and first person references to his (her) intention to rid the countryside of English invaders. Therefore, this dramatic reconstruction transfers the realm of personal experience to that of an already authorized document, confirming the spectators' knowledge of and confidence in that authority. And, significantly, for the purposes of the present analysis, this affirmation takes place while a mute Joan stands beside the cleric on stage.

The authority extended to Joan in the *Mistére du siége* is based, in large part, on reiterating the orthodox, and outwardly visible, nature of her spirituality. In the same way that the compiler constructs a *procès de paradis* that shapes the historical story line by staging the divine mandate, he builds an authoritative Joan.[30] The compiler's recreation of the Poitiers episode further illustrates an intentional reconstruction of Joan's experience. The *Mistére du siége*'s compiler stages a preliminary deliberation in which Charles VII, in Chinon, seeks the advice of four Counselors regarding a young maiden who has arrived to "bouter les Anglois dehors du royaulme" [kick the English out of the kingdom].[31] The anonymous Counselors find this maiden unusual, and, fearing a possible deception, they suggest that by sending her to Poitiers the King might not be held responsible for any undesirable consequences. The Counselors then accompany Joan to Poitiers, where four *Présidents* and one Inquisitor are waiting to interrogate her.

In the first of two series of questions, the First Poitiers President asks Joan where she comes from, what has motivated her to come to France, if she realizes what she is suggesting, and finally, what might be her intentions. These questions recall, quite clearly, two pertinent documents that may well have served as the compiler's sources, either directly or indirectly: first, the Rehabilitation testimony of Jean d'Alençon,[32] and, secondly, *The Poitiers Conclusions*. The latter, a document duly diffused throughout the kingdom and beyond, reports that Charles's counselors interrogated Joan as to "sa vie et sa naissance,. . .ses moeurs, son caractère et ses projets" [her life and birth,. . .her habits, character and her plans].[33] These questions, and Joan's responses in the *Mistére du siége*'s reconstruction, recall, at least superficially, the *discretio spirituum* implemented by the Poitiers judges in order to determine that Joan's upbringing conformed to the Christian standard and that her mission was politically and morally justifiable. Joan, as the *Mistère du siège* text recounts, is from Barrois, a region then loyal to France; her father is an honest and faithful man. God has commanded her to come to France. As he makes things possible, she does as he requests. Her intentions are to raise the siege at Orléans and to lead Charles to Reims to be crowned. Freeing France of its enemies is Joan's ultimate objective.[34]

In the second half of the *Mistère du siège*'s Poitiers interrogation, the Inquisitor focuses on two equally familiar issues. First, he reminds Joan that God does not need violence to achieve his will. This admonition, followed by Joan's retort that she will not need many men to accomplish the task, constitutes one of the most cited incidents from the Rehabilitation records[35] and signals a statement that Joan will repeat in her letter to the English. Next, the Inquisitor questions Joan's transgendered appearance. Her male dress had been a contentious issue on both sides of the political map. *The Poitiers Conclusions* had specifically addressed this issue. Other contemporary documents, including the *De quadam puella*, had debated this controversial manifestation of Joan's mission. The Rehabilitation judges too argued against the Condemnation trial's conclusions in this regard.[36] The *Mistère du siège*, however, places the question of the Maid's dress in God's mouth. Thus, when Joan subsequently informs the Inquisitor that God himself has mandated her to wear male clothing and that it is more practical for the task at hand, she is only repeating a divine imperative to which the spectators have themselves been witness. Having thereby dismissed any apparent obstacles to Joan's orthodoxy, there is no further need for debate on this issue. Instead, the *Mistère du siège* reenactment provides only the consensus expressed in *The Poitiers Conclusions*. The Inquisitor and the Presidents determine, not surprisingly, that the Maid is "prudente et savante" [carefully spoken and knowledgeable][37] and that she is indeed God's creature.

The scant orthodoxy produced in this staged recreation of the Poitiers interrogation focuses, first, on the miraculous nature of the military victory that Joan will win through God's intervention and, then, on confirming, rather than testing, the orthodoxy that characterizes God's agent in this endeavor. In dealing only with Joan's life circumstances and her dress, this recreation only partially reflects *The Poitiers Conclusions*. Having rendered visually on stage as historical truth the voice or counsel that Joan and the authoritative documents had identified,[38] the compiler need not ask Joan to explain her inspiration. In like fashion, the sign or signs that appear as a prevalent theme in *The Poitiers Conclusions* and in the trial records,[39] is played out in the *Mistère du siège* reenactment before an audience fully cognizant that the Orléans victory had indeed constituted proof of her divine authority. Unlike the contemporary judges who approved Joan only provisionally, the *Mistère du siège* does not hesitate to claim, in Deborah Fraioli's words, that Joan "was indeed sent by God."[40] While the Poitiers judges had probed the personal Joan in search of an appropriate profile,[41] the compiler shifts public attention further away from testing a personal Joan to a simple affirmation of the tangible and visible dimensions of the divine plan in which Orléans and the Maid are inextricably linked. The authority of the record itself replaces the personal experience of the historical individual who was destined to become the Maid.

Comparing this staged episode to the three narrative chronicles already named reveals some intriguing differences. The *Journal du siège d'Orléans* places the Poitiers episode within the same chronological parameters as does the *Mistère du siège*, including the use of uncharacteristically vague references to dates and times for these events.[42] However, the *Journal du siège* reports only one question in its description of the Poitiers interrogation: that of the Inquisitor, or "docteur jacobin"[43] who informs Joan that God does not need violence to achieve his will. The *Geste des nobles francoys* summarizes the Poitiers interrogation in only a few words,[44] while the *Chronique de l'établissement de la fête du 8 mai* does not even mention Poitiers.[45] Despite having been written or revised after 1452, and despite the fact that two of these chronicles rely partly on Rehabilitation testimony, as does the mystery play, these prose sources, unlike the mystery play, do not fully integrate this nonlocal event.

These chronicles nonetheless inform the mystery play's Poitiers recreation in a uniquely local way. The *Chronique de la Pucelle* and the *Journal du siège* both reiterate that the French administration had relocated, so that Joan was accompanied to Poitiers "où estoit la court de Parlement" [where the Parliament was located][46] and where could be found several doctors in theology, as well. The *Geste des nobles francoys* further stipulates that Joan was interrogated in Poitiers by parliamentary as well as theological experts.[47] The *Mistère du siège*'s compiler follows these contemporary versions, contending that Charles wants the case explained to the Parliament[48] in Poitiers and that the counselors there who "tiennent parlement" [are seated in Parliament][49] will resolve the issue of Joan's intended mission. Thus, the compiler designates the Poitiers judges as four Presidents and a single theological doctor in order to maintain that Joan was interrogated there by parliamentarians, as well as by clergymen.

In so doing, the compiler commits what Pierre Boissonnade and others have called an apparent error.[50] The Rehabilitation evidence clearly demonstrates that the interrogators in Poitiers were theologians rather than civil lawyers.[51] Thus, the compiler's decision to grant approval to Joan by both church and state representatives via a single mechanism, though inaccurate, has nevertheless some basis in local lore. Other written sources repeated this coincidence and the Orléans public had apparently accepted this version as proof that the Court too had approved Joan's mission.[52] Evidently, the play's compiler valued the double authorization to be gleaned from this local version of the events, despite having included in the *Mistère du siège*'s quasi-civil reenactment questions inherent instead to the theological *discretio*.

The conscious selectivity that characterizes the *Mistère du siège*'s reliance on its various sources, especially in reference to Joan's presence, must fulfill a thematic necessity. Obviously, this selectivity hinges on the fact that the play was intended for a commemorative performance at least one generation removed from the siege itself,[53] so that a certain measure of hindsight enabled personal recollections to fuse with a public mandate. As such, the *Mistère du siège*'s reconstruction of the Maid is characteristic of those Rehabilitation era texts, like Elie de Bourdeille's treatise, that justify after the fact a righteous Maid whose victory paved the path to a French victory. According to Jane Marie Pinzino, Bourdeille's hindsight enabled him to narrate "a realized salvation history of the French people with Joan of Arc in the leading prophetic role, guiding the French people and struggling in the name of God to fulfill his plan for establishing an independent French people."[54] Likewise, the *Mistère du siège*'s Joan is a willing and obedient agent who, when informed of God's design, accepts despite her initial fear, because, in her words:

A Dieu je vouldroye obeÿr
comme je doy et est raison,
et tres humblement le servir
a mon povoir, sans mesprison.

[I would like to obey God
As I should and as is right,
And very humbly serve Him
With all my might, without erring.][55]

Once she accepts the authority of her mission, Joan performs as a fearless and public figure in the *Mistère du siège*. Her subsequent actions and her words are intended as proof of the fulfillment of a divinely ordained mission for France. The "Dame Jehanne" to whom the other personages on stage speak predicts the two parts of her mission as previously determined by God himself on stage. She predicts the imminent victory at the Tourelles fortress in the same informed manner. While these predictions have been rendered literally on stage because they are directly related to the mystery play's intention, others, such as the reference to Glasdale's bloodless death, are relegated by the compiler to the astrologer Jean des Boillons,[56] perhaps to avoid diffusing the mission's focus. Joan's military leadership, on the other hand, is fully relevant. This quality earns the respect of her fellow soldiers, for whom she is: "en conseil si bien disposee / de guerre, qu'on ne pourroit mieux / de ce qu'elle dit et proppose" [in council of war so well prepared / that one could not hope for better / than what she says and proposes].[57]

Joan's own words, in deferring to God's authority rather than her own,[58] underscore the complementary traits of humility, piety, and charity that were so oft-repeated in the Rehabilitation documents.[59] Joan's spirituality is thus realized, first and foremost, in the public demonstration of traits relevant to her mission. Even her martyrdom, though ridiculed by the English soldiers, is confirmed by God's promise that Joan's soul will find solace.[60]

In the hands of our compiler, this rehabilitated Joan is also the catalyst for a local revival in which the Orléans's residents might participate. Thus, in the *Mistère du siège*, Joan attends mass at Sainte Croix cathedral in Orléans, as local sources had maintained. She also stands center stage, symbolically clad in a "robbe de drap d'or" [cloak of golden cloth],[61] to exhort the victorious soldiers to hear mass and to remember the significance of the day's victory. In addition, late in the play, she again admonishes the citizenry to participate in the victory procession and celebratory mass.[62] This admonishment is unhistorical,[63] as already noted, but it allows the compiler, once again, to implicate the Maid fully in local concerns.

This implication, however, does not extend to reiterating those popular images of the Maid found in the local chronicles. For example, both the *Mistére du siége* and the *Journal du siège* recount Joan's arrival in Orléans on the evening of April 29, 1429. The mystery play account describes the following staged activity: "et viendront a la porte Bourgoigne et a l'entrée, la Pucelle fait porter son estandart, au soir, a torches devant elle, armee et montee sur ung gros cheval blanc, et chacun de la ville va devant d'elle" [and they enter by the Burgundy gate, and at the entrance the Maid has her banner displayed, in the evening, with accompanying torches, and is armed and mounted on a large, white horse, and the people all go to meet her].[64]

Thus, the play gives to Joan's arrival the status of a princely entry, as the choice of props readily demonstrates. This entry is followed by appreciation speeches uttered first by the count of Dunois, who is leading the city's defense, and then by the Maid herself. The *Mistère du siège* then moves directly to a discussion of Joan's missing messenger. However, the *Journal du siège*'s account actually provides more details of the ceremonial entry, including the order in which various warlords and city leaders joined the procession and were received by the Maid.[65] Moreover, this prose version of Joan's entry also embraces popular reaction to the Maid's arrival. The men, women, and children present, overjoyed by Joan's arrival, looked upon her with great affection, and "y avoit moult merveilleuse presse à toucher à elle, ou au cheval sur lequel elle estoit" [they all pressed forward to touch her, or even the horse she was riding].[66] Unfortunately, in their enthusiasm, the crowd jarred a torchbearer, who inadvertently ignited Joan's banner. The Maid rapidly turned on her horse to quench the flames, to everyone's amazement. Following this surprising display, the Maid was accompanied to her intended host's home, surrounded by ecstatic people from all walks of life. Despite its dramatic potential, this sequence is not exploited in the compiler's reenactment.

In fact, according to the *Journal du siège*, common people followed Joan wherever she went in the city, prompting its author to comment that the people "se saoulaient de la voir" [they were intoxicated with seeing her].[67] Characteristically, then, this chronicle recalls a Joan who participated in and had an impact on the lives of the local inhabitants in nonofficial ways. The mystery play, as a public reenactment, prefers a more distant and public perspective. The *Mistère du siège* does state that the people are overjoyed at Joan's arrival, but, in its folios, the city leaders express, somewhat officiously, public appreciation for Joan's efforts on their behalf.[68] While the *Mistère du siège*'s Joan refers to Orléans's brave residents and thanks them for their hospitality,[69] the only commoners who come into direct contact with this Joan are the messengers she dispatches and receives as part of her mission.

It appears that unlike the commemorative play, which places Joan center stage commanding the local leaders before a crowd of spectators, the chronicles revel instead in remembering Joan as having been present in the crowd itself. The *Mistère du siège*, on the other hand, follows a public mandate in which Joan's spirituality is a "piété agissante" [activist piety], as Pierre Lanéry d'Arc termed it.[70] The *Mistère du siège* therefore relegates superstitions and rumors to its English characters and to commoners who do not encounter the Maid.[71] This marked difference between popular veneration, as expressed in the local chronicles, and the public mandate staged on the *Mistère du siège*'s folios, is so obvious as to negate early criticism about the play's being nothing more than a chronicle in verse.[72] Their different perceptions actually illustrate the city's need to recreate a Joan responsive to local needs.

Furthermore, the *Mistère du siège*'s performance mandate also seems to respond to an unstated public policy. Among its principal characters the *Mistère du siège* counts several members of the local municipal council, which was composed of twelve *bourgeois* elected biannually to manage the city's affairs.[73] Their participation in this reenactment is essential, since they represent the city's interests. As civilian and secular managers reacting to a military leader who has been granted full authority in their defense,[74] they assure the Maid that "obbeyr vous voulons" [we want to obey you].[75] However, the Joan whom they address on stage is essentially the "puissante dame" [forceful woman][76] who, in leading the military defense, was responsible for the city's liberation.[77] Moreover, while the mystery's Joan does hear mass in Orléans,[78] she never encounters the two ecclesiastical leaders, Jehan de Saint Michel, bishop of that city, and Regnault de Chartres, who appear but once in this otherwise detailed reenactment.

Instead, not surprisingly, the officious nature of the relationship between the municipal leaders and Joan the Maid in the *Mistère du siège* finds some parallels in the *Comptes de ville et de forteresse*. The public mandate that characterizes the city council's record-keeping is analogous to the *Mistère du siège* to the extent that official reaction to Joan disassociates her politico-military role from any personal spirituality. Unlike those official records, however, the *Mistère du siège* places Joan center stage as the catalyst for the city's commemorative celebrations, rather than assigning this role to the city leaders who actually organized and financed them. A richly dressed Maid calls on all those present to ring the city's bells and to sing *Te Deum laudamus* in the *Mistère du siège*. Historically, Dunois, as the city's appointed military leader, actually led the spontaneous procession in which all present must have participated on May 8, 1429,[79] although one chronicle did state that Joan called for music on the battlefield.[80] In assigning to Joan the role of instigating and then commending to the local population annual processions and masses, the compiler has fulfilled his local intention, drawing spectators to the commemorative events being staged and in which they should participate. And, perhaps, by rewriting Joan into the city's commemorative tradition, the compiler, like the Rehabilitation witnesses, reveals an intention that extends beyond the play's construction to the very heart of its message.

During the victory celebration that constitutes the culmination of the *Mistère du siège* reenactment, the city council expresses its gratitude to the Maid for her efforts in valiantly winning the battle against the English.[81] The Maid subsequently expresses her appreciation to the city for the hospitality that has been extended to her, but also reminds its leaders that their thankfulness is due God, not herself. Then, despite the Maid's conscientious acknowledgment of Orléans's generosity, a *bourgeois* inexplicably apologizes for not having adequately accredited the Maid.[82] His words, in admitting some unnamed, but grievous, error, (". . .la deffaute / Que devers vous avons mesprise" [. . .the error / that we committed against you]) are strangely out of kilter with the supposedly contemporary scene being depicted. The historical Joan had been well received in Orléans during the siege and in subsequent visits, as even her character on stage admits. This oddly placed passage may reflect a public moment in Orléans's history when the city had not responded adequately to Joan's role in the decisive events of the siege. It may even reflect the belated acknowledgment afforded Joan in the city's commemorative activities, just as the rehabilitated Joan on stage is out of kilter with the 1429 events being reenacted.

Conclusion

The local chronicles, the city's *Comptes*, and the *Mistère du siège* all point to an evolution in the city's perception of Joan's place in its history. Each, though in different ways, reacted to the Rehabilitation energy that rewrote history and created the Maid as we know her. On one hand, it is true that the *Comptes*'s consistent references to the *fête de la ville* and to the *procession des Tourelles* deny any specific role to the Maid before, and even long after, the Rehabilitation era. Nonetheless, there is evidence that the city eventually responded to public opinion by centering its celebratory activities on Joan. The *Mistère du siège d'Orléans* responded to this same evolution by enacting on stage a revised public, and therefore orthodox, view of the Maid.

The local chronicles, in reflecting public opinion in the form of reconstituted episodes that may have taken place in the city, revived instead a more personal Joan. They accepted the coincidence in the Maid of both an orthodox and a popular spirituality. Their collective memory of the Maid's local experience placed her among them, on the streets and battlefields of Orléans. Although these works incorporated in varying degrees the revised Johannic material that emanated from the Rehabilitation documents, they nonetheless reflected a renewed interest in justifying, or venerating, Joan's role both locally and nationally.

These chronicles provided the *Mistère du siège* with not only a chronological narrative, but with thematic threads that were well known to the local population. François Guessard postulated in 1862 that the population of Orléans had performed a simpler version of the mystery spectacle before 1456.[83] If that is true, they did so despite the virtual moratorium concerning Joan that characterized the years between the two trials, and, they did so without the Rehabilitation records that apparently informed much of the play's characterization of the Maid. Without that authority, and without the divine justification included in the *procès de paradis*, we must wonder which "Joan" was depicted in that early version. Instead, the extant version of the *Mistère du siège* coincides with a post-Rehabilitation evolution in the depiction of Joan's participation in the city's history, as its reliance on revised local accounts and on official traditions demonstrates.

The coincidence of so much revision regarding Joan's historical presence, and in favor of granting her a newly justified place in local (and French) history, reflects changes in official, or public, activities that were perhaps reactions to the more popularized chronicles in which the personal

Joan was remembered. For instance, on May 30, 1432, the city had instituted a procession to remember Joan's death.[84] That procession, which led to Saint-Samson church, was interrupted permanently in 1439, when the city learned that Jeanne des Sermoises was making her way to Orléans as Joan.[85] Perhaps the memory of that trickery prompted the city officers to lead the Rehabilitation trial's commissioners in a procession to the same church in 1456. And perhaps, in the *Mistère du siège*'s reenactment, an authoritative Joan reasserts her influence on the history of Orléans so that the city might honor that memory, perhaps to the point of apologizing for past sins. Claims by various characters that "au monde n'en fut onc de telle" [never has there been anyone like her][86] single out this Joan to serve a uniquely public mandate. Many characters in the play, including the *bourgeois* themselves, point to Joan's everlasting renown, claiming that it will not diminish "tant que le monde sera estable" [as long as the world remains constant][87] as if hoping to rekindle a forgotten ember. If that is the case, then in the folios of the *Mistère du siège*, the compiler has created a Maid who will serve in perpetuity the city's collective need to ritualize its own spirituality.

Notes

1. *Le Journal du siège d'Orléans*, ed. Jules Quicherat, *Procès de condamnation et de réhabilitation de Jeanne d'Arc, dite la Pucelle*, 5 vols. (1841–49; New York: Johnson Reprints, 1965), 5:79.
2. The *Journal du siège* is a composite chronicle based on a daily register written during the siege. It was amended with material gleaned in part from the Rehabilitation witnesses. Historians including Jules Quicherat 5:79, have pointed out that the *Journal* and the mystery play of the same name follow very similar chronologies and that in many scenes the lists of participants, incidents and even times of day are identical in both works.
3. In 1467 the city leaders of Orléans commissioned the *Journal du siège d'Orléans*; a *quittance* for that year states that the city paid a cleric named Soubsdan to compile the chronicle, apparently using a contemporary text. See Quicherat 4:94.
4. Quicherat 4:204, names Charles d'Orléans, but Auguste Vallet de Viriville, *Chronique de la Pucelle* (Paris: Delahays, 1859), p. 40, prefers Jean d'Orléans, count of Angoulême, who received an early copy of this journal.
5. Auguste Vallet de Viriville, "Examen critique du *Mystère du siège d'Orléans*," *Bibliothèque de l'Ecole des Chartes* 5 (1864): 5.
6. Historians in the nineteenth century attempted to assign the authorship of this contemporary account to Guillaume Cousinot and others. See Françoise Michaud-Fréjaville's preface to Vallet de Viriville's edition of

La Chronique de la Pucelle (1859; Caen: Paradigm, 1992), p. 11, for a related discussion.

7. *La Chronique de la Pucelle*, p. 102.
8. The *Chronique de l'établissement de la fête du 8 mai* accompanies copies of the *lettres patentes* that offered indulgences to loyal Orléanians who attended the commemorative masses and processions in 1452 and subsequent years. See Quicherat 5:299–308.
9. Auguste Vallet de Viriville, "Examen critique du *Mystère du siège d'Orléans*," p. 9.
10. *La Chronique de l'établissement de la fête du 8 mai*, ed Jules Quicherat, *Procès de condamnation et de réhabilitation de Jeanne d'Arc, dite la Pucelle*, 5 vols. (1841–49; New York: Johnsons Reprints, 1965), 5:296.
11. *La Chronique de l'établissement de la fête du 8 mai*, ed. Quicherat 5:297.
12. *Le Journal du siège d'Orléans*, ed. Quicherat 4:153.
13. *Le Journal du siège d'Orléans*, ed. Quicherat 4:125.
14. *La Chronique de l'établissement de la fête du 8 mai*, ed. Quicherat 5:291.
15. *La Chronique de l'établissement de la fête du 8 mai*, ed. Quicherat 5:290.
16. *Le Journal du siège d'Orléans*, ed. Quicherat 4:171.
17. Pierre Mantellier, *Le Siège et la Délivrance d'Orléans* (Orleans: A. Gatineau, 1855), p. 122.
18. Mantellier, *Le Siège*, p. 99.
19. First published by Denis Lottin in 1836, Quicherat also reproduced this *motet* (5:313–16).
20. Denis Lottin, *Recherches historiques sur la ville d'Orléans, depuis l'Aurélien, l'an 274 jusqu'en 1789* (Orleans: A. Jacob, 1936), p. 279.
21. The *motet* cited in note 19 refers to Joan as having chased away the English troops, in the style of Judith and Esther. See Quicherat 5:315.
22. Lottin, *Recherches historiques*, p. 311.
23. Lottin, *Recherches historiques*, p. 313.
24. Lottin, *Recherches historiques*, p. 313, states that Charles VII financed this monument in Joan's honor in 1458. However, Jacques Debal, *Histoire d'Orléans et de son terroir*, 3 vols. (Roanne/Le Coteau: Editions Horvath, 1983), 2:254, maintains that the first such monument was probably constructed as late as 1502.
25. Graham A. Runnalls, "Form and Meaning in Medieval Religious Drama," *Littera et Sensus: Essays on Form and Meaning in Medieval French Literature*, ed. D.A. Trotter (Exeter: University of Exeter, 1989), pp. 99–100.
26. Alan Knight, *Aspects of Genre in Late Medieval French Drama* (Manchester: Manchester University Press, 1983), p. 19. Knight describes mystery plays as "historical in the sense that they were externally referential" with a linear model of time.
27. Jean-Pierre Bordier, "*Le Mystère du siège d'Orléans*, de la politique à la religion," *Perspectives médiévales* 18 (1992): 54–66, discusses a three-pronged thematic approach to this work.
28. Robert L.A. Clark characterized the letter's inclusion in the *Mistère du siège* as a dramatic monologue during an International Joan of Arc Society

session entitled "Joan of Arc and Modes of Late Medieval Chivalry" at the Kalamazoo Medieval Institute's annual congress in 2000.

29. Historically, Jean Erault, one of the Poitiers judges, performed the function of scribe and editor of the Maid's letter to the English.
30. This theatrical device dates from the mid-fifteenth century. It is characterized by a debate that takes place among heavenly beings regarding the outcome of events on earth. See Grace Frank, *The Medieval French Drama* (Oxford: Clarendon Press, 1954), p. 180.
31. *Le Mistère du siège d'Orléans, édition critique*, ed. V.L. Hamblin (Geneva: Droz, 2002), p. 421. This and all subsequent translations are my own.
32. Régine Pernoud and Marie-Véronique Clin, *Jeanne d'Arc* (Paris: Fayard, 1986), p. 46.
33. Quicherat 4:487.
34. *Le Mistère du siège d'Orléans*, pp. 426–28.
35. Séguin Séguin attributed this question to Guillaume Mery (Aymeri). See Pernoud and Clin, *Jeanne d'Arc*, p. 49. The two local chronicles to be revised in the Rehabilitation era also include this incident.
36. *Documents et recherches relatifs à Jeanne la Pucelle: La Réhabilitation de Jeanne la Pucelle; L'Enquête ordonnée par Charles VII et le Codicille et Guillaume de Bouillé*, ed. Pierre Doncoeur and Yvonne Lanhers, 5 vols. (Paris: Librairie d'-Argences, 1956), 3:82.
37. *Le Mistère du siège d'Orléans*, p. 433.
38. The chronicles spoke of a counsel or voice that was not identified until the Condemnation trial records were made available. The *Mistère du siège* includes Saint Michael as God's emissary to Joan. God's heavenly court, though, includes the Virgin Mary and Orléans's two patron saints rather than the personal saints (Catherine and Marguerite) named by Joan during the trial.
39. Pernoud and Clin, *Jeanne d'Arc*, p. 49.
40. Deborah Fraioli, *Joan of Arc; The Early Debate* (Woodbridge: Boydell, 2000), p. 54.
41. Fraioli, *Joan of Arc*, p. 52.
42. The Joan material included in the *Journal du siège* has been inserted in the daily register and is introduced by terms such as "environ ces jours" (Quicherat 4:126).
43. *Le Journal du siège d'Orléans*, ed. Quicherat 4:129.
44. Vallet de Viriville, *La Chronique de la Pucelle*, p. 94.
45. *La Chronique de l'établissement de la fête du 8 mai*, ed. Quicherat 5:289. Vallet de Viriville, "Examen critique du *Mystère du siège d'Orléans*," *Bibliothèque de l'Ecole des Chartes* 5 (1864): 5, contended that a revision of the mystery play and this post-1452 narrative were composed during the same era.
46. *Le Journal du siège d'Orléans*, ed. Quicherat 4:128.
47. *La Chronique de la Pucelle*, ed. Auguste Vallet de Viriville, p. 94.
48. *Le Mistère du siège d'Orléans*, p. 424.
49. *Le Mistère du siège d'Orléans*, p. 425.

50. Pierre Boissonnade, "Une étape capitale de la mission de Jeanne d'Arc; le séjour de la Pucelle à Poitiers, le quadruple enquète et ses résultats," *Revue des questions historiques* 17 (1930): 26.
51. For a recent discussion of this issue, see Fraioli, *Joan of Arc*, p. 48.
52. Octave Raguenet de Saint-Albin, "Les Juges de Jeanne d'Arc à Poitiers; membres du Parlement ou gens d'église?" *Lectures et mémoires de l'Académie de Sainte-Croix d'Orléans* 7 (1894): 427. Saint-Albin cites Martin Le Franc's poem, written in 1442, as a contemporary example of this apparent error.
53. The nineteenth-century editors of the *Mistère du siège* manuscript believed that the play had been performed initially in the decade after the siege, then later revised. See François Guessard and Eugène de Certain, eds, *Le Mistère du siège d'Orléans* (Paris: Imprimerie impériale, 1862), p. xv. However, according to Barbara Craig, "The Staging and Dating of the *Mystère du siège d'Orléans*," *Res publica litterarum* 5.2 (1982): 82, the play was probably composed in the 1450s. My analysis of the play's content and its linguistic features is in agreement with the latter hypothesis. See V.L. Hamblin, ed., *Le Mistère du sige d'Orleans, édition critique*, p. 31.
54. Jane Marie Pinzino, "Speaking of Angels: A Fifteenth-Century Bishop in Defense of Joan of Arc's Mystical Voices," *Fresh Verdicts on Joan of Arc*, ed. Bonnie Wheeler and Charles T. Wood (New York: Garland, 1996), p. 172.
55. *Le Mistère du siège d'Orléans*, pp. 312–13.
56. *Le Mistère du siège d'Orléans*, p. 113.
57. *Le Mistère du siège d'Orléans*, p. 607.
58. E.g., *Le Mistère du siège d'Orléans*, p. 577.
59. Doncoeur and Lanhers 3:72.
60. *Le Mistère du siège d'Orléans*, p. 512.
61. *Le Mistère du siège d'Orléans*, p. 569.
62. *Le Mistère du siège d'Orléans*, p. 783.
63. The speech in question occurs after the June 1429 battle in Patay. In speaking to the people of Orléans, the Maid cannot be referring to the spontaneous celebrations that took place on May 8 and 9 of that year. Her speech is intended to remind them of a yearly commitment to thank God for the city's victory against the English troops.
64. *Le Mistère du siège d'Orléans*, pp. 480–81.
65. *Le Journal du siège d'Orléans*, ed. Quicherat 4:153.
66. *Le Journal du siège d'Orléans*, ed. Quicherat 4:153.
67. *Le Journal du siège d'Orléans*, ed. Quicherat 4:170.
68. *Le Mistère du siège d'Orléans*, p. 577.
69. *Le Mistère du siège d'Orléans*, p. 579.
70. Pierre Lanéry d'Arc, *Le Culte de Jeanne d'Arc au XVe siècle* (Orléans: Herluison, 1887), p. 9.
71. While Joan's supernatural contact is literalized and justified on stage, the English characters discuss their dreams and consult with an astrologer. Likewise, scenes with commoners, intended as diversionary, are contrasted with the Maid's seriousness of purpose.

72. Quicherat 5:79.
73. For a history of this council, see Rémy Boucher de Molandon, *Les Comptes de la ville d'Orléans des XIVe et XVe siècles* (Orleans: Herluison, 1880).
74. The municipal leaders refer repeatedly to Joan's "vaillance" (p. 550), her "gloire" (p. 577), and to her "excellance" (p. 550). Furthermore, in each encounter they submit to Joan's authority in the ways of war.
75. *Le Mistère du siège d'Orléans*, p. 479.
76. *Le Mistère du siège d'Orléans*, p. 577.
77. In v. 16, 809, a *bourgeois* does repeat that God sent the Maid to Orléans, but this fact is certainly not their focus, as is demonstrated by their many references to Joan's authority.
78. *Le Mistère du siège d'Orléans*, p. 496.
79. Mantellier, *Le siège*, p. 96.
80. *La Geste des nobles francoys*, ed. Quicherat 4:110.
81. *Le Mistère du siège d'Orléans*, p. 550.
82. *Le Mistère du siège d'Orléans*, p. 580. Here are those apologetic lines: "Plaise pardonner la deffaulte / Que devers vous avons mesprise, / Dont a vous, personne tres haulte, / N'avons pas la chose premise / Qui vous appartenoit, et mise, / Pour vous servir comme devions; / dont en ce que avons mesprise, / dame, s'i vous plaist, l'amendrons" [Please forgive the error / That we committed toward you, / Such a worthy person, / When we did not discharge / That which was rightfully yours, / And that we should have seen to; / For that which we have failed, Madam, if it please you, we will make amends].
83. Guessard and de Certain, *Le Histère*, p. xv.
84. Lottin, *Recherches historiques*, p. 279.
85. Lottin, *Recherches historiques*, p. 286.
86. *Le Mistère du siège d'Orléans*, p. 682.
87. *Le Mistère du siège d'Orléans*, p. 550.

PART FOUR

JOAN AS MODEL

CHAPTER 12

THE PRINCESS AND THE MAID OF ORLÉANS: SCULPTING SPIRITUALITY DURING THE JULY MONARCHY

Nora M. Heimann

This chapter explores the impact of Marie d'Orléans' popular sculpture, "Joan of Arc in Prayer" (ca. 1834–39), as a resonant image of spiritual faith during a time of resurgent anticlericalism in France.

Two women—Joan of Arc (ca. 1412/13–31) and Princess Marie d'Orléans (1813–39)—offered images of spiritual faith that resonated across the political and social spectrum of French society during the July Monarchy (1830–48), a time of resurgent iconoclasm and anticlericalism. One young woman was a provincial peasant and charismatic mystic who turned the tide of the Hundred Years War; the other, born four centuries later, was a young amateur artist and a princess of the realm (figure 12.1). Despite their marked differences in class and chronology, both became linked in the public imagination by the Princess's *Joan of Arc in Prayer* (ca. 1834–39, bronze, Orléans, H: 6′ 2″) (figure 12.2), one of the most widely emulated representations of the Maid of Orléans in the nineteenth century.[1]

Marie d'Orléans's *Joan of Arc in Prayer* portrays the Maid slightly larger than life size, standing alone in a moment of rapt spiritual devotion, her slender frame clad simply in medieval armor and her boyishly coiffed head bowed humbly in prayer with the hilt of her sword held like a cross pressed against her heart. While the work acknowledges Joan's controversial cross-dressing,

12.1 Ary Scheffer, *Princess Maria d'Orléans in her Studio*, ca. 1838. Oil on fabric. The Cleveland Museum of Art. Photo courtesy of the Shepherd Gallery, New York.

it de-emphasizes it by placing a modest skirt over the armor covering the Maid's lower limbs. Instead, the sculpture focuses on other remarkable aspects of Joan of Arc's life story—her modest origins, tender youth, and female gender, and her anomalous status as a military leader who claimed God's own command as the origin of her authority. Devoid of any overt allusions to patriotic pathos, militant nationalism, royalist fealty, or even organized religion, this spare yet compelling image of a young maiden

12.2 Maria d'Orléans, *Joan of Arc in Prayer*, ca. 1834–36, cast in 1840, bronze, Orléans: Hôtel Groslot (former Hôtel de Ville). Photo courtesy of Nora M. Heimann.

soldier absorbed in solitary prayer expresses Joan of Arc's mystical faith in a manner at once fervent, introspective, and intimate.

The bronze, Marie d'Orléans's first large-scale sculpture, was begun at the urging of the artist's father, King Louis-Philippe I, as a replacement for an unsuccessful commission for a life-size rendering of the Maid for the new Musée historique at Versailles by one of the leading sculptors of the day, James Pradier (1790–1852).[2] While to modern eyes this work may seem to verge on the sentimental in its poignant, melancholic tone, in the mid-to-late nineteenth century (when religious art often recalled either the Byzantine or the Baroque in its stiff "hieratic" stylization or florid emotional effusion),[3] *Joan of Arc in Prayer* was enthusiastically embraced by the court and the public alike as a poignant and morally uplifting image. Even the Comtess de Boigne, a critic of the princess—who described Marie in her *Memoires* as too liberal in her taste, too unconventional in her preference for modest dress, and too uncouth in her avoidance of courtly rituals and pleasures—admitted the young artist's "remarkable talent for sculpture," noting the warm reception the Joan of Arc statue enjoyed when it was unveiled in 1837: "I do not think that there was any flattery in the general admiration which it aroused when it was subjected to public inspection at the opening of the Palais of Versailles."[4] Similarly, the prominent painter Ary Scheffer praised both the artistic success and the personal virtue of his young student, Marie d'Orléans, after her sculpture (which Scheffer helped the princess to model in wax) was publicly unveiled:

> Despite all the difficulties [the princess had in making the figure], the statue came out the finest modern statue at Versailles. The nobility, the simplicity, and an admirable feminine character [of this work] distinguish it from the vulgar productions around it; because it bears the imprint not only of talent, but also the expression of the author's elevated soul! The success which attended the appearance of this statue was prodigious. The most flattering applause was lavished upon it, yet I never saw flattery received with greater indifference than by this Princess. Though always manifesting, more or less plainly, her contempt for the "Official Tribe" around her, she was as delighted as would have been any child, at the success of her work among the *people*; and more than all, with the admiration bestowed on it by the soldiers.[5]

Perhaps the least biased assessment of the princess's sculpture may be evidenced by its widespread reproduction over more than five decades (enduring long after the princess's premature death at the age of twenty-five and the fall of her father's regime in 1848). Following the inauguration of the plaster original and a marble copy of *Joan of Arc in Prayer* at Versailles in 1837, a life-size bronze was founded for the town of Orléans in 1840, followed by casts of the sculpture rendered in varying dimensions and materials for churches, public buildings, and public squares throughout France, including large-scale copies for the Maison natale de Jeanne d'Arc in Domremy, the Église Sainte-Vincent-de-Paul in Paris; the Bibliothèque municipale in Rouen, the Musée Vivenel in Compiègne, the Hospice de Janville, and the Fontaine Jeanne d'Arc in the town square in Noisey-le-Sec.[6] For private consumption, Marie d'Orléans's sculpture of *Joan of Arc* was also replicated in miniature as a collectable porcelain by Sèvres in the 1840s; and both large- and small-scale replicas in plaster, marble, and bronze were advertised for sale by commercial vendors through the early twentieth century.[7] It inspired book illustrations, popular prints, and commercial advertisements.[8]

Marie d'Orléans's *Joan of Arc* was even carved on pen and pencil sets, and modeled in miniature as the decorative handle for handbells.[9]

The remarkable popularity of *Joan of Arc in Prayer* derived, at least in part, from the princess's novel approach to the subject, which differed in two subtle but significant ways from earlier renderings of the Maid. The first was in the artist's careful attention to archival detail in her portrayal of her protagonist's appearance; the second was in her treatment of Joan of Arc's faith. In depicting Joan with a short, boyish haircut and a relatively accurate period costume, the princess offered one of the first historically based treatments of the Maid's appearance in French sculpture.[10] Among the persuasive details that lend credence to this portrayal are a number of authentic components of early fifteenth-century European armor, including *pauldron* (plate defense for the shoulder), a *cuirasse* (joined back and breastplates), *cubitière* (elbow armor), a *fauld* of *lames* (armor attached to the bottom of a breastplate to protect the abdomen composed of horizontal strips of plate designed to allow flexible movement), *jambière* (plate armor for the shin), *soleret* (metal plated shoes), and a *bassinet* (an open faced helmet) shown resting on the stump of a tree beside Joan with a pair of gauntlets.[11] This adherence to accurate historical detail reflected both a growing contemporary cultural concern for history,[12] and the personal passion of the artist for the medieval past.

The princess's keen interest in the Middle Ages began with a taste for the poetry of Byron, the historical plays of Shakespeare, and the romantic writings of Johann Christophe Friedrich von Schiller, Johann Wolfgang von Goethe, and Walter Scott. Indeed, Scott's *Ivanhoe* (1819) was the first novel the closely chaperoned young royal was permitted to read.[13] From this historical fiction Marie found an interest in medieval costumes and culture. She began to collect antiques, which she researched, as well as troubador-style *object d'arts* and furnishings, with which she decorated her apartments in the Tuileries Palace in a mixed neo-Gothic and Renaissance revival style.[14] She even designed and installed a medievalizing oratory in her private chambers complete with stained-glass windows and a rood screen with flamboyant finials.

Among the historical studies that Marie d'Orléans read in pursuing her interest in the Middle Ages was Alexandre Buchon's abridged, but highly important early documentary study of the Maid's life and trial, *Chronique et procès de la Pucelle d'Orléans* (1827).[15] The princess's passionate response to Buchon's *Chronique* was recorded in a letter dated May 29, 1834, in which she wrote:

> It's charming! It's simple! It's touching! The character of this poor girl is so natural, so free of all sentimental romance! She cried at the sight of the dead, and this old Frenchman [Buchon] lends a new charm [to her life story].[16]

It was almost certainly the inspiration of Buchon's *Chronique* that led Marie to sculpt her first image of the Maid as an equestrian figure weeping at the sight of her fallen enemy—*Joan Weeping at the Sight of the Wounded* (n.d.).[17] Produced shortly after Marie took up sculpting in the early 1830s, this small terra cotta (h: 520 cm [20.8″], later cast in bronze), was modeled in three, rather than two, dimensions at the instigation of the princess's painting master, Ary Scheffer, who believed that sculpting might help his young student master the proportions of human anatomy in the absence of being allowed to study from a nude model for reasons of propriety.[18] Thus when the Princess began her first large-scale sculpture, *Joan of Arc in Prayer* (around 1834 or 1835), at the urging of her father, she had already completed an equestrian sculpture of the Maid; she may also have already completed an undated plaster sketch of Joan of Arc as humble peasant (now in Dordrecht).[19]

The warm public reception that the Princess's portrayal of *Joan of Arc in Prayer* received derived not only from the perception that her work was historically accurate; it also came from the artist's poignant portrayal of the Maid's mystical faith, a focus lacking in the only two major monuments to Joan of Arc produced in France during the prior century—Paul-Ambroise Slodtz's grand *Joan of Arc as Bellona* (1756, formerly Rouen, destroyed in 1944) and Edme-Étienne-François Gois *fils*'s bellicose *Joan of Arc in Battle* (ca. 1801–04, Orléans) (figure 12.3). These statues, from the Ancien Regime and the Napoleonic regime respectively, both cast Joan of Arc as a latter-day goddess of war in a flowing gown with long hair. Marie d'Orléans's prayerful image of the Maid marked a departure from these earlier, wholly secular, and less archivally informed monuments.

While the idea of portraying Joan of Arc in life-size came from the artist's father, the impetus for portraying the Maid in a moment of prayer almost certainly did not. The duc d'Orléans, an avowed agnostic and a pragmatic politician, distanced himself and his court from the Roman Catholic Church (the largest organized religion in France and the Bourbon monarchy's closest auxiliary) after he came to power with the collapse of the last Bourbon regime in July 1830. In an effort to distinguish his new constitutional monarchy from the ultra-conservative Catholicism and absolutist excesses of his deposed Bourbon cousins, the new "Citizen-King" adopted the secular symbolism of the Republic by refusing a sacral ceremony at Reims Cathedral (preferring instead for his investiture as Louis-Philippe I, "King of the French," a simple oath sworn before the Chamber of Deputies in August 1830), and by ordering that the revolutionary Tricolor replace not only the royal white flag and fleur-de-lis of the Bourbons, but also all crosses in the courtrooms and churches of France.[20] It is thus less likely that Louis-Philippe would have chosen to promulgate such an overtly religious

12.3 Edme-Étienne-François Gois *fils*, Joan of Arc in Battle, ca. 1801–04, Orléans: Place Dauphine. Photo courtesy of Nora M. Heimann.

image in the mid-1830s (when Princess Marie began her sculpture of the Maid praying), than that the artist herself chose to portray the subject in an expressly religious manner. By all accounts, the princess—unlike her father—was very enthusiastic in her religious beliefs, and very faithful in her devotional practices.[21]

Marie d'Orléans, of course, did not invent the iconographic image of Joan of Arc praying. Indeed, the first monument to the Maid erected in Orléans in 1502 (destroyed in 1792) took the form of a *Calvaire* with King Charles VII and Joan of Arc kneeling on either side of the crucifix and the mourning Virgin Mary.[22] Rather, Marie d'Orléans was innovative in the manner in which she portrayed Joan of Arc's pious virtue and faithful devotion. Here the decisive elements were not in what the artist included in her portrayal of Joan of Arc so much as what she managed to avoid—both overt references to religious convention and to French royalty. Absent in this rendering are any of the grand, royalist trappings—such as a white plumed hat, or a fleurdelisèd bodice, skirt, or standard—that prevailed in Joan iconography from the sixteenth century forward. No king kneels nearby; and no conventional religious imagery—such as a crucifix or pietà—is placed beside Joan to establish her as a definitively Roman Catholic and monarchical identity. Rather, modestly dressed in a decidedly unresplendent suit of armor, Marie d'Orléans's *Joan of Arc* seems humble, pious, and yet unmarked by any overt class identification, political affiliation, or religious denomination.

In its simplicity, Marie's Maid becomes mutably accessible to many different interpretations. Her clasped sword, for example, can be read simply as an unsheathed weapon by those preferring to see this maiden simply as a warrior contemplating how to save her country, while those seeking an image of faith can interpret the hilt above her hands as a cross. Even her costume can be read, at once, as a warrior's armor and as a woman's dress. As Léonce Dupont wrote in 1861, praising the town of Orléans's bronze casting of *Joan of Arc in Prayer*:

> See, rather, her hands joined together and leaning against her steel-clad chest, clenching there the hilt of her épée. What thoughts are in this embrace! Is it steel that she grasps? Is it the cross she has set in the hilt [of her sword]? Is it the memory of her thatched cottage that she seizes in passing and to which she accords a final good-bye? It is perhaps all these things at once. . . . There is everything in this pose. In the costume, there is, mixed together, the woman and the warrior. The wings of her breast-plate cover her [as much] like a dress as like the buckled breast-plate of a man-of-arms; her coat of mail is puffed up almost like a skirt. It is iron, but an iron that seems to have lost its hardness in contact with the body of a young girl.[23]

Gently pious without seeming too overtly Catholic, historically accurate enough to be recognized in her armor and short hair, yet softened and made feminine in her demeanor and her skirted costume, the princess's sculpture offered a subtle and brilliant negotiation between the many compelling—and at times competing—royalist, populist, secular, military, and religious elements of Joan of Arc's remarkable life and legacy. It offered, that is, an image that could appeal to all those who wanted Joan of Arc to represent by turns patriotic sacrifice to one's country, loyalty to the French throne for which Joan fought, and the power of the people to whom she belonged. Above all, *Joan of Arc in Prayer* offered an embodiment of fervent personal faith, at a time when religious expression in France seemed compromised, for many, by the Catholic Church's close association with the failed Bourbon regime. As Heinrich Heine, chronicler of the age, declared baldly, summarizing Catholicism's problematic situation after the fall of the Restoration, "The old religion is completely dead. It is already dropping away into dust and most French people do not want to hear any more about the corpse. They hold their noses when the Church is mentioned."[24]

During the first years of the July Monarchy (as before, during the first French Revolution, and again, during Napoleon's years in power), Joan of Arc was remembered and celebrated in secular terms as a woman warrior, redolent of French national integrity and military might rather than mystical faith or monarchical fealty. In 1792, for example, after the first monument to the Maid in Orléans was attacked by revolutionary vandals and was melted down to make cannons, the revolutionary government saw fit to inscribe one of the weapons "Joan of Arc," because it would share the Maid's "noble destiny of striking down the enemies of France."[25] Similarly, during the Consulate, Napoleon granted a petition by the Municipal Council requesting the reestablishment of a monument to the Maid's memory in Orléans as a warlord in the midst of battle (rather than as prayerful companion to the king at Calvary) with these famous words, praising Joan of Arc as a symbol of martial strength and national unity: "This deliberation is very pleasing to me. The illustrious Joan of Arc proved that there is no miracle that the French genius cannot produce when the conditions are propitious or when our national independence is endangered. United, the French nation has never been vanquished."[26] Similarly, it was as a revolutionary archetype that the Maid was called to mind during the first "glorious days" of the July revolution in 1830, when a fearless young working woman who fought on the barricades in Paris was described in contemporary accounts of the battle as "une jeune fille, nouvelle Jeanne d'Arc":

> A young girl, a latter day Joan of Arc, fought with extreme valor on the Place de la Bourse. There, despite the hail of bullets, she secured a piece of artillery. Her companions in this glorious moment, marvelling at her behavior, carried her to a throne in the Hôtel-de-Ville and crowned her with laurels. Then, on the 29th [of July], in the evening, she was placed in a triumphal chariot adorned with palms, laurels, myrtle, overturned white flags, victorious tricolor standards and the spoils of the conquered army, and paraded throughout Paris. Young men drew the chariot along. . . The picturesque ceremony took place by torchlight and amid cheers, cries of joy and singing.[27]

While this heroine of the July uprisings (later identified as a young woman named Marie Deschamps)[28] was celebrated as a modern Maid of Orléans, she was also honored in a manner that recalled the revolutionary festivals of 1789–90 in which personifications of Liberty (and similar republican allegories) were glorified in such triumphal parades.[29] Thus ironically, Joan of Arc, embraced by the royalist right during the Restoration as a martyr for her efforts to save the French monarchy,[30] was identified during the revolution that led to the Bourbon's final fall as a latter-day republican insurgent, able to embody the courage and power of the people.[31]

With Marie d'Orléans's sculpture, the spiritual—rather than political or military—aspects of Joan of Arc's life were finally brought back to the fore. Within two years of the unveiling of *Joan of Arc in Prayer* at Versailles, however, the artist died of consumption and complications related to childbirth; she was only twenty-five. The public response at Princess Marie's death was enormous. As one contemporary observer, the baron de Barante, wrote, "People from all classes cried;. . .they spoke of [Marie d'Orléans] and bought common reproductions in plaster of the statue of Jeanne d'Arc; [Marie] lived on in a very pure and very noble oeuvre."[32] As Marie d'Orléans's work became recognized posthumously through the popularity of her sculpture of *Joan of Arc in Prayer*, so in turn did the profound role that Joan of Arc's faith in God begin to be recognized again in the work and words of artists and authors, scholars, and politicians alike. Among the many who went on to celebrate Joan of Arc as a religious role model was the novelist Alexandre Dumas père (1802–70), author of *The Count of Monte Cristo* and the *Three Musketeers* (both 1844), whose romantic account of the Maid's life, *Jehanne, la Pucelle, 1429–1431* (1842), was dedicated to the memory of Princess Marie d'Orléans. In Dumas's account, Joan of Arc's virtuous piety and profound spirituality are cited as the miraculous source of her greatest accomplishments.[33] Indeed, the Maid's birth is made messianic, complete with a falling star and wonder-struck peasants who run joyfully into the streets of Domremy on the night of her birth. In describing the equally remarkable end to Joan's life, Dumas evoked images of holy wonder and divine sacrifice. Joan spends her last nocturnal hours before battle in Compiègne (as if prescient that she will be taken captive there) praying "like our Savior upon the Mount of Olives,"[34] and later still, after her death at the stake, Joan of Arc's executioners become struck with remorse upon finding her heart whole and unburned, while "the soul of the martyr" ascends to heaven in the form of a dove rising from the ashes of the woodpile like the Holy Spirit.[35] In these images, we see the apotheosis of Marie d'Orléans's prayerful maiden: remembered for a time only as a latter-day Bellona or a medieval Marianne, Joan of Arc is fully reborn here as a spiritual savior—"the Christ of France," as Dumas wrote, who redeemed "the sins of the monarchy as Christ redeemed the sins of the world."[36]

Also following in the princess's footsteps was a veritable legion of visual artists who, from the second half of the nineteenth century on, similarly focused upon Joan of Arc's spiritual aspect in their paintings and sculptures. In literally hundreds of works produced after Marie's lifetime, Joan can be seen similarly standing or kneeling in prayer, attending to the angelic voices of her divine inspiration, and often clutching a sword at the hilt like a raised cross.[37] Among the many finely crafted images, as well as many modest quality emulations of the Maid in the same pious pose, may be numbered Prosper d'Epigny's *Jeanne d'Arc au sacre* (1902, Reims), Antonin Mércié's *Jeanne d'Arc* (1906); André-César Vermare's *Jeanne d'Arc au sacre* (1909, Paris); and Henri-Émile Allouard, *Actions de grâce* (ca. 1898, Louveciennes); of the many lesser quality and often anonymous renditions of the *Joan of Arc in Prayer* (such as the polychromed *Jeanne d'Arc* in Chateaugay), scores still stand today in small churches throughout France.

Even though Princess Marie's sculpture became one of the most emulated and popular images of Joan of Arc in the mid-to-late 1800s, little critical attention has been given to this artist and her work in the last century. This may be due, at least in part, to both the sculptress's royal status, as well as her gender, for the princess was not only forbidden to study from a live nude model—the hallmark of every serious academic art education in the mid-nineteenth century—she was hampered in her ability to establish herself as an artist by not being allowed to exhibit at the Salon des Beaux-Arts.[38] Above all, perhaps, the political fallout engendered by the collapse of the July Monarchy, and the exile of the princess's parents following the revolution of 1848, virtually guaranteed the official neglect of the princess's oeuvre in France in the later nineteenth century.[39]

Mourned at her death as one of the most "brilliant" and popular members of the royal household, Marie d'Orléans was remembered by her friends and family for her high spirits and quick wit, her romantic enthusiasm for medieval chivalry, her religious piety, and her passionate love of art.[40] Fellow artists, celebrated her as the maker of *Joan of Arc in Prayer* in numerous commemorative paintings, prints, drawings, and sculptures.[41] Auguste Vinchon, a favored painter to the July court, memorialized Marie d'Orléans's work in 1848 in his image of the royal family solemnly gathered contemplating the princess's sculpture of the Maid in the darkened galleries of the Musée de Versailles.[42] Similarly Franz-Xavier Winterhalter, the most prominent royal portraitist in Europe, painted King Louis-Philippe in 1841 standing in the new Galerie des Batailles at Versailles with a prominent miniature of *Joan of Arc in Prayer* placed beside his left hand, evidence of a father's pride in his daughter's sculpture and the significance of the Maid of Orléans to the July Monarchy. Although her name was all but forgotten in official art circles by the end of the nineteenth century, the profound impact of the princess's image of *Joan of Arc in Prayer* was recognized by at least one scholar; as F.E. Desnoyers, author of *L'Iconographie de Jeanne d'Arc*, who wrote in 1891:

> Before 1830, it must be courageously admitted, France had almost forgotten its liberator. . .It is to the Princess Marie that we owe the definitive awakening of France; this remarkable work was the clap of thunder that shook off a general sleep, and since this epoch, France has gloriously made amends for its neglect.[43]

Yet despite this outpouring of commemorative artwork in the immediate aftermath of the princess's death, by the end of the nineteenth century, her talent as an artist was all but forgotten; and her name—when it was recorded—was remembered only as that of a daughter of the last reigning monarch of France. Aside from the cursory praise of a few twentieth-century Joan of Arc scholars, who have noted the princess's sculpture of the Maid praying only in passing, Marie d'Orléans's life and legacy have been largely ignored by the general public and historians of art and culture alike.[44] Joan of Arc might have met with a similar fate had it not been for Marie d'Orléans's compelling image of her in prayer. For by commemorating the Maid of Orléans's faith in God in a new and resonant manner, the princess of Orléans helped to reestablish a conception of the spiritual, rather than merely martial or royalist aspects, of a life that would later be sanctified by canonization in 1920. Perhaps by reawakening awareness of the Princess Marie's small but significant contribution to Joan of Arc's iconographic fortunes, we may make amends for the relative neglect of this talented, if tragically short-lived young woman.

Notes

Unless otherwise indicated, all translations are the author's.

1. Although thrown from its base and perforated by shelling during the allied invasion of Orléans in World War II, the princess's life-size bronze statue of *Joan of Arc* remains stalwart, if war-battered and now tarnished by time before the Hôtel Groslot (the historic former Hôtel de ville) in Orléans. Because the artist never exhibited at established artistic venues, such as the annual Salon des Beaux-Arts in Paris, precise dating of the princess's sculpture is difficult. The earliest recorded reference to this work can be found in a private letter from the princess to her nursemaid, Mme de Malet, dated October 3, 1834, in which she inquires after both her art instructor Ary Scheffer (a prominent painter to the court) and the state of her sculpture of "*Jehanne*" (Marthe Kolb, *Une correspondance inedite de la Princesse Marie d'Orléans, Duchesse de Wurtenberg, publiée avec une Introduction et des notes* [Paris: Ancienne Librairie Furne, Boivin & Cie, éditeurs, 1937], p. 228).

2. James Pradier, *Correspondance*, v. II (*1834–1842*), ed. Douglas Siler (Geneva: Librairie Droz, 1984), p. 96; see also Harriet Lewin Grote, *Memoir of the Life of Ary Scheffer* (London: John Murray, 1860), p. 43.
3. Here, one might compare Marie's sculpture to both the more stiffly hieratic religious imagery of Victor Orsel (such as his neo-Byzantine painting of *Good and Evil* [1836]) or Dominique Papety (such as his primitivising *Cyprien and Justine* [ca. 1837]), or the more melodramatic and grandiose paintings of Théodore Chassériau (see, e.g., his mural painting of *The Apotheosis of Ste-Marie-L'Egyptienne* for the Church of Saint-Merri [1842–43]) or Eugène Devéria (as exemplified by Devéria's *Glorification of the Life of Saint Geneviève* [1836]). For a discussion of the "hieratic mode" in religious painting in France during the second half of the nineteenth century, see Michael Paul Driskell, *Representing Belief: Religion, Art and Society in Nineteenth-Century France* (University Park, Pa.: The Pennsylvania State University Press, 1992); for a more general introduction to the complex eclecticism of art produced during the July Monarchy, see also, *Art of the July Monarchy: France 1830 to 1848*, ex. cat. (Museum of Art and Archeology, University of Missouri-Columbia, Columbia, Mo.: University of Missouri Press, 1990).
4. Charlotte Louise Éléonore Adélaïde Boigne, comtesse d'Osmond, *Récits d'une tante, mémoires de la comtesse de Boigne, née Osmond, publiés d'après le manuscrit original par M. Charles Nicoullard*, ed. Charles Nicoullard (Paris: Librairie Plon, Plon-Nourrit et Cie, 1907), trans. anon. under title: *Recollections of a Great Lady* (New York: Charles Scribner's Sons, 1912), p. 176.
5. Grote, *Memoir of the Life of Ary Scheffer*, pp. 45–46.
6. The plaster original of Marie's *Joan of Arc in Prayer* is now in the Ary Scheffer Museum in Dordrecht. In response to a request made in 1839 by the citizens of Orléans, a bronze cast of the work was founded in 1840, and donated to Orléans in 1841 by King Louis-Philippe; this casting was formally inaugurated ten years later—on September 12, 1851—before Orléans's Hôtel de Ville. See Pierre Fontenailles, "Chronique historique: La Jeanne d'Arc de l'Hôtel de Ville et la Princesse Marie d'Orléans," *Republique du Centre* (April 23, 1947), n.p.; and "Les Monuments: A Jeanne d'Arc," *Le Gaulois* (May 10, 1895), n.p.; Archives, Centre Jeanne d'Arc, Dossier 821.
7. A 29-inch-high bronze cast of *Joan of Arc Praying*, modeled ca. 1834–36 and cast after 1843, now in the collection of the Dahesh Museum of Art in New York, was one of several mid- and large-sized editions produced by the *maison d'éditions* Susse Frères, one of the most prominent bronze-foundries in France in the nineteenth century. Among the many commercial replicas made of the princess's *Jeanne d'Arc* was also a porcelain miniature rendered by Fischbach for the Manufacture nationale de Sèvres in 1841 (C.F. Vergnaud-Romagnési, *Mémoire et documents curieux inédits sur les anciens et sur les nouveaux monuments élevés a la mémoire de Jeanne d'Arc à Orléans, à Rouen, à Domremy, etc.* [1861], p. 106; for examples of copies after the princess's sculpture, see also: *Images de Jeanne d'Arc: Hommage pour le 550e anniversaire de la libération d'Orléans et du sacre*, ex. cat. [Paris: Hôtel de la

Monnaie, 1979], cat. 120, p. 92; and Marcel Marron, ed., *Encyclopédie Johannique* [Orléans: Librairies Jeanne d'Arc, ca. 1910], pp. 54, 80).

8. Nora M. Heimann " 'What Honor for the Feminine Sex': A Cultural Study of Joan of Arc and the Representation of Gender, Religion, and Nationalism in French Nineteenth-Century Paintings, Prints and Sculpture" (Ph.D. diss., City University of New York, 1994), pp. 353–54, n. 633, and pp. 483–85, figures LXXXIX, XC, XCI; see also Léonce Dupont, *Les trois statues de Jeanne d'Arc, ou Notices sur les monuments élevés à Orléans en l'honneur de Jeanne d'Arc* (Orléans: H. Herluison, Libraire, 1861), p. 29.
9. [Albert Marie Léon] Le Nordez, *Jeanne d'Arc: Racontée par l'image* (Paris: Hachette & Cie, 1898), p. 228; *Images de Jeanne d'Arc*, p. 284; Marron, ed., *Encyclopédie Johannique*, pp. 85–87.
10. As the eminent Joan-scholar Régine Pernoud noted: "The statue of Joan of Arc by the Princess Marie d'Orléans, daughter of Louis-Philippe, marked the first progress accomplished towards an iconography that was very faithful to known historical accounts; it was followed some years later by Ingres's grand portrait. Joan, from now on, wears the armor of her time, and is coiffed 'à la Joan of Arc.' Her attitude, at once meditative and resolved, is effective. The image in this way was made to stand out; it was approximately contemporaneous with Quicherat's publication of the Maid's trial. The nineteenth century was decidedly 'the history century of Michelet' " (Régine Pernoud, *Jeanne d'Arc* [Paris: Éditions du Seuil, 1981], p. 85).
11. These armored gloves are actually the most notable of the few small inaccuracies in Marie d'Orléans's portrayal of the Maid's harness (or suit of armor), for hand armor in which each finger was protected by its own separately articulated set of steel *lames* was not common in France until the later fifteenth century. In the first decades of the 1400s, during Joan of Arc's lifetime, "hour-glass gauntlets"—curved metal cuffs that protected the sides and top of the hand ending at the knuckle—prevailed; only in the mid-century were "mitten gauntlets" introduced consisting of a curved plate encircling the forearm and wrist that was shaped to the base of the thumb, and often riveted with articulated laminations covering the fingers (Edge, *Arms & Armor of the Medieval Knight*, pp. 81, 103–104, 106, 109; and Régine Pernoud, *Jeanne d'Arc raconntée par Régine Pernoud* [Paris: Perrin, 1997], p. 43). It might be noted that such anachronistic inclusions were common in Joan iconography from the late fifteenth century on. Born perhaps of the convention in the Middle Ages and the Renaissance of portraying prominent historic, religious, and literary figures in the costume of the present day (regardless of what age they came from), many of the images of the Maid from the fifteenth through the eighteenth centuries show Joan of Arc in clothing and armor that were not produced until decades, at times even centuries, after the Maid's death in 1431. Among the many prominent French artists who included similar anachronistic gauntlets in the nineteenth century was J.-A.-D. Ingres, who placed a red-throated pair in the foreground of his canvas *Joan of Arc at the Coronation of Charles VII* [1854, Louvre]. Ingres, it might also be noted, chose to portray the Maid with

abundant hair bound back into a long pony-tail, despite his knowledge of the well-established historic evidence that Joan (while a warrior) wore "her hair cropped short and round about the ears like a young [fashionable boy]" (W. P. Barrett, trans. *The Trial of Joan of Arc* [London: George Routledge & Sons, 1931], p. 152). That Ingres was aware of the Maid's short hair style when he painted his canvas of 1854 can be established by his earlier portrayal of Joan of Arc with a boyishly cropped haircut (like that evidenced in Marie's *Joan of Arc in Prayer*) in his illustration for Mennechet's *La Plutarch français* in 1846. For further discussion of these images and the treatment of Joan of Arc's hair in nineteenth-century art, see Heimann, "What Honor for the Feminine Sex" (Ph.D. diss., 1994); for an extensive study of Joan of Arc's harness (or suit of armor), see Adrien Harmand, *Jeanne d'Arc: ses costumes, son armure, essai de reconstitution* (Paris: Librairie Ernst Leroux, 1929); for more recent research on European weapons and armor from the eleventh to the sixteenth century, see David Edge and John Miles Paddock, *Arms & Armor of the Medieval Knight: An Illustrated History of Weaponry in the Middle Ages* (New York: Crescent Books, 1996); finally, see also Régine Pernoud and Marie Véronique Clin's short, but informative essay on "Joan's Armor," in *Joan of Arc: Her Story*, trans. Jeremy duQuesnay Adams, ed. Bonnie Wheeler (New York: St. Martin's Press, 1998), pp. 224–25.

12. This "rise in history," as Stephen Bann put it, was manifest in the first half of the nineteenth century by a pervasive taste in Europe and America for historical genre in literature and art, by a fashion for historical revivalism in architecture and design, and by a rise in systematic, scholarly archival research as an academic and intellectual pursuit. A considerable body of literature has arisen in recent years investigating this phenomenon in relation to changing conceptions of history and historiography in Western culture. Among the most useful research to my own work on the iconographic fortunes of Joan of Arc in French art and culture have been the following: Stephen Bann, *Romanticism and the Rise of History* (New York: Twayne Publishers, 1995); Hayden White, *Metahistory: The Historical Imagination in Nineteenth-Century Europe* (Baltimore: The Johns Hopkins University Press, 1973); Robert Gildea, *The Past in French History* (New Haven: Yale University Press, 1994); Stanley Mellon, *The Political Uses of History: A Study of Historians in the French Restoration* (Stanford: Stanford University Press, 1958); and *Realms of Memory: The Construction of the French Past*, ed. Pierre Nora, 3 vols., trans. Arthur Goldhammer (New York: Columbia University Press, 1996–98).
13. Boigne, *Recollections*, p. 169.
14. Madeleine Deschamps, "Decor à la Cathédrale," in *Romance & Chivalry: History and Literature Reflected in Early Nineteenth-Century French Painting*, ex. cat. (London: Matthiesen Fine Art Ltd and Stair Sainty Matthiesen Inc., 1996), pp. 227–28.
15. J.-Alexandre Buchon, *Chronique et procès de la Pucelle d'Orléans, d'après un manuscrit inédit de la Bibliothèque d'Orléans, accompagné d'une dissertation de l'Abbé Dubois* (Paris: Verdière, 1827); Kolb, *Ary Scheffer*, pp. 23–24. Buchon's

Chronique, it might be noted, influenced Jules Michelet in writing his account of Jeanne d'Arc's life (Margolis, *Joan of Arc in History*, p. 19, cat. no. 72).

16. Quoted by Pierre Lebrun, *Notice sur la vie de Madame la Princesse Marie d'Orléans, duchesse de Wurtemberg* (Paris: Imprimerie Royale, 1840), p. 51; also quoted by Kolb, *Une Correspondance inedite de la Princesse Marie*, pp. 24–25, n. 1.
17. Early references to this sculpture indicate that it was entitled variably: *Jeanne pleurant à la vue des blessés* and *Et considérant la grande destruction d'Angloys. . .se prist a plourir la Pucelle.* The city of Orléans requested that a bronze casting of this equestrian sculpture be made as a companion piece to *Joan of Arc in Prayer* after it was installed before the Hôtel Groslot in Orléans in 1851. With the authorization of the artist's mother, Queen Marie-Amélie, who was in exile in England following the revolution of 1848 (the artist herself had already died in 1839, as had King Louis-Philippe in 1850), a copy of *Jeanne pleurant à la vue des blessés* was founded by Charnod from a copy of the princess's equestrian figure in the possession of Ary Scheffer. Given to the city of Orléans in 1851, this statue was installed in the grand salon of the Hôtel de ville, where it remains today (*Images de Jeanne d'Arc*, cat. 118, pp. 91–92, and Anne Pingeot, "80 ans de Jeanne d'Arc sculptées," cat. 259, p. 246). The plaster-proof cast from Scheffer's copy of *Jeanne pleurant* (from which the Orléans's bronze copy was made) was also given to the Musée Jeanne d'Arc in Orléans in 1853 (Philippe Mantellier, *Notice des collections composant le Musée de Jeanne d'Arc* [Orléans: H. Herluison, Libraire-Éditeur, 1880], cat. 118, pp. 90–91).
18. Grote, *Memoir of the Life of Ary Scheffer*, pp. 40–41.
19. *Joan of Arc dressed as a peasant with bare feet* [*Jeanne d'Arc en habit de paysanne, pieds nus*], n.d., H: 49 cm, signed Marie d'Orléans (Dortrecht: Ary Scheffer Museum). Marie d'Orléans may have sculpted further images of the Maid. Much of the Princess's oeuvre, however, has been lost, both in the 1838 fire that destroyed her home after her marriage in Gotha (in Thuringia, Germany), and in the destruction done to the royal residences in Paris during the revolution of February 1848 (Marthe Kolb, *Ary Scheffer et son temps, 1795–1858*, Ph.D. diss., Université de Paris (Paris: Boivin & Cie, éditeurs, 1937), p. 26, n. 2; Grote, *Memoir of the Life of Ary Scheffer*, p. 43).
20. From the very beginning of the July Monarchy, the Catholic Church was made to suffer for the many protections and privileges it enjoyed under the last of the Bourbon kings. During the reign of Louis XVIII (1814–24), these included a royal order inducing court attendance at daily Mass; police ordinance enforcing public observance of Sundays and Holy days; and state censorship suppressing newspapers that offended public morality, challenged the divine right of kings, or endangered "respect due religion." Under Charles X (1824–30), state sanctions supporting the Gallican Church became even more repressive; indeed the sacrilege laws of 1825, which imposed life imprisonment for the profanation of sacred vessels, and death for the desecration of the consecrated host, verged on the draconian. Reprisal for these repressive ordinances came swiftly during the hot days of

summer insurrection in 1830 for which the July regime was named. Churches and seminaries were looted, calvaries were destroyed, and sanctuaries were desecrated. For a time, priests were forced to adopt lay attire to protect themselves from assault; and many prelates fled France (Elizabeth Kashey, "The Catholic Church in Nineteenth Century France" in *Christian Imagery in French Nineteenth Century Art, 1789–1906*, ex. cat. [New York: Shepherd Gallery, 1980], p. 5; and Adrien Dansette, *Religious History of Modern France*, v. I [New York: Herder and Herder, 1961], pp. 183, 207–208; François Furet, *Revolutionary France, 1770–1880* [London: Blackwell, 1988], p. 305; Driskell, *Representing Belief*, p. 20).

21. Marie's religious devotion exceeded even that of her mother, a woman well known for her piety. Following the marriage of her elder sister Louise in 1832, an event that left Marie bereft at the loss of her closest childhood companion, her faith deepened to a point that seemed almost exaggerated to some observers (Boigne, *Recollections*, p. 171). Although Marie's pious devotions gradually abated as her grief lessened, the princess remained devout; as Boigne wrote: "The tendency to mysticism gradually disappeared, and though her religion preserved a somewhat more enthusiastic character than that of her mother and her sisters, she abandoned the exaggerations which she had almost reached" (Boigne, *Recollections*, p. 172). Ary Scheffer later recalled that "in the heart of this Princess dwelt a religious faith, such as became a noble, womanly heart" (quoted in Grote, *Memoire of the Life of Ary Scheffer*, p. 47).
22. Damaged by iconoclastic Calvinists during the wars of religion in the 1560s, this calvary scene was reconstructed in the 1570s by the bronze founder Hector Lescot, who transformed the scene into a pietà by removing the figure of Christ on the cross with Mary, and replacing these figures with the body of Christ held in the lap of his mother, the mourning Virgin Mary. This pietà was restored again from the ravages of time and weather in 1771, before being damaged beyond repair in 1792 by revolutionary vandals. The monument was melted down to make cannons in the war effort by order of the *Conseil général de la commune* in Orléans in 1792 (Heimann, "What Honor for the Feminine Sex?" pp. 20–21, n. 25; see also Pierre-Marie Brun, "Le premier monument à Jeanne d'Arc sur l'ancien pont d'Orléans," in *Images de Jeanne d'Arc*, pp. 27–34; and Pierre Marot, "De la réhabilitation à la glorification de Jeanne d'Arc: essai sur l'historiographie et le culte de l'héroine en France pendant cinq siècles," in *Mémorial de Jeanne d'Arc, 1456–1956*, ed. Joseph Foret (Paris: Jospeh Foret and Comité national de Jeanne d'Arc, 1958), p. 88 [pp. 85–164].
23. Dupont, *Les trois statues de Jeanne d'Arc*, pp. 20–21.
24. Dansette, *Religious History*, p. 208.
25. Charles Aufrère-Duvernay, *Notice Historique et critique sur les monuments érigés a Orléans en l'honneur de Jeanne d'Arc* (Orléans: *Imprimerie de Pagnerre*, 1855), p. 2021.
26. Quoted in *Le Moniteur universel* 148 (28 pluviôse an XI [February 17, 1803]), p. 596.

27. Maurice Agulhon, *Marianne into Battle: Republican Imagery and Symbolism in France, 1789–1880*, trans. Janet Lloyd (Cambridge: Cambridge University Press, 1981), pp. 41–42.
28. T. J. Clark, *The Absolute Bourgeois: Artists and Politics in France, 1848–1851* (Princeton: Princeton University Press, 1982), p. 17.
29. For further discussion, see Mona Ozouf, *Festivals and the French Revolution* (Cambridge: Harvard University Press, 1988).
30. Concerning of the rise of the Maid's image during the Bourbon Restoration, see Norman D. Ziff, "Jeanne d'Arc and French Restoration Art," *Gazette des Beaux-Arts* 93 (January 1979): 37–48; see also Heimann, " 'What Honor for the Feminine Sex,' " ch. 8, pp. 228–96.
31. Regarding Joan of Arc's image and that of Liberty (also known as "Marianne"), and their role in both the revolutionary festivals of 1789–90 and in Napoleonic culture, see Heimann, "What Honor for the Feminine Sex," ch. 2 and 6, esp. pp. 22–28, 162–65.
32. Baron de Barante, *Souvenirs* (Paris: Calmann Lévy, 1983), Vol. VI, p. 170; also quoted in Marie d'Orléans, *Une Correspondance inédite de la princesse Marie d'Orléans, duchesse de Wurtemberg*, ed. Marthe Kolbe (Paris: Boivin & Cie, éditeurs, 1937), p. 45.
33. As Dumas wrote in his dedication: *A la mémoire de S.A.R. Princess Marie. Hommage de respect à la fille de France; Homage d'admiration à l'Artiste européené*, Alex[andre] Dumas, *Jehanne, la Pucelle, 142–1431* (Paris: Magen et Comon, 1842), n.p.
34. Alex[andre] Dumas, *Joan, the Heroic Maiden*, trans. Louisa C. Ingersoll (Philadelphia: E. Ferret & Co., 1846), p. 84.
35. Dumas, *Joan, the Heroic Maiden*, pp. 106–107.
36. Dumas, *Joan, the Heroic Maiden*, pp. 9–10; see also Nadia Margolis, *Joan of Arc in History, Literature and Film* (New York: Garland, 1990), no. 1196, p. 314.
37. For an illustrated listing of these works, see Anne Pingeot, "80 ans de Jeanne d'Arc sculptées," in *Images de Jeanne d'Arc*, pp. 185–261.
38. Understanding the relatively little social value placed upon her life and work as an unmarried female artist, Marie d'Orléans confided in her friends that she was afraid she might never marry: "When I appear before God with my sculptures in my arms, what shall I say when He asks me, 'Was it for that I sent you upon the earth?' " (quoted by Boigne, p. 178).
39. When Marie d'Orléans's sculpture *Jeanne d'Arc en prier* was erected before the town hall in Orléans in 1851, there were no inaugural ceremonies because of the sculptress's association with the recently fallen July Monarchy. See Pierre Fontenailles, "La Jeanne d'Arc de l'Hôtel de ville et la Princess Marie d'Orléans," *Republique du Centre* (March 23, 1947), n.p., and Dupont, *Les trois statues*, p. 36.
40. Alfred-Auguste Cuvillier-Fleury, *Journal Intime de Cuvillier-Fleury, publié avec une introduction par Ernest Bertin*, Vol. 1: *La Famille d'Orléans au Palais-Royal, 1821–1831* (Paris: Plon-Nourrit et Cie, 1900); Grote, *Memoirs of the Life of Ary Scheffer*, p. 47; Kolb, *Une correspondance*, p. 7; Boigne, *Recollections*, pp. 166–67.

41. These images include Achille Deveria's sepia and gouache image of *Jeanne et Marie d'Orléans* [reproduced in *Images de Jeanne d'Arc*, cat. 119, p. 92], Adolphe Mouilleron's lithograph of *La princesse Marie dans son atelier devant la statue de Jeanne d'Arc*, repro. in Pierre Marot, *Le culte de Jeanne d'Arc à Domremy: son image et son développement* (Nancy: Palais Ducal, Éditions du Pays lorrain, 1956), p. 36, and Sébastien Delarue's *Marie d'Orléans avec la statue de Jeanne d'Arc*, repro. in Thomas W. Gaehtgens, *Versailles: De la résidence royale au musée historique. La galerie des Batailles dans le musée historique de Louis-Philippe*, trans. Patrick Poirot (Antwerp: Mercatorfonds, 1984), p. 162.
42. For more information on Vinchon and his award-winning painting of *Boissy-d'Anglas* (Salon of 1835) for the Chamber of Deputies at the Palais-Bourbon, see Michael Marrinan, *Painting Politics for Louis-Philippe: Art and Ideology in Orléanist France, 1830–1848* (New Haven: Yale University Press, 1988), pp. 93–94; for a description of Vinchon's *Sacre de Charles VII, à Reims (juillet 17, 1429)*, painted on commission for Versailles, see Émile Arthes, *Liste chronologique des ouvrages de peinture, sculpture, architecture, gravure & litho graphie concernant Jeanne d'Arc, qui ont été admis aux expositions annuelles de Paris, de l'origine à nos jours* (Orléans: H. Herluison, 1895), p. 12; and for a critical view of Louis-Philippe's program at Versailles, see also Albert Boime, "The Quasi-open competitions of the quasi-legitimate July Monarchy," *Arts Magazine* 59 (April 1985): pp. 94–105.
43. F.E. Desnoyers, *L'Iconographie de Jeanne d'Arc* (Orléans: H. Herluison, 1891), p. 14.
44. Among the few twentieth-century scholars to single out Marie d'Orléans's *Joan of Arc in Prayer* for attention are Régine Pernoud, who (as has been noted earlier) devoted one sentence of praise to the princess's sculpture in her 1981 study *Jeanne d'Arc*, and Marina Warner, who gave less than a paragraph to Marie's statue of the Maid praying (more generously, she also devoted a page to the princess's small equestrian statue of the *Pucelle*) in her over 300-page investigation of the Joan of Arc's image over time (Pernoud, *Jeanne d'Arc*, p. 85; and Marina Warner, *Joan of Arc: the Image of Female Heroism* [New York: Alfred A. Knopf, 1981], pp. 181, 259).

CHAPTER 13

LE TRIOMPHE DE L'HUMILITÉ: THÉRÈSE OF LISIEUX AND "LA NOUVELLE JEANNE"

Denise L. Despres

This chapter considers Saint Thérèse of Lisieux's last convent drama, "The Triumph of Humility," as a reflection of the personal influence of Joan of Arc on Therese's spiritual and literary imagination, as well as on nineteenth-century French devotional culture.

The writings of Thérèse Martin (1873–97), known to the world as Saint Thérèse of Lisieux, reflect Joan of Arc's popularity as a symbol of royalist Catholic France among the pious and politically conservative of the Third Republic.[1] Yet for Thérèse, the youthful Joan, who had yet to be canonized, provided a personal model of female sanctity both to emulate and against which to define and measure the efficacy of the hidden life of Carmel in the modern world. Thérèse's representations of Joan in her creative writings thus help us comprehend the evolution of Thérèse's own distinctive contribution to modern Catholic spirituality, known as her "little way."

In Thérèse's early poems and plays, Joan figures as a romantic model of sanctity and agency. Thérèse's final play, *Le Triomphe de l'humilité* [*The Triumph of Humility*], echoes the invocation of Joan of Arc in the much publicized, contemporary account of Diana Vaughan, using it to explore the possibility of a heroic sanctity in the modern world. The play's reworking of Vaughan's story—supposedly a factual, first-person account by Diana, but actually a deceptive fiction by Léo Taxil—provides us with a specific context in which to situate Thérèse's anxieties about the persecution of the

Church and its disestablishment in the Third Republic. In Thérèse's play, Taxil's sensational story of diabolical conspiracy and covert evil is the vehicle for a larger, theological problem: how can the faithful be holy in the present, apocalyptic landscape of illusion, deception, and nihilism? In the modern world, where the very existence of evil is rationalized away, who is sufficiently vigilant to be the "new" Joan of Arc? The play proclaims the triumph of a humility that Thérèse was soon afterward challenged to master in real life, when Taxil's hoax was revealed and her unwitting part in it publicly exposed. Deceived by Taxil's cynical and depraved fiction, even as Joan had been misled by her jurors, Thérèse finds the greatest heroism in humility. "The Triumph of Humility" ultimately offers the prayerful, hidden life of Carmel as the frontline of the battle between good and evil. Similarly, Thérèse's final hymn to the imprisoned Joan reflects a spiritual maturation brought about by physical suffering and the humiliation resulting from the Diana Vaughan affair.[2]

Playing Joan, Portraying Diana: Thérèse's Search for Heroic Models

Joan of Arc figured in an important way in Thérèse's creative writings from beginning to end, and her onstage portrayal of Joan, preserved in photographs, came to play an unexpected part in the unfolding of the Vaughan affair. Thérèse's high spirits and creative bent as a writer from her youth earned her the privilege of composing eight short plays for performance in her community, in continuance of a long-established theatrical tradition within Carmelite culture. Her sister Céline took the famous photographs of Thérèse, enchained and looking pensive, as she herself played Joan of Arc on January 21, 1895, in an ambitious production she staged entitled *Joan of Arc Fulfilling Her Mission* (figure 13.1).[3] Carmelite scholar Guy Gaucher notes the twenty-two-year-old's fervor in identifying with the suffering Joan: "Five photographs taken by Céline show a twenty-two-year-old Thérèse wearing a brown wig, with banner and sword in hand, intensely living the part. She had, as it were, become the heroine whose part she was playing. . . .really identifying herself with the young imprisoned girl."[4]

Playing the part of Joan in a Carmelite play allowed Thérèse to combine symbolically Joan's life of heroic, public action with the greater, hidden life of spiritual sacrifice. Already as a schoolgirl Thérèse had defined her vocation in comparison to Joan's. In her spiritual autobiography, *Histoire d' une ame* [*Story of a Soul*], she writes:

> When reading the accounts of the patriotic deeds of French heroines, especially the *Venerable* JOAN OF ARC, I had a great desire to imitate them; and it seemed I felt within me the same burning zeal with which they were

13.1 Photograph of Saint Thérèse as Joan of Arc. Reproduced with the permission of the Office Central de Lisieux.

> animated, the same heavenly inspiration. Then I received a grace which I have always looked upon as one of the greatest in my life. . .I considered that I was born for *glory*. . .[God] made me understand my own *glory* would not be evident to the eyes of mortals, that it would consist in becoming a great *saint*.[5]

Similarly, in a letter dated April 25, 1987, to l'abbé Bellière, a young priest who sought prayer and spiritual counsel, Thérèse wrote humorously:

> Well! I shall make you smile once more when I tell you that I dreamt in my childhood of fighting on the fields of battle. . .When I was beginning to learn the history of France, the account of Joan of Arc's exploits delighted me; I felt in my heart the desire and the courage to imitate her. It seemed the Lord destined me, too, for great things. I was not mistaken, but instead of voices from heaven inviting me to combat, I heard in the depths of my soul a gentler and stronger voice, that of the Spouse of Virgins, who was calling me to other exploits, to more glorious conquests, and into Carmel's solitude.[6]

Thérèse's letter confirms that her youthful adulation of Joan was that of a schoolgirl, a wistful admiration, perhaps, of a bolder, more visible girl whose singular path to sanctity could never be duplicated in less heroic, less religious times. Thérèse's affectionate, childlike love for her widower father, Louis Martin, whom she named her "king," gives an indirect expression to her identification with Joan of Arc, for like Joan, who brought Charles VII to his coronation at Reims in 1429, Thérèse wanted to secure the coronation of beloved Papa: "I cannot say how much I loved Papa; everything in him caused me to admire him. When he explained his ideas to me (as though I were a big girl), I told him very simply that surely if he said this to the great men of the government, they would take him to make him *King*, and then France would be happy as it had never been before."[7]

Thérèse was more than content to keep her devout father, who was worthy to be "*King of France and Navarre*" as "[her] King alone," however.[8] The domicile of the Martins thus allowed her to imitate Joan in a domestic kingdom that foreshadowed the Carmel at Lisieux. Certainly the model of the Holy Family at Nazareth and its quiet sanctity prevailed among the French middle class of Thérèse's time, providing a powerful bulwark against skepticism, republicanism, and secularism to Catholic families who were affected in a variety of ways by the State's virulent anticlericalism.[9] Thérèse's youthful claim that her conquests would be "more glorious" than Joan's martial achievements ought to be taken at full value, however, for in 1897 she had worked through her own radical spirituality, the "little way" of holiness necessary for the least powerful in the world, for the cloistered Carmelite as well as the lonely believer struggling against the malaise of nineteenth-century nihilism.

Thérèse's faith in her new spirituality was tested during the last, difficult years of her life. The beloved father whom she honored as her king, and who was for her an earthly image of God the Father, suffered a paralysis that affected him mentally and made him in 1889 a patient in a psychiatric hospital in Caen. In *Story of a Soul*, Thérèse describes her empathic share in her "Papa's three years of martyrdom" as a treasure of suffering more valuable to her than "all the ecstasies and revelations of the saints."[10] From April 3, 1896, Thérèse entered into a new period of interiority intensified by the ominous sign of rapidly degenerative tuberculosis. During the night of Holy Thursday, Thérèse felt a froth of blood bubbling at her lips; the haemoptysis left her with a brief sense of joy at her imminent death, shortly followed by a "dark night of the soul" that remained with her until she died on September 30, 1897. This final purgation of the soul from earthly attachments, described in detail in Saint John of the Cross's spiritual teachings, is the sober foundation of Thérèse's last play. During the early months of this period of intense suffering, more spiritual and psychological than physical, when excruciating doubts about God's existence and thus the meaning of her own life tormented her, Thérèse turned to the newspaper accounts of the spectacular Diana Vaughan for consolation and confirmation of God's dramatic, palpable presence in individual lives.

Diana Vaughan, the contemporary heroine whom Thérèse celebrates as the "new Joan," was the notorious refugee from freemasonry whose conversion story had captivated Catholic readers and even made its way to the sanctuary of Carmel. The "book" the young woman supposedly penned, *The Memoirs of an Independent, Fully Initiated, Ex-Palatine: Unveiling the Mysteries and Satanic Practices of the Luciferian Triangles*, was published in 1895 and created an immediate public stir. The young woman, virginal and orphaned, fought over by the powers of good and evil, assumed the part of a Joan-like France in the popular imagination of Catholics. At first sight, the Vaughan narrative served to validate the destructive power of freemasonry and to substantiate papal directives and popular fears that had been mocked by rationalists as paranoid and fictitious. It seemed to confirm the dark works invisibly undermining the powers of the Church that Pope Leo XIII had addressed in his encyclical *Humanum genus* [on freemasonry, promulgated on April 20, 1884] and to the Italian people in *Custodi di quella Fede* [*Guardians of That Faith*, on freemasonry, December 8, 1892].[11]

Critical to understanding Thérèse's late writings, in which she poignantly refers both to her own struggle against impending death and skepticism and to Diana Vaughan's conversion from freemasonry, is our awareness of the apocalyptic mentality that prevailed among faithful Catholics who felt, and indeed were, institutionally oppressed by political forces at work effectively and finally to separate Church and State. For families like the Martins, who sent all five daughters into the religious life and rejected secular education, the heavy taxation of religious orders and the various means employed by the State to reduce the numbers of the priesthood and to dismantle parochial schools made credible the widespread accusations that conspiratorial forces were at work to destroy the fragmented, postrevolutionary Church Militant. The Second Administration, which prevailed from October 1895 to April 21, 1896, was especially anticlerical, and nine of eleven of its members were freemasons.[12] Due to its secretive nature, its alliance with Republicanism, anticlericalism, and antiauthoritarianism, freemasonry was perceived as a diabolical expression of Enlightenment precepts, most specifically of secular humanism rooted in naturalism.

Viewing social and economic forces rather than spiritual, eschatological truths as the organizing force of history, proponents of these new intellectual views evoked an even more rigid authoritarianism from French Catholics, where Ultramontanism (literally, looking beyond the mountains to the Vatican for order) originated. The loss of the Papal States in September 1870 seemed a grievous blow in an apocalyptic struggle between good and evil, played out on a political stage that assumed cosmic proportions to ordinary Catholics. Papal documents like the *Syllabus of Errors* by Pius IX (1878) attributed the spread of liberalism, naturalism, and absolute rationalism to socialism, communism, and secret societies like the freemasons, and they forbade Catholics to participate in the latter.

In *Custodi di quella fede*, the pontiff cautioned of freemasonry: "In a matter of such importance and where the seduction is so easy in these times, it is urgent that the Christian watch himself from the beginning. . .Every Christian should shun books and journals which distill the poison of impiety and which stir up the fire of unrestrained desires or sensual passions."[13] The sensational case of Diana Vaughan allowed the Catholic press to counter the propaganda of freemasonry with a supposedly factual exposé of its seductive evils. Thérèse's uncle, Isidore Guérin, a journalist and surrogate father after Louis Martin's death (July 29, 1894), promoted the story in *Le Normand*. Guy Gaucher speculates that the Lisieux Carmel was exposed to the Diana Vaughan affair "possibly through the influence of Father Mustel, editor of *Revue Catholique de Coutances*, and an out-and-out supporter of Diana Vaughan."[14]

In the recesses of the Lisieux Carmel, an impressionable Thérèse listened eagerly to Taxil's fabrication and devoutly copied out passages from Vaughan's widely publicized prayer, "The Eucharistic Novena of Reparation."[15] Ironically, Catholic newspapers and journals became the unwitting conveyers of Taxil's sensationalistic tale. Although individual prelates and even Orders, most notably the Jesuits, spurned the story as fabulous, the reportage of the shadowy underworld of freemasonry clearly intrigued a wide audience whose fascination with lurid details might be mitigated, given Vaughan's conversion and the imprimatur of the Catholic press. The sensuality of the narrative and the romantic language may seem distinctly sexual to post-Freudian readers and thus peculiar fare for chaste Carmelites, but bridal mysticism and the erotic idiom of the biblical Song of Songs has a distinguished place in the contemplative writings of both men and women in the Catholic tradition. Saint John of the Cross (1591), Thérèse's favorite writer, composed sensual meditations on union with Christ rivaled in elegance only by the *Sermones super Cantica Canticorum* by Saint Bernard of Clairvaux (1153).[16]

Thérèse herself fashioned a "wedding invitation" for her espousal to her heavenly husband that reflects the tendency in nineteenth-century female devotionalism to "domesticate" spiritual relationships.[17] Among the laity as well as religious, the figure of Christ "as ideal husband and lover was expressed in various forms."[18] In his exploration of popular schoolgirl piety in nineteenth-century France, Thomas Kselman analyzes the psychological ramifications of "a deck of playing cards designed for Catholic school girls. . . .There were thirty-three cards in the deck, one for each year of Christ's life, and each card bore a title, a secret, and a prayer. Theoretically, the girls would choose a card each day and use it to help them meditate on their association with Christ. Among the titles were some that described the romantic stereotype of the modern wife: The Lover, The Conquest, The Ideal Companion, The Captive, The Victim."[19]

The last two resonate deeply with Thérèse's own religious sensibilities; nonetheless, Thérèse's perception of herself as a "victim" of love is not self-punitive or masochistic, but rooted in her own admiration of genuine historical martyrs, not only Joan, but more recently the Carmelites of Compiègne (the site of Joan's capture), who were among the last to be guillotined among the thousands of religious martyrs of the Reign of Terror. Further, her own desire to travel to Indochina as a missionary, and her correspondence with missionary priests whose deaths, such as l'Abbé Bellière's at age twenty-seven, of fever and exhaustion, were almost certain, made the concept of sacrificial victim a concrete reality rather than a flight of fancy.

In *Story of a Soul*, Thérèse marvels at how her childhood dream of becoming a martyr for the faith has not only remained alive within her but also intensified since her enclosure within the walls of Carmel. Significantly, she concludes the list of those martyrs with whom she especially identifies with the name of her "dear sister," Joan of Arc: "*Martyrdom* was the dream of my youth and this dream has grown with me within Carmel's cloisters. But here again, I feel that my dream is a folly, for I cannot confine myself to desiring *one kind* of martyrdom. To satisfy me I need *all*. Like You, my Adorable Spouse, I would be scourged and crucified. I would die flayed like St. Bartholomew. . . .and like Joan of Arc, my dear sister, I would whisper at the stake Your Name, O JESUS."[20]

In Diana Vaughan, Thérèse found another spiritual "sister," someone who shared her devotion to Joan of Arc. Vaughan's conversion, eagerly published by widely read Catholic papers like *La Croix*, appealed deeply to Thérèse, for Diana claimed in her supposed autobiography to have converted under the intercessory prayer of the blessed Joan of Arc, thus offering proof of Joan's sanctity. Taxil's outrageous story of the young woman, half-French and half-American, raised by rationalists to espouse freemasonry, galvanized conservative Catholics by reviving well-worn tales of diabolical conspiracy and ritual desecration. In this lurid, mildly erotic confession, Diana Vaughan describes her betrothal to the beautiful Asmodeus, servant of Lucifer, and her initiation into a French Masonic Lodge presided over by her nemesis, the lovely and headstrong Sophie Walder. Diana, the daughter of a distinguished American freemason, is fêted in Paris until she refuses to participate in one of the central rituals, earning Sophie Walder's enmity. On March 25, 1884, significantly the Feast of the Annunciation, Vaughan witnessed the Luciferians engaged in ritual host desecration: bearing poinards, the sect knelt at the feet of the grand Priestess, while she swore an oath to Lucifer. Then, bearing a Host in a chalice,

"Elle crache sur la divine Eucharist et invite la récipiendaire à l'imiter" [She spit on the Holy Eucharist and invited the membership to do likewise].[21]

Vaughan, disdainful of such superstition, for it assumed the power of the Real Presence, rationally refused to spit on the Host. This episode, reminiscent of medieval Christian anti-Judaic myths of host profanation, reflects Diana's future conversion. Diana goes on to describe how on June 6, she sat alone in her chamber, meditating upon a letter she had received from a "priest-professor" that had touched her heart. He had asked her to promise not to mock the Blessed Virgin. As she considered this request, she gazed upon the statue of Joan of Arc that she kept, for she, like Thérèse, had a particular devotion to Joan, and she prayed: "Vous aimez Marie de toute vôtre coeur, o Jeanne, pendant cette glorieuse et trop courte existence que j'admiré tant. . .Eh bien, c'est à vous, douce et sublime héroine, c'est à vous que je veux prêter le serment de respecter à jamais le nom de Marie, mère de Christ" [You love Mary with all your heart, O Joan, during your glorious and very brief existence that I so admire, and indeed it is to you, sweet, sublime heroine, that I wish to make an oath to respect forever the name of Mary, the mother of Christ].[22]

Vaughan's oath never more to abuse the name of the Virgin is highly charged, for it suggests the power of Joan's intercession on behalf of persons, as well as her enduring force in the battle against the Antichrist on behalf of royalist and Catholic France. The Virgin is the patroness of Carmel, and Diana's tentative oath to respect "the name of Mary" seemed to Thérèse (as her subsequent invitation to Vaughan in *The Triumph of Humility* attests) to be a prophetic step toward the convent. As soon as she had taken this vow, the first time ever upon her knees, Vaughan began to weep, although not knowing why. This sign of feminine transformation, new to the witty and steely Vaughan, undoubtedly signaled for the greater part of Taxil's audience a conversion to normative female tenderness as well.

Diana's oath to Joan of Arc results in the terrifying apparition of four devils. According to her supposed memoir, Diana invoked the name of Jeanne when the demons attacked her: "Jeanne, Jeanne, défends-moi," effecting the transformation of these spirits from their disguises as angels of light (which is how they appear to the freemasons and how they seduced Diana) to hideous monsters, "avaient queue et cornes; bref, vrai diables" [with tails and horns, in sum, real devils]. Simply calling upon Joan's name wounds the devils, and roaring in dismay, they disappear. After Diana sees the demons for what they are, she mysteriously disappears from public (or the Press), retreating into a convent, for fear that the freemasons will try to assassinate her before she reveals her knowledge of their secret rituals.

For conservative Catholics, Vaughan's highly publicized narrative of spiritual depravity and freemasonry confirmed an apocalyptic sense of

France's role in a struggle against modernity played out on a national stage. Her "confession" legitimized the association of freemasonry, and thus republicanism, with satanic forces in league to destroy the powers of order and light in the present time. Catholic newspapers, such as *La Croix*, openly equated secularism and republicanism with apocalyptic signs, such as the persecution of the Church and the appearance of Antichrist.[23] The Catholic Right fully anticipated France's providential role in the impending battle between good and evil outlined in anti-Masonic writings.[24]

Thérèse, whose search for a unique sanctity intensified in her final difficult year, invested the character of Diana Vaughan with both a personal and eschatological meaning.[25] Thérèse's final play, *The Triumph of Humility*, evokes the prevalent apocalyptic spirit, as it pits the Carmelites, staunchly protected by their patroness—the Virgin Mary—against the forces of Satan; the Carmelites become the bulwark of Christian society in this battle. It is an eschatological drama wherein her favorite subject—Joan's battle to free France from its English oppressors—is translated into a cosmic struggle in which France must resist a more powerful, because internalized and intellectualized, darkness. In this last play, Thérèse offers purity and prayer in battle against diabolical forces, representing atheism, republicanism, and freemasonry.

For Thérèse, Vaughan's account suggested that the heroic enterprises of God's saints, even those accomplished in secret, would prevail in the modern world. The hidden way need be no less valorous than martial heroism in the world. Thus, despite the typical sentimentality of Thérèse's idiom, which can create an impression of naïveté and insularity, Thérèse's play, like her final hymn to Joan, is rooted in the stark realism foundational to the Carmelite contemplative life.

Thérèse's "Triumph"

Thérèse composed *The Triumph of Humility* for performance on June 21, 1896, the feast day of the prioress, Mother Marie Gonzague. The one-act play's central theme is the unifying force of humility and the efficacy of Carmelite prayer. Early in the play, Thérèse cites Diana Vaughan's own conversion as evidence of intercessory prayer's power to defeat evil. The drama opens in the convent recreation room, where Thérèse, as novice mistress, indulges in a playful conversation with Sisters Marie Madeleine and Marie du St. Esprit. Acknowledging their own aridity in prayer, they wonder at the courage of souls whose spiritual lives are dramatically graced with consolations, visions, or even diabolical threats that test faith.

Clearly, the play refers to Diana Vaughan's own spurious biography, as the play at this point includes a comical encounter with Vaughan's own diabolical fiancé, Asmodeus. Saint Michael, an archangel especially associated with Joan of Arc as one of her voices, appears on stage in response to their imaginings, followed by an enchained Lucifer, Beelzebub (Baal-Zeboub), and Asmodeus, whose prideful boasts and vulgar threats underscore their enslavement. Under Saint Michael's protection, the nuns turn their backs to the demons, hearing the confrontation but never being defiled by evil. The devils in Thérèse's play comically quarrel, in imitation of the divisions among the freemasons in Vaughan's report, but also as a portent of the ultimate dissension that is a chief characteristic of hell and essentially antithetical to community. Beelzebub accuses Asmodeus of impotence, noting that his beloved freemason Diana Vaughan has converted through the intercession of the virgin Joan of Arc.

Just as Thérèse had played the historical Joan in previous plays, now she imagined the confrontation of Diana, whom she calls "la nouvelle Jeanne," with palpable evil.[26] Taxil's account was undoubtedly read directly to Thérèse at some point, for she clearly derived the inspiration for the comedy from Diana's description of the farcical and grotesque energy of demons: "ils me menaçaient, pleins de rage, comme si j'avais été un ange d'Adonaï, c'est à dire comme ils faisaient dans leurs comédies de guerre. . .mais je comprends maintenant que leur fureur contre moi n'était pas feinte" [Full of rage, they menaced me, as if I had been an angel of Adonai, it was done as in their playacting of battle. . .but I understand now that their anger against me wasn't feigned].[27]

The demons rail against holy virgins, most especially Carmelites, whose unified prayers render them ineffectual. They rally with empty threats of attacking Carmelite monasteries and convents, but Saint Michael invokes the Virgin's humility and conquers them. In the face of Carmelite poverty, chastity, and obedience, they are ineffectual. Saint Michael then sings the "Canticle of the Sacred Heart," driving the demons back to the underworld. The sisters acknowledge their collective roles as the "new Joans" who will chase the foreigner—Satan—from the realm. They renew their collective purpose with a prayer to the Virgin, after which angels arrive on stage to sing a Carmelite song of triumph.

Although at first sight, the brief play might appear to glorify the exploits of Vaughan and resistance to the tangible presence of demons, Thérèse's play is subtler, more searching than this. Instead, it ultimately celebrates a complete trust in God's protection, symbolized by the screen, which prevents the Sisters in the play from viewing the demonic presence. If Diana Vaughan is "la nouvelle Jeanne," the play argues, then the Carmelites aspire to resist evil in the darkness, without even the benefit of material evidence that would substantiate its existence. Diana is like Joan in her privilege of receiving voices and her witness to God's intervention in human history, but in her flight from the world to the convent—and thus imprisonment, darkness, and anonymity—Diana is metaphorically united to both Joan and Thérèse in Carmel.

In *The Triumph of Humility*, Thérèse expresses her wish that the young woman join her in the Lisieux Carmel: "My greatest desire would be to see you unite to Jesus in our little Carmel when your mission is finished."[28] This desire suggests that she identified with Diana personally, investing in her dramatic conversion and retreat from the diabolical life of freemasonry her own anxieties, and ultimately faith, in a life of contemplative prayer undistinguished by the dramatic visions and voices that both Vaughan and Joan of Arc experienced. The play explores the nature of humility in a faith unconfirmed by supernatural evidence of God's direction. Thérèse's affirmation of faith in the absence of miracles runs counter to nineteenth-century religious sensibilities but offers a paradigm of modern Catholic faith, both to cloistered religious and the laity.

One of the critically exciting elements of Thérèse's drama is its ability to represent imaginatively the Lisieux community and her role in it at a specific historical moment. Thérèse thus acts in the play, but plays a version of herself as novice mistress, where her task is to gauge and gently instruct the distinctive vocation of each soul in her charge. The characters of Sister Madeleine and Sister Marie du St. Esprit are subtly drawn by one familiar with the spiritual desires and maladies typical of the enclosed life—a desire for visions (or at least the elocutions of which the foundress also writes), the aridity of prayer, spiritual timidity. Although partially expunged by Mother Agnes of Jesus (or someone else under her direction) during the Process of Beatification in 1910, some references to Diana Vaughan remain; after Thérèse introduces the subject matter of Vaughan's conversion and her role as "une nouvelle Jeanne d'Arc," Soeur Marie-Madeleine identifies Vaughan as one whom God has privileged with ecstasies and revelations, a theme of significant interest for the ailing Thérèse who had entered into a period of spiritual dryness and darkness at Easter of 1896.

In the play, Thérèse cheerfully rebukes her sister, reminding her of Saint John of the Cross's assertion that a desire for consolation is a venial sin, for Christ himself said, "Bienheureux ceux qui n'ont pas vu et qui ont cru" [Blessed are they who have not seen and yet believe].[29] Besides, even if the Sisters should be granted a glimpse of the demons, Thérèse assures them, "les démons ne sont pas plus à craindre que les mouches" [Demons are no more to be feared than flies]. Saint Michael, however, grants them the experience of "hearing" the demons at the very gates of hell; the demons parade and threaten on stage for the audience, removed from the presence of evil by the farcical nature of the "play" that distinguishes this Carmelite drama from the genuine, blasphemous ritual of the freemasons who invite Lucifer into their presence. Folios 2v, line 24 through 4r, line 21, contains a number of lacunae where the text has been expunged, clearly in response to the Diana Vaughan affair. The character Asmodeus, however, was perhaps unfamiliar to the Carmelites of Lisieux before 1896, when he figured prominently in the spurious memoirs as Diana's jealous fiancé. Despite the missing text, clear references to the freemasons remain, as well as a pointed description in Beelzebub's speech in 3r, lines 35–40, of Diana appealing to Joan for help: "d'un nom comme celui de Jeanne, Jeanne. . .ennemie, dont le seul nom nous fait fremir!!!" [Of a name like that of Joan, Joan. . .enemy, whose name alone causes us to tremble].[30]

The references to Diana, however, serve merely as a prologue to the larger drama Thérèse explores: the diabolical intention Lucifer pronounces to destroy the convents, whose seeming invincibility has foiled his plans to destroy the Church. He is not frightened by individual Carmelites with their holy water and crucifixes and prayer, "mais unies à leur Dieu elles sont aussi terribles que Lui" [But united with their God they are as terrible as He].[31] Only a Carmelite at Lisieux could have known how directly Thérèse's references to dissent and unity were, in the wake of the Mother Prioress's bitterly contested recent election. The mock battle between Saint Michael the archangel and the easily routed demons exemplifies the power of the three Carmelites, who beg his protection on their knees in a manner reminiscent of Diana's invocation of Joan. At the play's conclusion, the novice mistress underscores the message: only by humility and a community united in the Service of "Notre Mère" will the Carmelites be invisible heroines of the modern world: "nous saurons nouvelles Jeanne d'Arc, chasser l'étranger du royaume, c 'est à dire empêcher l'orgueilleux Satan d'entrer en nos monastères" [We shall know new Joan of Arcs to drive the stranger from the kingdom, that is to say to prevent prideful Satan from entering our monasteries].[32] The purging of the realm (France) of evil in these latter days will be a Carmelite task, for the Carmelites are the last bastion against a corrosive humanism, exemplified by "Orgueil, Indépendence, Propre Volonté" [Pride, Independence, and Individual will or freedom]—all core values of republicanism antithetical to convent life, which is now a model of community.[33]

Diana Vaughan's courage and conversion in lonely battle with the demons is not so much rejected in this play as superceded by another kind of heroism, a united force of Carmelites whose anonymous, but powerful, prayer can save a Church undermined by the diabolical pride of the modern world and secular humanism. The world may not know of their determination and heroism, but the Carmelites are the real "Joan of Arcs" whose resistance to despair and darkness, in anonymity and existential imprisonment, is the heroism of the nineteenth century.

In this context, "the new Joan" of the play Thérèse penned for Mother Marie Gonzague's feast day reveals in a comic medium the searching for a vocation amidst nothingness that Thérèse confesses in her spiritual autobiography. The "new Joan" is a meditation, in a time of crisis, on Joan's witness, confirmed through her visions and "voices" early on in her life and even more so by faith during the dark night of her imprisonment. Thérèse's intriguing connection between the spurious Diana Vaughan and Joan, and the consideration of the valor of both in the metafictional play space of Carmel, nonetheless disallows any equation of the two women, as well as any simple reduction of Thérèse's admiration for either woman to mere hero-worship. Thérèse evolved her own, mature vision of holiness in a probing exploring of both young women, who provided her with working models of female agency.

Through the Darkness: Following Thérèse's "Little Way" of Holiness

Unknown to Thérèse, her fellow Carmelites, and the French reading public, Diana Vaughan was the literary creation of Léo Taxil, a cynic with penetrating psychological insight into the mythic appeal of both Catholicism and freemasonry as ordering narratives fulfilling deep needs for modern audiences suffering in the wake of intellectual, spiritual, and cultural deconstruction.[34] On April 19, 1897, Taxil could no longer evade a public appearance; he was ready to expose his hoax and agreed to a press conference on Easter Monday before a select audience at the Paris Geographical Society. His revelation and glee at hoodwinking august prelates and even the pope himself, who had shown interest in this fantastic conversion, enraged the public. During his exposé, an enlarged photograph of Thérèse was displayed on the wall; Taxil made certain of Thérèse's own humiliation and cruel exposure to the world when he revealed his true identity and pointed to the photograph Thérèse had sent "Diana" of herself playing Joan of Arc—their mutual protectress—as evidence of Catholic irrationality and gullibility. The young Carmelite, moved by Vaughan's courage, had requested and was granted permission by her superiors to correspond with her. She had sent Diana Vaughan a photograph of herself, dressed as Joan of Arc, as an encouragement to the convert, who had reportedly offered herself as reparatory victim on June 13, 1895. Thérèse had even received a response from Vaughan, expressing her gratitude. At the discovery of her betrayal, Thérèse ripped up her precious letter from "Diana."[35]

From Easter of 1896, Thérèse had been suffering from a spiritual darkness, an acute anxiety that she had placated herself with illusions of a secret heroism; her "little way" might be, after all, nothing more than a self-deception in the face of modern nihilism. This "dark tunnel," a "thick fog" of pitch-black darkness, is at once a spiritual, psychological, and philosophical state undoubtedly exacerbated by the Diana Vaughan Affair.[36] Thérèse reminisces about a period prior to her trial of darkness in which she lived in a blissful state of spiritual childhood: "I was unable to believe there were really impious people who had no faith. I believed they were actually speaking against their own inner conviction when they denied the existence of heaven, that beautiful heaven where God Himself wanted to be their Eternal Reward. During those very joyful days of the Easter season, Jesus made me feel that there were really souls who have no faith and who, through the abuse of grace, lost this precious treasure, the source of the only real and pure joys."[37] Her passion, although attended by genuine physical pain, could be characterized as metaphysical, for now her back was turned not to darkness and evil but to the light itself: "My torment," Thérèse writes, "redoubles; it seems to me that the darkness, borrowing the voice of sinners, says mockingly to me: 'You are dreaming about the light, about a fatherland embalmed in the sweetest perfumes; you are dreaming about the *eternal* possession of the Creator of all these marvels; you believe that one day you will walk out of this fog which surrounds you! Advance, advance; rejoice in death which will give you not what you hope for but a night still more profound, the night of nothingness.' "[38]

Rather than despairing in this imprisonment, Thérèse claims, "I no longer have any great desires except that of loving to the point of dying of love."[39] The passages in her spiritual autobiography that follow contain her most profound teachings on martyrdom and suffering in wholly modern terms; they constitute the essence of her "little way" and have earned Saint Thérèse the title of Spiritual Doctor of the Church along with her beloved Saints Teresa of Avila and John of the Cross.

In May 1897, after the humiliation of the Diana Vaughan affair, Thérèse wrote yet another hymn to Joan of Arc:

Quand le Dieu des armées te donnant la victoire
Tu chassas l'étranger et fis sacrer le roi.
Mais ce n'était encor qu'une gloire ephémère
Il fallait à ton nom l'auréole des Saints.
Au fond d'un noir cachot, chargée de lourdes chaines
Le cruel étranger t'abreuva de douleurs.
Jeanne, tu m'apparais plus brilliante et plus belle
Qu'au sacre de ton roi, dans ta sombre prison
Ce céleste reflet de la gloire eternelle
Qui donc te l'apporta? Ce fut trahison.[40]

[With the God of armies giving you victory
You drove out the stranger and had the king anointed.
But this was still only an ephemeral glory.
Your name was due the halo of the Saints.
Deep in a black cell, burdened with heavy chains

The cruel stranger heaped sorrows upon you.
Joan, you appear to me more brilliant and beautiful
in your dark prison than at the coronation of your king.
That celestial gleam of eternal glory
Who brought it to you? That was betrayal.]

The poem, when read in the context of "la nouvelle Jeanne" and *The Triumph of Humility*, is an affirmation of Jeanne's heroism in imprisonment and martyrdom, rather than her heroic exploits on the battlefield. Young, betrayed, enchained in a "noir cachot" that resonates with Thérèse's dark tunnel, Jeanne triumphs in humility through faith and a tenaciously willed love. The poem explores a spiritual maturation Thérèse instinctively claimed and understood as the final stage in Joan's sanctity because it brought both young women to the threshold of Christ's own passion and resurrection.

In her own humiliation, both personal and public, Thérèse modified the text of the play. Later, in 1910, Mother Agnes of Jesus would expunge further references to Diana Vaughan prior to the Process of Beatification, so embarrassing was the legacy of this event, which exposed the Saint's vulnerability and capacity for error. From a historical distance, however, we can recover the way in which Thérèse's admiration of "la nouvelle Jeanne" allowed her to arrive at a full understanding of spiritual poverty in the depths of humility. She came to locate Joan of Arc's holiness not in visible acts of courage on behalf of France, but in the young peasant's inglorious, ignominious death. This genuine triumph of faith in the face of the anonymity and nihilism of modern life is the essential message of *The Triumph of Humility*, where she concludes that she and her Carmelite sisters will know—indeed become—the new Joan of Arcs.

Notes

1. I am grateful to my colleague, Professor Jane Marie Pinzino, for her helpful responses to my essay and contribution of fluid translations; Father Kurt Nagel was also a generous and thorough critical reader. Thérèse Martin was canonized in 1925 and pronounced a Doctor of the Church on October 19, 1997. For a brief overview of her life, see Bernard McGinn, *The Doctors of the Church* (New York: Crossroad, 1999), pp. 169–73. The political and religious importance of Joan in nineteenth-century France is set forth in Marina Warner, *Joan of Arc, the Image of Female Heroism* (1981; repr. Berkeley: University of California Press, 2000), pp. 255–75.
2. Thérèse's involvement in the Vaughan affair is described by Carmelite historian Guy Gaucher, O.C.D., *The Story of a Life* (New York: Harper Collins, 1987), pp. 166–83.

3. Figure 13.1, a photograph of Saint Thérèse as Joan of Arc, is reproduced with the kind permission of the Office Central de Lisieux. Other photographs taken by Céline are reproduced in Gaucher, *Story of a Life*, plate 23, p. 145 and in *Poesies Et recreations pieuses de Thérèse de Lisieux, Le Triomphe de l'humilite* (Les Editions du Cerf et Desclée De Brouwer, 1975), plates 1 and 4.
4. Gaucher, *Story of a Life*, p. 142.
5. Thérèse of Lisieux, *Story of a Soul: The Autobiography of St. Thérèse of Lisieux*, trans. John Clarke, O.C.D., 2nd ed. (Washington, D. C.: ICS [Institute of Carmelite Studies] Publications, 1976), p. 72.
6. Letter 224, in *Letters of St. Thérèse of Lisieux*, 2 (1890–97), trans. John Clarke, O.C.D. (Washington, D. C.: ICS Publications, 1988), p. 1085.
7. *Story of a Soul*, p. 48.
8. *Story of a Soul*, p. 48.
9. Although Thérèse's nineteenth-century sentimentalism suggests to modern readers a distasteful infantilism, her letters reveal an adult's awareness of the grievous impact of punitive taxing of already impoverished religious orders (the law called *d'accroissement*, instituted December 28, 1880); in July 1986, she wrote to her aunt in reference to political persecution, "We seemed to be flying already to martyrdom. . ." (*Letters*, p. 969). See also *Letters*, p. 4.
10. *Story of a Soul*, p. 157.
11. These papal texts have been made available to the net by Professor Paul Halsall and can be found at http://www.newadvent.org/docs/.
12. See Thérèse's topical references to such anticlericalism in a letter to her Aunt Guerin, dated July 16, 1896, in *Letters of St. Thérèse of Lisieux* 2 (1890–97), p. 971.
13. Pope Leo XIII, *Custodi di quella fede*, articles 12 and 16. See note 11.
14. Gaucher, *Story of a Life*, p. 166. The play's critical editors, however, suggest that Uncle Guérin made the text accessible to the Lisieux Carmel. See footnote 1r, 31–33, p. 44.
15. Gaucher, *Story of a Life*, p. 166.
16. See Guy Gaucher, *John and Thérèse, Flames of Love: The Influence of St. John of the Cross in the Life and Writings of St. Thérèse of Lisieux* (New York: Alba House, 1999), pp. 117–43.
17. Thomas A. Kselman, *Miracles and Prophecies in Nineteenth-Century France* (New Brunswick, N. J.: Rutgers University Press, 1983), pp. 98–99.
18. Kselman, *Miracles and Prophecies*, p. 98.
19. Kselman, *Miracles and Prophecies*, p. 98.
20. *Story of a Soul*, p. 193.
21. Quoted in Eugen J. Weber, *Satan franc-maçon: La Mystification de Leo Taxil* (Paris: René Juillard, 1964), p. 38.
22. Weber, *Satan franc-maçon*, pp. 100–102.
23. See Kselman, *Miracles and Prophecies*, p. 127.
24. Kselman, *Miracles and Prophecies*, p. 92.
25. Kselman, *Miracles and Prophecies*, p. 92.
26. *Le Triomphe*, p. 20: "maintenant qu'elle est devenue une nouvelle Jeanne d'Arc. . . ."

27. Weber, *Satan franc-maçon*, p. 101.
28. *Le Triomphe*, p. 20: "Mon plus grand desir serait lorsque sa mission sera terminée de [la voir] s'unir à Jesus dans notre petit Carmel."
29. *Le Triomphe*, p.45, see note 1v, lines 9–18. Thérèse quotes John 20:29.
30. *Le Triomphe*, p. 25.
31. *Le Triomphe*, p. 27.
32. *Le Triomphe*, p. 31.
33. *Le Triomphe*, p. 30.
34. Eugen Weber has set forth Taxil's bizarre life most completely in *Satan franc-maçon*. It holds interest for the cultural critic because Taxil so astutely gauged popular anxieties about diabolical conspiracy, Jews, feminism, and a host of other issues that are reminiscent of other periods gripped by apocalyptic fervor. As Weber comments in his introduction, Taxil's creation tells us much about the impending fascism of the twentieth century (p. 18). Indeed, Taxil's more lurid reportage, published under the respectable name of "Dr. Bataille" and scientifically entitled *Le diable au XIXe siècle*, is a remarkable compilation of Western myths reflecting the cumulative fear of alterity that would result in the scapegoating of Jews under Hitler.
35. See Gaucher, *Story of a Life*, pp. 181–82; and *Le Triomphe*, pp. 115–16: "Diana Vaughan et 'L'Epreuve de la Foi.' "
36. *Story of a Soul*, p. 212.
37. *Story of a Soul*, p. 211.
38. *Story of a Soul*, p. 213.
39. *Story of a Soul*, p. 214.
40. Reproduced in *Le Triomphe de l'humilité*, p. 113.

CHAPTER 14

FORCE OR FRAGILITY? SIMONE WEIL AND TWO FACES OF JOAN OF ARC

Ann Pirruccello

This chapter analyzes Simone Weil's belief that popular interpretations of Joan of Arc convey unskillful spirituality, while Weil's alternative reading of Joan emphasizes purity and compassion for a fragile France.

Simone Weil (1909–43) spent much of her philosophical life trying to separate unskillful models of spirituality from more helpful ones. Sifting tirelessly through world traditions of historical, literary, philosophical, artistic, and scientific texts, and never straying far from her own experience, Weil's desire was to understand the necessities that shape human life and define its possibilities. Turning to literary figures like Antigone, and historical persons such as Joan of Arc, Weil reflected critically upon traditional models of spirituality. These models were her teachers, the treasures of cultural traditions, and they provided material for her philosophical judgments about what counts as genuine and what counts as ersatz spirituality. Often, Weil did not accept what received literary or historical traditions had to say about a particular figure or narrative, instead reversing, reinterpreting, and retelling traditional stories in light of her own understanding and purpose.[1] This Weilian trademark can be seen in her treatment of Joan of Arc. Journals and essays written during the early 1940s show Weil reflecting upon Joan of Arc with a sensibility sharpened by the circumstances of war and the exigencies of a refugee's life on the run.

Before speaking more specifically of Weil's thoughts about Joan of Arc, a brief sketch of her own life may suggest similarities between Weil and her medieval predecessor, both of whom are known as strongly mystical figures. Born in Paris in 1909, Weil identified early on with those she perceived as impoverished, endangered, oppressed, or suffering, even as she enjoyed a rather privileged upbringing.[2] Weil's superb philosophical training at the best schools in France deepened her concern with the nature of justice and the causes of oppression, and she undertook experiments in factories and agriculture in order to understand better the conditions endured by French workers. In 1936 she joined other European and American intellectuals participating in the military fight against fascism in Spain, and survived, it seems, only because an accident sent her back to France for medical treatment.[3] Often described as a Christian mystic, Weil's religious life deepened considerably during the last decade of her life (Weil died in 1943 at the age of thirty-four), and her mystical experiences have been related in some of her letters.[4] In one of these letters, Weil confides to a Catholic priest that in 1938, during her recitation of a poem, "Christ himself came down and took possession of me."[5]

The German occupation of France forced Weil and her parents to leave the country in 1942, and after a short stay in the United States, Weil crossed over to London to work for the Free French until her death from tuberculosis in 1943. Weil was hoping to be assigned to a combat mission, as she was determined to share in the hardship and danger being experienced by people all over the world. She was disappointed to be put to work writing and evaluating ideas concerning postwar France.[6] One of her favorite projects during the last year or so of her life was her plan to parachute nurses to the warfront to care for wounded soldiers. These nurses, who would almost certainly perish in the line of duty, would serve as a reminder of the fragile values, land, and traditions being defended in battle. Weil, of course, wanted to be the first volunteer sent. The plan was never implemented, and it is reported that De Gaulle thought Weil must be mad for proposing it.[7]

While Weil speaks relatively little of Joan of Arc, what she does say suggests the medieval saint played a powerful, even archetypal role in her philosophy and psyche. Sometimes it is taken for granted that Weil did not admire Joan of Arc, but a close reading of her work does not support this. The notebooks she kept and a long political essay written near the end of her life reveal two enormously different kinds of reference to Joan of Arc: one refers to the story of Joan as presented in popular or political accounts, opinion, and myth, while the other speaks of Joan of Arc as Weil herself "read" (*lecture*) the actions and spiritual condition of the historical Joan. In what follows, I present Weil's two Joans, and show how one is rejected as a model of spirituality, while the other is embraced.

The Joan of Arc of Popular French Culture

Writing for the Free French in London in 1943, Weil writes that "Joan of Arc's popularity during the past quarter of a century was not an altogether healthy business; it was a convenient way of forgetting that there is a difference between France and God."[8] This evaluation sums up much of Weil's criticism of the contemporary interpretive practices associated with Joan of Arc. She does not name specific traditions, or particular writers and sources on Joan, and seems instead to be concerned with accounts that were popular and "in the air" in France during, and prior to, the time of writing. Certainly it is possible that she was also responding to appropriations of Joan of Arc made by the French Right in the name of national unity (e.g., Action Française and Marshall Pétain) and by the extreme Left in the name of the people (Popular Front).[9] At any rate, Weil finds a common theme running through popular Joan accounts. In each case, Joan of Arc is identified with the kind of glory enjoyed by a nation or people that wields superior force. The blinding luster of force, granted and guaranteed by God himself, is what popular opinion reads and finds absolutely irresistible in the Joan narrative. This is why Weil claims that recent interpretations of Joan of Arc have something "essentially false" about them: Joan's voices are "bound up with prestige."[10] The Maid of Lorraine serves as a cloak to nationalist idolatry because what many are encouraged to read in her are the promise of Roman-style greatness and the glory of the modern French nation state.

Weil illustrates what she takes to be the falseness of the popular Joan stories by comparing them to the Indian classic, the *Bhagavad Gita*. This narrative describes the spiritual struggles of Arjuna, one of the Pandava brothers, who is about to go to war against a faction of his own family. Arjuna is taught the truth of his own condition and receives mystical teaching from his charioteer, who turns out to be none other than Krishna, an incarnation of the god Vishnu. After a long and remarkable lesson, Arjuna enters the battle and carries out his *dharma* or duty. One of the things Arjuna learns is that his own action is the result of the operations of nature (*prakriti*), including the law of cause and effect (*karma*), and he must not believe that such action is the work of Atman or divine reality. Weil is convinced of the authentic spirituality of the *Gita*, and plays it off the Joan of Arc account to help illuminate both narratives.

Weil notes the "[d]ifference between the spirit of the *Bhagavad Gita* and that of the Story of Joan of Arc, a fundamental difference: he makes war although inspired by God, she makes war because inspired by God."[11] This difference is crucial for several reasons. First, the Joan story appears to make God a partisan in war, and the protector of a chosen people. As we will see, this idea, which Weil traces to the early Hebrew Scriptures, is simply unacceptable to her. Second, this partisanship is bound up with enduring illusions about the nature of force, which Weil thinks must be dispelled whenever they arise. Third, the Joan of popular culture is mistaken about the potential of her own action to accomplish an ultimate good for the people of France; and fourth, the source of Joan's action is seen to be divine, whereas Weil thinks her actions are the expression of natural forces.

According to Simone Weil, the idea of a partisan God is simply the work of the imagination, which, as a part of nature, cannot tolerate a void: "In no matter what circumstances (but sometimes at the price of how great a degradation!) imagination can fill the void. This is why average human beings can become prisoners, slaves, prostitutes, and pass through no matter what suffering without being purified."[12] Weil is claiming that whenever a person or a people is threatened by a sense of diminishment due to events, real or imaginary, the fantasy-manufacturing part of the imagination can step in to fill the void and restore a fuller sense of self.[13] Very often, what fills the void is the exercise or promise of force. This is likely what Weil sees at work in the Hebrew Scriptures and, presumably, in any context where God is identified with force and seen as championing a chosen people.[14]

Weil's own theological researches conclude that God is a completely impartial being who has relinquished some of his own power in order to let something other than himself exist.[15] This something else is the world, and while God withdraws his power to be everything, he inscribes a completely impartial Necessity or wisdom as the order of the world.[16] Weil's work suggests that the idea of a God who intervenes preferentially in the events of history should be downplayed, as the void-filling imagination can too easily and falsely construe events as the work of personal providence. While Weil leaves open the possibility of such providence, she seems to think it is defined by a kind of impulsion exercised on a few human souls, and not by intervention in historical events. It is much better, Weil thinks, to emphasize the impersonal and impartial order of things.[17]

The Joan of Arc legend, with its promise of national glory in partnership with God, fills voids quite well, and in Weil's France everyone was experiencing the void created by the country's fall to Germany in June 1940. Moreover, Weil is strongly concerned with the illusions about force entertained by people throughout history. Chief among these illusions is that it is possible to possess force, rather than having it solely on loan, subject to ever-changing circumstances.[18] This is a particularly dangerous illusion, because it permits people to get trapped in the mechanism of force, which consists of the compulsive blows and counterblows characteristic of drawn-out conflicts such as we now see in the Middle East and in Northern Ireland. The illusion of force convinces one that force will fill all voids suffered, that one can use it without using it up, that one can handle it without being hypnotized and defiled by it.[19] Weil's commentary on the *Iliad* illustrates the illusions of force as the Greeks and Trojans alike sustain them during the Trojan War. Neither side can walk away from the conflict, and whenever there is an opportunity to do so, each decides to stay and try to fill the void of losses they have suffered.[20] Such a psychology prevents a measured use of force, a use that would seek to limit its exercise to what is the bare minimum for attaining a given end, such as the return of Helen to the Greeks.

Joan of Arc, as popularly read, feeds all of these illusions because Joan represents a force backed up by God, and her goal is to fill the void of the French people by restoring the luster and glory of national power. She is not defiled by her contact with force; rather, she seems ennobled by it. Weil claims, however, that "[c]ontact with force, from whichever end the contact is made (sword handle or sword point) deprives one for a moment of God."[21] In part, she means that one is closed up in one's own fantasies or suffering, and the ability to witness the world as it is and thus to love God (since "to love God, is nothing else than a certain way of thinking on the world") is temporarily impossible.[22] This is one of the reasons why the Joan story has the ring of falseness to it. Joan's uncertainty about her status and her own degradation is replaced by certitude and fantasy. Joan wields force and submits to it, but is supposedly not defiled by it: "Joan of Arc: we read in her story what is dictated by contemporary public opinion. But she herself was uncertain."[23] The popular and confident Joan resembles certain accounts of the Christian martyrs: they were so full of imagined rewards as they went to their deaths that they were unable to witness the truth of the world.

The Joan propaganda story carries other illusions as well. Weil claims that the lesson of the *Gita* is that we must not seek good in action.[24] Before Arjuna, the hero of the *Gita*, is enlightened by Krishna, he believes that his own action can accomplish good for himself and his community. Weil interprets this as referring to an absolute good, the kind of good that makes us whole and complete. But as Arjuna learns, this is not up to our wills; God alone is the source of such good. Weil believes all one can do is prepare to receive the highest good by practicing a kind of attentiveness or openness to the world, but ultimately it must be given by grace.[25] In the Joan narrative, Joan's own action and God's action are conflated. The promise of some good—the might and glory of France—replaces the infinite good, which has nothing to do with force or national greatness or glory.

According to Weil, one of the most serious errors transmitted by the Joan of popular opinion has to do with a failure to see nature as the source of Joan's actions. As mentioned earlier, one of the lessons Arjuna learns in the *Bhagavad Gita* is that his own actions are the work of natural causes, not his divine Atman or Self; that would require something wholly different.[26] Weil believes that normally all of our actions are a result of necessity, the natural forces that compose the world around us. These natural forces are themselves obedient to the invisible limits placed upon them by divine wisdom, but human beings experience them as blind constraints on the will. Ultimately, our freedom consists in the ability to be attentive to the world and to the impulses that would move us. If we are habitually inattentive, we are simply the puppets of natural (including social and psychical) forces, and these have their characteristic mechanisms, such as the compulsion to fill the void.[27] The general result of our blind obedience to these forces is that we act on impulses that are self-aggrandizing. This is why people pursue "riches, power and social consideration."[28]

On the other hand, if we practice deep attention and cultivate it to the utmost, our impulses, which are expressions of how we read situations, obey a higher necessity. According to Weil, the highest form of attention is actually a form of consent to the reality of the world, to the existence of all things, just as they are.[29] When this attentive consent is added to the mechanism of natural necessity, a new necessity is enabled to operate.[30] Such necessity is in accord with justice, and when turned toward human beings, its exercise is an enabling love or compassion.[31] The sign that the legendary Joan is moved by natural necessity alone, and not "supernatural" necessity or justice, is that she invokes a partisan God. This suggests a self-aggrandizing (where the self has been transferred onto France) way of reading and consequently of responding to events:

> *Gita* and the legend of Joan of Arc. To fight the English was Joan of Arc's dharma, although a woman and a shepherdess (if we do not take the caste system in a strictly social sense), but it was Nature which infused her actions (prakrti), not God (Atman). (*Gita*, XIII, 29.) One may not debase God to the point of making Him a partisan. In the *Iliad*, the gods are partisans, but Zeus takes up his golden scales.[32]

In conclusion, Weil thinks that Joan of Arc as read by popular French culture does not provide a model of genuine spirituality. Part of the evidence Weil accepts for this conclusion is the fact that Joan of Arc failed to inspire the French people to take actions that might constitute risks to their own well-being. More concretely, relatively few were moved to defend France when the Germans marched in during June of 1940. While many dreamed of a restored French glory, only a tiny fraction were willing to spend the energy—accept a larger void—to defend France. Ian Ousby describes France at that time as "a country of civilians who no longer wanted to be part of any war and of *fuyards*, soldiers not in retreat but in open flight, soldiers who no longer wanted to be soldiers at any price."[33] And as Weil observes: "Joan of Arc's statue was occupying a prominent place in every church throughout the country, all through those terrible days when Frenchmen abandoned France to her fate."[34]

Joan of Arc as a Model of Skillful Spirituality

The foregoing discussion should function, in part, as a kind of *via negativa* as we try to understand Weil's ideas about what a skillful spiritual model might look like. While Jesus of the Gospels, Job of the Hebrew Scriptures, and Antigone of Greek literature are most frequently cited by Weil as worthy spiritual paradigms, Joan of Arc also plays a role in the spiritual archetype Weil is defining. Her positive models are not ruled by the imagination and its void-filling impulses; the "proof" of this is that their action is performed even in the face of profound danger and lack of assurance of well-being. Each is described as motivated by love or compassion, not force, and each is moved by a desire to see justice done.

Before going further, it seems necessary to note that it is puzzling, to say the least, that Simone Weil would even offer an alternative reading of Joan of Arc. After all, some of Joan's pronouncements seem to confirm the interpretation of her life that Weil sees as embodying a false spirituality. For example, while Joan claims not to know if God loves or hates the English, she does say during her interrogation of March 1, 1431, and again on March 17, that God will send victory to the French.[35] In her letter of March 22, 1429 to the English high command, she says that she is "sent from God, King of Heaven, to chase you all out of France, body for body [every last one of you]."[36] In the same letter she goes on to say that she believes firmly "that the King of Heaven will send the Maid more force than you will ever know how to achieve with all your assaults on her and on her good men-at-arms; and in the exchange of blows we shall see who has better right from the King of Heaven."[37]

To problematize matters more, we cannot say with certainty what portions, if any, of the literature of Joan's trial, letters, or witnesses were known to Weil. She has left behind a childhood essay—perhaps an original composition, perhaps a dicté—which suggests a fairly extensive familiarity with Joan's story.[38] At any rate, it seems reasonable to assume that Joan of Arc's claims about God's intention to send victory to the French would be well known to a French scholar of Weil's caliber, breadth, and interests.

Perhaps the best way to respond to the fact of Joan's words confirming the claim of partisanship of God is to consider Weil's remarks on the reading of history. A lengthy passage from *The Need for Roots* is helpful:

> History is founded upon documents. The professional historian won't allow himself to form hypotheses which don't rest upon something. That seems to be very reasonable; but in reality it is far from being so. For, since there are holes in documents, a balanced judgment requires that hypotheses which haven't any basis should be present to the mind, provided they be there in that capacity, and that there be several of them in connexion with each particular point.
>
> All the more reason why when dealing with documents it is necessary to read between the lines, allow oneself to be transported entirely, with a complete forgetfulness of self, into the atmosphere of the events recalled, keep the attention fixed for a very long time on any little significant details and discover exactly what their full meaning is.[39]

Weil adds later that professional historians are not inclined to do this, and we might add that this is perhaps even less likely for the nonhistorian. Moreover, Weil states, "documents originate among the powerful ones, the conquerors. History, therefore, is nothing but a compilation of the depositions made by assassins with respect to their victims and themselves."[40]

It seems admissible to assume that Weil approached the historical Joan of Arc in the manner recommended here, and scholars familiar with the corpus of Weil's work can no doubt find many examples where she attempts to enter the atmosphere of long-past events. So we should not be surprised if Weil's reading of Joan of Arc differs in important respects from what might appear to be obvious interpretations of documents pertaining to her. And what Weil says about Joan does seem to hinge on the "little significant details" mentioned earlier.

If "to love God, is nothing else than a certain way of thinking on the world," as mentioned earlier, it should not be surprising to learn that some of Weil's most mature reflections on spirituality are within the context of the task assigned to her by the Free French in London, 1943: to explore ideas on how to inspire and regenerate France. The profound result of this assignment, *The Need for Roots* (*l'Enracinement*), includes discussions that show that Joan of Arc possessed the key to reviving a people whose disillusionment and demoralization had reached an infinite depth.

Simone Weil produces a remarkable sketch of French history that traces a number of themes across the centuries. She is concerned with the condition of patriotism in France, in part because the scandal of June 1940 threw into relief the lack of any sentiment that would rouse more than token resistance to the Germans. As she traces the various currents of patriotism as they rise and disappear, she finds that by the nineteenth century, the only existing object of loyalty and basis for patriotism is the cold, repressive nation state.[41] It is no longer possible to practice fidelity to the king (even the memory of the monarchy is tarnished by its brutality), the ideals of the French Revolution (sadly killed by those obsessed with progress rather than the ideals leading to the events of 1789), or the Church (it had made an irreparable mistake by becoming the bedfellow of the monarchy).[42] As Weil writes in 1943, all that offered itself to the French as an object of patriotism was "the very self-same inhuman, brutal, bureaucratic, police-ridden State bequeathed by Richelieu to Louis XIV, by Louis XIV to the Convention, by the Convention to the Empire, and by the Empire to the Third Republic. And what is more, it is instinctively recognized and hated as such."[43]

In Weil's analysis of the state, she concludes that it had set itself up as an absolute value and thus became an object of loveless idolatry. It was served as such during World War I, and the toll exacted from the French people had been too great. The result was revulsion for the state, and consequently, the French were left with nothing to love or serve as the object of fidelity.[44]

If the lack of anything to love was at the root of France's humiliation, Weil thinks the solution is fairly obvious: give France something to love.[45] In the ensuing pages of her treatise, Weil describes a new sort of patriotism, one inspired by compassion for France. Briefly, Weil thinks that a tender feeling for her country—its history, traditions, people, aspirations—which includes an acknowledgment of its very fragility, is the only sentiment appropriate to France at the moment. Appeals to past glory only insult those who are suffering deeply, and a patriotism based on pride is exclusive and abstract. Weil believes the Christian virtue of humility must be present, for humility is at the core of charitable love, and compassion for France can find daily expression. Compassion for the country does not exclude warlike energy, Weil claims, and it is not a product of the compulsive desire for filling voids:

> Compassion for France is not a compensation for, but a spiritualization of, the sufferings being undergone; it is able to transfigure even the most purely physical sufferings, such as cold and hunger. Whoever feels cold and hunger, and is tempted to pity himself, can, instead of doing that, from out of his own shrunken frame, direct his pity towards France; the very cold and hunger themselves then cause the love of France to enter into the body and penetrate to the depths of the soul. And this same compassion is able, without hindrance, to cross frontiers, extend itself over all countries in misfortune, over all countries without exception; for all peoples are subjected to the wretchedness of our human condition.[46]

But does France have any resources in its culture that might resonate with such a form of patriotism? Weil is emphatic: "We have a glorious respondent. It was Joan of Arc who used to say she felt pity for the kingdom of France."[47] While she does not elaborate on Joan's pity, it is clear that Weil reads it as a form of compassion for suffering and fragile France. Joan is thus a model of one who can honor the world of her country, but whose love embodies a humble, self-emptying love at its heart. For all Joan of Arc's words about force and victory, Simone Weil reads through them an enduring love, which suggests the presence of something superior to natural impulses.

Yet there is more to admire in Joan of Arc, and again we see Weil amplifying one of those "little significant details" of the historical record. This concerns Weil's characterization of Joan as uncertain: "Joan of Arc: we read in her story what is dictated by public opinion. But she herself was uncertain. And Christ. . .[.]"[48] It is not easy to be precise about Weil's meaning here. Given her reference to Christ, and later to Antigone, who "doubts," it seems that Weil might be referring to Joan of Arc's fear of the stake that prompted her abjuration. This would suggest to Weil that Joan was not like the Christian martyrs of legend: she was not convinced of a reward, identified with a supernatural power, or sure of her own immortality so that she could accept death blithely. Nor did she have unambiguous public support, as Weil points out.[49] Joan of Arc experienced the true absence of God. And later, in the midst of that absence, she nullifies her abjuration, knowing the penalty will be the stake. For Simone Weil, the miraculous and authentic consist in being able to accept a void. This, she believes, requires divine grace:

> To accept a void in ourselves is supernatural. Where is the energy to be found for an act which has nothing to counterbalance it? The energy has to come from elsewhere. Yet first there must be a tearing out, something desperate has to take place, the void must be created. Void: the dark night. [. . .] To love truth means to endure the void and, as a result, to accept death. Truth is on the side of death.[50]

Interestingly, this indicates that Joan's abjuration was evidence of her high spiritual condition. Although she claimed that the voices told her she did wrong in abjuring, for Simone Weil, the abjuration, coupled with its subsequent nullification, counts as evidence of Joan's authentic spirituality because it signifies that she has fully acknowledged the fragility of her life and the possibility that she may cease to exist as an "I" or self. One who experiences such a prospect will naturally recoil from it, and if Joan had not abjured, it would be less clear that she had indeed realized the possibility of not existing in any manner at all. This last qualification is added because Weil thinks it is only possible to conceive of life, even an afterlife, as a physical one.[51] The reason an acknowledgment of one's possible nonexistence is crucial, in Weil's view, is that pure love for God is made of the acceptance not to be. As long as one is holding onto life, even by the slenderest of threads, God's being is not affirmed. This is because the life of God, in part, is the world of necessary laws and operations that may destroy or afflict a person at any moment. To refuse this possibility for oneself amounts to refusing God. Joan of Arc had to realize the possibility of nonexistence in order to accept it truly, otherwise her love for God would be less than perfect: "If we find fullness of joy in the thought that God is, we must find the same fullness in the knowledge that we ourselves are not, for it is the same thought."[52]

Lastly, Simone Weil reserves for Joan of Arc an epithet that she rarely applies, and never without great reverence—purity:

> If one were to look for names which are associated with real purity, one would find very few. In Greek history, one would only be able to name Aristides, Dio, Plato's friend, and Agis, the little socialist king of Sparta, put to death at the age of twenty. In French history, would one be able to find any other name besides that of Joan of Arc? It is doubtful.[53]

It seems that Weil is able to call Joan pure because she has learned how to act without attachment to her own idea of her self. When Weil discusses pure actions, she usually cites examples where one has been willing to give up one's life rather than see a terrible injustice committed.[54]

This does not mean that the natural impulses of the human being are cancelled or nullified. Rather, something new is added to them, as mentioned earlier, such that a superior form of necessity operates. Joan of Arc, as Weil reads her, was not fighting for glory, but for justice, the other face of her compassion for France. Her actions took a military form because the dynamic of force had already been set into motion: the English were exercising force against the French; to refuse would have been simply to allow the country to be defiled by contact with the sword blade.[55] Joan of Arc acts according to the natural requirements of the existing situation, but she is not hypnotized by force: she does not fall to the illusion that the blow of her sword will compensate the void experienced by the French people. As Weil reads her, it is the fragility and beauty of France that move Joan, not national glory or an idea of greatness inherited from Rome.

Conclusion

Simone Weil says tantalizingly little about Joan of Arc. Yet we see that she felt strongly about the historical Joan's virtues and the legendary Joan's illusions. It might prove helpful to try to tie together some of Weil's more positive characterizations of Joan of Arc to see how they add up.

Simone Weil believed that the most important task any human being can undertake is to train the imagination methodically through action.[56] The reason, again, is that the imagination commands our readings of events, and our readings command our actions. In the end, our bodies, our actions are the pointer on the scale that weighs up our impulses.[57] As long as the imagination is untrained, it will operate in an egocentric manner, and the reality of the world will be concealed by a veil of self-aggrandizing readings.

It is hard to say how Joan of Arc's imagination was trained, in Weil's sense. Perhaps it was a matter of her intense religious devotion, a kind of devotion that culminated in what Weil calls "attention."[58] Attention in its highest form is the ability to be open to the world in all its impersonality and to consent to its existence, just as it is. As discussed earlier, since the world is impartial and might destroy us at any moment, Weil thinks consent to the existence of the world is also consent to our own nonbeing.[59] For her, this is the highest expression of love of God that can be practiced by anyone.

The actions of Joan of Arc, in Weil's estimation, suggest that she loved the world to the point of consenting to her own death. She was "absent" from her actions, and wholly obedient to the requirements of a supernatural form of necessity. Joan of Arc was not great because she affirmed and exercised free choice in some robust manner. Weil would never make a kind of existentialist out of her. Rather, Weil thinks she is great because she was in touch with a necessity that left her without choice. But this necessity is none other than that of compassionate justice, and Joan of Arc stands as an archetype of this human possibility.

Do we learn anything about the spirituality of the historical Joan of Arc by considering Simone Weil's ideas? This is far from clear. Weil's reading of history has its leaps and over-universalizing tendencies. Often she does not embrace the alterity of non-Christian traditions and reduces them to what is recognizably Christian and explicitly valued by her. But we cannot deny that her consideration of Joan of Arc raises crucial questions that are still highly relevant about cultural values. Arguably, many contemporary societies suffer from the same loveless idolatry and fascination with force that Weil highlights in her criticism of the popular Joan of Arc. And we get an interesting insight about Weil herself: Joan of Arc probably functioned as an archetype for Weil for nearly all of her compressed life. She was there, no doubt, when Weil carried out her painful factory and farm experiments; surely it was she who moved Weil to leave the safety of New York in order to join the Free French in London.

In summary, Weil, as usual, gives us much to ponder as we try to integrate our social, political, and spiritual lives. Like Weil, Joan of Arc is claimed by so many that we do not know how to recognize her. Each woman attests to the riches and range of our readings.[60]

Notes

1. For more on Simone Weil's relationship to narrative and the prose style that figured so strongly in her philosophy, see Joan Dargan, *Simone Weil: Thinking Poetically* (Albany: State University of New York Press, 1999); Christine Ann Evans, "The Power of Parabolic Reversal: The Example in Simone Weil's Notebooks," *Cahiers Simone Weil* 19.3 (1996): 313–24; Ann Pirruccello, "Simone Weil's Violent Grace," *Cahiers Simone Weil* 19.4 (1996): 397–411.
2. For the most complete account of Weil's life in English, see Simone Pétrement, *Simone Weil: A Life*, trans. Raymond Rosenthal (New York: Pantheon Books, 1976)
3. Pétrement, *A Life*, p. 278.
4. Simone Weil, *Waiting for God*, trans. E. Craufurd (New York: G. P. Putnam's Sons, 1951; Harper Colophon, 1973), pp. 61–83.
5. Weil, *Waiting for God*, p. 69.
6. Pétrement, *A Life*, p. 482.
7. Pétrement, *A Life*, p. 514.
8. Simone Weil, *The Need for Roots*, trans. Arthur Wills with a preface by T.S. Eliot (London: Routledge and Kegan Paul, 1952, ARK Edition 1987), p. 126.
9. For more on ways in which Joan of Arc was appropriated for political purposes during and prior to World War II, see Nadia Margolis, "The 'Joan Phenomenon' and the French Right," in *Fresh Verdicts on Joan of Arc*, ed. Bonnie Wheeler and Charles Wood (New York: Garland Publishing, 1996), pp. 265–87; Nicholas Atkin, *Church and Schools in Vichy France, 1940–1944* (New York: Garland Publishing, 1991), pp. 78–80; Joan Tumblety, " 'Civil Wars of the Mind': The Commemoration of the 1789 Revolution in the Parisian Press of the Radical Right, 1939," *European History Quarterly* 30.3 (2000): 416–17 [389–429]; Ian Ousby, *Occupation: The Ordeal of France, 1940–1944* (New York: Cooper Square Press, 2000), passim.
10. Simone Weil, *Notebooks*, 2 vols., trans. Arthur Wills (London: Routledge and Kegan Paul, 1956), p. 25.
11. Weil, *Notebooks*, p. 25.
12. Simone Weil, *Gravity and Grace*, trans. Arthur Wills (New York: G. P. Putnam's Sons, 1952, Bison Books Edition, 1997), pp. 63–64.
13. Weil, *Gravity and Grace*, pp. 62–64.
14. For example, see Weil, *Gravity and Grace*, p. 55; Weil, *Notebooks*, p. 565; Simone Weil, *Pensées sans ordre concernant l'amour de Dieu* (Paris: Gallimard, 1962), p. 48.
15. Simone Weil, *Intimations of Christianity Among the Ancient Greeks*, trans. E. Geissbuhler (London: Routledge and Kegan Paul, 1957, ARK Edition, 1987), p. 193.
16. Weil, *Intimations*, pp. 184–95.
17. Weil, *Gravity and Grace*, pp. 44–45; *Roots*, pp. 250–51.
18. Simone Weil, *The Iliad or The Poem of Force*, trans. Mary McCarthy (Wallingford: Pendle Hill, 1991), pp. 11–25.

19. Weil, *The Iliad*, pp. 11–19.
20. Weil, *The Iliad*, pp. 15–18.
21. Weil, *Notebooks*, p. 25.
22. Weil, *Notebooks*, p. 25.
23. Weil, *Notebooks*, p. 195.
24. Weil, *Notebooks*, pp. 289, 316.
25. Weil, *Waiting for God*, pp. 105–16.
26. Weil, *Notebooks*, pp. 55–56.
27. Weil, *Notebooks*, p. 57.
28. Weil, *Intimations*, p. 175.
29. Weil, *Intimations*, p. 190.
30. Weil, *Intimations*, p. 194.
31. Weil, *Intimations*, p. 177.
32. Weil, *Notebooks*, p. 55.
33. Ousby, *Occupation*, p. 31.
34. Weil, *Roots*, pp. 126–27.
35. Régine Pernoud, ed., *Joan of Arc by Herself and Her Witnesses*, trans. E. Hyams (New York: Scarborough House, 1982), pp. 186, 174–75.
36. Régine Pernoud and Marie Véronique Clin, *Joan of Arc, Her Story*, trans. and revised J. duQuesnay Adams (New York: St. Martin's Press, 1998), p. 34.
37. Pernoud and Clin, *Joan of Arc, Her Story*, p. 34.
38. Simone Weil, "Jeanne d'Arc," unpublished essay contained in the notebook entitled *Omnium Brouillon*. Many thanks to Christine Ann Evans for furnishing me with a copy.
39. Weil, *Roots*, p. 214.
40. Weil, *Roots*, p. 215.
41. Weil, *Roots*, pp. 98–125.
42. Weil, *Roots*, pp. 98–125.
43. Weil, *Roots*, p. 122.
44. Weil, *Roots*, pp. 122–23.
45. Weil, *Roots*, p. 150.
46. Weil, *Roots*, p. 166.
47. Weil, *Roots*, pp. 162–63.
48. Weil, *Notebooks*, p. 195.
49. Weil, *Roots*, p. 99.
50. Weil, *Gravity and Grace*, p. 56.
51. Weil, *Gravity and Grace*, p. 84.
52. Weil, *Gravity and Grace*, p. 84.
53. Weil, *Roots*, p. 221.
54. Weil, *Roots*, p. 220, e.g.
55. Weil, *Notebooks*, p. 25.
56. For more on this aspect of Weil's thought, see Ann Pirruccello, "Making the World My Body: Simone Weil and Somatic Practice," *Philosophy East and West* 52.4 (October 2002): 479–97.
57. Weil, *Notebooks*, p. 57.

58. Weil, *Waiting for God*, pp. 105–116.
59. Simone Weil, *On Science, Necessity and the Love of God*, trans. Richard Rees (London: Oxford University Press, 1968), pp. 184–88.
60. Many thanks to Christine Ann Evans, Lesley College, who generously provided me with a number of relevant materials for this project.

CHAPTER 15

SHE GETS INSIDE YOUR HEAD: JOAN OF ARC AND CONTEMPORARY WOMEN'S SPIRITUALITY

Anne Llewellyn Barstow

This chapter suggests several ways that Joan of Arc is a comforting role model for contemporary women. Thirty-three women tell what the story of Joan of Arc means to their lives and their spirituality, raising new questions about how we draw conclusions from the documents and the legend.

History has produced many images of Joan of Arc. We have made of her memory what we need it to be. Her figure calls up strong representations: from innocent girl among peasants to curious prodigy at court, from magical virgin to witch and whore. Among these many Joans are some we would deem bizarre, even offensive to her memory. For example, I have recently come across "Joan, the Militant Kamelia," written in the 1920s for the women's order of the Ku Klux Klan; it claims that "voices like unto those that commanded Joan of Arc" now speak to American women, telling them to establish the supremacy of the white race.[1] Yet no matter how far from the historical Joan this appropriation by the KKK may take us, still we must acknowledge the way the Maid of France exerts influence over societies far removed from her own.

For the history of how women respond to Joan's story, there is not much point in searching before the first women's movement in the nineteenth century. Most of the voluminous writing about Joan before that date is by men.[2] With the beginning of feminist writing, however, women began expressing themselves about the story of Joan. Two nineteenth-century responses—liberal and conservative—to her story illustrate how it inspired very different types of women.

In the first public address of her career, at the Seneca Falls convention in 1848, Elizabeth Cady Stanton used Joan of Arc to illustrate that women should be allowed to be active in the public realm. In that historic speech, Stanton observed that men do not object to women or blacks appearing in public, provided they are there to serve them. By way of contrast, she asked, "What man or woman has a feeling of disapproval in reading the history of Joan of Arc? The sympathies of every heart are at once enlisted in the success of that extraordinary girl." Stanton adopted Joan's mysticism to her own reformist faith. Noting "when all human power seemed unavailing, the French no longer despised the supernatural aid of the damsel of Domremy," she justified Joan's strategies for reform-minded women: "'Voices' were the visitors and advisors of Joan of Arc. Do not 'voices' come to us daily from the haunts of poverty, sorrow, degradation and despair, already too long unheeded? Now is the time for the women of this country, if they would save our free institutions, to defend the right [to do so]." She exhorted her audience to recall: "the same religious enthusiasm that nerved Joan of Arc to her work nerves us to ours." Stanton warned that the path to reform would not be easy, but concluded that when fired with a prophetic spirit women would defeat those entrenched behind the bulwarks of custom.[3] In the same vein, Roman Catholic women in their earliest organized demands for equal rights in 1911 named their group the St. Joan's International Alliance.[4]

Besides this liberal nineteenth-century position, there was another, quite different school of thought about Joan. Believers in "true womanhood" were challenged by the first women's movement to restate their female ideals. In rising to defend the traditional image of women in the home, conservative women invoked Joan's memory on their behalf. A Roman Catholic treatise written by Isabel O'Reilly in 1894 praises Joan's "gentle unassertiveness," her pious childhood, and especially her ability to spin.[5] O'Reilly contrasts Joan's martyrdom with the selfishness of modern women "who want victory not for their country or for God's cause but for a more selfish motive" (i.e., self-assertion). She admires Joan for avoiding having sex. Since O'Reilly's main point is that women's place is in the home, she appears to have wandered far from the actual life of Joan of Arc. But no, in a complete turnabout, she declares that Joan can still be the model for traditional Catholic women, even though she left home; Joan qualifies because she is the exception to this dictum—because she was commanded by God to enter public life.

The first women's movement of the nineteenth century, in both its liberal and conservative expressions, thus invoked not Joan the martyr but

Joan the powerful visionary. Yet the second women's movement of the twentieth century has not until recently utilized Joan's life as one of its models. A look at what one of the movement's leading theoreticians wrote about Joan may help to explain why. Opining that "Joan of Arc's adventure. . .was only a brief escapade," Simone de Beauvoir in *The Second Sex* concludes, "most female heroines are oddities . . . [W]e see that their greatness is primarily subjective: they are exemplary figures rather than historical agents."[6] In the eyes of de Beauvoir, the Maid was too exceptional in the patriarchal context of her own time to have been a pathbreaker for women in the cause of social change.[7] De Beauvoir thus goes against the grain of almost all recent appraisals of the Maid in denying that she was a historical agent.

In this chapter I explore the question whether Joan has found a new place in the spirituality of contemporary women and, if so, for what reasons. My interest in what motivates women to turn to the story of Joan began in the 1970s, a time when feminist scholars were eagerly reinterpreting historical women. I noted the lack of feminist writing about Joan at that time and surmised that feminists were not drawn to her.[8] Several factors might indeed put us off: her mysticism, her love of military life, her violent death, and our own ambivalence about women who are powerful.

The marked feminist indifference toward Joan in the 1970s stands in contrast to her current omnipresence as a cultural icon. In order to account for her widespread appeal and to understand better the meanings that Joan of Arc has for women today, I surveyed several groups of women to learn if the recent ferment of women's consciousness-raising had led them to ask any new questions in regard to Joan. I drew up the following statement: "I am seeking testimonies about Joan of Arc's influence on modern women's lives, especially their spirituality. If you are aware of being influenced by the life of Joan of Arc in any way, would you write about it?" Sending out this question to about 250 women, I received thirty-two replies.[9] While my method is completely unscientific, I find the results richly suggestive.[10]

I learned from the responses that women today do still turn to Joan; they do so in order to seek support in becoming independent, self-defined persons. They are drawn to her heroic, larger-than-life career in order to conceive of *their* lives in new and nontraditional ways. Women drawn to paths usually closed to or frowned upon for females take inspiration from her.

How, then, is Joan of Arc inspiring women today? In turning now to the testimonies of contemporary women, I first note what women are *not* thinking about Joan. They write little about Joan's valor as a warrior, her mystical experience, or her sainthood. One woman praises Joan for "her unique image as a woman warrior," and for being "a great soldier [who] saved her country." Another admits that when she was thirteen, "Joan, teen warrior-martyr, inspired more energy and passion in me than Mary, docile virgin-mother." A Catholic woman from Belfast confesses that "it even embarrasses me a little to acknowledge how deeply I responded to this peasant girl who dressed up as a boy and led men into battle. Battle against the English, no less." Apart from these testimonies, however, the survey indicates that Joan's love for battle and the military scene, so prized by filmmakers, plays little part in her appeal.[11]

As for Joan's voices, few of the respondents mention them. When they do, it is to reflect that the "voice" was God's voice within Joan, and to stress that she held to it despite the doubts and pressures of the world. One writes that Joan "is an inspiration to me to listen to my own 'inner voice,' which prompts me to follow what I really believe." Another observes: "What a magnificent inner light must have been in that Soul. . .There comes a time when one must. . .follow that inner voice and act upon it. In my divorce proceedings all I have to do is tell the truth. And through it all I will gain a stronger sense of who I am. I have no doubts that in the end, as Joan was standing in that inferno, she knew exactly who she was."

The phenomenon of voices is not totally unknown to these women. Two women report that they, like Joan, hear voices. One, a former Mormon and a writer, explains: "Voices tell me what to write, give me no peace until I've done it—and then more speak up." Another, an artist and poet, writes: "All of my poems develop during sleep; I awaken around four in the morning with the lines running through my head. . .It's an experience I am unable to will to happen."

More typical of the comments about Joan's mysticism and miraculous legend are remarks indicating that (in the words of one respondent) "the 'voices' and Joan's more exotic qualities were not so relevant to me." Another woman puts it this way: "the fact that she looked to God for the strength to go on,and received it. . .that is the miracle that touches me, not the beating heart left in the ashes."

As for Joan's sainthood, it simply was not mentioned by the respondents. A number remark that they first learned of "St. Joan" as children attending parochial schools, but as adults they do not seem to associate her with the saints. In fact, one comments: "I have left the Catholic Church, and the lives of the saints seem even more removed from me than they did when I read them in primary school. But Joan remains real, an earthy young woman touched with the divine, courageous, vulnerable, resolute, and ultimately, touchingly human and accessible."

Thus, three of the classic categories connected with Joan are not of articular interest to most of the respondents. Considering modern women's ambivalence about becoming empowered, I had questioned also if they would accept Joan's strength, or prefer, like Isabel O'Reilly, to see

Joan as obedient and "unassertive." Would the story of this young woman who made her voice heard in the world of powerful men be threatening to today's women? But this quality turns out to be precisely what draws women to Joan today. What women do find relevant in this story is Joan as a role model for becoming an independent woman and, as we will see, Joan as source of comfort and strength when that struggle becomes very hard.

Let us look first at Joan as a model for women struggling to become autonomous. Many respondents to my survey question mention Joan's courage in holding to her convictions. In heeding her inner voice, Joan shows how to be true to one's beliefs, to say no to peer pressure, to take risks. One respondent is thrilled at Joan's assertion at her trial that the voices had commanded her to "answer boldly." She translates this command as an imperative for herself: "Do not speak coyly, do not prevaricate, do not be persuaded that your truth is not important." Another confesses that from Joan she has learned how to assert her individuality. Joan was a woman "who did heroic things when women were not expected to." This comment was written by a Catholic woman who concludes her testimony with the declaration that Joan "was why I became a feminist theologian, not an expected path to choose." One woman reports, nonetheless, that while she loves Joan's certainty, she is still overwhelmed by it; she cannot identify with a certainty so absolute that it led Joan to her death.

Further proof of Joan's courage for the respondents is that she succeeded in the public realm, even inspiring a nation. Although some of these women refer to their admiration as "romanticizing"—because not many women can lead an army—still they insist that they need a heroine and are grateful to Joan for filling that need. One respondent learned from Joan's story "to be fearless, to say what I think." Another sums up Joan's political importance by writing: "I don't know many people who can tell you the name of the king Joan helped, but *everyone* knows about Joan of Arc!"

Joan is a powerful, direct influence on some women. A Presbyterian minister wrote that "Joan's story was formative in my own sense of call, to work for social justice and to become a minister. In fact, she helped me to understand the concept of vocation and to focus on it in my life."

A former Catholic nun who left the convent at age fifty-one writes: "Now, after all these changes, I am trying to have a life and spirituality of my own. What does all this have to do with Joan of Arc? I had never given her much thought. Then last year I saw *The Passion of Joan of Arc*. . .I was so moved by Joan's steadfastness when confronted by all those male representatives of church authority and certitude. She spoke to me as I struggled to claim my own truth as more central than any claim that the church and community had the right to make on me."

Understandably, Joan's story seems to affect people most strongly when they are teenagers—like her. One reports that Joan's influence was most powerful on her from age fifteen to about twenty-five, when Joan was for her an image of what a young girl could accomplish: "I was just beginning to reach political awareness. I admired her courage and intensity. Her story—of what an impact one person can make on history—helped me not to be overwhelmed as I learned about the evil of the Holocaust." Another, who rebelled against her family's wishes by choosing "Joan" as her Confirmation name, believes that this act of self-assertion saved her from losing contact with the Church. She had been a cynical, rebellious adolescent, but this act of choosing her name enabled her to assert her individuality and thus to carve out a bit of space for herself within the Church, an institution that she felt otherwise denied her any chance for self-definition.

One woman reports that she had been profoundly affected by Joan when she was nine years old. She developed the feeling that she *was* Joan. So strong was her identification with Joan of Arc—as a tomboy, and, more dramatic, as a martyr at the stake—that she has continued to be "visited" by Joan off and on into middle age. The lesson for life that she has learned from Joan is "Don't diverge from your vision."

Several others recall that attending a summer camp dedicated to Joan's legend, Camp Jeanne D'Arc in the Adirondacks, was a turning point in their lives. Performing a play about Joan, seeing her pictures and statue everyday, praying daily to her, being instructed to emulate Joan's heroism—all helped the girls to see that "we, like Joan, could do anything we put our minds and bodies to." One respondent, who went on to do "relatively unconventional work as a feminist theologian," believes that her work has been nurtured by her exposure at camp to the values of Joan of Arc.

All of the effects of Joan's life are not perceived as positive. One woman rejects the image of Joan presented to her in parochial school, seeing Joan's "simpering, syrupy piety" and "obligation toward martyrdom" as profoundly unhealthy. She finds Joan's chastity and simplicity as much too limiting for women's lives today. She describes her "distaste for Joan as pretty visceral." Joan's death at the stake, she reports, even gave her a morbid fear of fire. (Another woman relates similarly that she cannot bear the sight of fire that looks like a pyre.) And yet this woman took the time to answer the survey question. Despite her earlier, negative reaction to Joan, she reports that now that she is teaching Medieval Studies, she is beginning to see what she calls "Joan's protean possibilities."

Several respondents say that Joan's story has revealed to them that the world of the Church can be a frightening one. This insight helped one when she was forced to break an abusive marriage. Her priest told her that she had to leave her husband for the safety of her children, but that if she divorced him, she could not continue in the Church. "Just when I needed God most, God was denied me," she writes. As she painfully worked her way out of her dependence on the world of men—Church, husband, and so on—she came to see that the real message of Joan's life was that the world puts a high price on independence for a woman. After she had to leave the Church, she "discovered that God was inside me and not in a church. I often prayed to Joan for courage during the years after my divorce. A relationship developed for me with the God I discovered inside me who not only loved me for my femaleness but also had created me exactly the way I was meant to be. Competitive. Capable. And able to cry."

Other women write of receiving a mixed message from Joan's story—that if one speaks up, there will be the fire. One observes that she recognized the Church's fallibility for the first time when she reflected that the same church that canonized Joan also had condemned her.

As for Joan's sexuality, responses to it run in a contradictory blur through these comments. One woman writes: "She violates every sexual stereotype—she dresses like a man, acts like the most manly of men, is a leader of men, and yet she is a virgin. In the end, what is she—totally androgynous and totally herself because totally given to God." For some, Joan's appeal lies in her manliness. One respondent shares this childhood memory: "She had been a great soldier. . .My tomboy heart was thrilled with the story. I needed Joan of Arc. I loved her." Another, writing from a community of lesbian and gay clergy and laity, reflects: "Joan blends a young masculinity with that of the wild woman." Yet several respondents identify strongly with Joan as a virginal woman. Joan's sexuality was one area of clear disagreement in the surveys—just as it was during Joan's lifetime.

A number of women mention that they turn to Joan when they encounter hostility. One, discriminated against and misunderstood at her parochial high school because of her lesbianism, identified closely with Joan: she was falsely accused as Joan had been, she held on to the truth when persecuted as Joan had done. When angrily attacked by the faculty, she even asked herself, "If I had lived in Joan of Arc's time, would I too have been burned at the stake?" Another, harassed on her job, found the strength to stand up for herself by recalling the way Joan was true to herself even when threatened by death. Still another recounted that when her work takes her out into the city late at night, serving the homeless, "thinking of Jeanne gives me strength to take care of myself as I care for others."

One writer shares the following story. Having breakfast in a diner early one morning, she overheard a woman exclaim, "Look what they did to Joan of Arc!" This was said in response to a comment critical of the Catholic Church, and meant, "See, they will do anything." The writer goes on to reflect: "Yes, look what they did, what they're still doing to our visionaries, our militant women of justice! Just today the Bishop of San Diego excommunicated a woman of conscience. Joan of Arc! You haven't been forgotten. Early morning, in a diner, a woman sings your cause."

Finally, the question—my original question—about spirituality. A number of respondents did not refer to it directly. Since I had asked specifically about spirituality, I have to assume that the question is one that some women cannot or prefer not to speak about. But a dozen did so. They report that Joan is part of their prayer life. "I feel spiritually connected to her," says one, "I include her in my daily prayers, and call on her to intervene for me in tough places."

Another woman writes that she has developed an extraordinary identification with Joan as her feminist consciousness has deepened. This in turn has led to a religious reawakening: "Although I had 'left' the church as a practicing Catholic for some time. . .an intrinsic part of my childhood spirituality arose within me—as if Joan's voice was calling me." Now, "faith in something, I know not what, keeps me going." Women who attended Camp Jeanne D'Arc years ago still remember the exact words of their daily prayer to Joan: "St. Jeanne D'Arc, exemplar of faith, endurance, courage, and confidence, pray for us."

Others speak of the importance to them of her oneness with the will of God; this is an inspiration to them to search for God's will for themselves and to be faithful to it. One confesses that the act of meditating on a powerful statue of Joan challenges her complacency, urges her on when she feels too small or ill-equipped to do the task at hand. Joan's remarkable achievements encourage her to be an activist, as well as a contemplative. Another has a different take on the question of Joan's will: "I resent the attempts to make her [boring] by deciding what God had in mind first and then foisting it onto her narrow shoulders. . .I don't agree that Joan was a good Catholic girl, and that if you want to understand her you must understand Catholicism." Another, now drawn to neo-paganism, remembers that years ago, before female images of the divine were as available as they are now, she used to place a box top from "Joan of Arc brie cheese" on her personal altar. Its picture of Joan charging on her white horse represented for her the power of femaleness in the divine.

A lesbian writes that early in her life she decided to seek spirituality without male guidance. In this way, she says, she is like mystics such as Joan, who found their spiritual authority inside themselves, and who are proof that there can be autonomous female spiritual experience.

Most memorably, a clergywoman writes: "I identify with her in a way I don't with Jesus. I can't aspire to 'be like Jesus,' but I have aspired to be like Joan of Arc. But that's a secret! I am aware that the world would ridicule such an aspiration." Was her emulation of Joan necessary for her to find the courage to become ordained? Or to perform her work of social justice? Or perhaps to do something else entirely? (This was one of the times I wished I could e-mail back and say "Please write more.")

That many respondents did not mention a direct spiritual connection *to the person of Joan* may mean that Joan works on us through a different, more subliminal way. At this point my own story may be useful.

I finished writing my book, *Joan of Arc: Heretic, Mystic, Shaman*, in 1983. Writing about Joan had been such a pleasure that I was actually sorry when I completed the project. But I turned then to other matters and did not think often about her again. In 1987, at the age of fifty-seven, I surprised myself—and my family—by becoming for the first time a political activist; in the next three years I was arrested three times for performing nonviolent civil disobedience, actions that I considered part of my religious commitment to the peace movement. It was not until my fourth arrest, which brought me to the possibility of a six-month jail sentence, that I remembered Joan. Had her story been working on me, quite without my knowing it? Had she gotten inside my head? I have to agree with what one of my respondents wrote: "Her story seeps in over time." The mysterious process by which Joan becomes a role model, an enabler whose example makes possible changes in the lives of others—perhaps this "explains" my otherwise inexplicable transformation.

All of the women who replied to my question describe themselves as struggling to shape their lives along new lines. If I had asked my question of conservative women like Isabel O'Reilly, I might have received very different replies. O'Reilly, you will remember, turned to her image of Joan to affirm that women should be gentle, unassertive, pious, and self-sacrificing. None of those words appear in any of the responses, with the exception of one brief mention of Joan as martyr. On the contrary, my respondents claim that Joan was assertive and believed absolutely in herself. This striking turnabout must be a response to the challenges of our times. One woman observes: "In the 1970s, when the women's movement was in full swing, we were sure that we, like Joan, could do anything we put our minds to." Another declares: "If Joan were alive today, she would be fighting for women's issues and not afraid to stand up to the establishment." And so, another generation of women has claimed Joan for itself and its cause.

As has always happened, the images of Joan that this role-modeling produce vary greatly. Some of them may not fit our own images of Joan; I know that I am dubious about some of the assumptions that my respondents made. But that is not the point. Out of experiences such as those recorded here are emerging new images of Joan that hint at new emphases in interpreting the historical role that Joan played. These images move us away from the battlefield, urging a different definition of heroism, that of holding to one's truth, even unto death. They reveal our interest in Joan as one who not only fulfilled norms of faithfulness, but also broke norms. The respondents revel in Joan's propensity for larger-than-life goals, for challenging the ordinary, the expected.

Finally, these responses provoke us to search her records for every sign of an active and creative spirituality, one that uses the traditions but does not stop there. Since contemporary personal testimony adds insight to our understanding of historical figure, working with this kind of evidence can help us to interpret texts. The chief texts for Joan's life, the Rouen trial record and the retrial records, are themselves a mixture of both legal procedure and personal testimonies. While scholars have long struggled with the problem of interpreting this mix, they have not entirely solved it.[12] Joan's story and the protean legends surrounding her continue to furnish us with new work to do.

Notes

1. Frankie Folsom Jones, *Joan, The Militant Kamelia* (Atlanta: The Kamelia, a patriotic, benevolent, educational, and historical order of the Native, White, Protestant Women of America, n.d.). The organization was later known as "The Women of the Ku Klux Klan." My thanks to Glenn Zuker for a copy of this pamphlet.
2. Christine de Pizan in 1429 and Madeleine de Scudery in the mid-seventeenth century are notable exceptions.
3. Elizabeth Cady Stanton, "Address Delivered at Seneca Falls and Rochester, N.Y., 19 July and 2 August 1848" (New York: Robert J. Johnston, 1870). I owe this reference to Mary Pellauer.
4. *New Catholic Encyclopedia*, vol. 12. The Alliance was founded in London.
5. Isabel M. O'Reilly, "The Maid of Orleans and the New Womanhood," *American Catholic Quarterly Review* 19.75 (July, 1894): 582–606. My thanks to Carol Duncan for this reference.
6. Simone de Beauvoir, *The Second Sex*, trans. and ed. H.M. Parshley (New York: Bantam Books, 1952), pp. 96, 121–22, 269. For her attitude to Joan, see my *Joan of Arc: Heretic, Mystic, Shaman* (Lewiston, N. Y.: Edwin Mellen Press, 1986), pp. 131–32.
7. De Beauvoir's characterization of Joan of Arc is similar to that of Virginia Woolf, who identified with Joan as an inspired woman like "Shakespeare's sister," driven to madness by a patriarchal society. On this topic, see Ann W. Astell, *Joan of Arc and Sacrificial Authorship* (Notre Dame: University of Notre Dame Press, 2003), pp. 162–69.
8. Not many writers were working on Joan from any perspective. This indifference has changed dramatically since the 1970s. In 1999 alone, we received a made-for-television mini-series (*Joan of Arc*, produced by Peter Bray) and a film (*The Messenger: The Story of Joan of Arc*, produced by Patrice

Ledoux)—cinematic productions that followed close on new scholarly work, such as *Fresh Verdicts on Joan of Arc*, ed. Bonnie Wheeler and Charles Wood (New York: Garland Publishing, 1996). The following year saw the publication of a new biography by Mary Gordon, *Joan of Arc* (New York: Viking, 2000). The level of gender awareness and feminist analysis in these works varies widely, from nonexistent to sophisticated.

9. How to use this material was a problem. Accustomed as I am to working on long-dead people, who cannot correct my interpretation of their words, I was unsure how to analyze the replies I received. Because I had asked a personal question and received some intimate answers, I felt compelled to respect the experience of my informants. I could not, therefore, interrogate this material as if it were, say, a legal text. Each generation brings its own questions to history, and these questions in turn influence the historian's work. I therefore granted my respondents the possibility of throwing some new light on our understanding of Joan's story.
10. My thanks to the following women who responded: Robin Burdulis, Ann Chamberlin, Kathleen Cavanaugh, Joan Challinor, Elaine Connolly, Jane Darin, Claire Deroche, Ann Marie Dzolan, Jehanne Edwards, Maria Fama, China Galland, Joan Gibson, Dana Greene, Jeanine Hathaway, Mary Hunt, Laura Jervis, Kasundra Kasundra, Karolyn Kinane, Jeanne Klein, Marie Kopin, Mary Leslie, Suzan Lipson, Nancy S. Murray, Sr. Marianne Nordstrom, Barbara O'Neill, Mary Ann Reed, Kay Sparling, Jane Leahy Stockhausen, Renee Williams-Reeb, Stefanie Zadravec, and two anonymous authors. Except for one from the United Kingdom and one from Sweden, all of the writers are from the United States. Special thanks to Mary Hunt and Bonnie Wheeler for making their e-mail lists available to me.
11. Two recent films, *The Messenger* (director, Patrice Ledoux) and the made-for-TV *Joan of Arc* (director, Peter Bray) glory in long, violence-explicit scenes.
12. See Karen Sullivan, *The Interrogation of Joan of Arc* (Minneapolis: University of Minnesota Press, 2000). Sullivan helpfully separates the words of the clerics from Joan's, showing the cultural bias in the former and pointing out the very different assumptions that each of the protagonists brought to the trial. Going further, she maintains that every reader of the trial must factor in her own assumptions as she tries to find "the truth" about Joan.

CONTRIBUTORS

Heather M. Arden, professor of French at the University of Cincinnati, has published on the medieval theater and courtly romances. Her current research focuses on Marie de France, the *Roman de la Rose*, and Christine de Pizan. She also has written on Harry Potter and the Middle Ages for *Arthuriana* 13.2 (2003).

Ann W. Astell earned her doctorate at the University of Wisconsin-Madison in 1987. Professor of English at Purdue University, she is the author of numerous books and articles on medieval literature and spirituality, including *The Song of Songs in the Middle Ages* (Cornell University Press, 1990), and the editor of two collections of essays on spirituality: *Divine Representations: Postmodernism and Spirituality* (Paulist Press, 1994) and *Lay Sanctity, Medieval and Modern: A Search for Models* (University of Notre Dame Press, 2000). Her most recent book is *Joan of Arc and Sacrificial Authorship* (University of Notre Dame Press, 2003). The recipient of a John Simon Guggenheim Memorial Foundation fellowship in religion (2001–02), she is currently completing a book-length study on medieval eucharistic spirituality and theological aesthetics.

Anne Llewellyn Barstow is now retired from SUNY College at Old Westbury, where she taught European medieval history and courses in Women and Religion. She is the author of *Joan of Arc: Heretic, Mystic, Shaman* and *Witchcraze: A New History of the European Witch Hunts.*

Denise L. Despres is Director of Humanities and a Distinguished professor of English at the University of Puget Sound in Tacoma, Washington. She has written on medieval lay devotionalism, mysticism, Jewish–Christian relations, and religious iconography. She is currently exploring visual semiotics and meditation in English Books of Hours.

Kelly DeVries holds a Ph.D. in Medieval Studies from the Centre for Medieval Studies at the University of Toronto and is professor of History at Loyola College in Maryland. He is the author of six books, including *Guns and Men in Medieval Europe, 1200–1500: Studies in Military History and Technology, Joan of Arc: A Military History, The Norwegian Invasion of England in 1066, Infantry Warfare in the Early Fourteenth Century: Discipline, Tactics, and Technology*, and *Medieval Military Technology*, and several articles on medieval military historical and technological subjects. He serves as the Secretary General of the United States Commission of Military History, editor of *The Journal of Medieval Military History*, and series editor of The History of Warfare for Brill Publishers.

Deborah Fraioli is professor of French at Simmons College. She is the author of *Joan of Arc: The Early Debate* and is currently working on a book on the Hundred Years War. Her other current research investigates the authenticity controversy about the correspondence of Abelard and Heloise.

Vicki L. Hamblin is professor of French language and literature at Western Washington University. Her research centers on French mystery plays of the fifteenth century and, specifically, on the performance data gleaned from the play texts themselves. Her critical edition of the *Mistère du siège d'Orléans* was recently published by Droz (Geneva). The results of her research have also appeared in a number of international journals, including *European Medieval Drama*. She participates regularly in international conferences on medieval theater, such as those sponsored by the Société internationale du theâtre médiéval and the Centre d'études supérieures de la Renaissance (Tours, France). Her current project focuses on stage directions and music in mystery play texts.

Nora Heimann wrote her dissertation on the image of Joan of Arc in nineteenth-century French art and culture at the City University of New York. She is an assistant professor of art history at the Catholic University of America; and she is currently completing a monograph on Joan of Arc in French Art and Culture: From Medieval Maiden to Modern Icon.

Henry Ansgar Kelly is the Director of the Center for Medieval and Renaissance Studies at UCLA. His most recent book, *Inquisitions and Other Trial Procedures in the Medieval West* (2001), includes essays on Joan of Arc. He is a contributor to the *New History of Penitence* (Brill).

Nadia Margolis studied medieval French literature and culture in both the United States and in France. She has published widely on Christine de Pizan and Joan of Arc, most recently coediting (with John Campbell) the volume of essays, *Christine de Pizan 2000* (Rodopi, 2000), and the essay on

Joan in the *Cambridge Companion to Medieval Women's Writing*, ed. Carolyn Dinshaw and David Wallace. She has taught and lectured at many institutions in the United States, Canada, Europe, and the United Kingdom.

Brian Patrick McGuire holds the chair of Professor of Medieval History at Roskilde University, Denmark. Since 1976 he has published eight books and about a hundred articles on various aspects of medieval monastic life and spirituality, including *Friendship and Community: The Monastic Experience* and *Brother and Lover: Aelred of Rievaulx*. His latest work, a biography of church reformer Jean Gerson, is entitled *A World Reborn: Jean Gerson and the Last Medieval Reformation 1350–1450*.

Yelena Mazour-Matusevich is associate professor of French at the University of Alaska, Fairbanks. Her book *L'âge d'or de la mystique française* was recently published by Archè (Paris–Milan). Her publications include articles on Nicolas of Cusa (Brill, 2002), Jean Gerson and Petrarch (C.N.R.S., France, 2003), feminine spirituality (*Magistra*, 2001) and a comparative study of Zola and Dostoyevsky (France, 1999). Her current project, *Problems of Definition of Culture*, focuses on the legacy of the famous medievalist Aron Gurevich and the European History of Mentalities school.

Jane Marie Pinzino holds a Ph.D. in Religious Studies from University of Pennsylvania and has written several works on Joan of Arc's posthumous nullification trial. Her forthcoming monograph by Palgrave Press, *The Grand Inquisitor, a Bishop and the Maid: Joan of Arc's Nullification Trial and the Reform of Inquisition*, assesses the nullification trial as a surprising source of proto-Enlightenment thought directed beyond the single case of Joan of Arc toward internal reform of medieval inquisition for its abuses against the laity. She has taught in the Religion Department and Humanities Program at University of Puget Sound in Tacoma, WA.

Ann Pirruccello (Ph.D., Purdue, 1992) is associate professor of Philosophy at the University of San Diego. She has published a range of articles on Simone Weil and is interested in philosophy of the body and comparative philosophy. She is currently working on a manuscript dealing with traditional Asian and European conceptions of the body.

George H. Tavard, born in Lorraine (Jean of Arc's province) on February 6, 1922, is a priest in the congregation of the Augustinians of the Assumption. He has taught theology and religious studies in seminaries and universities. He has written fifty-four books in the areas of theology, ecumenism, and spirituality, notably *Woman in Christian Tradition* (University of Notre Dame, 1973) and *The Spiritual Way of St. Jeanne d'Arc* (Liturgical Press, 1998).

Bonnie Wheeler directs the Medieval Studies Program at Southern Methodist University. She writes and teaches about medieval literatures and culture, and she is the editor of the journal *Arthuriana*. She is series editor of The New Middle Ages, in which this volume appears, and for which she recently edited *Listening to Heloise: The Voice of a Twelfth-Century Woman* (2000) and coedited *Eleanor of Aquitaine: Lord and Lady* (New York: Palgrave, 2003).